Conversations

# Conversations

with
Jesus, Mary and Thérèse of the Child Jesus

**Marcel Van**

Translated into French and introduced by
Father Antonio Boucher, CSsR

English translation by
Jack Keogan

With a Preface by
Cardinal Christoph Schönborn
Archbishop of Vienna

GRACEWING

Originally published in French as
*Colloques*, Marcel Van Complete Works Volume 2
by Éditions Saint-Paul, BP652 – 78006 Versailles CX

This edition published in 2008

Gracewing
2 Southern Avenue
Leominster
Herefordshire HR6 0QF

All rights reserved. No part of this publication may be reproduced, stored in a retrieval system, or transmitted in any form, or by any means, electronic, mechanical, photocopying, recording or otherwise, without the written permission of the publisher.

Original text and this translation © *Les Amis de Van* 2001
English edition © Gracewing Publishing 2008

The right of Marcel Van (Joachim Nguyen tan Van) to be identified as the author of this work has been asserted in accordance with the Copyright, Designs and Patents Act, 1988.

ISBN 978 0 85244 629 4

Typesetting by
Action Publishing Technology Ltd, Gloucester, GL1 5SR

Printed in England

# Contents

*Supplemented with relevant notes by Father Antonio Boucher*

| | |
|---|---|
| Preface by Cardinal Christoph Schönborn | xxiii |
| Novitiate Life at the Time of Van, by The Friends of Van (*Les Amis de Van*) | xxxiii |
| Introduction by Father Antonio Boucher | xxxvii |
| Foreword by The Friends of Van (*Les Amis de Van*) | xxxix |
| Chronological Notes | xli |

CONVERSATIONS

| | |
|---|---|
| Before 7 October 1945 (1) | 3 |
|    Mission confided to Brother Marcel (1 & 2) | 3 |
|    Kisses (3) | 4 |
|    You will write in your free time (4) | 4 |
|    Love of Jesus (6) | 4 |
|    Marcel, mother of souls at the cost of great suffering (7) | 5 |
|    Vow of friendship between Jesus and Marcel (8) | 5 |
|    You are fortunate not to be a priest (10–11) | 6 |
|    Little apostles of my love (12–13) | 6 |
| 7 October 1945 (15) | 7 |
|    Your life will be short (15) | 7 |
| 8 October 1945 (16) | 8 |
|    Love consumes faults and imperfections (16) | 8 |
|    The cause of your sadness (17) | 8 |
|    My little flower, how beautiful you are (18) | 8 |
|    Forbidden to write (18) | 8 |
| 22 October 1945 (19) | 9 |
|    Never doubt the truth of my words (19) | 9 |
|    The Blessed Virgin's army (19–20) | 9 |
|    Fear of Pride (20) | 9 |
| 23 October 1945 (21) | 10 |
|    I am saving great sufferings for you later (22) | 10 |
| 24 October 1945 (23) | 11 |
|    Autobiography (23) | 11 |

26 October 1945 (24) ........................................................... 11
  Humility of heart (24) .................................................... 11
  How can a priest lose the faith? (25–26) ........................ 12
27 October 1945 (28) ........................................................... 13
  As witness of the love I have for priests (28) ................ 13
28 October 1945, Christ the King (30) ............................. 14
  The reign of Love (30) ................................................... 14
  The work I expect from my spouse (30) ...................... 14
  You must love my Mother (31) ..................................... 14
  Jesus, are you sometimes sad because of me? (33) ...... 14
  Jesus banker, Jesus chief telegrapher (33–34) ............. 15
30 October 1945, France (38) .............................................. 17
  Marcel, go quickly and look at the aeroplane (38) ...... 17
  Someone needs to hold the wheel (38) ......................... 18
31 October 1945 (40) ........................................................... 19
  Kiss, ardour of Jesus' love (40) ...................................... 19
  Are priests also your spouses? (41) ................................ 19
  It is difficult to keep the secret with two in the same room (43) ... 20
1 November 1945 (45) .......................................................... 20
2 November 1945 (47) .......................................................... 21
  Secrecy concerning what is said (48) ............................. 22
  You will have to suffer much from your brethren (49) ... 22
  The absence of Jesus (50) ............................................... 23
  Interior sufferings (56) .................................................... 24
  Your vocation, your perseverance (56) .......................... 25
4 November 1945 (57) .......................................................... 25
  Precious pearl (57) ........................................................... 25
  Jesus, do you speak only to me? (58) ............................ 25
5 November 1945 (59) .......................................................... 26
  Sorrowful child of my love (59) ...................................... 26
6 November 1945 (62) .......................................................... 27
  Go and make your Stations of the Cross (62) ............. 27
  Days of suffering are days of intimacy (62) .................. 27
  Dryness, fatigue, lack of appetite (62) ........................... 27
7 November 1945 (64) .......................................................... 28
  The spouses I love the most? (64) ................................. 28
8 November 1945 (65) .......................................................... 28
  Your little sister will become a Redemptorist sister (66) ... 29
  Your director will have to suffer a lot in this business (67) ... 29
  He will have to appear as a witness (67) ...................... 29
9 November 1945 (68) .......................................................... 29
  Have you been tired for several days? (69–70) ............ 29
  Healthy atmospheres (72) ............................................... 30
  My love in the world is so weak (73) ............................. 31
  Only a few minutes remain (73) ..................................... 31
  France, the country I love the most (74) ...................... 31
  The vision of Jesus receiving messages from different countries (78) ... 32
10 November 1945 (81) ........................................................ 34
  My little flower, write what follows (81) ....................... 34

| | |
|---|---|
| The feast of Saint Stanislaus, song in the novitiate common room (82–84-a) | 34 |
| 11 November 1945 (83) | 35 |
| Following Jesus on the way of perfection (Poetry) (84–1) | 35 |
| Why, Magdalene, were you kneeling exhausted at my feet? (85) | 36 |
| My child, your particular role is to be the apostle of my love (86) | 36 |
| My love is always limitless, tell this to souls (87) | 37 |
| I would gladly sacrifice my life to bear witness to the truth of these words (87–88) | 37 |
| 12 November 1945 (92) | 38 |
| Prayer for France (92) | 38 |
| Jesus, I do not really understand your words which you address to France (97) | 39 |
| Do not be afraid to reveal my marks of affection to souls (98) | 40 |
| Why does my sister Thérèse not speak to me as often? (98) | 40 |
| Prayer intentions for each day of the week (102–103) | 41 |
| 13 November 1945 (104) | 42 |
| When you see that Jesus is sad (104) | 42 |
| You are always the dear little brother of Thérèse (106) | 43 |
| What your sister Thérèse does for you, you must also do for France (107) | 43 |
| Marcel, a second Thérèse (108) | 43 |
| Union between France and Vietnam (109) | 44 |
| 14 November 1945 (110) | 44 |
| Prayer for France (110) | 44 |
| What saddens me (116) | 46 |
| 15 November 1945 (117) | 47 |
| Jesus, why am I so weak? (117) | 47 |
| Do you intend to make me sad? (118) | 47 |
| If I leave you these weaknesses (119) | 47 |
| You do not want me to love you more than my brothers? (119–120) | 47 |
| The smaller your love for me, the more mine will envelop it with its intimacy (122) | 48 |
| To the Canadian Redemptoristines (123–1) | 48 |
| 16 November 1945 (124) | 49 |
| On France (124) | 49 |
| My sister Thérèse, why were you crying so much? (127) | 50 |
| 15 November 1945 (128–1) | 51 |
| Vision about France (128–1 – 128–4) | 51 |
| 18 November 1945 (133) | 53 |
| The sufferings that Jesus wishes to send are near (133) | 53 |
| Poetry of Thérèse: Peace in suffering (135–1) | 54 |
| Prayer for France (135-b) | 55 |
| Vision of France: Jesus, crying, looks at France (137–140) | 55 |
| Thérèse's counsel: Do not worry, offer up your weakness (141–143) | 57 |
| Thérèse's poems: While waiting for the God of Love (of the Beloved) (143–144) | 58 |
| Other counsels: Call me 'saint' (and not 'sister') (146) | 59 |

viii  *Conversations*

  Poem: Remain strong in love, retain your smile and
   peace of heart (147–148)   59
 20 November 1945 (149)   60
  O my little brother (Poem) (149)   60
  My sister, I am very sad (150)   60
 21 November 1945 (151)   61
  Poem of Thérèse: Wait in peace for the object of your desire (153)   61
 23 November 1945 (154)   62
 24 November 1945 (155)   62
  Vision: Jesus, clothed in priestly garb pursued by priests (155)   62
  I feed you with a mixture of sweet and bitter (155)   63
  Although I feel distaste, my heart remains joyful (157)   63
 25 November 1945 (159)   63
 26 November 1945
  A threatening voice heard while he was sweeping a corridor (161)   64
  Vision: Jesus crosses France, sometimes sad, sometimes joyful (162)   64
  Thérèse pulls a funny face to make him forget his sadness (162)   64
1  December 1945 (163)   65
  The vision of a closed fist lifted close to Jesus' face (163)   65
2  December 1945, First Sunday of Advent (167)   67
  Prayer for France (168)   67
 13 December 1945 (169)   68
  Pains like little thorns stuck in the end of the toes. Disgust (169)   68
 25 December 1945 (171)   69
  The three Christmas Masses (171–172)   69
  Who made this habit? (172)   69
  Jesus: Marcel, sing so that your little Jesus may be joyful (176–177)   71
  Who would be able to understand such figurative language? (177)   71
  To understand, that is your Director's business (178)   71
  Am I causing you much pain? (178)   72
  Little Jesus, you are eight years old and I see that you are
   still very mischievous (179)   72
  You speak of tearing to bits the flower whose beauty you praise (179)   72
  It is necessary that I tell my director what happened last night (180)   72
  Account of the night's vision (A large cradle for two) (181)   73
 26 December 1945 (183)   74
  I got up late from my siesta (183)   74
  I have heard that in France there are numerous parties? (186)   76
  Prayer to Jesus and Mary for France: Reign in the hearts of
   French priests (188)   77
  In the little way it seems that all is joyful and pleasant (189)   77
  You are very clever, little Jesus (189)   77
  Wish to throw away the bitter herbs (189)   77
 27 December 1945 (191)   79
  To prove your love for me, you have to do only two things (192)   79
  I am now teaching you how to sigh for love of me (193)   79
  I was a little sad a moment ago (194)   80
  The wren's occupation is to sing for me every day (195)   80
  Song of Thérèse of the Child Jesus: 'Be joyful little brother' (195–1)   81

|   |   |
|---|---|
| 28 December 1945 (196) | 81 |
|   Feast of your Holy Name (196) | 81 |
|   Today, 28 December, feastday of the Holy Innocents (196) | 82 |
|   Certain brethren are astonished at what they find in books (197) | 82 |
|   God is, at the same time, Father, Friend (Spouse) and Master (197–198) | 82 |
|   Little Marcel, do you love me? (199–200) | 83 |
|   Now, Marcel, do you want something? Why are you sad? (200) | 83 |
| 29 December 1945 (202) | 84 |
|   Marcel, it is necessary for you to know that you have not the least virtue (202) | 84 |
|   Do you wish to speak to me? Speak to me in French (202) | 84 |
|   Thérèse, is she with me? She does not speak to me (203) | 85 |
|   Drawing of patrons for the new year (203–204) | 85 |
|   Marcel, have you finished your work yet so that you can write? (205) | 86 |
|   To love and to work, that is your duty (206) | 86 |
| 30 December 1945 (208) | 87 |
|   Fragrant warmth in the mouth at communion (208) | 88 |
|   Later, there will be times when you will wish no longer to eat me (208) | 88 |
|   Happiness for you, Marcel, is … being the apostle of my love (209) | 88 |
|   Confide these functions to priests (210) | 88 |
|   A new kind of suffering that you have never experienced (211–212) | 89 |
|   Has my sister Thérèse known this kind of suffering? (213–214) | 90 |
|   Thérèse confirms: Suffering is not our task (215) | 90 |
|   Thérèse, are you now weaker than me? (215) | 90 |
|   I am sad at not being able to practise mortification like you (215–216) | 91 |
|   Poverty (217–218) | 91 |
|   Jesus, I love you: Song of love (220–221) | 93 |
| 31 December 1945 (222) | 94 |
|   How is it that some brethren say they have a great fear of you? (223–224) | 95 |
|   I understand absolutely nothing (226) | 96 |
| 1 January 1946 (227) | 96 |
|   Saint John Eudes, patron saint of the year (227) | 96 |
|   Why did you not present yourself yesterday to be my patron saint for another year? (229) | 97 |
|   Pray especially during this month for the priests of France (231) | 98 |
|   Thérèse to her brothers, the priests of France (231–232) | 98 |
|   Jesus, do female saints love you with a warmer love than their male counterparts? (232–233) | 99 |
|   Marcel, you, the little flower of Vietnam, you are very fragile (235) | 100 |
|   You are tired. Go and rest (237) | 101 |
| 2 January 1946 – Meditation on Jesus crying in his crib (238) | 102 |
|   Marcel, do you love me? (238–239) | 102 |
|   I really love the little flower of Vietnam (239) | 102 |
|   Jesus, why am I sad this evening? (241) | 103 |
| 3 January 1946 (243-a) | 104 |
|   I feel much disgust but I have the Blessed Virgin to chat with (243) | 104 |
|   Vision of the Virgin Mary (243-1) | 104 |

| | |
|---|---|
| My Mother Mary, I love you dearly (245) | 106 |
| I, your Mother, I love you and I have pity on you (248) | 107 |
| 4 January 1946 (249) | 108 |
| But what will my sister Thérèse do? (249) | 108 |
| Mary: 'My child, what name do you wish me to call you?' (250) | 108 |
| First Saturday of the month. Recommendation to you and your director (250–251) | 108 |
| My reign will come after that of the Love of Jesus (251) | 108 |
| Marcel, in heaven, you will be like a second Thérèse of the Child Jesus (251) | 109 |
| 5 January 1946 (252-b) | 109 |
| Mother, following my sister's example, I love you dearly (253) | 110 |
| Later, in heaven, I will achieve my wish to make you loved (253) | 110 |
| Marcel, your mission on earth (254–255) | 110 |
| 6 January 1946 (258) | 112 |
| Is it true that the end of the world is close? (258–260) | 112 |
| In which country do you especially choose your apostles? (262) | 113 |
| Give to me the name Mother of the Universe (264–265) | 114 |
| Rosary, distractions (266) | 115 |
| Simplicity of the little member of the Juniorate (268) | 116 |
| I think of the souls of children (269) | 116 |
| 7 January 1946 (271) | 117 |
| Mother, what does little Jesus love the most? (272) | 117 |
| Jesus' sleep (275) | 118 |
| Mary, my Mother, hide my sadness from little Jesus (279) | 120 |
| 12 January 1946 (281) | 120 |
| Marcel's sadness. Mary consoles him (281–285) | 120 |
| End of January 1946 (286–1) | 123 |
| Prayer for France (286–1) | 123 |
| 2 February 1946 (Têt) (287) | 123 |
| Têt, days of festivities, days of sin (287) | 123 |
| 3 February 1946 (289) | 124 |
| Mary, you see me suffering (291) | 125 |
| 4 February 1946 (293) | 125 |
| 11 February 1946 (298) | 127 |
| Mother, you know my weakness (307) | 130 |
| Game of hide and seek (309) | 130 |
| 3 March 1946 (311) | 131 |
| Adoration during the pre-Lenten days (311) | 131 |
| 10 March 1946 (313) | 132 |
| Letter to Mary. Thérèse's words (314) | 132 |
| 14 March 1946 (315) | 133 |
| Sufferings are crosses and crosses are roses (315–316) | 133 |
| 15 March 1946 (316) | 133 |
| A little consolation, these past few days (317–318) | 133 |
| Prompted by pictures on his table he speaks with Mary (319–323) | 134 |
| 17 March 1946 (323) | 136 |
| Daddy, God; mammy, Mary (324) | 136 |
| 22 March 1946 (326) | 137 |

|     | Ardent desire for Lucifer to recognize you as his mother (327) | 137 |
| --- | --- | --- |
|     | 25 March 1946 (331) | 139 |
|     | Jesus does not deign to open his mouth to speak to me (331) | 139 |
|     | 26 March 1946 (332) | 140 |
|     | Brother Basil has just learned to sew (332) | 140 |
|     | 27 March 1946 (333) | 140 |
|     | The spirit of darkness wants to disturb me (334) | 141 |
|     | A brother said I was virtuous in word only (335) | 141 |
|     | 28 March 1946 (336) | 141 |
|     | I met some children (336) | 141 |
|     | To teach souls, above all, to teach children to love Jesus (337–337-a) | 142 |
|     | 29 March 1946 (337-b) | 143 |
|     | Suffering does not leave me (337-b) | 143 |
|     | Jesus wishes that I take the trouble to go in search of souls (337) | 143 |
|     | 30 March 1946 (340) | 143 |
|     | In heaven, when I want to ask the Father a 'favour' (341) | 144 |
|     | 31 March 1946 (342) | 144 |
|     | The love of Marcel for children (343–348) | 144 |
|     | He does not dare to give Saint Alphonsus the name of Father reserved to God (348) | 146 |
|     | My father, Saint Alphonsus, I love you dearly (348) | 147 |
|     | Mother, will I be more powerful that my father Saint Alphonsus? (349) | 147 |
| 2   | April 1946 (350) | 147 |
|     | Jesus, three months without speaking to me! With no reason (350) | 147 |
| 3   | April 1946 (350) | 148 |
|     | Little Marcel, do you love me? (350) | 148 |
|     | Reciprocal teasing ... brotherly love (352–353) | 148 |
|     | 'The kingdom of heaven belongs to children' as you said in the Gospel. Jesus, what did you do at Nazareth? (358) | 159 |
|     | Little bird, sing loudly so that the other birds know that (359) | 150 |
|     | Now, I will show you my love as a friend to his little friend (359) | 150 |
| 4   | April 1946 (360) | 150 |
|     | Questions on Jesus' childhood (360–362) | 150 |
|     | What is it about the flower that you adorn it with all the colours? (363) | 152 |
|     | Gunfire (364) | 153 |
|     | Did you laugh? Cry? (364) | 153 |
|     | According to my divine nature (365) | 153 |
|     | From the moment that I took on human nature in Mary's womb (365) | 153 |
|     | If a child never laughed, it would cause its family to be sad (365) | 153 |
|     | Brother Anthony scolded us, and it was your fault (367) | 154 |
| 5   | April 1946 (374) | 155 |
|     | Marcel, my life was one of suffering (368) | 155 |
|     | Playfulness (372) | 157 |
|     | Little Jesus, how is it that your gaze is so powerful? (374) | 158 |
|     | Marcel, the glance of your weakness is yet more powerful than mine (374) | 158 |
| 6   | April 1946 (374) | 158 |
|     | The love of Jesus for children (375–376) | 159 |
|     | I am the true path which leads men to heaven (376) | 159 |

Pray a lot so that children may understand my love (377)    160
Jesus, speaking of Mary (380)    161
Mother, was Jesus very obedient? (381)    161
7 April 1946, Passion Sunday (382)    162
Mother, what does the word 'naïve' mean? (382)    162
Little Jesus is very fussy (384)    163
Do not worry, Marcel (385)    163
The sighs of love divert the arrows of sinners which target my heart (387)    164
Has the reign of love already begun in the world? (388)    165
It is your sister Thérèse who is the universal apostle of the apostles of my Love (388)    165
Is the end of the world close, as people say? (388)    165
Thérèse, why do you no longer speak to me? Are you angry with me? (390)    166
From now on, little brother, I will remain silent (391)    167
Jesus, Saint Gerard's diver (392)    167
Jesus, if you had preached in Vietnamese (393)    167
Translation of the Bible into Vietnamese (393–394)    168
In such heat you want me to close my door and write (394)    168
Some men say, 'We cannot believe that Mary is the Mother of God' (396)    169
8 April 1946 (397)    170
Little Jesus did you eat bananas? (397)    170
Little Jesus spoke to me again last night (398)    170
Broken plate (398)    170
Canonization (399)    171
Accept cheerfully the harsh words that Brother Augustine addresses to you (399–400)    171
Marcel, be joyful, I do not like to remain with sad children (401)    172
Mother, your little one makes me sad (403)    172
9 April 1946 (405)    174
Jesus and Thérèse (404–405)    174
Looking at Jesus (407)    175
Vision: Jesus cries (407–408)    175
Looking at me with a very joyful expression, Jesus shows me the cross (408)    175
Jesus, are you pleased with little Toa? (409)    176
10 April 1946 (411)    177
Jesus, why do you speak to me so little? Teasings (411)    177
There is still too little confidence in my Love (412)    177
Pray for the Redemptoristines (412)    178
Little Jesus, do you love my father, Saint Alphonsus? (413)    178
Playing: 'which Carmelite novice is in this flower?' (414)    179
Jesus likes only to play with those who are happy (415)    179
Jesus, why do you make me speak to you as if I were your 'little brother'? (417)    180
Will our relations be the same in heaven as they are now? (417–418)    180

|     |     |
| --- | --- |
| I really like my new place in the Novitiate oratory (419) | 181 |
| 11 April 1946 (419) | 181 |
|    Today, on the Father Provincial's feast day, I have eaten really well (420–421) | 182 |
|    In the past, little Jesus, did you eat cake? (421) | 182 |
|    Was your family as poor as mine? (422) | 182 |
|    Marcel, you must not ask yourself anxiously if you have been deceived (423–424) | 183 |
|    Mary's faith (425) | 184 |
|    Hope and love like Mary (426) | 184 |
|    Forgive, little Jesus! (427) | 185 |
|    Little brother, without Mary it would be impossible for me to love you (428) | 185 |
|    Am I very proud? (428) | 185 |
|    I do not wish you to understand all the words that Love addresses to you (428–429) | 185 |
|    O, my very little brother (429) | 186 |
| 12 April 1946 (429) | 186 |
|    Today, Jesus no longer speaks to me. I feel very sad (429–430) | 186 |
|    Today, the feast of the Seven Sorrows, have you done anything to console me? (430) | 186 |
|    I am taking all the love of my heart … to love you, Mother (431) | 187 |
| 13 April 1946 (432) | 187 |
|    Jesus, why these terrible threats against those who scandalize children? (433) | 188 |
|    The souls of children are perfectly pure temples inhabited by the Trinity (433–434) | 188 |
|    Palm Sunday. Entry into Jerusalem. See, little brother (436) | 189 |
|    Little Jesus, today I received a penance in the dining room (437) | 189 |
| 14 April 1946, Palm Sunday (440) | 191 |
|    Little Jesus, I am very tired. I no longer wish to write (440–441) | 191 |
|    Why do you say that the glance of my love is stern? (441–442) | 192 |
| 15 April 1946 (443) | 193 |
|    I am less tired today (443) | 193 |
|    If you had faith the size of a mustard seed (444–445) | 193 |
|    A short while ago I had to extract a tooth (446) | 194 |
| 16 April 1946 (448) | 196 |
|    I have a soutane which I dislike a great deal (449) | 196 |
|    Observation to Brother Augustine on the soutane's length (451) | 197 |
|    Pray for sinners today (454) | 198 |
| 17 April 1946 (455) | 199 |
|    Little Jesus, has the devil got faith? (455–456) | 199 |
|    A very deep sadness in the heart (456) | 200 |
|    Little Jesus, this year I am not going to serve Mass at the Carmel (457) | 200 |
|    This year my voice has changed, little Jesus (457–458) | 200 |
|    I am, therefore, very weak. One could not be more so (458) | 200 |
|    At one time, I would have liked to enter Carmel (458–459) | 201 |
|    Today, Mother, little Jesus has not given me collation (460–461) | 201 |
| 18 April 1946, Holy Thursday (462) | 203 |

| | |
|---|---:|
| To assuage the sorrows of my heart ... no remedy comparable to the sighs of love (463–464) | 204 |
| Playfulness on the subject of medication (465–466) | 204 |
| Today, what have you to comfort me? (466) | 205 |
| Marcel, you no longer belong to yourself, it is to me that you belong (467–468) | 205 |
| Marcel, when the true Father in heaven sends you crosses (469) | 206 |
| Brother John Baptist and I, we like each other a lot (470) | 207 |
| Little Jesus, you said just now that my will was already in you (471) | 208 |
| Mother Mary, I have had to remain on my knees a long time before the altar of repose (473) | 208 |
| In the presence of Jesus at the same time as the children (473) | 208 |
| Little Jesus, do you want to allow me to fast tomorrow? (474) | 209 |
| 19 April 1946, Good Friday (475) | 209 |
| Jesus obliges Van to wear socks all day (475) | 209 |
| I go to confess (475–476) | 210 |
| You must pray for priests today (477) | 210 |
| The voices of priests must be raised to protect my love (477) | 210 |
| Little Jesus, tell me why you love priests so much (478) | 211 |
| Oh! Today, I completely forgot to wear the *cuissard* (479) | 211 |
| It is the day when I gave my Mother to you to be your true Mother (479–480) | 212 |
| 20 April 1946, Holy Saturday (481) | 213 |
| Mother of Sorrows (482) | 213 |
| Problems with Brother Mark (484–485) | 214 |
| But if I cried at your crucifixion, would you forbid me to cry? (485–486) | 215 |
| Brother Augustine does not stop crying when making the Stations (486) | 215 |
| 21 April 1946 – Vision of Good Friday | 216 |
| Fear of being sent away because of his health (489–490) | 217 |
| Why did you cry a short while ago? (491) | 217 |
| Happy feast day for Father Marquis (494) | 219 |
| Holy Saturday. The unveiling of Father Alphonsus' statue (494) | 219 |
| The office of Saturday. Brother Gregory lacks simplicity (497) | 221 |
| 22 April 1946 (499) | 222 |
| Little Jesus, have I really got a sickness of the heart? (499) | 222 |
| Today, you feel disgust (500) | 222 |
| Marcel, where have you just come from? (502) | 223 |
| Scruple ... dubious fault (503–505) | 223 |
| France and Vietnam (508–509) | 226 |
| 23 April 1946 (510) | 227 |
| I am a brother of the Congregation but I do nothing worthwhile (510) | 227 |
| I called you to the Congregation to be a brother (510) | 227 |
| Translation of spiritual books ... difficult reading (511) | 227 |
| I must choose many apostles for the expansion of the reign of my Love (512) | 228 |
| Today, ask permission to write to your little sister (513) | 228 |
| Playfulness (514) | 228 |

|   |   |
|---|---|
| Little Jesus was boasting in front of me, Mother, during the washing of the linen (514) | 228 |
| Marcel: 'Tell me Mother, am I beautiful?' (515) | 229 |
| 24 April 1946 (516) | 230 |
| Conversations with Mary (517) | 230 |
| You allowed the scissors to fall on my bad foot (519) | 232 |
| 25 April 1946 (521) | 232 |
| Floor cloth for washing the floor (521) | 232 |
| Little Jesus, I love you unreservedly (524) | 234 |
| Interior sufferings (526) | 235 |
| 26 April 1946 (529) | 236 |
| Result of medical examination: there is nothing wrong with my heart (529) | 236 |
| 'I will sacrifice myself joyfully for your Love' (531) | 237 |
| For the month of May, prayer for France (532–1) | 238 |
| Mother, I am really sad, I do not know what to say (532–533) | 238 |
| Sadness and sufferings (533) | 238 |
| I offered myself as a victim for the Love of Jesus (533) | 239 |
| 22 April 1946, (end) (534) | 239 |
| If the French did not use aeroplanes (534) | 239 |
| 28 April 1946 (535) | 239 |
| A day when I had nothing to say to little Jesus (535–537) | 239 |
| All souls are my spouses (538) | 241 |
| Brother Eugene's exaggerations (541) | 242 |
| Mortification, fasting, novitiate, community … family (543–545) | 243 |
| Children are not yet aware of sin (545) | 244 |
| Little Jesus, you have a very difficult nature (546) | 244 |
| Little Jesus, you said to me the other day (547) | 245 |
| Bearded Jesus imitated you in obliging me to smile before dismissing me (548) | 245 |
| Kisses (549–551) | 246 |
| Did my father Saint Alphonsus love you a lot under your title of the Child Jesus? (552) | 247 |
| Why did he write mainly about your Passion? (552) | 247 |
| The interior sorrows of the Child Jesus (553) | 248 |
| 29 April 1946 (554) | 248 |
| I would really like to join the ranks of the communists (554) | 248 |
| What function would you accomplish among the communists? (555) | 249 |
| Difficult questions to which I do not at all know how to reply (555) | 249 |
| If you posed the same question to me as you did to Saint Peter (555) | 249 |
| What was it you had to complain about a short time ago? (556) | 249 |
| Did you have your director's permission to make this sacrifice? (556) | 249 |
| Now, my little brother, guess why I am plumper than you? (557) | 250 |
| So, what could I do to prove my love for you? (558) | 250 |
| Is it possible, that the saints who fasted did nothing good? (558) | 250 |
| 30 April 1946 (559) | 251 |
| The obedience of Jesus (562) | 253 |
| It seems that, outwardly, you never suffered as much as Saint Gerard (563) | 253 |

| | |
|---|---|
| The value of the penances of the saints (564) | 254 |
| Little Jesus, I understand absolutely nothing! (564) | 254 |
| So, little Jesus, tell me what 'victim of Love' means (564) | 254 |
| Problems with Brother Mark (566) | 255 |
| I am coughing a lot, I am not able to go to communal meditation (567) | 255 |
| Do you want your sister Thérèse to act the fool to make you laugh? (568–569) | 256 |
| 1 May 1946 (570) | 257 |
| Interior poverty (570–571) | 257 |
| Little brother, you must never work to acquire merit (572) | 258 |
| Children who have just been baptized (572–573) | 258 |
| 2 May 1946 (573) | 258 |
| Example of poverty (578) | 260 |
| In heaven, all of the virtues are to be found in charity (580) | 261 |
| You say that God the Father, being the Infinite Being, is also infinitely poor (580) | 262 |
| Go and take your copybook to bearded Jesus and rest yourself (582) | 262 |
| What passage did you read in the Story of your sister Thérèse? (582) | 263 |
| Why that? (583) | 263 |
| 3 May 1946 (584) | 264 |
| Little Jesus, I was very angry yesterday (584) | 264 |
| Where did you get the audacity to say that the translator was proud? (586) | 265 |
| Today, I feel really hungry. I spoke of it to bearded Jesus (587) | 265 |
| 4 May 1946 (589) | 267 |
| Mother, on this day specially dedicated to you (589) | 267 |
| Mother, I love you dearly (589) | 267 |
| Mary, little Jesus is very lazy. He shares the same room with me (590) | 267 |
| My child, your soul is a living room (590) | 267 |
| Mary, I feel, from time to time, a great sorrow in my heart (592–593) | 269 |
| Anointing of the sick (593–594, 622) | 269 |
| Troubles. My child, I am going to teach you a new method of sacrificing yourself (595) | 270 |
| 5 Mother 1946 (597) | 271 |
| Mother, at prayers this morning I wanted to avoid sleeping (597) | 271 |
| Prayer is the only means of saving the country from communism (599) | 272 |
| Little Jesus, what did our sister Thérèse give to us this morning? (599–600) | 272 |
| Little Jesus, why was I so ill at ease a moment ago? (602) | 273 |
| Why do you worry so, little brother? (602) | 273 |
| Little Jesus, last night I spoke to Brother Mark and he made fun of me (603) | 274 |
| From now on, no longer repeat any of the words I address to you (603) | 274 |
| In this case what will there be for me to say to the brethren? (604) | 274 |
| This pen has a very contrary temper (608–609) | 276 |
| So who will be attentive to my soul? (610) | 277 |
| What will you give to them in the way of alms? (610) | 277 |
| Brother Augustine has new sandals. Little Jesus, you spoil him more than me (611) | 277 |

|   |   |   |
|---|---|---|
| 6 | Mother 1946 (612) | 278 |
|  | Thérèse's playfulness (612) | 278 |
|  | Humility (613) | 278 |
|  | Why don't you teach me to paint so I can do your portrait? (616–617) | 280 |
|  | Mother, men make very ugly paintings of you (618–619) | 281 |
|  | Disgust: sandals, sore feet, etc. (619) | 281 |
|  | Mother, I would like you to give me a kiss (620) | 282 |
|  | Do you feel disgust? (621–622) | 282 |
|  | The other day, little Jesus pretended to give me the sacrament of the sick (622–623) | 282 |
| 7 | Mother 1946 (624) | 284 |
|  | Little Jesus, take pity on little Toa ... badly treated by Phúc (624) | 284 |
|  | Today, I had to serve at table. I was very tired (627) | 285 |
|  | I do not understand how God the Father can be infinitely poor (631) | 286 |
|  | And who asks you to understand? (631) | 286 |
|  | My sister, I want to tell you what happened this morning (632) | 287 |
| 8 | Mother 1946 (634) | 288 |
|  | It is obvious that you must hate sin. It is necessary that you pray for France (635) | 288 |
|  | Now, my sister, I love France again and I do not cease praying for her (635) | 288 |
|  | Brother Eugene continues to insist that women only are your spouses (635) | 288 |
|  | Do you know why I consider myself the Spouse of all souls? (640) | 290 |
| 9 | Mother 1946 (640) | 291 |
|  | Anger against the choir brothers who dirty the floor (640) | 291 |
|  | Sad? Do you not remember that you are weak? (641) | 291 |
|  | I hurt the brothers (641–642) | 291 |
|  | What do the words 'phu phụ' mean? (642) | 291 |
|  | In the past, I knew many strange words without understanding their meaning (643) | 292 |
|  | New sandals (644) | 292 |
|  | If I no longer wish to be one with you? (644) | 293 |
|  | It is very difficult for a soul to fall into hell (646) | 293 |
|  | New pen (649) | 294 |
|  | Is the doctor saved? (650) | 295 |
| 10 | Mother 1946 (651) | 295 |
|  | Serving at table (651) | 295 |
|  | Your weakness has not disappeared for all that (652) | 296 |
|  | Little Jesus, I have something here that you really like a lot (652–653) | 296 |
|  | Little Jesus, here are my fatigue and disgust, I am giving them to you (653) | 297 |
|  | What do you want in return? (654) | 297 |
|  | Marcel does not like suffering. Neither does Jesus like to cause suffering (655) | 297 |
|  | Marcel, I am very pleased. Continue to accept suffering patiently (655) | 298 |
| 11 | Mother 1946 (655) | 298 |
|  | Baptism of Mrs. Giác (655–656) | 298 |
|  | Teasings: Marcel and Jesus (657) | 298 |

| | |
|---|---|
| To comfort a soul in sadness (658) | 299 |
| You remember the time when your sister Thérèse looked at you with only one eye (659) | 299 |
| 12 Mother 1946 (659) | 300 |
|   Our Mother loves you a lot because you are weak (660–661) | 300 |
|   I am eating a lot. I am almost as fat as you (661) | 301 |
|   I want to sit down during meditation (661) | 301 |
|   Little Jesus, would you eat some soup? (662) | 301 |
|   Brother Augustine is very sad. Why don't you console him? (662) | 301 |
|   You must not make such assumptions (664) | 302 |
|   There, my bowl of soup is finished (665) | 303 |
|   Suffering! Love (665) | 303 |
|   What did bearded Jesus just say? I did not understand it (665–666) | 303 |
|   Mary is a Mother who speaks with goodness, even of the devil (667–671) | 304 |
| 13 Mother 1946 | 307 |
|   Mr Diệm, a refugee in the Hanoi monastery (676) | 308 |
|   Mr Diệm: 'Without France we can do nothing' (677) | 308 |
|   Does he recognize Mary as his true mother? (678) | 308 |
|   Sadness, disgust (680) | 309 |
| 14 Mother 1946 (681) | 310 |
|   Sufferings from his brethren (682–683) | 310 |
|   Little Jesus, Brother Augustine told me that I was very fierce (683) | 311 |
|   Little brother, you really have a fierce demeanour (683–684) | 311 |
|   As for this sweetness of character which allows itself to be intimidated by children (684) | 311 |
|   A paper on his table was moved (686–687) | 312 |
|   Do not hit children (687) | 312 |
|   Do not imitate the dog that only knows how to get angry (687) | 312 |
|   Do not be angry with Brother Mark (687) | 313 |
|   Time is up, little Jesus. I am leaving (688) | 313 |
| 15 Mother 1946 (688) | 313 |
|   Mother, I feel again a pain in my heart (688) | 313 |
|   My child, it is not right to complain (688) | 313 |
|   Little Jesus, I hear what sounds like cannonade (689) | 314 |
|   I must look after you more (689) | 314 |
|   Little brother, you asked me about the poverty I spoke of in the Gospel (689) | 314 |
|   Offer everything to the Trinity without holding anything back (690) | 315 |
|   Why was the young man not pleased with Jesus' words? (690–691) | 315 |
| 16 Mother 1946 (692) | 316 |
|   Brother Vitus compares Father Vaillancourt to Father Romeo Gagnon (692) | 316 |
|   In speaking in this way, has the brother spoken badly about Father Gagnon? (693) | 317 |
|   Judging externally, Brother Vitus lacks true wisdom (693) | 317 |
|   Little Jesus, you know that I truly love only you (694) | 317 |
|   Yes, it is true. Also, I love you dearly (694) | 317 |
|   Bringing to mind the sufferings caused to me by my parents (694) | 317 |

|   |   |
|---|---|
| Mother, today I feel an extreme disgust (694) | 318 |
| 17 Mother 1946 (695) | 318 |
| I have had to remain hungry (695–696) | 318 |
| 27 Mother 1946 (696) | 319 |
| 'Jesus, accept France's confidence' (696) | 319 |
| 6  June 1946 (696) | 319 |
| Solitude, desolation (696–697) | 319 |
| 20 June 1946 (697) | 320 |
| Brother Augustine and Brother Gregory have left (697–698) | 320 |
| 27 June 1946 (698) | 320 |
| Prayer for France (698) | 320 |
| 24 July 1946 (699) | 321 |
| On the subject of children who die without baptism (699–702) | 321 |
| 28 July 1946 (703) | 325 |
| 8  August 1946 (703) | 325 |
| Desire for heaven (703) | 325 |
| Mother, I love you dearly (703) | 326 |
| I have received already a pair of new shoes (703) | 326 |
| Spiritual nuptials (704) | 326 |
| There are twelve huge fish bearded Jesus has asked me to pray for (704) | 326 |
| 10 August 1946 (705) | 327 |
| Mother, I am praying today for your little apostles (705) | 327 |
| After reflection, to please him I replied (705) | 327 |
| Mother, I shall soon go to heaven with you (705) | 327 |
| 12 August 1946 (705) | 327 |
| Mother, today I was allowed to enter Carmel (705) | 327 |
| The funeral of a deceased sister (705–707) | 328 |
| 16 August 1946 (707) | 328 |
| Mary, I see that this world is full of misery and weakness (707) | 329 |
| 19 August 1946 (708) | 330 |
| Love of God among the saints (708–709) | 330 |
| 22 August 1946 (709) | 330 |
| The devil's voice, temptation of pride (709) | 330 |
| 23 August 1946 (710) | 331 |
| After my novitiate I wish to go to heaven (710–712) | 332 |
| 24 August 1946 (712) | 332 |
| Jesus, give generosity to the priests of France (712–715) | 332 |
| Here I am on retreat but I do not feel any fervour (713) | 334 |
| 27 August 1946 ( 715) | 335 |
| Serving at table (717) | 336 |
| Little Jesus, the day of our union is already close ( 718) | 337 |
| Your infinite Love is equally my infinite Love (718) | 337 |
| To be a spouse is to join two lives together (721) | 339 |
| 28 August 1946 (722) | 339 |
| I wrote yesterday without understanding anything (722) | 339 |
| Carmel (723–724) | 341 |
| 29 August 1946 (725) | 342 |
| An easier way to say the rosary (725–726) | 342 |

xx    *Conversations*

| | | |
|---|---|---|
| 1 | September 1946 (726) | 343 |
| | Mother, Jesus' voice does not stop calling me to go to heaven (727) | 344 |
| | Today, feast of the Vietnamese martyrs (728) | 344 |
| 2 | September 1946 (728) | 345 |
| | I have decided to make Vietnam a country that belongs to you (728) | 345 |
| 3 | September 1946 (731) | 346 |
| | The preacher spoke about exaggerated nationalism (731) | 346 |
| | Mother, I dearly love my country (732) | 347 |
| | Why are you so cruel, little Jesus? (732) | 347 |
| 4 | September 1946 (733) | 348 |
| | Mother, I have just made a general confession (733) | 348 |
| | Jesus, keep my love unceasingly in all its purity (734) | 348 |
| 6 | September 1946 (734) | 349 |
| | In two days I will be able to call myself little Jesus' spouse (734) | 349 |
| | On that day, together, we will enter into an eternal friendship (734–735) | 349 |
| | The idea came to me to give Thérèse the name of mother (737) | 350 |
| | Mary, the first Redemptorist sister (737–738) | 351 |
| 7 | September 1946 (738) | 352 |
| | Mary, tomorrow is the feast of your nativity (740) | 353 |
| 8 | September 1946, Religious Profession (741) | 354 |
| 10 | September 1946 (742) | 354 |
| | Little Jesus, it is still raining (742) | 354 |
| | Thoughts on his little sister Tế and his older sister Lê (743) | 355 |
| 11 | September 1946 (744) | 356 |
| | I am confirmed as the Novitiate brother (744) | 356 |
| 13 | September 1946 (744) | 356 |
| | I will go to have my photo taken (744) | 356 |
| 15 | September 1946 (746) | 357 |
| | The photo taken the other day is very beautiful (746) | 357 |
| | The newly-professed move into the community (746–747) | 358 |
| | As for me, I am still working as the tailor (747) | 358 |
| 29 | September 1946 (748) | 359 |
| | So arrange things that France and Vietnam are animated by a mutual trust (748) | 359 |
| 6 | October 1946 (749) | 359 |
| | Father Minister forgets to give him a picture of Our Lady of Perpetual Succour (749) | 359 |
| | At Saigon there are some fathers who treat the brothers as ordinary coolies (750) | 360 |
| | 'Those who speak in this way are not true Redemptorist brothers' (750) | 360 |
| 13 | October 1946 (751) | 361 |
| | I see myself in a dream at the Hữu-Bằng presbytery (751) | 361 |
| 17 | October 1946 (753) | 362 |
| | Is it possible to imitate Saint Gerard? (753) | 362 |
| 20 | October 1946 (755) | 364 |
| | Jesus, make the reign of your Love spread (755) | 364 |
| | Prayer for children (755) | 364 |

| | |
|---|---|
| 23 October 1946 (756) | 364 |
| Ordain things so that Vietnam, my country, knows and loves only the truth (756) | 364 |
| 3 November 1946 (756) | 364 |
| 'Be cunning as serpents and innocent as doves' (756) | 364 |
| 10 November 1946 (757) | 365 |
| Is it Jesus' will that religious leave the Congregation? (757–758) | 365 |
| 17 November 1946 (758) | 366 |
| I wish to die very quickly to go to heaven with little Jesus (758) | 366 |
| Sweet taste when I receive Jesus (759) | 366 |
| 27 November 1946 (760) | 367 |
| Expressions used by Jesus when speaking of his apostles and those close to him (760) | 367 |
| Prayer for December: that the French and Vietnamese have but one heart (761) | 367 |
| 1 December 1946 | 368 |
| I am sure that my Holy Father (Pius XII) is deeply distressed (761–762) | 368 |
| 8 December 1946 (762) | 368 |
| Jesus said that it is never necessary to hit children (762) | 368 |
| 24 December 1946 (762) | 368 |
| Figment of my imagination or trick of the devil (762) | 368 |
| 4 January 1947 (763) | 369 |
| Ardent desire to see Jesus. Serious wound of love! (763–764) | 369 |
| 11 January 1947 (764) | 369 |
| Jesus, make Vietnam and France enjoy mutual peace (764) | 369 |
| 12 January 1947 (765) | 370 |
| Where is my eternal Beloved? Who is He after whom I sigh? (765) | 370 |
| 14 January 1947 (766) | 371 |
| Little Jesus, the more I desire to see you, the more I have the feeling of having been deceived (766) | 371 |
| 15 January 1947 (767) | 371 |
| 15 February 1947 (767) | 372 |
| 19 March 1947 (769) | 372 |
| If he stumbles he does not fall since the Lord holds him by the hand (Ps. 36, 24) (769) | 372 |
| 30 March 1947 (769) | 373 |
| I dreamt that I was at the point of death (769–771) | 373 |
| One just man would be enough for Jesus not to destroy France (771) | 374 |
| 13 May 1947 (772) | 375 |
| Mary, my sad heart waits for the Beloved (772) | 375 |
| 15 May 1947 (772) | 375 |
| My Father, how can I express to you the feelings of my heart? (772) | 375 |
| 25 August 1947 – Letter (772) | 375 |
| To Jesus, the little Lord of my heart (772–773) | 375 |
| Appendix | 377 |

# Preface

'What is your secret, little Van?'* This question, to which the authors of a volume of essays bearing the same title have tried to respond, takes on a more particular meaning when one begins to read the *Conversations* which form the second tome of the *Complete Works*. What is the 'status' of these conversations in which Jesus, Mary and Thérèse speak with the young and small Vietnamese novice? What rank can be given to these 'private revelations'? How should they be read? How can one distinguish in them between what is the message from heaven and what the 'receiver' and 'sender' brings from his own personality, his own sensitivity, his own intelligence and his own experience?

Before trying to reply to these questions it is necessary simply to read these conversations, to try to receive from them the message, to listen to their tonality, to garner from them, without prejudice, that which touches us, while at the same time being attentive to their doctrinal content.

What strikes us first of all in these conversations is, according to the words of Father Boucher, the Brother's novice master and spiritual director – to whom we owe a debt of gratitude for having collected so carefully this legacy of Marcel Van – 'the incredible familiarity ... the tenderness of which Brother Marcel has been the object on the part of his heavenly interlocutors.'† This young man who has experienced

---

\* *What is your secret little Van?* A series of essays by celebrated theologians: Georgette Blaquiere; R. de Tryon Montalembert; Fr de Kermadec, MRI; Fr J. Lê Phung, CSsR; Fr D. Joly CSsR; Fr P. Descouvemont; Mgr Guy Gaucher; Fr M.-D. Molinie, OP; Fr T. de Roucy, SJM; Fr O. de Roulhac, OSB; Fr Bruno-Marie Simon, OP; Br Silouane; Fr F. Frost; Fr J. Mimeault, CSsR; Fr Thibault; Fr A. Birot. Edited by Anne de Blaÿ. Editions Saint-Paul, 2000.

† See below, Introduction by Fr Antonio Boucher, CSsR, p. xxxvii.

many emotional wounds during his childhood and youth has been 'weaned' by the tenderness of his heavenly Mother, of his beloved Jesus and of his sister Thérèse, who was so incredibly close to him. That 'little Jesus' showers him with kisses, that Mary takes him on her knees, that he snuggles up against her breast, all these marks of affection would surprise us, nay, disturb us, if they were not encapsulated in that which is at the heart of little Van's experience and message: his unbounded confidence in Him who is Love.

In these conversations Jesus and Van often appear to us as mischievous children playing their childish games and this can seem somewhat disconcerting. But it is in this way that the whole of his life as a novice becomes a 'relationship of love'. The daily sacrifices (such as the soutane that is too small, too narrow and uncomfortable [449], his hunger and his tiredness), the numerous physical, psychological and, above all, spiritual trials, are all 'subjects for dialogue' with Jesus, with Mary, with Thérèse.

What strikes one first of all in the *Conversations* is that everything in Van's life: the most ordinary things, the sad memories of his family, of his childhood, his frequent sadnesses, his feelings of disgust of which he speaks so often, his physical weaknesses, hunger and fatigue, all, really all, are lived with Jesus, with Mary his Mother, with Thérèse his sister. They are not 'elevations', beautiful spiritual thoughts that fill these pages, but really the enactment of what is probably the true secret of little Van:

> I used to think, that to be holy, to seek perfection meant a life full of charm, like a wonderful springtime ... I thought that holiness was perpetual joy without the shadow of sadness. But with time, the more I advance the more I see that sanctity is a life in which it is necessary to change sadness into joy (Correspondence 28 January 1951).

The *Conversations* are, throughout his novitiate, this 'laboratory of faith' of which the Holy Father spoke to youth at the time of the evening gathering of Tor Vergata at the Jubilee of Youth: a laboratory where the reader can see, in the daily life lived in the friendship of Jesus, this transformation of sadness and suffering into a happiness which, too often, we believe impossible and beyond our reach. The *Conversations* are the putting into practice the 'grace of Christmas' of 1940:

> I found the most precious treasure of my life at that moment ...
> My soul was transformed in an instant. No longer did I fear suffering. God had confided a mission to me: that of changing suffering

into happiness. I had not to suppress it but to change it into happiness (Autobiography 439).

That it is possible in spite of all our natural repugnance towards suffering ('I do not like suffering,' says the little brother, Conv. 654), that it is possible to change suffering into happiness, this book of the *Conversations* gives us a simple assurance: 'That's the point, little brother, continue to accept suffering patiently. That is to love; why worry?' (Conv. 655) 'Oh Mother, I love you, make me suffer joyfully' (Conv. 695).

The secret of this transformation is called love. And Brother Marcel has the vocation of an apostle of the love of Jesus, for him, for his country Vietnam, for France the enemy, for priests, for everyone: 'Little child of my love, one can never measure my love,' Jesus said to him (Conv. 40). Jesus calls him, 'Little apostle of my love' (Conv. 69).

And here we have the school of Thérèse bearing fruit in the life of Brother Marcel. Jesus calls him 'his little flower', so fragile

> ... that I never dare depart from you. Is that not an advantage for you? It is precisely because of your weakness that you are, on my part, the object of a much greater love ... Remember always that you must never be sad because of your weakness. And no matter how great your weakness, always remain in peace, believing that my love would never have the heart to separate itself from you, my little flower (Conv. 82).

If, therefore, little Van experienced such attention on Jesus' part, he to whom Jesus wished to teach, 'that really you do not have an ounce of virtue' (Conv. 651–2), how could one not confidently take courage?

> Little brother, always remember that you are truly a destitute and poor soul. Do not be preoccupied by your weakness, as your sister Thérèse has told you and as I myself have told you many times. It is in knowing your nothingness that your confidence in me will have to be really strong (Conv. 652).

To be discouraged by your weakness, 'what sadness that would be for me,' Jesus tells him (Conv. 35). 'Pray that men in great numbers are animated by an unshakeable confidence in my love. If, in a sinner, I still find the word confidence, this sinner already belongs to me' (Conv. 35).

Here is an important consequence of this teaching on confidence:

> **Marcel**: Little Jesus, according to what you are saying, I think that

it is not certain that a soul can fall into hell. I still think that it is certainly very difficult for the devil to snatch a soul from your hands, that it is almost impossible.

In reply there follows a text of dazzling power (Conv. 646–50) worthy of the great pages of Thérèse. It suffices here to quote a few lines in order to send the reader back to the complete text.

*Jesus*: Sin never offends my Love; there is absolutely nothing which offends my Love, except the lack of confidence in my Love ... Even the devil must despair of a soul in which the word 'confidence' is still found ... [there follows an exchange on the little occurrences of daily life which is normal in the *Conversations*] ... Later, in heaven, people will be very surprised to see among the ranks of the saints a great number of souls that one believed to be damned ... It is, perhaps, very easy for man to get to heaven while it can be very difficult ... to fall into hell; since Love can never suffer a soul to lose itself so easily.

A false guarantee of being saved quasi-automatically does not follow from this.

*Jesus*: However, little brother, these words must not be shown to all souls indiscriminately; it is necessary to do it prudently for fear that certain souls, knowing that, might become hardened in evil ... And as a consequence lose confidence in me and no longer have any confidence.

This call to confidence, to 'unshakeable confidence in my love' (Conv. 35) recalls the pressing appeals received and transmitted by Sister Faustina, canonized by the Holy Father on the second Sunday of Easter in the Holy Year.

This call does not minimize the weight of sin. At the beginning of the *Conversations* there is the image of the stick with which someone beats Jesus. 'The stick is the occasion of sin. To seize the opportunity to commit sin is to strike me' (Conv. 35). And these are the wounds received from sinners that Jesus wishes to share with souls who give themselves to him (Conv. 37).

Little Van has had to accept the sacrifice of never becoming a priest. He has had to endure the unhappy experience of the presbytery at Hữu-Bằng. This terrible sentence that Jesus speaks to Van is to be understood against this sombre background: 'Many priests use my name to lead a great number of souls to their ruin ... Pray for these unfortunate priests ... I still love them and I wait for them ... My child! Love me in their place ... '(Conv.10).

It is in this direction that Brother Marcel's vocation will receive its specificity. It will be characterized by two terms which for a young religious are, at first sight, surprising: to be the 'spouse' of Christ and to be 'mother of souls'. From the beginning of the *Conversations* these terms indicate the double vocation of the little brother:

> Very little spouse of my love, do you wish to lead to my love a great number of souls? Do not forget that this will be at the cost of great suffering. I have chosen you to be the mother of souls; now it is through the power of suffering that the mother succeeds in making worthy people of her children (Conv. 5).

In the volume of collected essays, edited by Anne de Blaÿ, *What is your secret, little Van?* two studies are more especially devoted to these two terms of spouse and mother: that of Father Francis Frost, 'Van and the spousal relationship with Jesus', and that of Father Jules Mimeault, 'My soul is a Mother'. The doctrinal balance, the biblical roots and the spiritual tradition of Van's usage of these terms emerges forcibly.

That the soul in her relationship with Jesus may be a spouse, called to live a spousal union with the Only Spouse, is a theme which is cherished in the Christian tradition, at least since the time of Origen. Used largely in the commentary on the Canticle of Canticles, it is clear that this spousality of the soul is not reserved solely to women: 'I have already spoken clearly of these things in the Gospel. I have not spoken particularly for women but for all souls ...' (Conv. 638). And Jesus explains to the brother who does not admit that his soul can be the spouse of Christ:

> If in one's relations with Jesus one has not got the feelings of a spouse with regard to his spouse, one will lack, also, the other feelings of the child towards his father, of the pupil towards his master, of the friend regarding his friend.

In brief, 'One is no longer even a man' (Conv. 635–6). It is really a question of the relationship of the creature towards his Creator, Father and Master who makes himself so close to us that the soul is called to friendship, to spousal love, to the union of love. The message that little Van transmits to us is of a theological and spiritual accuracy which far surpasses his own intellectual knowledge.

It is the same regarding the theme of the maternity of the soul. Here again the biblical entrenchment is evident. We need only think of the expressions of Saint Paul's maternal spirituality with regard to his communities. Little Van, who has not been called to become a priest as he had first of all wished, saw himself charged with being 'the little apostle of my love' (Conv. 20), the instrument that Love uses to spread the confident love in Jesus and, by that, to be 'mother of souls' (Conv. 27) and to draw to Jesus 'a great number of souls' (Conv. 48).

What we manage to get out of the *Conversations* is very far from exhausting the richness of images, of symbols, of themes and perspectives. In conclusion I return, however, to the question posed at the beginning: what is the status of these conversations, of these 'dictations' from heaven? What is the significance for the reader of the *Conversations* of this command of Jesus: 'Little apostle of my love, be for me like a pencil for my use. One I wish to make use of to write or to leave it in a corner, it is the same to it' (Conv. 20). What is the part of this pencil in Jesus' hand? If it has an instrumental role, an *instrumentum animatum*, as Saint Thomas Aquinas would say, it is an instrument which places all its being at the disposition of the Lord by a love which gives itself totally and whose joy is to do only the will of the Beloved.

The question of private revelations has been treated recently in a magisterial manner by Cardinal Joseph Ratzinger in his *Theological Commentary* on the 'Third Secret of Fatima', made public on 13 May 2000.* It is necessary to remember first of all that there is a difference not only in degree but also in nature between 'public revelation' and 'private revelations'. The former indicates the revelatory action of God intended for the whole of humanity. Its literary expression is found in the Bible, in the Old and New Testaments. It is accomplished with Christ in whom God gives us the definitive and impassable Word. There will be no other new revelation before the glorious return of Our Lord.† But the Catechism adds an important observation: 'Yet even if Revelation is already complete, it has not been made completely explicit; it remains for Christian faith gradually to grasp its full significance over the course of the centuries' (*CCC*, 66). This is done by meditation on the mysteries of faith, by experience of Christian life, by the work of theologians. And it is here, also, that is placed the role of 'private revelations'. This is what the Catechism says about it:

---

\* Published in *Documentation Catholique* no. 2230, 16 July 2000, pp. 678–83.
† Cf. *CCC*, 66.

Throughout the ages there have been so-called 'private revelations', some of which have been recognised by the authority of the Church. They do not belong, however, to the deposit of faith. It is not their role to improve or complete Christ's definitive revelation, but to help live more fully from it in a certain period of history. Guided by the Magisterium of the Church, the 'sensus fidelium' knows how to discern and welcome in these revelations whatever constitutes an authentic call of Christ or his saints to the Church' (*CCC*, 67).

If Revelation demands our faithful adherence, private revelations are an aid to faith, but we should not accord them nor demand for them the faith due to God who speaks to us through Revelation. The message of a private revelation can help us to live the Gospel better and point us more intensely towards Christ. 'It is a help which is offered but of which it is in no way obligatory to make use'.\* However, no one will neglect such an aid, all the more so when it often brings an enrichment and a deepening of popular piety, which is an inestimable treasure for the life of the Church.

The Church has at all times received by such 'messages', new impulsions, calls to conversion to a more authentic Christian life, encouragements and consolations in the trials of life here below. If it falls on the magisterium of the Church to make a discernment on 'private revelations', it is no less true that the *sensus fidelium* knows by the instinct of the Holy Spirit 'how to discern and welcome in these revelations whatever constitutes an authentic call of Christ or his saints to the Church' (*CCC*, 67).

But let us dwell briefly on the anthropological and psychological aspects of these messages. How are they received and transmitted? Little Van speaks often of 'dictations' for which he knows himself and wishes to be the simple 'pencil'. How does he receive them? By locutions and visions? By interior voices? This reception is certainly hidden from others and Brother Marcel takes great care to keep it secret. But he submits everything to his spiritual father in total confidence. The latter encourages him and follows him with wisdom and humility, and it is not the least merit of Father Boucher to have known so well how to accompany his novice.

What Cardinal Ratzinger says on the subject of visions (with the emphasis on Fatima) has value also for the locutions which Brother Marcel has enjoyed:

---

\* Card. Ratzinger, *Documentation Catholique*, p. 679.

To see interiorly does not mean that it is a question of fantasy, that which would only be an expression of subjective imagination. It means, rather, that the soul is brushed by the touch of something real, even if it is suprasensitive, and it is enabled to see the non-sensible, the non-visible to the senses – a vision with the 'interior senses'.

And the Cardinal adds a remark which applies well to little Van: 'One will perhaps understand why it is specifically children who are the privileged recipients of such apparitions; the soul is still little spoiled, its interior capacity of perception is still hardly damaged.'*

What is then the role of the instrument, of the 'pencil'? It is used 'with its physical potential, with the characteristics and perceived forms which are available to it.'

There is, therefore, a 'process of translation in so far as the subject, in an essential manner, is participating in the formation, under the form of pictures, of that which emerges. The picture can take shape only according to his capacities and means.'† This is true in the same way with words, with concepts, and in the case of the 'dictations' of Brother Marcel: they also carry in themselves the limitations of the subject who perceives.'††

Let me conclude with a word from the great Cardinal in his masterly exposé on Fatima and private revelations: 'The images (the visions of the three secrets) are rather, so to speak, a synthesis of the impetus which comes from On-High and the potential of this made available from the subject which perceives, in this case the children.'§ I believe that it is legitimate to apply this exposé to the *Conversations* to which this preface wishes to be a simple introduction.

If it is true that 'private revelations' should not be read in a spirit of curiosity which looks to draw from them some novelty, some sensational and unusual things, but always in a disposition to allow oneself to be led to the centre of our faith, towards God and his will, towards Christ and his love, then there is no doubt that the *Conversations* will lead us right to the centre, to the immeasurable love of Christ ('one can never measure my love,' Conv. 40) and they invite us, through the little apostle of his love, to become such in our turn.

Under these conditions, what riches of themes, of insights and experiences are found overflowing in these *Conversations*, nourished by this

---

\* Card. Ratzinger, *Documentation Catholique*, p. 680.
† Ibid.
†† Ibid.
§ Ibid., p. 681.

central message and illustrating it. We are only at the beginning of what Van has to say to us, has to do here below:

> O Mary, my personal mission is to be the apostle of souls and the apostle, especially, of children ... But my humble position as a Brother of the Congregation of the Most Holy Redeemer does not allow me to fulfil this mission immediately. It is only later in heaven that I will be able to fulfil it perfectly (Conv. 347).

Christoph Cardinal Schönborn, OP
Archbishop of Vienna
Bayeux, 10 July 2001
(52nd anniversary of Van's death)

# Novitiate Life at the Time of Van

Some months after his arrival Van is admitted to the group of postulants. A year later he begins his novitiate under the direction of Father Antonio Boucher. The period of the *Conversations* covers Van's novitiate and the following year. These few notes will give the reader an idea of Van's regime and will give some explanations on the customs of the Redemptorists.

When Van is finally admitted to the community of the Redemptorists at Hanoi he becomes a postulant and receives at this time a new name, Marcel. This symbolizes his death to the world and his new life. After a year of postulancy he begins his novitiate on 8 September 1945. For their formation at that time the novices were divided into two groups: the choir Brothers and the lay or assistant brothers. Van was part of the second group.

The chorists followed a course of religious instruction and studied the Constitution and Rules in French and said the office in Latin while the lay brothers used only Vietnamese. The offices bringing together the whole community took place in the main chapel and the exercises proper to the novitiate took place in the novitiate chapel.

Saint Alphonsus, in founding the Congregation, had in mind the evangelisation of the poor and more abandoned. For that end he invites his sons to imitate the divine Redeemer in all things. The Fathers are trained for the missions and for preaching so as to follow the example of Jesus in announcing the Good News. As for the brothers, they try by their humble service to follow Jesus more particularly in his hidden life at Nazareth.

The time of the novitiate is often a time of trials. Under the vigilant direction of the Master of Novices the Brothers devote themselves to becoming religious by spiritual combat, prayer, mortification, intellectual training, silence and the fraternal life. The daily timetable encourages this objective by regulating at every moment the novice's occupation: prayers, meditations, reading, time of manual work (longer for the brothers), rest and recreation.

Rising at 4.30, the brothers begin the day by reciting the *Angelus* and by meditation with the whole community in the main chapel. After Mass, always followed by thanksgiving, is the time for breakfast and doing the dishes. At 7.30 the novices begin their manual work: (housework, work in the kitchen, looking after the linen, etc.). At 9.00 they all assemble for a short conference (half an hour) given by the Novice Master or his assistant, *Father Socius*. This is followed by free time for private devotion (visits to the Blessed Sacrament, rosary, etc.), in the small novitiate chapel. Then the whole community assembles in the main chapel for the first examination of conscience. At midday, after the Angelus, everyone meets for lunch in the large refectory of the community. The brothers serve the meals and the choir Brothers and one of the Fathers assist them on Fridays. After an hour's siesta the brothers begin the afternoon with a time of spiritual reading and meditation, each one in his own room. At 3 p.m. the rosary is recited in common in the small novitiate chapel. There follows time for each one's individual devotions, Work recommences at about 4 p.m. At 5 p.m. free time commences and at 6.30 the whole community assembles in the main chapel for a half-hour's meditation, followed by the *Angelus* which precedes dinner. After the washing-up the lay brothers meet with the choir Brothers in the novitiate room for communal recreation. At 8 p.m. evening prayer signals the beginning of the great silence for the night. Lights out is at 10 p.m.

At this time the asceticism is hard: fasting, the discipline and the wearing of little chains. (These corporal mortifications were, in the spirit of the time, a means of uniting oneself to the sufferings of Christ during his Passion.) At the final recreation of the day each one draws by chance a number which corresponds to one from a little list of penances, which will be carried out the following day. After the novitiate, with the exception of Friday discipline, particular penances have to be decided with the spiritual Father.

In all of the novitiates, the 25th of each month is a feast day. Each novice is invited to celebrate Christmas. This day is a day of rest, which gives more time for meditation on the life of the Child Jesus and for writing a letter to him. In the morning the Mass of Christmas is celebrated. At the end of the day the letter is placed in the crib during the adoration of the Child Jesus. On this particular day, speaking is allowed during the meals (normally meals are in silence so that one can listen to the reading) and all the novices assemble for a little treat.

At least once a month the novices have a spiritual interview with the

Master of Novices. The Rule invites them to open themselves freely to him; for they have to see in him, with eyes of faith, the Divine Redeemer himself.*

The entire day is spent in silence. Silence is observed during work, except in case of necessity, and it is punctuated every quarter of an hour with an invocation. Manual work is reserved more particularly for the brothers: the bursar's office, the tailor's workshop, the infirmary, the kitchen, the dining room, the sacristy and the reception; and the novices help the brothers in their work.

So as to encourage a spirit of humility, a practice existed which surprises us today. In turn a novice was nominated as zealator. His function, as his name suggests, was to encourage zealous behaviour. He had to observe any infringements of the Rule made by anyone and, each week, at the chapter of faults, he had to reprimand the brothers who were guilty of these infringements. The latter had to accept these reprimands humbly without attempting to justify themselves, even if the reprimand was unjustified. A new zealator was appointed on the 25th of each month. At the end of the novitiate the brothers pronounce their first vows of obedience, chastity and poverty. Six years later (before the expiration of their temporary vows) they could commit themselves by means of perpetual vows after a retreat of six months. This retreat is what is called the 'second novitiate'.

The Friends of Van (Les Amis de Van)

---

* This is why Van affectionately called Father Boucher 'bearded Jesus'. In fact all missionaries wore beards.

# Introduction

The translation of the confidential writings in these pages has been made from a Vietnamese text written by Brother Marcel during his novitiate, 1945–6, and a little more during the rest of his life.

Since this Vietnamese text was written on both sides of sheets of very ordinary paper (it was wartime), I believed it prudent to copy them personally on to student copybooks so as to preserve them more easily. It goes without saying that I took the greatest care to omit nothing nor to change the original text.

In making the translation, so as to make reading easier, I allowed myself to identify and clearly underline the name of the speaker who was indicated only by a dash in the Vietnamese text.

Given the fragility of this first-hand document and not foreseeing what was going to happen to Vietnam in the following years, I thought it good to confide it to Father Benoît Hoàng-Quang Lương, the Provincial of the new religious Province of Vietnam at the time of his visit to Canada on 9 September 1969.

My intention was that the Vietnamese text be preserved in the archives of the Vietnamese Province in Saigon, all the more so since Jesus, from his first conversation with Brother Marcel, expressed to him his wish to choose him to serve as an intermediary of his love for his Vietnamese countrymen. I do not know what has become of this text but I am confident that it is safe and that one day it will be able to serve as evidence in favour of the cause of Brother Marcel Van. I confide it, therefore, to the keeping of the Lord whose mysterious intentions escape us.

In my capacity as master of novices and spiritual counsellor, I testify that I have lived, day by day, and at the side of Brother Marcel, all the events and little facts related on the small pages that he gave to me regularly each week. On reading these texts, I sensed that this very small brother whom Jesus, Mary and Thérèse were leading by the hand would have a role to play in the Church and in the world. I also felt myself constrained not to allow anything to be lost from the treasure which was unfolding before my eyes, by his hands and his heart. I humbly recognized that Brother Marcel taught me more on the spiritual life than I was able to teach him.

First of all, I have been profoundly moved by the unbelievable familiarity and tenderness of which Brother Marcel has been the object on the part of his heavenly interlocutors. On the other hand, his exemplary life, his limpidity of soul, his perfect obedience to his director and his generosity in face of sacrifice favourably impressed me regarding his truthfulness and the authenticity of his communications; this, obviously, with all the reserve necessary, not wishing in anything to anticipate the final judgement which belongs by right to the authority of the Church.

Antonio Boucher, CSsR

# Foreword

'Love of Jesus' that is what Jesus calls the message that he confides to Van for his compatriots and all little souls.* Van is therefore charged to write this message.

The original manuscripts are of different shapes and sizes:

89 pages, 15 x 11cm, with writing on both sides;
60 pages, 13 x 20cm, with writing on both sides, and then;
475 exercise book pages, 17 x 22cm of which some are loose and some are attached. In general the paper is of very poor quality. The first sheets are written in turquoise or blue ink, the copybooks, generally, are written in violet ink. Certain pages are sometimes written in black pencil.

The translation offered under the title of *Conversations* is the second tome of the *Complete Works of Van*. It follows the *Autobiography*. Father Boucher completed it on his return to Canada in 1964. As a privileged witness of Van's spiritual life and mandated by Jesus to help Van in the work that was confided to him,† Father Boucher is therefore the person who can accomplish better than anyone this difficult work which is the transfer of the Vietnamese culture into Western culture.

For the current edition we have allowed ourselves certain 'touching up' in altering some antiquated expressions, some heaviness of style and, in accordance with Father Boucher's wish, by employing the more familiar mode of address in the conversations.†† This has been done the

---

\* Cf. Conv. 6–7 and 12.
† Cf. Conv. 28.
†† It is impossible to translate the numerous degrees of respect between the generations, much more numerous than in French which are limited to two.

better to illustrate Van's simplicity and intimacy with Jesus and the saints whom he loved to invoke. Further, we have added some explanatory notes at the bottom of some pages. The pieces in italics are commentary notes by Father Boucher. We have considered it useful to keep them in the body of the text in view of their importance.

So as to make reference as simple as possible, we have chosen to keep the numbering of the original pages so as to facilitate a reference to the original text. These references are placed in the margins within parentheses, e.g. (251). Sometimes an extra leaf is inserted in the middle of another one. For example, on page 135 Van speaks of a poem he has written on a different sheet. We have, therefore, begun the first part of page 135 with the reference (135-a), then we have inserted the poem with the reference (135-1) and then we have continued page 135 with the reference (135-b). In our example, if the poem had had 3 pages it would have had the references (135-1) (135-2) and (135-3). Certain pages are not mentioned. These correspond to blank pages.

At the end of the work the reader will find a list of Redemptorist Fathers and Brothers that Van had rubbed shoulders with at the time of the *Conversations*.

The Friends of Van (*Les Amis de Van*)

# Chronological Notes

| | | |
|---|---|---|
| 1928 | 15 March | Birth at Ngăm-Giáo (Bắc-Ninh Province) Baptized the following day |
| 1932 | | Birth of Anne-Marie Tế |
| 1932–1934 | | Stayed with his Aunt Khánh, 18km from Ngăm-Giáo, with occasional visits to his parents |
| 1934 | | First Communion. Confirmation |
| 1935 | May | Departure for Hữu-Bằng. Van is confided to Father Nhã |
| 1937 | | Van dislocates his knee and is cared for by Mrs Sáu |
| 1938 | | Van's family is reduced to poverty. He becomes the 'boy' of the parish priest. His first attempt to flee from Hữu-Bằng |
| 1940 | 10 May | Obtains his certificate of studies |
| | Summer | Sent to Thái-Nguyên then runs away to his parents' home. His mother takes him back to Hữu-Bằng |
| | Autumn | Third escape. Roaming around Bắc-Ninh for a fortnight. Stays for two weeks at his Aunt Khánh's and then returns to Ngăm-Giáo |
| | Christmas | Interior illumination: 'to change suffering into joy' |
| 1941 | Jan/May | Stays at his aunt's |
| | June | Returns to his family until the parish priest of Hữu-Bằng takes him back to Hữu-Bằng |
| | October | Vow of virginity. Foundation of the 'Angels of the Resistance' |
| 1942 | January | Arrival at the junior seminary of Lạng-Sơn. |
| | Summer | Closure of the junior seminary. Van is admitted to the presbytery of St Thérèse of the Child Jesus at Quảng-Uyên |

|      |           |                                                                                      |
|------|-----------|--------------------------------------------------------------------------------------|
|      | October   | First meeting with Saint Thérèse                                                     |
| 1943 | June      | Expelled from Quảng-Uyên. Goes to his parents and then to Hữu-Bằng                   |
| 1944 | 2 August  | Admitted as gardener's helper at the Redemptorists' at Hanoi                         |
|      | 17 Oct    | Admitted to the community                                                            |
| 1945 | 8 Sept    | The taking of the habit at the beginning of the novitiate                            |
| 1946 | 8 Sept    | Temporary Vows                                                                       |
| 1950 |           | Leaves for the monastery of Saigon                                                   |
| 1952 |           | Second Novitiate at Đa-Lạt                                                           |
|      | 8 Sept    | Perpetual Vows                                                                       |
| 1954 | 14 Sept   | Returns to the Hanoi Monastery by the last aeroplane from the South to the North     |
| 1955 | 7 May     | Arrested in Hanoi                                                                    |
| 1956 | May       | Judged and condemned to fifteen years of re-education                                |
| 1959 | 10 July   | Van dies, at midday                                                                  |

# Conversations

## Before 7 October 1945

*Jesus*: Marcel! Humble child of my love, listen to the words I am saying (1) to you here and put them into writing. Do the same work that Sister Benigna Consolata* is accomplishing. I want you to serve as an intermediary of my love with your Vietnamese compatriots. My child! You will certainly feel a certain disquiet on hearing me speak like this ... Indeed, when I spoke to you previously your confessor told you that it was not appropriate to concern yourself with those things ... But since I have made you see and understand in what way I converse with Sister Benigna, how can you still doubt the manifestations of my love to all those souls who are sincere with me? ... Remain, therefore, in peace. The words that I am speaking to you here are words of truth that only the simple and the humble are able to understand.

*Brother Marcel confided to me that he hesitated to agree before consulting his director. And Jesus said to him:*

That's fine. I allow you to ask your director's advice; however I am (2) certain that he will agree also ... Now I am speaking to you. Write down what you can remember.

*Marcel*: The time is up; I will go to work with my brethren.

*Jesus*: There are some minutes left still, keep on writing. Each sentence that you are able to write adds to my glory. If you wish to glorify me, continue writing. I wish to seek my glory in the words that you are writing here.

*Marcel*: My Jesus, my handwriting is terrible.

*Jesus*: That is not important. Listen and continue to write; remember well that I never attach importance to external beauty; such things (3) never have the power to move my loving heart; only souls who love me with the sincerity of a child are capable of drawing my love. I accept you as my spouse; that is possible although you are a man ... As I told you I attach no importance to what is external.

Humble child of my love, do you love me? I am the Spouse of your soul ... At this time are you not experiencing much disgust? This is the

---

\* Sister Benigna Consolata (1885–1916) was a religious of the Visitation of Como (Italy). She loved to converse with Jesus who had asked her to be his little secretary. Van spoke of her often to his brothers in the novitiate.

price you will pay to taste the delights that I will reserve for you later. Offer this disgust to me so that during this time of trial I may give joy to those souls who find themselves in an arid state. This is a sacrifice that I wish always from you.

Now that you have some time, write what follows. Each time that you say: 'My Jesus, I love you' or other words expressing the tenderness of your love, I am impelled to give you a kiss. Little child of my love, I want you to tell me of your love always in this way in order to give you the kisses that the world repulses and does not wish to receive. There you have what your Jesus wishes, conform yourself to his will; nothing is more beautiful than to do the will of the one whom one loves.

(4) Have you felt for some time a lot of dryness in going to communion? Accept it cheerfully, it is my will. You doubtless think that the moments of perceptible fervour devoted to conversing familiarly with me are the only times when you can receive my favours. Not at all. Listen to me carefully so that you will not sigh deeply when you feel disgust. In giving you favours, I pay no heed to your state of dryness or fervour; all I demand is confidence in me, and this constant love which, even in face of difficulty, knows how to remain courageous and remain unshakeably faithful to the Beloved ...

Marcel, there you are, troubled concerning the words that you must write. My little child, I do not want you to trouble yourself in this way; no I do not wish that you cause yourself as much pain as Sister Benigna. It will suffice that you write when you have some free time. I have not told you that it will be necessary to neglect your duties in order to write my words. All that I have told you is this, listen carefully so that you will remember it: 'When it is possible for you to write, I will speak to you and you will only have to write what you have retained.'

(5) Very little spouse of my love, do you wish to lead a great number of souls to my love? Do not forget that it will be at the cost of great suffering. I have chosen you to be the mother of souls; now, it is by suffering that the mother succeeds in making worthy people of her children ... That is enough, what follows concerns you personally; there is no need to write it, it is sufficient to remember it.

In asking you to be the intermediary of my love with your compatriots, my intention was that you write not only the words that I dictate to you, but also those that you speak to me. Since there are many who only listen to what I say without daring to converse quite frankly with me as children, under the pretext that it is not proper ... tell them that I gladly listen to ordinary conversations, even the simplest ones, and I take pleasure in hearing them. There, that is all I expect from souls who (6) love me ... Continue to write my words down and call them 'Love of Jesus'. As for the words you address to me, you will call them 'Love of

Marcel'. I do not look for elegant words as do people of the world, only childlike words coming from a loving heart have the gift of charming my ear. And you, my child, always act in this way since I find much attraction in the words that you address to me here; I never tire of listening to them ...

Stop writing now; it is time for spiritual reading. You will continue when you have time. Oh my child! How I love you! Seeing that the words 'Jesus I love you' are always on your lips, I never cease to place my lips against your cheek. My child, love me incessantly because in that is my will.

Ah, my child, do you hesitate to write. Do not let that discourage you. If I gave the name of 'Fatherly Recommendations' to the message addressed to Sister Benigna, I will call the one that I am now addressing to you, 'Love of Jesus'. And in thus showing you my love, my great (7) wish is to see you draw towards me a great number of souls who will love me as you do ... Oh! My spouse, how many souls there are waiting for the words that you are writing to learn how to love me. Continue to write therefore and be really convinced that these words will later draw in large measure the souls of your compatriots.

Is it not true that certain people criticize you, saying that you have a very nasty look on your face and that you can never become a saint? Oh my little flower, to comfort yourself listen to the words of your loving friend which will be able also to comfort those who are suffering from some external infirmity ... I have told you already: external charms can in no way attract my love; only a sincere friendship and an unshakeable confidence are capable of touching my heart ...

Little friend of my love, when I contemplate your soul I am delighted by its beauty. What name would you like me to give it? I shall call it: 'My little flower'. And I shall warm this little flower by the sun of love and I (8) shall make the dew of grace fall on it. Oh, my little flower, exhale your scent before my throne. When I look at you in your purity, what a joy it is for me and how I wish that all souls were like yours.

Humble child of my love, while writing, recite this phrase which will be a pledge of the love between the two of us: 'My beloved Jesus, I love you and because I love you, you have chosen me to be your spouse for all eternity; and I, Jesus, I shall never allow my little friend to leave my so gentle arms.'

Marcel, my child, I am now giving you this recommendation: never be afraid of your spiritual director. Doubtless it is necessary to show him external marks of respect, but it is also necessary to be joyful with him. Seeing you happy will delight him as I delight in it also. Your director (9) is the bond which joins your love closely to mine ... Do not be afraid, therefore, to let him know all that happens to you, including my love for you ... He must know these things to maintain the purity of your soul ... Do you understand my child? Always maintain this manner of behaving with your director; put all timidity to one side and be sincere with him as you are with me ...

I am now going to speak to you about priests. Remember what I am going to say to you. Shame on the directors of conscience who, seeing in the souls of their charges a bond of friendship being forged with me, far from tightening this knot, cause it to be loosened to the extent that these souls end up by distancing themselves from me ... My child, pray a lot for these unfortunate spiritual directors; if many souls do not know how to love me, they alone must carry the responsibility ...

(10) Happy are you not to be a priest ... Many priests acting in my name allow a great number of souls to be lost ... I tell these priests: 'I thirst for souls', nevertheless, they do not take care to give them to me. Imitating the torturers, they give me vinegar to drink, and not daring to come close to me they give me this drink by means of a reed ... Oh! ... How I suffer from such behaviour ... Pray for these unhappy priests ... I love them still and I wait for them but, for their part, they only know how to receive my love without loving me in return. They abuse the time I give to them in order to insult me. My child! Love me in place of this kind of priest.

(11) However, one thing does comfort me a lot. It is that many priests still know how to love me ... Truly, these priests gather round me like a shield which protects me against the arrows coming from those unfortunate priests ... I have a predilection for these good priests, I fix my gaze on them, I rejoice with them, I do not cease to be their guide and support ... I do everything to favour them ... They are always at my side without ever distancing themselves from me. Oh! Child of my love, how I wish there were many priests who act in the same way towards me ... My child, find such priests for me (First Friday of the month of September 1945).

(12) Now write down these words which are important to me: 'From the time that a soul possesses a little real love for me, it will draw to itself all of the fire of love which burns in my heart and, thus transformed into a burning bush, it will be consumed and purified by it ... It will then become so closely united to my love that it will form but one heart with me ... It is, therefore, impossible to separate me from this heart so closely united to mine. Can you understand, my child, the immense love that I have for these souls! ...'

Oh my little apostle! It is because I love you that I give you this name of little apostle. The words I am dictating to you are destined solely for the little souls who abandon themselves totally to my will and who never consent to distance themselves from me ... It is only humble and simple

souls who are capable of understanding these words I am repeating to
you ... Later other souls will do, like you, the work that I will confide (13)
to them; they will follow each other without interruption and I will call
them also, my 'little apostles, the little apostles of my love'. I am reserv-
ing this name for the souls who will listen to the words that you are
writing here; they are my words and they will benefit the souls who will
listen to them ...

Later, you will see, I will have a whole army of apostles and all I will
teach them will be to love me as you yourself, love me. But I need
someone to serve as intermediary ... You, therefore, will be this intermediary. My 'little apostle', do you accept this role? It will suffice to
write down my words and afterwards there will be other apostles who
will enable them to be put into practice by everybody. So, therefore,
your work will be accomplished and my love will spread ... If it does
not, my love will be extinguished among men ... What I said previously (14)
to Sister Benigna Consolata ... My little flower, my spouse, little apostle
of my love, I recall it now for you ... Nothing is more beautiful than to
do the will of the one who one loves ... Accept, therefore, to do my will.
My child, I am taking you in my arms, I am lifting you to my lips and I
am giving you a kiss. Seeing your soul burning with love for me, I am
beside myself and my sole desire is to see many souls love me as you do
... My spouse, there is nothing so beautiful as to do the will of the one
one loves. There are still many things that you must write and that I will
tell you later ... Little apostle of my love, the words that I am dictating
to you here, do you find them beautiful? ... As for me, I find them very (15)
beautiful as they are coming from a heart overflowing with love.

### 7 October 1945

*Jesus*: The work that I have confided to you, do it quickly as I will not
leave you long in this land of exile. So, dedicate all your free time to
writing down my words. When you have time, I will speak to you and I
will do so for as long as it will be possible for you to write ... It is only
after I have called you to me, that the world will know and put into
practice the words I have asked you to write down ...

Little apostle of my love, be patient still for a little while and you will
taste the joy of resting in my arms. You will be able to show me then
your feelings in perfect freedom; no longer will it be as it is now.

That's enough. Go and walk in the garden with your brothers for fear (16)
that one of them might know what you are doing ... It is necessary to
be prudent so as not to allow anything to be obvious ... Be on your
guard a little.

## 8 October 1945

*Jesus*: My little flower, those souls which do not burn with love for me are very unfortunate; if they happen to commit faults, these faults do not cease to accumulate in them ... But, on the contrary, in the souls inflamed with my love, I do not see any imperfection because as soon as they commit a fault, this fault is immediately consumed in the fire of love, so that they are always pure in my eyes ... These souls are very dear to me; I hide them in the depths of my heart, considering them as very expensive jewels which belong to me, and nothing can extinguish in them the fire of my love.

(17) Oh, my little friend, I see that you are very sad ... Do you know, my spouse, the cause of this sadness? It is nothing other than the love which consumes you. You will excuse me, my child, my little friend. Yes, you will excuse me, since to see you in this state only adds to my joy, and this joy has the gift of making me forget even the sufferings that my spouse is enduring at this moment ... It happens, therefore, that with my spouses who love me with a sincere heart, I am in the habit of practising this kind of forgetfulness in order to test the strength of their love, as people in the world do. My little child, do you understand me? Try to understand and welcome this sadness cheerfully. Wait for me a little bit longer and I will come back to you. Do you agree? My little soul, chase away sadness, dry your tears; the day will come when the sight of my love for you will make your tears flow ... As in the past ...

(18) Never will I separate myself from you, my spouse.

My little flower, how beautiful you are! But I do not want your beauty to appear externally ... I will use the appearance of your simplicity in order to hide you in my hands ... My little flower, never allow your beauty to appear externally so it may be something reserved for your only-beloved who finds his joy simply in contemplating you ... That is his great desire ... My little flower, the more beautiful you are, the more you will be smothered with caresses.

*(In order to try Brother Marcel's obedience, I asked him to discontinue writing down the words he said he was receiving from Jesus. He immediately gave me the little sheets that he used for his writings. I lifted this restriction after two weeks and he resumed writing from 22 October.)*

## 22 October 1945

*Marcel*: Jesus, speak to me again ... (19)

*Jesus*: My child, has your sadness gone away? Since your director is allowing you to continue your writing, I am continuing to speak to you so that you may write. As for you, my little spouse, be happy to write and never doubt the veracity of my words. Pay a lot of attention to what I am saying. I am repeating for you once again: if the words that I am saying to you were not true, how could I ever allow a soul who loves me and confides himself to me without reservation to fall into error? Furthermore, be really convinced of this and never forget it. In speaking previously to Sister Benigna, I predicted to her that there would exist later an army of little apostles of my love who would teach people to love me and who would save souls for me. And you, my little apostle, it is thus at this very moment that I have chosen you and, with you, many others who will follow one another in order to continue in the world the work that I wish to accomplish. I assign a different task to each one. These apostles are still hidden at this moment, waiting to show themselves on the day fixed by my will.

Later there will also be an army of the Blessed Virgin. Remember to pray from this moment for this weak army since, hardly will it be (20) thrown into battle when all hell will rise up united against it so that it will appear impossible to stand up against them. But, eventually, hell will suffer a resounding defeat and then the Blessed Virgin will be glorified on earth. So you must pray a lot for this army so that it can fight with keenness and courage right to the end. This army does not actually exist yet but it will exist later ...

*Marcel*: Jesus, I am afraid that the words you are addressing to me will give rise to feelings of pride in me.

*Jesus*: Do not let that worry you since it is only after having first delivered you of this vice that I have shown myself to you. Little apostle of my love, be for me like a pencil for my own use. One that I may wish to write with or leave to one side, it is all the same to it; that I use it in such or such a manner when I wish to write a word, it must follow the movement of my hand. To that extent, what have you got to be proud about? Be, therefore, this docile pencil for me and I will never have to be impatient with you.

## 23 October 1945

(21) **Marcel**: My beloved Jesus, you do love me a lot, don't you? My sister Thérèse said to me quite correctly: 'Jesus grows tired more quickly at having to wait for us than we do at having to wait for him' ... Indeed, dear Jesus, after having made me wait for a little more than ten days you were in a hurry to come back to me immediately. I was very sad during that time and I cried a lot but perhaps you were even sadder than I was at having to hide your love from me. It sometimes happened that my sister, Saint Thérèse, and my sister Benigna cried at this thought. It must be very painful for you who are Love not to be able to show your love. If I have cried also it is only because you left me alone, abandoned. Besides, you know well, Jesus, that I am still very weak, incapable of putting up with this sadness, this weariness. So my sister Thérèse had to follow me all day to remind me of this and that. My mother Mary equally took pity on me; she came each day to comfort me and to help me to be braver. While you remained hidden they both came to my aid and I am really privileged to be so loved by everyone. I must recognize however that it is solely because of my weakness and my misfortune that I receive such marks of affection. It is you, yourself,

(22) Jesus who said to me: 'Marcel, if you were not weaker than the saints, your brothers and sisters, my love would never have shown itself externally to you.' Yes, I am really miserable not knowing how to do anything worthwhile, if it is not to love you, Jesus, and to place all my trust in you.

Today I have had some free time, why do you not speak to me, Jesus? Perhaps you have to wait for another time.

**Jesus**: My little friend, I am still saving many sufferings for you later but I must first of all ask you if you are ready to accept this joyfully. Without taking this precaution I would be afraid when the moment had arrived to send them to you, that you would not accept them and then I would not know to whom to send them. Besides, when I send sufferings, I do not send them suddenly but little by little so that they are easier to bear. If, on the contrary, I were to send them all at the same time, the sight of these sufferings would, without doubt, frighten you. My little friend, accept, therefore, sufferings with joy. Concerning my apostles and my spouses, there is nothing which pleases me and fills me with joy so much as the joyful acceptance of suffering through love. If, therefore, you

(23) want to please me, act always in this way and I will help you and you will never have to fear that I will ever abandon you.

**Marcel**: I do not know why when it is the afternoon I experience such disgust and I do not feel like working. Jesus, come to help me; I want to work with joy for love of you.

## 24 October 1945

*Jesus*: My little child, so, you have a slight interior pain. Wishing to give the grace of easier conversion to a sinner, I have taken all his hesitation from him by allowing you to suffer in his place. Had you not accepted, much more time still would have been necessary before this sinner returned to me. All I ask of you so that I can save souls is that you accept little sacrifices of this nature.

## 25 October 1945

*Jesus*: My little apostle, you are still engaged today writing the story of your vocation, the story of the love I have shown to you. First, finish this work and then I will speak to you so that you can write. All work done through love for me is pleasing to me; moreover, this work about your vocation will serve to make known the love that I have for all souls as well as for you.

## 26 October 1945

*Jesus*: My little flower, do not hesitate to accept the sufferings that I am sending to you; neither hesitate to welcome the joys which come to you from my hand. Whether I make the pearls of a gentle dew fall on you, or I allow the worms of the soil to make you suffer, my little flower, always retain your freshness. And I, seeing you in this state, I can only take pleasure in all that you do. (24)

*Marcel*: Jesus, I would like you to speak to me about humility of heart.

*Jesus*: My child, this is my reply. This morning I spoke to you for a fairly long time, which troubled you did it not? I will now summarize in a few words. Remember each sentence and write it clearly. Your formation in humility is not your affair; it is the business of your director. In the same way as you are united to me you must also be with your director ... Your director, he is me, he is my spirit, do whatever he wishes you to do. I said to you the other day that you must become as a pencil for my use. Listen to me well. No matter where or how my will, that is to

(25) say, your director, places you, it is I who places you there, and the only thing you have to do is to forget yourself in order to accept the decisions of my spirit. There you have it; that's humility. Have you understood?

*Marce*l: Yes, I have understood.

Jesus, today I heard the novice master ask for prayers for priests, saying that certain priests seem to have lost the faith ... How can a priest lose the faith? Since without faith it is impossible to love you and also impossible to save souls. That must make you so sad, Jesus. What can I do to comfort you and what means can I use so that priests can become more helpful to the Church? It is truly strange. Why does such a disorder exist among the clergy at this time?

*Jesus*: My child, little apostle of my love and my little friend, do you love me? What you understand on the subject of priests is very little. If I let you see the pain that priests cause me every day by their conduct, you would perhaps ask me to chastise these unhappy priests here and now ... Apostle of my love, try to pray and to practise little sacrifices to console my loving Heart. Pray also that the time I give to these priests, 
(26) in the hope that they will come back to me, will be lengthened a little more so that they may profit from it and be converted. My little child, if priests are in revolt against me, to whom will my love go to seek a little comfort? Pray that priests may be full of zeal for me; ask that, each day, they will come closer to me, to comfort my love and to protect me from the injuries that bad priests inflict upon me. My little apostle, I need priests who are full of zeal for me; it is only thanks to them that I will be snatched from the hands of these priests, and that these latter will be led back to my love. My child, pray therefore, pray as if you, yourself, had to submit to my unhappy lot. My little friend, all I ask of you is to do me a favour, and this favour, whatever it may be, offering or word, if it is done with the intention of comforting me, I will accept it gladly ... Go and rest. Time has passed ... (last Friday)

(27) Little apostle of my love, it is now dark but since you have a lamp, I am asking you to make an effort to write again what follows: to escape the darts which sinners throw at me, I shall take refuge among priests. I am imploring their help then, making known to them my unhappy fate. I am begging them to console my abandoned love. Alas there are those among them who treat me without respect and show me the door, thus showing that it is not convenient that I show my love to them and that my words of love are too much. By such behaviour it happens that the souls who are entrusted to them lose confidence in me. Little apostle of my love, nothing wounds my heart so much as to see someone lose confidence in me.

Faced with such a situation I have to withdraw to the little souls and, once installed in them, I recognize them as my spouses. I take them into my service and confer on them the dignity of mother of souls that I want to save. I give them marks of affection, I even make known to them my unhappy fate ... My little friend, I also find in these souls in diverse ways many consolations.

Little apostle of my love, make known to your director how I suffer because of the conduct of priests and ask him to comfort me in my love (28) for all priests. Ask him to help you in the work I am confiding to you and I myself will join with you in pressing your request ... I am asking him also to pray that other directors understand clearly the love I have for the souls confided to their care.

*Marcel*: My Jesus, yesterday I really had to hurry since you spoke to me right up till the time scheduled for the Stations of the Cross ... I have already forgotten everything. You must really forgive me.

## 27 October 1945

*Jesus*: Little apostle of my love! I wish again to give to priests signs of my love but the words I am addressing to you are still far from the reality. As evidence of the love I have for priests, I will choose from their ranks an apostle of my love. Pray for this apostle. I will speak to him exclusively of priests so as to lead these latter to really believe that my love is limitless ...

It does not matter if you do not understand anything of what I am saying. To understand is the business of your director; your role is simply to write. Write again today the words I am addressing to priests. (29)

There is something which is even more deplorable, there are priests who use the following procedure. Placing me on one side and the world on the other, they hold souls in their hands. If the world asks for some of them, they give them readily and are even ready to help these souls ... But if I, on my part, ask for some of them, they answer me: 'Who will be the master of these souls?' And I must resign myself to gaze after them in spite of my ardent wish to possess them. And if, sometimes, they offer me one, they only place it at my side, leaving it to its own devices in that which concerns its conduct towards me. Too bad for me if I wish to use this soul in some way. That is why a great number of souls abandon me to follow the way of the world.

My little apostle, if I have invested priests with my authority, it is with the sole intention that they use this authority to lead souls to me in such a way that they can unite themselves intimately with me. But the reality is that these priests dare to use my name to lose souls. Little friend of my love, since I am but one with you, you must suffer just like me the treatment that I am subject to. To comfort my love and expiate the sins that priests do not cease to commit against me, accept cheerfully the sufferings that I send you at the time when I should send you joys and sweetness.

## 28 October 1945
### (*The feast of Christ the King*)

(30) **Marcel**: Jesus, today on the feast of your universal kingship, I ask that you reign in the hearts of all men. Does that please you? That's all I know how to say. I cannot find anything better.

**Jesus**: You will repeat this prayer throughout today: 'Jesus, King of love, may the reign of your love be deeply rooted in the hearts of priests.'
  The work I expect of my spouse is that she will go in search of souls. Even if this gives you a lot of pain in writing all the words that I am dictating to you and praying all your life in order to save a single soul and offering it to me, I will welcome this soul with all my heart as I would do for a million other souls who would come back suddenly to me. My little apostle, never allow yourself to be afraid by the effort that you must impose on yourself to write. Even if the words I am saying to you were useful only to a single soul, that would already be sufficient.
  The behaviour of my spouses in their relations with me must also be the same in their relations with my Mother. Mary, being my Mother, and my spouses being but one with me, it follows that my Mother is (31) equally the Mother of my spouses. It seems, however, that many of my spouses show evidence of indifference towards my Mother. Little friend, listen carefully to what I am going to say to you; do not be distracted. It is thanks to Mary that my spouses can unite themselves to my love in an intimate and lasting fashion. My little friend, never forget it: you must love my Mother just as I love her myself.
  (My Father, that's all Jesus has said to me today. He has left the rest of the time to me to write what you asked me to ... )

(33) **Marcel**: Jesus, are you sad sometimes because of me?

**Jesus**: My child, if that ever happens it is only when I see you sad. When you are happy, how could I be sad? So, be happy always. A single one of your joys suffices to console me very much.

*Marcel*: Jesus, does it ever happen that I cause you pain?

*Jesus*: Why not? Nevertheless, your negligences are like grains of dust in my eyes which tarnish your soul a little, but which disappear completely as soon as they have passed through the fire of my love. That is why I said to you: 'The soul which burns interiorly by the fire of my love is always white with purity in my eyes.'

*Marcel*: Jesus, my sister Saint Thérèse gives you the name of banker.* So, do men confide to you many spiritual treasures every day? I love you a lot, dear Jesus, and my only wish is to confide huge spiritual treasures to you every day, while asking you to distribute them to souls. I admit that my spiritual goods have neither any importance nor any worth; but be happy, however, to accept them since that is all I possess. I know that, already, you understand me very well without my having to speak to you of it.

*Jesus*: Little child of my love, listen to me. In truth the tabernacle in which I reside resembles a telegraph room where news from everywhere arrives continually. And I, like the chief telegrapher, must stay there all the time, always listening. News comes to me every day, some sad, some happy; and although the latter are often of no consequence, they are still able to please me to such an extent as to make me forget all the bad news. (34)

Let us suppose that news from sinners comes to my ears from everywhere; some blaspheme my love, others address hard reproaches to me and speak all the evil they can of me. But if at the same time the words of my spouses come to me from divers places, these words make me forget all the blasphemies, they even make me forget to punish the sin of the blasphemers. As if under the spell of a charm, I am unaware that they have offended me, so that I give to them all the graces of which my hands are full. My child, do you know what these words are which charm me so much? They are none other than parcels of sighs of love which are sent to me by my spouses. This is fortunate for sinners since, if I had not received these words making my heart happy, I would have chastised them already.

---

\* Cf. Letter 142, 6 July 1893 to Celine: 'Your Thérèse is not in the best of form at the moment but Jesus teaches her, "to profit from all *the good and the bad* that she finds in herself." He teaches her to play at the bank of love, or rather, no he plays for her without telling her how. He does so because that is his business and not Thérèse's; what concerns her is to abandon herself, to give herself without holding anything back, not even the pleasure of knowing how much the bank yields to her.'

(35) It is not only sinners who act in this way; even among my spouses there are some who treat me in the same manner. This is a subject of great bitterness for me since here it is a question of someone I love with a special love ... At this precise moment when I am speaking to you, the message from one of my spouses has come to me. Allow me to read it to you: 'Lord, there was a stick close to my hand but I was as if blinded not seeing that you were close to me; then I grabbed the stick and hit you with it. Forgive me, Lord.' There is at least one thing here that comforts me: it is that this soul, my 'spouse' still has confidence in me and she is sorry for her fault. If, on the contrary, she became discouraged, what sadness that would be for me. Pray so that men in great numbers are animated by an unshakeable confidence in my love. If in a sinner I still find the word confidence, this sinner already belongs to me. My child, I am continuing to speak to you of news of everyday things; listen to me.

*Marcel*: Incidentally Jesus, what is the meaning of the stick you mentioned?

*Jesus*: The stick is an occasion of sin. To seize the occasion in order to commit sin is to hit me. Do you understand?

(36) *Marcel*: Yes, I understand. However Jesus, because you speak figuratively, I find it a bit difficult. A moment ago I asked myself why I was so sad. I believed that you were absent again. But, I did not cry; I smiled but sometimes my smile was accompanied by tears. I have a question for you: why do I often think of women? I have had enough of it. I do not manage to chase away these thoughts. What can I do? I have had enough. But you, Jesus, do what you wish but I, I do not wish to have such thoughts, I've had enough.

*Jesus*: I, I am leaving it to your director to answer that question. When these thoughts come, think of me ... If you are unable to think of your invisible Beloved, offer these thoughts to me and I will accept them. My little child, do you understand that is all you have to do.

*Marcel*: Did my brothers and sisters have such thoughts?*

*Jesus*: Everybody is the same, everybody is carnal as you are, but the saints fight against these temptations ... But you, my little child, all I ask of you is to offer these thoughts to me. That is sufficient ...

\* By this expression Van means the saints.

*Marcel*: Was it the same for saint [Thérèse] my dear Jesus?

*Jesus*: You are so scrupulous. Right, I am going to make use of your director to explain this question to you and then you will understand it. Don't be scrupulous; that makes me sad. Remain in peace and please me, that's enough. You asked me previously if you could become a saint. Nothing is more beautiful than to follow the will of the one you love. These sentences are reserved for your director because they do not concern other souls. And I, I am answering you ...

*Response to various questions from Brother Marcel but not written down.*

*Jesus*: My child, listen carefully to what I am telling you here: this business is your director's affair and not yours. Don't you worry about it ... (37)

Do you know how I respond to sinners at this time? Calmed by the words of my spouses, words of love which ring in my ears, instead of replying to sinners by threats of chastisement, I reply to them with gentleness and love. And the graces that I give to them are precisely the graces sent by my spouses that I have accumulated in my heart. As for the hurt that sinners have inflicted on me, each of my spouses receives their little part: to some I send external sufferings, to others interior ones ... etc. When I send interior ones to a spouse, it is a sign that she has a greater love for me. Do you understand, my little child? When I send you interior or external sufferings, accept them joyfully. Don't be sad to have to endure sadness.

(Jesus told me many other things but I have forgotten them all; holy hour of 18 October 1945.)

## 30 October 1945

*Jesus*: Marcel! Go quickly and watch the aeroplane. *(He was sweeping a corridor at the time)* Can you see how fast it is? Why this speed, my child? Listen to me while you are working, I am going to explain to you. If the aeroplane can fly so quickly, it is because there is a fire burning inside it. The greater the fire and the lighter the aeroplane, the more it can rise in the air. You are like this aeroplane, but to light the fire you do not need petrol; it is sufficient for you to recall the love of my heart that burns in your soul and it will fly straight to heaven. In a short time, it will repose in my arms. There it will have no need to fly further. Having reached its end it will remain secure forever in order to be consumed in the fire of my love. (38)

*Marcel*: But, my Jesus, someone needs to hold the steering wheel.

*Jesus*: It is my hands, (that is to say, your director's) that will hold the steering wheel and that will drive you straight to heaven.

*Marcel*: Ah! Yes, I understand. I find nothing astonishing in that as my sister Thérèse has already told me: 'It is the fire of love that is the engine of our faculties.'

(39) *Jesus*: It is equally the same for other souls: the more they burn interiorly with the fire of my love, the more quickly they fly to the heights. The words that I am addressing to you here are far from expressing all the love that I bear for souls. I do not know what human language to employ to translate the full intimacy of this love. The intimate words that I address as well to other souls, I borrow from the language that people ordinarily use to express their feelings. If I used the intimate language that is more suitable for me to use when speaking to you, you would understand nothing. Indeed, my child, humanly speaking, my words are the expression of the deepest love; but I, I regard them as being only a simple glance of my love. My child, I do not know what words to use to succeed in making you understand more. Little one, do you understand? Allow me to explain things to you still more clearly. If I spoil you to that extent, can you wish for more? My little child, write without stopping while listening to me.

(40) Firmly believe that I am always pleased with you. I have never said to you that an action had offended me. I have said to you, simply, that things that are troubling you at present, are simply grains of dust. Do you understand? Be at peace, you have not offended me ... Listen therefore, I am speaking to you.

Little child of my love, my love can never be measured. My love for you my child, and for souls, is still hidden; it is impossible for me to show it completely in this world. The day when one will see love, when one will be united eternally to love, is the only day when one will succeed in understanding it clearly. Has your sister Thérèse not told you, 'my love alone remains eternally'?

## 31 October 1945

*Jesus*: My little child, when I wish to give you a kiss, I must, first of all, contain my love before daring to give it to you. Because, if I give you a kiss putting into it all my love, in the wink of an eye your love for me would lose itself entirely in the depths of my love so that you would no longer be able to sit here to write the words that I am addressing to souls. When I do give you this kiss it will be the last. And this will happen only on the day when it will please me to unite your love to mine forever in a single love. The last kiss will, in truth, be the first kiss given to my spouse when I come to look for her ... Still a little longer and this kiss will be given to you, my little child.

Continue to write, but do not allow your exterior joy to be too apparent for fear that Brother Andrew might guess its cause. (41)

My child, listen to this again and try not to let it sadden you. Before receiving this kiss it will be necessary for you to endure much suffering, but I will choose this suffering in such a way that it is not beyond your strength. My child, reflect carefully on this: it's one thing if I must restrain the love I have for souls, but that there are still a great number of souls who do not wish for my love ... Oh what torture that inflicts on my love! ...

*Marcel*: Incidentally, Jesus, when you oblige me to suffer, how can you endure the pain it causes you?

*Jesus*: It is necessary then to make every effort to restrain my love a little ... I must close my eyes in order to give you a very gentle, little 'slap',\* which is still mixed with my love. Without this how could I bear the warmth of the infinite love which burns in my heart? ...

*Marcel*: Jesus, are priests also your spouses?

*Jesus*: My child, I have answered that question already but you have forgotten it. I will, therefore, answer it again so that you may understand; otherwise you will perhaps think I am not pleased with you. (42) Whatever a soul's situation may be, if full of confidence, it asks me a question, my love obliges me to reply – even if it asks me the same question a thousand times. My love needs to communicate with my spouses ... Now listen to my reply. Every soul that loves me is my spouse. Never forget that. Consequently, priests are also my spouses, and spouses I

---

\* That is, a little trial.

have chosen very specially to direct my little friends who do not fully know how to behave with their Divine friend. The result of this is that my love will unite itself more intimately with their love once again, thanks to these priests, my spouses, who, in my place, serve as guides to my other spouses.

**Marcel**: So then, my director is your spouse also?

**Jesus**: Yes, he is my spouse; he is the word of love I send to you at the same time as each little 'tap', and this word of love will help you bear the trial joyfully.

(43) My little apostle, there is one thing I really wish to communicate to you. It concerns your director specifically. You will pass it on to him, won't you? He is the only one in a position to arrange things so that we can easily exchange our feelings of mutual love. You must tell him that I do not wish that my love for you, my little friend, should be known to others at this time. Now, since there are two in the same room,* this is a disadvantage. And very often, at the time when you should be writing, you are prevented from doing so, regardless of the fact that it would be difficult to keep the secret for a long time. Tell this to your director; he will understand and will be able to arrange things to allow us to mutually express our love without anyone suspecting anything. However, my little friend, whatever your director decides or does, you must conform and I will do likewise.

## 1 November 1945

(45) **Marcel**: My dear Jesus, why am I so happy today? I am so happy that it is impossible for me to continue to write the story of my vocation. From the moment when I gave to my sister Saint Thérèse of the Child Jesus the name of 'sister', I have been overcome with such joy that it has been impossible to hold my pen firmly enough to write. This joy lasted all day, except after the siesta when I felt a slight headache that disappeared immediately.

Did my brothers and sisters† come down from heaven today to give me kisses? This morning, dear Jesus, before taking part in your Eucharistic banquet, I invited all of them to join me so that the feast would be more joyful. And so, after having received you in my soul, I

---

\* Normally the brothers each had their own rooms, except when there was a large number of novices.
† Cf. note on p. 16.

did not at all know what to say to you; the saints had all spoken so well that when my turn came, time was already up. Besides, even if time had remained, I would not have known what to say to you, since all that I intended to say, they had already said ... It is quite true that the lot of the youngest is to give way to others. You understand me don't you, Jesus?

Concerning the business you asked me to raise with my director, the latter is in the process of examining it for me. For myself, I am thinking all the time that if we both lived in the same room it would be just (46) what is needed, it would even be comfortable. At present, on the contrary, as we are, for practical purposes, three in the same room, it is a tight squeeze isn't it, Jesus? But that's enough. Since this business is not yet settled, you must watch so that your little apostle never lets the secret out of the bag because then it would be difficult for us to express our mutual love. At this moment the brethren still believe that I am writing the story of my vocation; but, later, how would it be possible to keep the secret? My Jesus, all you do is smile without saying anything to me. Ah! Now, I do not at all wish to become a 'saint', especially since, if I were a saint, I would no longer be permitted to stay here and write. I am, therefore, abandoning this wish.

*Jesus*: My little friend, it is now my turn to speak. The business I asked you to mention to your director, you need no longer concern yourself with it. In order for it to succeed, we have only to submit to 'my spirit' who will never allow our business to come out in the open. Remain in peace. Later, we will live together in the same room; but the most important thing is to obey 'my spirit'. You must always maintain this (47) line of conduct without ever forgetting it. And if, one day, you forget it, our project will end in failure ... It is suppertime already. Let me first of all give you a kiss and then take yourself off to the refectory ... Do not forget that I am sitting beside you at the table ... You can take your time, there are still five minutes ...

## 2 November 1945

*Jesus*: Did not your brothers contradict you yesterday on the subject of these words that your sister Saint Thérèse said to you: 'The fire of love effaces sins better than the fire of purgatory'? First of all, keep to yourself what concerns you only and if, accidentally, you let slip something of your love for me, even if the brethren disagree with you, remain silent and do not discuss it with them since that would doom to complete failure the work that I have committed to you ... Yes, be well

(48) aware of this, the brothers suspect something and there are some among them who think to themselves: except for the community exercises, he is no longer seen in the chapel. Nevertheless, to hear him speak, he gives the impression of someone who loves God ...

My little apostle, do not let that make you sad. Recognize that what they say and think about you is quite correct, since indeed, as you must accomplish the function of mother of souls, it is necessary that you withdraw to your room in order to write the words that your Beloved addresses to them ... Do not cry. What people think of you does not prevent you from loving me. Outwardly I must hide from the eyes of the world the beauty of the flower since, if the world knew its beauty, what brightness would it keep only for my eyes? Yes, I must keep it hidden for the moment; it is only later that I will let it be seen by the world so that it can know and covet it. Thus, it will draw a great number of souls to me ...

> *Explaining this passage Brother Marcel wrote:*
> *'For as long as I live on earth God wishes to hide the spiritual favours of which I am the object: my intimate conversations with him, the secret things he has allowed me to see. It will only be later, when I am in heaven, that he will show these things to souls. It is because of this that I shall be able to procure his glory and souls will be gripped with love for him.*
> *It is also his intention that I exercise a greater humility.'*

(49) **Jesus**: The time is up. You must now do your spiritual reading. I will speak to you again this evening.

I am returning to the question of your brothers so that you may understand this well. There are some brethren who have only to see your external behaviour to guess your intimate feelings ... When someone asks you what illness you are suffering from, how this, why that, weigh your words carefully before answering. Only your director knows your malady; you yourself are ignorant of its nature.

You will have to suffer a lot from your brothers and this type of suffering will serve to expiate the sins of priests who do not cease to repulse me. When the time for these sufferings comes, do not be sad and, even if I take the side of the brothers, never allow our mutual love to appear ...

My child, prepare your soul for trials. I am holding you in my arms at this moment, I am covering you with kisses; but the time will come when I must separate myself from you and allow your brothers to cause you suffering. You will cry a lot and if, after having exhausted all your (50) tears, you do not see my shadow anywhere, have the courage to wait for me, reminding yourself that at that very moment I am working to capture the hearts of priests ... My child, accept the fact that I will be absent for some time. It is this absence, an occasion of suffering for you, which will bear witness to the truth of my words and procure the good of souls. Child of my love, that time has not yet come. There is still time for us to exchange our feelings ... My dear child, I am showering you with kisses, my lips are pressed unceasingly against your cheek and I am holding you very tightly against my breast until the time of our separation will come, when my love will have to struggle to distance itself from you. My child, do not cry before the time comes ... Listen to my words ... Wipe away your tears and do not worry because I have not (51) yet left. I am only alerting you as lovers do in this world, in advance of the joyful or sad events which they foresee must happen. Thus warned, when the hour arrives, you will be more on your guard. My child, at that time, the words that I am saying to you now, far from increasing your happiness, can only add to your suffering ... Remember this well: 'You are not the only one that my love shows itself to, but it does, also, to other souls, and it is with souls in mind that I give you these signs of love.'

My child, at that time you will feel that your heart is separated from mine but it will be nothing of the kind. My heart will remain united to yours and the fire of my love, without burning within, will envelop you so completely that absolutely nothing that is bad will reach you since, (52) before reaching you, everything will have been consumed entirely by the fire of my love. Little child of my love, do not be preoccupied; the love I will send you with the sufferings, will be the 'director of your conscience'. Follow it with your eyes shut. My pilot will never allow the aeroplane to crash into the abyss.

My child, my love would dearly love to spare you from suffering but, on the other hand, this same love compels me to treat you as I do. My child, on my return, when I see your heart empty and alone, what kisses you will receive, not only on my behalf but also on behalf of priests whom I shall have already conquered by my love ... My child, these kisses will bring you, little by little, a last kiss, the first that I will give to (53) you and which will plunge you into the fire of my love from which no one will ever be able to snatch you.

My little child, it seems that you find the words I have just addressed to you very difficult. Do not worry about them. Your director is there to explain them to you. When the trial that I have predicted comes, ask your director to make you read the words that I am now saying to you so that they may comfort you a little. Really believe that I am not far away; I always care for you, holding you tightly in my arms and covering your cheeks with kisses.

Good. Let me now speak of something else. But first, dry your tears. But I see that the time is up. That's enough. Go and rest.

(54) ***Marcel***: My dear Jesus, I love you very much. How is it that the words you have just spoken to me have moved me so much? They have made me shed tears, and the cause of my tears is not the fear of suffering but rather because your words were so intimate. I know that your love would never be able to separate itself from me for a long time. Knowing my weakness and my deep misery, I cannot prevent myself from being a little moved but I also am certain that your love always remains and wraps itself around me, and the fire of this love will envelop me for all eternity. Yes, eternally. Oh! My feelings for you, you know them all dear Jesus. I have love only for you, my Beloved and I hand myself over completely, such as I am, to the flames of your love.

(55) ***Jesus***: My child, I cannot explain why, but I do not know what subject to raise in order to interrupt you. Allow me to speak if you please. And I will speak to you only on this subject: apart from the sufferings that will come to you from your brothers, you will have to endure interior sufferings once again, as I told you earlier, a short while ago. The tears of love that you are shedding now and those that you will shed during times of trial, I will garner and place to one side, only to unveil them on the day of our eternal union in love. It is then that, together, we will contemplate all their beauty ... My child, for souls who love me, not one tear is shed in vain.

***Marcel***: My Jesus! These days, each time that I think of you, I feel happiness. Yes, really, I am full of joy and, what's more, I shed tears readily: they flow as soon as my soul is overcome with joy.

(56) ***Jesus***: My little friend, you are, at this moment, crying tears of joy and you find happiness in thinking of me. In a short time, the more you think of me the sadder you will feel. My little flower, you are going to fade; your petals, so beautiful at present, are going to fall but, once fallen, new petals will unfold, more beautiful than the first ones because the faded flower will have been the object of greater care ... Little flower, so beautiful in my eyes, abandon yourself then to my hand: 'your director'. Let this hand adorn you as it wishes, in such a way that the master of the flowerbed finds his pleasure in admiring your beauty ... My child, it is my love that obliges me to treat you in this way. The time of temporary separation, not having yet arrived, I am always there to give you advice. My child, I love you, I spoil you, not wishing that anyone else should love you more than I do. When your heart is

hurting, do not forget to tell your director all that is happening since the enemy will choose precisely this occasion to try to harm the love that I am showing to souls ... Neither must you be preoccupied with your vocation and perseverance. It is your director's responsibility to concern himself with that instead of you. All you have to do is to follow him with your eyes closed, as now. Even if the circumstances change, 'my spirit' does not change. Maintain total confidence in your director as in myself; it is there then that you will find my love ... (57)

## 4 November 1945

*Jesus*: Little child of my love, I can only feel pity for the souls who, instead of having a 'link', that is to say a 'director' which attaches them strongly to my love, are deprived of this help simply because they lack confidence in their director ... To wish to unite themselves to my love while refusing to use the link capable of realizing this union, how could that be possible? Consequently, in spite of my desire to unite myself closely to these souls, it is impossible for me to do so. As soon as the link between them becomes a little loose, they undo it and go away so that there will never be a means of succeeding. My child, allow the bond of my love to remain tied as intended without worrying about anything. The more you remain one with this bond, you will not have to fear being separated from my love.

My little child, your soul is a precious pearl for me whose beauty delights me, and which I keep hidden at the bottom of my heart. But when that moment comes it will be necessary for me to drag myself away from it and resign myself to abandon it to itself. My child, do you think that I will regret it? Yes, I am going to regret it a lot, following it unceasingly with my gaze and I will have no peace of mind until the day when I see it once again resting in my heart. Oh, my precious pearl, it (58) is on condition that you are thus abandoned to yourself, outside of my heart, that other pearls will be able to find a place there. My little child, do not fear that your place will be left empty. On the contrary, how many pearls will your place be able to contain on the sole condition that you agree to be thus abandoned ... ?

*Marcel*: Jesus, is it to me alone that you are speaking, without speaking to other souls? I love you so much, so much ... I hand myself over to your love, leaving you completely free to treat me as you intend to. All I ask is to please you always.

*Jesus*: My child, listen. I am going to speak clearly to you so that you understand. All the words that I have spoken to you from the beginning until the last one I speak to you in the future – know that it is not to you alone that I am speaking, but to all souls. You see by this that I communicate with all of them. And if, like you, they are sincere in their relationship with me, then I am speaking also to them. It is not necessary that you understand this. Do not be afraid, therefore, if later somebody says that I spoke only to you ...

## 5 November 1945

(59) *Jesus*: Oh sorrowful child of my love may the days of suffering go quickly for you. My child, accept suffering to please me. The success of my work depends on your suffering; yes, your suffering is for me a defensive arm. My child, do not worry yourself during this time of trial if you do not know what terms to use to speak to me. Listen, I am going to dictate a formula that you will keep in order to read it when you do not know what to say to me. You will say, 'Oh Jesus, my only Beloved, as I have promised you, I offer you my heart, my sighs and my whole being. Dispose of them all as you wish so that your work will be accomplished perfectly. Oh my love, do you want still more? Since I have already given you all, what remains for me is only the little bit of love that you leave with me to comfort me; there remain only the sweet

(60) kisses and the tender caresses that you pour out in your love for me. If it is necessary, Jesus, take it all to do with as you wish. Or, if there is still a soul missing to complete the number you wish for, there is still my life, allow me to sacrifice it also to please you. Dear Jesus, my only desire is to please you ... Jesus, my love, I wish that the reign of your love comes to the hearts of priests without delay so that souls may share in the happiness of the peace which will follow. Act quickly, dear Jesus, so that we can demonstrate once more our love as we did before.'

..............................................................................

When you wish to speak to me use this formula. And if you happen to cry, recite it while wiping your tears or ask your Director to read it for you. Do not be sad prematurely. You are still enjoying, at this time, the caresses of my love; remain happy. When my love distances itself, then you will shed tears ... My child, you are now crying with joy but in a short time you will have to make an effort to smile in the midst of your tears.

(61) Dear child of my love, time passes very quickly. These days of suffering will be followed by days of intimacy when we will demonstrate our mutual love as we do now. It is then that I shall prepare the day of our mystical wedding ... Little friend of my love, your heart will be plunged

into suffering. If I have chosen a room for you where you may be alone, it is with the intention of hiding your tears so that others may not know your love. Now I have no more fear on that score. My child, I am kissing you, I am thinking of you at every moment. I notice each of your steps, each of your words, each of your tearful smiles. My child, give me a kiss; as for me, I never cease to give them to you without ever being satisfied. My child, close the door when you cry, for fear anyone notices. Now that your tears have flowed, offer them to me ... My child, this room will, from now on, be special since it will contain abundant tears fallen from the eyes of my spouse; it will be, also, my little friend, the witness of the happiness that we will taste together. (62)

Go and make your Stations of the Cross, it is already time. Do not allow anyone to see your tears.

## 6 November 1945

*Marcel*: My Jesus, I am not very happy today. At the time of meditation I do not know what to say to you. Moreover, you no longer speak to me when I am alone in my room and you need not fear any indiscretion. I wonder why, today, I feel a continuous fever. I am a little tired and I have no appetite. My Jesus, I love you so much, so much. I am stopping now. You are, doubtless, asleep, since you do not speak any more. Yes, so that your will be done ...

*Jesus*: My little apostle, remain in peace. If you are still tired today it is because of the kisses I am giving you ... It is very painful, my child; I must do everything to repress my love before daring to give you some kisses and, in spite of these precautions, my kisses still tire you. My little friend, what will happen when you receive the real kiss! The effect of (63) this kiss will be to draw your soul completely to unite itself directly to me; nothing less. If, because of all the kisses that I have just given you with so much care, you already have a red face, my little friend, it is because you are very weak; so, I must try to spoil you in a thousand ways. My dear child, accept the sadness just as you accept the caresses that I pour on you at this time.

Do not hold a grudge against me if I did not speak to you this morning. There will come a time when it will be necessary for you to wait even longer, and then what will you do to put up with this trial? Offer me these hours of waiting so that I may use them to win the hearts of priests.

My little apostle you must write yet more since what you have written is far from sufficient. You will experience moments of disgust when you will no longer wish to write; nevertheless, sacrifice yourself for my love. Whatever may be the intensity of your sufferings, you must remain silent without saying a word and put up with everything for love of me. My child, the time has passed, put down your pen. I will speak again to you tomorrow. It is painful ... Yes, very painful ... Offer me everything.

## 7 November 1945

(64) Jesus: My little friend, guess which spouses I love the most. Listen, I am going to tell you so that you may understand my manner of loving and that you may know how to act with me. The spouses I love the most are those who know best how to conduct themselves with me, those who take care to know what I like, what pleases me by its nature, look for it in order to offer it to me to please me. My little friend, do you understand what pleases me most? My greatest pleasure is to gather the sufferings and tears that you offer me in your sorrow.

My little friend, to know and to accept from my hand sadness and disgust in order to make them bear fruit, how that pleases me and how profitable it is for souls. The only thing that saddens me is that a good number of my spouses are happy to accept suffering cheerfully but refuse to let it bear fruit. Once they have accepted it, they leave it to one side without further attention; or again, if they think of pleasing me, it (65) is only when they enjoy my presence. As soon as I am absent they pay no more attention to me. Understand, if you are able to, how I must behave toward these spouses who, not content with rejecting pain, even use it as an opportunity to get annoyed with me. Consequently, even before my love might wish to abandon them, it is they who have already abandoned me. Do not neglect to pray for these spouses. As for you, my little friend, accept suffering cheerfully, just as much when I am absent as when I shower you with my consolations. It is in remaining always the same that you will prove to me your love ... My little friend, you are tired. Go and rest. So as not to tire you too much I will continue another time. I am kissing you and I will cradle you to make you sleep. Enough, my child.

## 8 November 1945

*Marcel*: I notice today that Jesus is speaking to me no more. This is what he said to me last night: 'My child, tell your director that I also wish to (66) call your little sister, that I wish to make her my spouse. Your little sister will enter the Redemptorist sisters. At the moment she understands absolutely nothing about her vocation; this is why I wish that your Director should be also your little sister's and that from this moment I wish to leave with my spirit the responsibility of looking after this business for me. I want him to direct my little friend in the same way that he directs you, my little friend. Your little sister will also have much to suffer before entering religion and, consequently, she will need external comforts. So, tell your director that it is my wish that he agrees to be the guide of this soul. My child, listen to me carefully ... It is necessary for you to pray for this delicate flower that I will pick very soon but that the world does not at all wish to allow me to have. Pray every day to your good father Saint Alphonsus that he really wishes, from on high, to keep safe for your little sister the grace of her vocation. Ask him to see to it that the foundation of Redemptorist sisters in Vietnam will come about promptly since there are a great number of souls who are waiting for the (67) words I am telling you here. All of these souls will agree to be my spouses but I wish for them to have a place to stay ... Your director will also have to suffer a lot for me in this matter. It is on this condition that my work will succeed perfectly ... My child, it will be only on the day when he sees himself in my arms that your director will know perfect bliss ... Pray for him also at this time so that he may have the courage to accomplish the work that I wish to confide to him. My little child, when you are united to my love, it will be necessary for him to endure very great sufferings ... My child, from now until that day it is not possible for us to forget him. He will have to come forward as a witness to the truth of the words that I am telling you for souls. My child, when I call (68) you to me, this will be the sign for your director that the time has come for him to endure sadness. But no matter what happens, my work, through him, will be crowned with success.'

## 9 November 1945

*Jesus*: Little apostle of my love, write down again the words of my love. (69) My dear little apostle, it is solely because of the kisses I have given to you that you have been tired for several days, which is very painful for you. So, from now on I will correct myself and I will no longer dare to give them to you so often. However, my child, I am not able to resign myself to abstain totally. Each time that I hear the words: 'Jesus, I love you' coming from your mouth I can only reply with a kiss of love, so how would I be able to suffer by not giving you this kiss? Allow me to do it, therefore, my child. Leave complete freedom to my love to show itself to you. And even if you have to allow several days to pass without writing, I will gladly bear it; but, to abstain from giving you kisses, what hardship would that be for my love! Judge for yourself; if it is painful for me to have to contain my love when I give you a kiss, how much more painful still would it be not to be able to give you this mark of affection.

My little friend, why are you inclined to blush so? You have nothing to be ashamed of since my kisses are not accompanied by any reproach. My little friend, you are really very weak. All you have to do is offer it all to me.

***Marcel***: But my dear Jesus, I have the feeling that you are looking at me and that is why I am blushing. And because of that I am very inclined to laugh, to such an extent that I must try continually to contain myself; otherwise the brothers would notice something, our love would be revealed and it is you who would be responsible. This weakness of laughing and blushing easily has only occurred recently; it was not like this before. My Jesus, I offer you this shortcoming and since you know that I am inclined to blush, try not to look at me so often. Can you resign yourself to that? If that is impossible for you, you may look at me as much as you would like and, regarding the kisses, give me as many as will please you. All I ask is to follow your will entirely ... These last days, seeing that you are not speaking to me, I am, naturally, a little sad but still I have not shed any tears. The happiness of the other day has not disappeared entirely so I can easily put up with this matter.

My Jesus, is the time for siesta approaching? You know that from now on I will have to accuse myself if I lie down late. It will be necessary, therefore, that you warn me in time; if not, when I accuse myself, I will not be able to stop myself from laughing which would be a serious sign of rudeness to the Father Master. Afterwards I would, with good reason, hold you responsible for this fault because you had not warned me ... Dear Jesus, when I chat with you, I could prolong the conversation indefinitely; but allow me to stop myself to allow you to speak in your turn.

***Jesus***: My little child, it is necessary when I speak that I do so for a long time, and so time is already up. What can we do? I will, nevertheless, speak to you in order to allow you to write; and, as time passes, there will be even more opportunity for you to renounce a little of your self-will ... Come on, and stop laughing. Quickly, there are only a few minutes remaining.

Souls that love me should be considered as so many healthful spheres which allow my love to breathe and live in the world ... If these healthful spheres were not in the world, my love would die there, asphyxiated. And if my love died in the world, what other lover could be found who would be able to support the world? Left without support, the world would only founder in the fire of love ... O, little sphere of my love, I must breathe through you; become for me a sphere that is always healthy. My child, when I inhale you, I inhale at the same time into my love other invigorating spheres. O little sphere of my love, truly the world has need of a great number of souls who love me; it has (73) need of these healthy spheres that allow my love to breathe. Without that it is lost. If one notices that my love is weak in the world, it is simply because there is in it only a small number of souls who love me and offer themselves for my love ... My child, keep watch so that I have a lot of good air to breathe. Do not forget that it is on this condition that the world will be able to escape perdition. Therefore, provide me with much fresh air since the stronger my love is in the world, the more will the world be stable. And even if hell vomits its smoke on the world, it will not be able to make it die of asphyxiation since it will already be set ablaze with the fire of my love against which the smoke of hell can do nothing. My child, if ever you see my wish realized, you will then know that my love is overflowing with joy ...

It is now time. Only a minute remains. Go and take your siesta otherwise you will forget again, you will have to accuse yourself and you will not be able to stop yourself from laughing ... My dear child, be happy (74) always. I am very pleased with you. Pass on to your director what I said to you on the day when I compared myself to a banker.*

## France

*Jesus*: My little apostle, a short time ago you did not have time to write on the subject of France. Now that you have, in order to allow you to obey 'my spirit', I agree to recall my words so that you may write them down. On that day you had heard so much that I knew very well that you would forget, and if you had not forgotten you would certainly have been very troubled. Listen to me now recall those things that I said to you and to which I will add others. Listen and do not fear that you will be short of time; be relaxed and when the time is up I will stop myself so as to continue tomorrow. Now write ...

Little flower of my love, do not forget the country that I love the most; you understand, the country which has produced the first little flower and which has given birth to many others since long ago. This (75)

---

* See note on p. 15.

little flower cherishes and indulges the other little flowers and she it is whom I have chosen to be, my dear little flower, your older sister. Do you know now who this little flower is? Here I wish only to call you little flower. My flower, consider that flower and understand this well: it is in France that my love first showed itself. Alas! my child, while the stream of this love was flowing through France and the universe, France sacrilegiously diverted it in the love of the world in such a way that it is diminishing bit by bit ... This is why France is unhappy. But my child, France is still the country that I particularly love and cherish ... I will re-establish my love there ... The punishment that I sent to it is now (76) finished. I am waiting now for only one thing to begin to establish my love in her: that enough prayers are said to me. Then my child, my love will extend from France throughout the world. I will make use of France to spread the reign of my love everywhere. (I had already made known these things to one or two souls but you, my little child, you were ignorant of them still; that is why I am telling you now.) But for this to happen many prayers are necessary because there are still many who do not wish to appear zealous for my cause ... Above all, pray for the priests of France since it is by them that I shall consolidate the 'reign of my Love' in this country ... My child, pray a lot. Without prayer numerous obstacles, painful to overcome, will be met and the reign of my love will establish itself only with difficulty. My child, I love France dearly and previously it was only because of her that my love nearly (77) died, stifled by the fumes mounting from hell. But because of her, I had, through mercy, to resort to a temporary punishment to dissipate the infernal smoke and allow my love to breathe more easily.

My child, once the reign of my love is liberated in France, I will make use of this country to extend this reign through the universe ... My child, France, you see, is a country that I particularly love and cherish. In contemplating the flower, your older sister, remind yourself to pray so that the country I especially love and cherish has the courage to sacrifice itself for the 'reign of love'. As for your own country, Vietnam, it is true that France is currently its enemy but, in the future, she [France] will become a country that will be a glorious witness to me. Pray my child, yes, pray so that France may be always faithful to the love that I have shown to her on this earth. Continue to pray for the intentions that your director has recommended to you.

(78) Begin now to tell him what I have revealed to you on the subject of France on the feast of my kingship ... Tell him all; if you forget something I shall remind you.

**Marcel**: My Father, on that day (*the feast of Christ the King*) I saw Jesus seated a little bent with a sad face and with some earphones on his ears.

Then voices were heard in the languages of different countries, even Vietnamese as I recounted earlier. When it was France's turn, Jesus spoke for a very long time so that I have forgotten everything and I was unable to remember it, whatever it was. It is only on the day when you asked me to pray for France that it came back to my memory and that Jesus reminded me in asking me to speak to you about it ...

My Father, when the voices were silent Jesus spoke to me. He was still seated, his head bent forward, a hand supporting his chin and the other placed on his chest, and he had a preoccupied air. I suddenly heard a (79) man's voice addressing him in French in a very insulting tone. (That is all I was able to understand.) At that very moment the Virgin Mary was also present, not ceasing to look at Jesus in a very sad manner. I then heard, coming from another side, a voice also speaking French and which was comforting Jesus. But this very weak voice was drowned out by the hurtful voice.

I then saw a quantity of large parcels which were returned to the sender. They bore these words: 'Parcels of sufferings which no one accepted'. And the Blessed Virgin, without stopping, had to untie all of these parcels. I saw then that Jesus turned to the side from where the words of love were coming ... then, little by little, flowers also began to arrive and then the hurtful words addressed to Jesus diminished imperceptibly. As for the flowers, Jesus took them and sent them somewhere, and I never saw them again. I then heard other voices whose sweetness made Jesus forget his sadness, as he had himself told me earlier. The Blessed Virgin had despatched all the parcels of sufferings ... And the words of love became more and more numerous and clear. Of the voices that I heard, the majority came from little souls which (80) repeated, above all, words of this kind (it is possible I may make a mistake in writing them): 'Dear Jesus, kiss me! Dear Jesus I love you.'*
At each of these words Jesus showed a very great joy; and a luminous ray of light escaped from his lips towards the place where the words came from. There was even a voice which asked if some sufferings still remained, and offered itself to endure them in Jesus' place. (But these sentences were too long and although I understood them well I cannot write them down.) Then the Blessed Virgin sent a parcel in the direction of the request ...

This vision lasted for about ten minutes. Until that time Jesus had never yet spoken to me about France, but the other day, when you advised me to pray for France, Jesus reminded me of what he had told me and he asked me to tell you all that I have just related.

---

* This was written in French in Van's text: 'Ô Jésus, embrasse-moi! Ô Jésus, je t'aime'.

## 10 November 1945

(81) **Jesus**: My little flower, write today only that which follows ... For the very delicate little flowers, a mild wind is enough to flatten them to the ground, and in their powerlessness how will they be able to get their petals to stand up again? They must wait for the gardener to come and lift them up ... My little flower; you should know that I love these delicate flowers more than the others. I am always close to them, to caress them and support them; and if they happen to fall, they cannot fall anywhere but into my hand and there, no matter what they do, it is impossible for them to escape the kiss from my lips. And even if at this time the mud that sticks to the flower should soil my lips, I would not hesitate to lean forward to give this kiss to this frail flower of my love.

**Marcel**: And I, dear Jesus, to what category of flower do I belong?

(82) **Jesus**: You, my child, you know that I always call you by the name of little flower. You, therefore, belong to the category of my little flowers and, in fact, you are a very fragile little flower; the slightest breath of wind is enough to make you fall at my feet. That is why I dare not depart from you. Is that not to your advantage? It is precisely because of your weakness that you are, on my part, the object of a greater love and that my lips are always ready to cover you with kisses. But you are very weak, so weak that you cannot even put up with my kisses. My little flower, remember always that you must never be sad because of your weakness. And no matter how great your weakness may be, be tranquil always, believing that my love would never have the heart to separate itself from you, my little flower.

(83) **Marcel**: By the way, my dear Jesus, next Tuesday is Saint Stanislaus' feast day. Now, on that day, every novice must sing a song in the common room. I do not really know where to find a song. I am leaving it to you then to sort it out as you wish, all the more since I already have your words to transcribe. I used to know a great number of songs but at this moment I have forgotten all of the words and I only remember the melodies, and my voice is far from being as beautiful as it used to be. My Jesus, I am therefore asking you to give me a song for that day and to allow my sister Thérèse of the Child Jesus to sing it with me. As for you, you will beat out the tempo. I am sure that your song will be very beautiful on that day and when you hear the two flowers performing this song you will doubtless not be able to stop yourself from smiling. But, for it to succeed you must, first of all, banish my unease. My Jesus, time is up ... Tomorrow, when I have time you will teach me

this song. Agreed? I love you a great deal, I love you above everything ... My Jesus, I ...

## 11 November 1945

*Jesus*: Yesterday, my child, you asked me to give you a song. I agree to give you one but I am placing on it a little condition. Do you agree to this condition? When you have agreed I will tell you what it is ... There is nothing very difficult but I see you still a little hesitant ... Ask the opinion of your director to see if he gives permission for you to sing this (84-a) song. If he does not give his approval you must obey him. Even if a song is not beautiful, once performed through obedience, it becomes very pleasing to my ear ... I am giving you a song, but you must say that it is a 'song through obedience'. My dear child, start writing; I will dictate this song to you.

*Marcel*: But Jesus, what melody shall I use?

*Jesus*: My child, why are you always in such a hurry? I must, first of all, give you a kiss ... That's enough, your face is already quite red ... provided that you are not going to cry ... You will take the melody of the song *Routier Maintenant*.* Use another sheet for writing. By this song you will be able to draw your father Saint Alphonsus to you ...

### In the Footsteps of Jesus on the Way to Perfection (84–1)

> The path which leads to perfection,
> Is the path of perfect love ...
> And of confidence in the God of Love.
> Dear Jesus!
> On the road that you formerly trod,
> Lead me gently in the scent of your fragrance.
> Soon I shall arrive at your home ...
> And no more shall we be separated.†

---

\* The title is in French in the text.
† As a variation, 'Draw me to the summit of love'. This variation replaces, 'Soon I shall arrive at your home ... And no more shall we be separated.' The explanation is given in section (114), p. 46.

>With one heart we shall walk side by side,
>Ascending towards the God of Love.
>May a fervent prayer accompany us,
>Which will draw men in our wake.
>Without respite we shall advance along the path of love,
>While gathering and offering roses;
>And later, in heaven, we will see the Beloved.

(84-b) My child, you will sing only two verses; otherwise the brothers would be able to guess your feelings and all would be ruined ... If your brothers
(85) should laugh because your song is too short, acknowledge your poverty and your misfortune ... This song is only a trivial thing and nevertheless I am the one who has had to give it to you. Do not forget my advice. If you do that you will be able to remain calm ... And if you wish that the brothers should not guess your feelings, you must introduce the song as being composed 'in accordance with the *Story of a Soul'*.

My little apostle, now that you have a song and that you even know its melody, you have to repay me by writing what I am going to dictate to you ...

Little child of my love, do you know why Magdalene was spellbound at my feet and found so much happiness close to me that she even forgot to come to the assistance of her sister Martha? Listen my child. The reason is that at that particular moment I was speaking only words of love to her as I am actually doing now with you. Magdalene was so enchanted that she even forgot the reproaches of her sister. But, supposing that she had not then been full of joy, she would have quarrelled immediately with her sister. However, because my words had
(86) taken her outside herself, she did not realize what her sister was saying to her and she satisfied herself by smiling, as you did yourself my child when I asked you if you wished to be my spouse.

My dear child, your role is to be the apostle of my love. For that you must not be happy simply to hear my words but you must also write them down for the good of souls. It is true it will be necessary to cause you a little pain; but since you love me, sacrifice yourself completely for my love ... If Magdalene at the time when she was listening to me had written down what I was saying to her, what words of love would have been shown to the world. My child, it is for this that I have said to your holy sister: 'It is not all at once that all my love reveals itself, but little by little'. Yes, my child, it is good that way. In the manifestation of my love to man I must observe a certain moderation; if I go much beyond this restraint, man will understand nothing ... My child, my love is limitless but a great number of souls do not believe this ... My child,
(87) you know how much I suffer because of such an attitude ... After all the

signs of love I have given to them, men have not yet understood; they have even dared to doubt my love ... My child, my love is always limitless; tell this to souls ... Yes, contrary to what people think, my love is always without limits. Little child of my love, if my love for souls ever ceased to exist, that would be the sign that I myself had ceased to exist. I have recalled this truth already many times, but each time I see those who doubt my love. I suffer a lot because of this and I complain of it to the souls who love me sincerely ... My child, comfort me. It is only close to my spouses that I hope to find some words of consolation ... If you do not know what to say to me, listen, I am going to teach you a short prayer that you will be able to repeat to me just as it is: 'Dear Jesus, my love, even if no one wished to believe the truth of your words of love that you are here dictating to me, I will gladly sacrifice my life to bear (88) witness to the truth of these words.'

My dear child, listen and write down what I am saying to you on the subject of France. My child, pray for the country I particularly love. Ah! France ... France ... If nobody prays she will be unhappy once again and the reign of my love will be able to establish itself there with difficulty. My child, do not doubt what I have just told you seeing that the situation is already a little more stable ... My child, I am speaking in this way so that France may be warned and know what precautions to take since the enemy wishes to create discord in this country. My child, much prayer is needed ... France! ... France! Do you promise to be (89) faithful to me? Have you decided to protect and extend the reign of my love in the world?

My child, France is the country that I love particularly. France, beware! You have need of many prayers ... If you see France enjoying peace, this will be the sign that many prayers have been said ... My dear child, pray for France ...

Can you see behind me a crowd of people holding a red flag in their hands and who are pursuing me? France, do you agree to spread the reign of my love? France, be on your guard so as never to be the victim of the poison of communism. France, it is necessary to pray and know how to be on your guard ... My child, it is my wish that prayers are said for France ... my dear child, little child of my love ... The reign of my love will spread in France but it is necessary that France prays; it is necessary that she is on the alert and knows how to take guard ... O (90) little apostle of my love, do not trouble yourself asking yourself if the words I have just said are true or not. Leave the responsibility of making a judgement to your director and be content to write down my words, that's all. My little flower, look at Thérèse of the Child Jesus who is trying to say something to you ...

Pray in a special way for France the country that I love with a particular love ... And, later, you will see me give a smile full of joy to France.

**Marcel**: My Father, while Jesus was speaking to me of France and seeing that that country was already at peace, I had a little doubt and felt a certain disquiet ... To punish me Jesus did not give me the customary kiss after having spoken to me ... I promised him I would correct myself ... He was pleased with that and gave me a kiss as before.

(91) Concerning the crowd with the red flag that Jesus had pointed out to me, I saw it suddenly before me without other signs ... At that moment, Jesus, his hands joined on his chest near his chin, and his head turned a little backwards, looked steadily at this crowd while continuing to speak to me. Behind me I saw a band of men holding red flags who were moving towards the place where Jesus was standing ... The latter's face was imprinted with goodness and mercy ... when he enabled me to see Saint Thérèse of the Child Jesus, I saw that she was smiling and she, also, seemed to exhort me to pray for France ... She then went through the motions of plucking a rose and offering it to Jesus ... I then saw Jesus reproach the French of Indo-China for having too little confidence in him ... And this lack of confidence saddened him greatly.

..................................................................

**Marcel**: My beloved Jesus, I love you a lot. You ask me to pray for France. Dear Jesus, if my director agrees I shall recite this prayer after each communion of your body and blood, after each spiritual commu-
(92) nion and after each formal prayers: 'O Jesus, king of Love, deign to solidly unite France and Vietnam by the bond of a charity which will last forever. O Love of Jesus, may your kingdom come in France and in the little country of Vietnam.'

**Jesus**: My child, you are suffering now because of the state of the reign of my love in France. My little apostle, I am giving you a kiss ... Time has passed by child.

## 12 November 1945

**Jesus**: Little apostle of my love, my love calls out for help throughout France. And what help is it asking. The unique help of prayer which, in reviving the flame of love, will make the hearts of the enemies of my love more malleable. Little friend of my love, if you love me how could you remain indifferent and not be anxious at the situation my love finds itself in? ... To do good wherever French people are one should, as I

wish, raise up towards my love the incense of prayer ... Little apostle of (93)
my love, write down these things I am telling you concerning France.
Yes, I want you to serve as my intermediary, even for France ... Fear
nothing. I am repeating to you ... 'There is nothing more beautiful
than to do the will of the one who is loved'. If you love me, do my will
... Alas! France, the country I especially love ... your duty towards me
is not an ordinary duty. France, I love you; and you, people of France,
do you really know the feelings of my heart towards you? Do you see
my tears, which mix with those of a foreigner engaged to write the (94)
words I am dictating to him for you?

France, I hold you tightly in my arms; I kiss you. It is not possible that
you should use this mark of tenderness to strike me full in the face.
French people, my children, have you really understood all the love I
have for you. You are the children of my love. Understand that my
anxious love, in company with a little foreign soul, is desolate concerning your country that I love. Alas! You the children of the country I
particularly love, how will you behave with regard to my love? Will you
deliberately reject it? (95)

Priests of the country of my special affection, I am a fugitive seeking
asylum with you. What welcome do you wish to save for my love? Will
I be thrown out or welcomed with open arms? My children be zealous
for my love. I do not wish my love to turn away from France. Alas!!! O
France! ... The country that I love more than others ... Hear the call
of my love. My love would not wish to separate itself from you for any (96)
reason, but if you repulse my love, what other love could you use to
raise France up? If there is no love to raise France up again, then
France will see itself covered with thick fumes coming from hell and in
this case she will become a country opposed to my love and she will end
up being destroyed. But, my child, humble child of my love, if prayers
coming from confident, simple and pure hearts rise to me, you will see
me smiling joyfully, later, at the country I love.

**Marcel**: My Jesus, I do not much understand your words addressed to (97)
France. Is that all right?

**Jesus**: My child, I have reminded you of that already, several times ...
But nevertheless I am happy to please you by replying, my little friend
... It is not necessary to understand everything; it suffices that 'my
spirit' understands ... Try to refresh your memory to see if, earlier,
your sister Thérèse of the Child Jesus did not say something to you on
this subject. Try to recall it for me just to see. You have studied at your
sister's school. I am now going to make you take your exam. Without
that you would still forget. So, answer ... you can do so by writing ...

**Marcel**: (*repeating Thérèse's words*) 'My little brother, I see that God has truly had pity on my little soul and he allowed me often to say many things for these souls I did not understand myself' ... She then added this advice: 'If, later, Jesus speaks to you and it happens that you understand nothing, do not become anxious. Do you hear me?'

My Jesus, when my sister spoke to me on that day, I understood nothing, which explains why I forget so easily.

**Jesus**: When she finished speaking to you, what did she do then? Tell me everything.

**Marcel**: She gave me a kiss and then she said she was offering me to you, Jesus.

**Jesus**: Little child of my love, never be afraid of revealing to souls the marks of affection which are shown to you by the saints and me. Do you hear me? Tell them in total frankness the feelings that move me with regard to a soul that loves me and has confidence in me. That will help you to be more humble. Do not forget, my child.

**Marcel**: My Jesus, why does my sister Thérèse not speak to me as often as she used to? I only hear her from time to time and still she speaks very little. Does she love me as much as before? Does she still give me kisses? Formerly, I would laugh often with her.

**Jesus**: My child, you ask me questions that also make me laugh. When, then, is Thérèse not with you? Do you not remember the day when I made you see the 'Crusades' ... ? Did I not say to you then that your Mother Mary and your sister Thérèse would come to help you in this matter? This being the case, how could Thérèse show indifference towards you? My child, remain at peace, do you hear? Thérèse is always beside you. She sometimes gives you kisses that you are unaware of ... Sometimes, also, when you pick roses in a distracted manner, before you have had time to offer them to me, she hurries to grab them to give them to me immediately for fear that they may get lost.

**Marcel**: My beloved Jesus, one more question. Is my father Saint Alphonsus pleased with me?

**Jesus**: So! My child you are so fussy ... However, do not be sad. Listen to what I have to say to you. Suppose that one of your questions did not merit an answer even from the least of men. Even so, if for love of me you ask me the same question until the end of the world, I will still gladly answer you ... My child, when I love you to such an extent, what more do you want? I love you and I spoil you in every way. If, after that you do not love me, who then will love you more than I do? But, before answering me I must give you a kiss. Without that you would not be able to understand the meaning of my reply ... My little flower, your father Saint Alphonsus is smiling on you all day; and each day and time that you turn your 'corolla' towards him he must give you his blessing. Do you understand the meaning of the expression 'to offer his corolla'? Look, I will explain it to you. By that I mean each time you recite the invocation, 'Saint Alphonsus'.* All the saints do the same thing when you invoke them ...

But, my child, ask your father Saint Alphonsus to found a convent of Redemptorist nuns on Vietnamese soil ... It is thanks to prayer that all (101) the difficulties will be resolved. I am waiting only for prayer. Not only must you pray but again it is necessary to tell your director that I want the whole community to pray. Many prayers. That is the necessary condition for the prompt realization of this project ... Your director will understand and attend to it. For you, my child, stay on my knees and I will grant to you immediately all you wish to ask for ... I have already chosen the Canadian Redemptorist sisters but they are still hesitant .... Truly they do not know what zeal for me and for souls is. My child, repeat to your director: 'What you wish to do, do it. Saint Alphonsus wishes to confide to you this project ...' I am holding everything ready in my hands; if there is need of anything, one has only to ask and I will agree there and then ...

However, no matter what happens, the words of my love may not be (102) divulged to souls before the foundation of the Redemptorist sisters.

*Marcel*: My Jesus, you recommend that I pray for many intentions. What can be done to help me remember everything?

*Jesus*: My child, there is not a lot ... It is a great pity, my little friend, that you get upset at the slightest thing and are thrown into a quandary. Let me tell you how to proceed. You will write down on another sheet, that you will leave on the table, the seven intentions that I am now recommending. There is one for every day of the week.

| | |
|---|---|
| **Sundays:** | For the reign of my love to spread throughout the world. |
| **Mondays:** | For France and Vietnam. Your director wishes also that you pray for Canada. I am happy for you to do so. |

---

* This was written in French in Van's text: 'Saint Alphonse'.

|  |  |  |
|---|---|---|
| | **Tuesdays:** | For sinners and non-Christians. |
| | **Wednesdays:** | So that the Redemptorist convent in Vietnam will soon be realized. On this day you may especially honour your father Saint Alphonsus. |
| (103) | **Thursdays:** | So that Christians in great numbers receive communion every day. |
| | **Fridays:** | So that priests overflow with zeal for my love. |
| | **Saturdays:** | For Mary to be the mother and special protectress of apostles who work to spread the reign of my love in the whole world. |

So, my child, you have only to follow this order and to do so without being troubled; otherwise I would not be pleased.

My child, I love you, I hold you against my breast, and I cover you with kisses and caresses. I do all this to intoxicate you with my love alone ... My child, time is up. I will continue tomorrow. I am kissing you. Go quickly, it is time. You have a passion for writing ... I will see you tomorrow my child.

## 13 November 1945

(104) *Marcel*: My dear Jesus, this is what my sister Thérèse said to me: 'When on your return to work you notice that Jesus is sad, you must try to please him. Go close to him and ask him a little question of this kind and, certainly, his sadness will disappear and he will give you a beautiful smile. You will say to him: "My Jesus, why do you look so sad? What news then have you received today? I dearly love you Jesus." And if you notice that he continues to be sad, repeat these words unceasingly: "You are the only one I love, Jesus." He is sad because there are too few who love him. Finally, if you see that his sadness still persists, call me immediately and both of us, together, will speak of love ... And, come what may, Jesus will be forced to smile ... One more word of advice. If at certain times Jesus is sad, it is because, more than ever, his love is

(105) trampled underfoot. There you have it, the sole cause of his sadness ... When, therefore, you see that he is sad, do not be sad because that will make him only sadder still. All there is to do in this case is to seek to make him forget his sadness.'

My Jesus, so you are allowing my sister Thérèse to instruct me once more, as she used to! I see that she loves me a lot since she still calls me her 'dear little brother'.

*Jesus*: Dear little brother of Thérèse, you deceive yourself in believing that because I speak to you Thérèse has no more interest in you. Nothing could be further from the truth. Naturally, the more my love involves itself with you, the less reason your sister has for speaking to you. On the other hand, perhaps you no longer believe that the words I speak to you really come from me. My child, remain composed. Do you understand? If Thérèse had not helped you in this matter, your feelings would have been unmasked on your entry into the community. (106) Remind yourself, for example, what happened last year. You opened your mouth more than once to tell your brothers many things she had asked you not to reveal to anyone. (That is understandable because you did not yet have a director.)

But, my child, what is troubling you now? You have no need to worry because at this moment the brothers have understood nothing of what you said. Thérèse, therefore, needs to speak to you less often, otherwise you would have asked her some question and the brothers would have known everything. But Thérèse would never agree to leave you. Consequently, my child, do not concern yourself; you will be always the 'dear little brother of Thérèse'. And remain convinced that when you are on my knees, Thérèse is also there close to you ... I am repeating this advice: from now on, Thérèse will speak to you again but when I tell you to write some words, do not fail to do so ...

My child, do not be sad about what I said earlier, do you hear? I did not intend to reproach you but only to warn you to be prudent. I love (107) you, my child and your brothers and sisters the saints love you also. I am kissing you, as are your brothers and sisters the saints. All that I do, they do also.

My dear child, what your sister Thérèse does for you, you must also do it for France. I wish that the union that exists between the two little flowers might be the symbol of the union I wish to see reigning between France and Vietnam. My child, remember that it is with France that your country, Vietnam, will succeed in consolidating the reign of my love. Remember to pray that the two countries only act together as one like the two flowers of France and Vietnam intimately united in my love ... My dear child, continue to follow your sister the little flower with docility in all the directions that she takes. I will make use of the union of these two (108) little flowers as a witness that will unite these two countries in my love.

My dear child! In my love I am giving you the name of the second little Thérèse. The function I will give to you in heaven, little Thérèse, will be to help your older sister to spread confidence in my love throughout the world. Little Thérèse of my love, you wanted to enter Carmel and you asked me to admit you there; but I have not yet given you my reply. I am giving it to you now. Listen, my child ... To be another Thérèse does not at all consist in being transformed into a woman ... Continue, therefore, to pluck roses in very great number so as to fill my heart with them and later, in heaven, you will, like Thérèse, have only one occupation: to make roses rain down on your country and on the entire world ... You are tired, my child. Rest a while ... I love you dearly but through love for souls you must suffer in this way. My child, I am kissing you ... My child, offer yourself as a victim to my love. How tired you are! That's enough. Go and rest ... Always do my will and you will comfort me ...

(109)

**Marcel**: My Jesus, I am also giving you a kiss.

**Jesus**: My dear child, first of all you will go and write some words that I am going to dictate to you; then you will copy out your programme and, if time remains, you will sing. You will be joyful, as I watch, in order to please me. To see you happy soothes the sadness that the enemies of my love cause me.

Many prayers are necessary to accomplish the union between France and Vietnam. The more prayers there are, the more the two countries will be tightly joined in my love ... My child, much prayer is necessary ...

## 14 November 1945

(110) **Jesus**: Listen, little child of my love; I am going to dictate a prayer to you and I want the French people to say this prayer to me ... 'Lord Jesus, have compassion on France. Graciously hold it tightly in your love and show it much tenderness. So ordain things that, full of love for you, it contributes to make you loved in all the nations on earth. O Love of Jesus, we now promise to remain always faithful to you and to work with a heart on fire to spread your reign throughout the universe. Amen.'

My dear child, tell the French people that this prayer is the one that I wish to hear them say. It comes from my heart burning with love and I want the French people to be the only ones reciting it. As for you, my child, I want you also to say it but you must also say it in French (your director will show you how) since I have wished, my little flower, that from the time that you began to grow you might be pointed towards the sun of my Love by the little flower of France.

(111)

My child, I wish but for one thing: that France spreads and protects my love in this country of Vietnam. I am not asking for France to govern it outwardly as before. All I ask of it is to protect my love ... My child, have you understood about whom I wish to speak to you? Let me explain. I mean to speak here of French priests who must make many sacrifices in the land of Vietnam to consolidate my love here. My child, pray that the French priests have the courage to sacrifice themselves in your country for my love. Make known to all French priests in what way Thérèse leads you so that they, themselves, may use the same method to lead Vietnam to my love ...

***Marcel***: Dear Jesus, my love, last night the brethren found my song very (112) beautiful but, unfortunately, my voice is on the verge of breaking so I could not reach the higher notes ...

So, I was a little embarrassed with my brothers but my sister Thérèse came immediately to chat with me, and I recovered my composure and I was happier than before.

***Jesus***: My dear little flower, later you will have a clear voice, you will sing in the company of your brothers and sisters the saints, you will be able to sing high notes and low notes freely and then your song will intoxicate you with joy; with such a joy that it would be impossible to put up with in the slightest here below. My dear child, do not be sad if I leave you with such an unattractive voice. Of all the songs last night, I found yours the most beautiful but I must allow things to develop, as you know, so as to teach you the lesson which is most important for you ... This lesson you heard yesterday evening from your sister (113) Thérèse ... However, my dear child, as souls do not yet know it, I want you to write now what your sister said to you last night.

***Marcel***: My dear Jesus, this is what my sister said to me yesterday: 'Dear little brother, the song you have just finished, in controlling your anxiety, has given much pleasure to Jesus; but the discomfort it caused you made you forget the kisses he has given you. The sentence he found the most beautiful was the last one, the one you spoke about yourself: "I cannot reach the high notes". So, little brother, do not be in a hurry to cry; allow me, first of all to say everything. Yes, little brother, this is as it is. Of course this song was given you by Jesus himself and you can in no way put into practice the things mentioned in it. You cannot climb a single degree; you are incapable of follow- (114) ing Jesus ... This is the reason why, towards the end of your song, Jesus allowed you to say these words: "I cannot reach the high notes" but without you understanding the meaning ... I shall now explain more clearly: it is impossible for you to ascend to God if God does not himself draw you to him. My dear little brother, these words came so naturally from your mouth without your paying attention to them. However, Jesus has understood well the meaning that he wished to give to you at the time when you were saying them ... Later, you will be more skilful in the art of singing. I am giving you a kiss and I wish you goodnight ...'

*Jesus*: My dear child, now that you have no more to fear having to sing the song I gave to you before your brethren, I want you to change the last verse in this way: 'Draw me to the summit of love' instead of, 'soon I shall arrive at your home, and no more shall we be separated.' You have no longer to fear that your feelings may be discovered ...

(115) *Marcel:* Why did you not give me more kisses this evening, dear Jesus? I am really sad. I have never felt anything like this. There must certainly be something that has hurt you ... Ah! I forgot the advice that my sister Thérèse gave me yesterday. Sad as I was, I am now happy ... Forgive me Jesus and tell me why you are so sad. I love you so much. I invite the whole of paradise to come down here to love you. I am even making use of your love to love you. Yes, dear Jesus, I love you a great deal ... There, without having had need to call my sister Thérèse I have succeeded in making you smile. Truly, you have a very charming smile.

Now, allow me to ask you a question. Why were you sad just now? Tell me. If I am unable to comfort you, I can at least say again that I love you always and that I love you dearly.

(116) *Jesus*: My little flower, when you see that I am sad, follow the advice of your sister and do not stop being happy; that is the only way to bring joy to me ... My dear child, what saddens me is to see huge amounts of clay enclosing magnificent pearls, which are very dear to me, pile up, condemning me to look at them from afar while no one thinks to offer them to me. Nevertheless, my child, if someone placed, if only for a moment, these clods of clay in my hand, they would become as many precious pearls in my eyes ... My dear child, do you understand the meaning of these words? Let me explain.

The clods of clay designate sinners. They allowed all the love I have given them to be lost in profane love and this profane love envelops them, making them similar to clods of earth ... Time has passed my child. That's enough. Go promptly

(117) My dear child, do you love these lumps of clay? If you love them, try to think of them always and offer them to me. These simple words: 'Jesus, I offer them to you' or any other loving words said with the intention of offering them to me is sufficient for me to receive them in my hand and there, my child, I will transform these ugly lumps of clay into many pearls as precious as diamonds.

## 15 November 1945

*Marcel*: My dear Jesus, why am I so weak? I am lacking in so many ways. After each omission I promise to correct myself the next time but, when the opportunity arises, it is always the same thing. My beloved Jesus, have pity on me ... And tell me if these negligences hurt you.

*Jesus*: Poor child of my love. If you really wish I will ask you a question and then I will reply to you ... when you are guilty of these lapses, do (118) you intend to hurt me? My dear child, listen to me. Why should you blush because of your weakness? Since you act simply for love of me, be assured that you never have the desire to hurt me, your Beloved. Besides, I have already told you: your weaknesses are only grains of dust which, passing through the fire of my love, disappear without trace ... Little friend of my love, firmly believe that I have never found in you anything of the slightest nature to sadden me. My dear child, offer these weaknesses to me so that I may make use of them to fuel the fire of my love in your heart ... My child, far from extinguishing in your heart the fire of my love, these weaknesses, on the contrary, only fan it (119) more as your sister Saint Thérèse has already told you. Moreover, if I leave you these weaknesses, it is because I wish that you might be in no way superior to your brethren ...

*Marcel*: So, you don't even want me to love you more than my brothers?

*Jesus*: My child let me speak. But, first of all I must give you a kiss for the extraordinary simplicity of the question that you have just asked me. This is my reply to your question ... Speaking truthfully, my child, if I compare your love for me with that of your confreres, I see that yours is hardly perceptible.

*Marcel*: Then why don't you show your love to a soul who loves you more?

*Jesus*: Not so fast. Allow me, first of all, to speak so that you understand. But now don't cry. I am saying to you that, in reality, your (120) brethren demonstrate to me a love superior to yours; however, I prefer to show myself to you because your love for me, although very weak, is, nevertheless, more sincere and simple. My dear child, have you understood? I will give you a comparison that will help you to understand better. Let's suppose a mother has many children. They all love her sincerely but each shows his love in a different manner ...

(121) the oldest, as a proof of their love, offer her very precious gifts; the youngest can only offer from his heart these simple words: 'Mammy, I love you a lot'. My child, compare the wonderful presents offered by the oldest with the ordinary and quite simple words that the youngest has drawn from his honest and confident heart, then, tell me, on whom will the mother shower her kisses? On the precious present or on her small child? My dear child, this mother will leave the precious presents of her oldest children where they are to go straight to her little one, covering him with kisses, pressing him against her heart and will use every means to let him know that she loves him as much as his brothers and sisters and even more ... As for the precious presents offered by the oldest to their mother, all the love of their hearts is concentrated therein ...

My child, you have there the manner in which I behave towards you. My child, if you loved me in the manner of your brothers, you would not receive my loving kisses, your heart would not rest so close to mine, you would experience neither my embraces nor my treats, nor the other manifestations of my love.

(122) My child, the smaller your love is for me, the more mine will envelop you with its intimacy. Let us suppose that the little one does not even know how to say to its mother the few words that I gave to him earlier and that he can only fix his gaze on her, be assured that he would receive from her marks of a love even more tender ... My dear child, my love envelops yours and will last until the time when your love loses itself entirely in mine ... My dear child, following the example of the little one, be happy to gaze on me and I will penetrate the depths of your heart more even than the mother penetrates that of her child; and throughout eternity, my love will never be separated from you. On the contrary, it will only make your love grow eternally ...

(123) My child! Without end and in every way, you will only receive marks of my love for you ... my dear little one, my love will never depart from you ... Oh loving child of my heart, look at me covering you now with kisses. My child, even if you looked for a means of divesting yourself of my love, you would never succeed because, already, you are wrapped and shrouded deeply in my love. My child, my dear child, it is no longer possible for you to escape from my love.

You are very tired, my child, that's enough, go and rest; you will write tomorrow. Dear little one, I feel a real sorrow for you. I am covering your brow with my kisses which intoxicate you with love ...

(123–1) **Marcel**: This is what Jesus said to me yesterday.

**Jesus**: My child, it is my wish that the Redemptorist sisters found a monastery first of all in Hanoi. Only afterwards will they go elsewhere. However, leave that to the judgement of your director. Today, I am letting you know also that I agree that my words concerning the Redemptorist sisters be publicized, but I want your director to do it prudently, otherwise this matter will end in failure ... Further, if my words are doubted, the project will only become more difficult ... Say what follows to the Canadian Redemptorist sisters : 'My spouses, I am waiting for you in this country for you to comfort me. It is only with your arrival that my sadness will be a little bit softened because you will be there to help me in the work of the salvation of the world. My dear spouses, come very quickly, why so much slowness? Do you not know that your Beloved waits for you here and that your little sisters also await you with impatience? Come, therefore, without delay to comfort the heart of your divine Friend. Your sweetheart.' (123–2)

Signed: Jesus

## 16 November 1945

*Jesus*: Little apostle of my love, write concerning France, the country I love especially ... French people, my children, and you my priests of France, I love you. Be on your guard, the enemy of my love is going to throw some poison at your head. Be on your guard once again my children so as to avoid it. This society, unlike the communists, will not harm you directly, my children; it will not destroy by a single blow the country I love but it will destroy it little by little. Yes, little by little it is going to spread, little by little it is going to belch its infernal smoke in order that you die of asphyxiation. It will act in such a way as to distance you, little by little from my love in order to bring you closer little by little to the love of the world. (124)

Yes, my children, it will act in this way, little by little. Be alert, therefore, so as to prevent this creeping misfortune. You my children whom I love with a particular love, have confidence in my love; consecrate your country to my love. Be on your guard ... It would be better for France to be governed by a man of the people with a dull-witted mind than by an enemy of my love who will lead it to total ruin by plunging it into the fire of the love of this world ... France, I love you ... The only advice I am giving you is to be on the alert, for fear that, later, it will not be possible for my love to live in the country I particularly love. My children let me remind you once more: be on your guard! Be on your guard for fear that the infernal poison does not reach your head and does not then lead your country, this country I love, to diminish little by little in my love, to eventually arrive at total destruction ... (125) (126)

France, you the most dear object of my solicitude, I hold you tightly in my love but it behoves you to take seriously the warnings I have just given you. My children, be alert and work with a burning heart to spread the reign of my love everywhere ... And you, my child, you will see me, later, smile with joy at the country I love.

*Marcel*: Today, Thérèse does not cease to repeat to me:

(127) *Thérèse*: My dear little brother, I am giving you this recommendation. If you love France, each time that you pray, when the clock sounds the quarter, add this prayer with me: 'Dear Jesus, we are consecrating France to your love.' Ask your director to make you recite it in French; it is more beautiful like that. My dear little brother, when you feel trouble in your heart, remind yourself to have recourse to the love of Jesus and do not neglect to speak to me also so that I can help you with my advice. Do not forget either that your worries are only about unfounded things. I am kissing you dear little brother, be happy always in the love of Jesus. Little brother remain peaceful. Formerly I also was inclined to worry, like you, but I regained my peace by obeying my director ...

*Marcel*: So why were you crying, so much yesterday, my sister Thérèse? I am deeply moved each time I recall the scene ...

(128) *Thérèse*: My dear little brother, you understand nothing about it. It is quite natural. I am a little flower, which blossomed in the country of France. Now, when I see my country in the depths of unhappiness, how could I pretend not to be concerned? Yes, I cry for France, since Jesus still loves it and without France you would not have me as an older sister. My dear little brother, you ask some very naïve questions and after such questions it is impossible for you to escape Jesus' kisses. Pray for France, little brother, pray that she becomes like the mother of the kingdom of Love throughout the world ... I continually give you kisses, since, hardly has Jesus given you his, than you receive mine also with Mary's. My dear little brother, such also will be the conduct of France in her relations with Vietnam.

Here is something I am recommending that you do. The prayer I advised you to say with me, ask your director to have it said by the Carmelite nuns in all the places where they have convents, and by French priests but not by people in general.

*Marcel*: But, my sister, why not have it also said by people of the world?

***Thérèse***: Dear little brother, you are not able to understand. It is Jesus who wishes it to be so; you have no need to ask questions. That suffices. I am giving you a kiss. Accept any sadness today for the love of Jesus. He is waiting until tomorrow to speak to you ... You can rest now, and, if you feel any disgust, dear little brother, accept this sacrifice cheerfully, and offer it to comfort love.

## Vision About France

### 15 November 1945

***Marcel***: During Benediction of the Blessed Sacrament I saw Jesus seated take me on his knees (I was the size of a small boy) and clasp me in his arms. I did not stop looking at him and he, on his part, looked at me also. Then, bringing his face close to mine, he kissed me. Then, indicating that I should look ahead, he said in my ear: 'Look, look at France.' I turned my head and looked in the direction he was indicating with his hand. I noticed a black flag, which was planted there. As for my sister Thérèse, with her left arm she clasped my left shoulder and did not stop looking at me, smiling as if she had not noticed the black flag in front of her ... A moment later Jesus looked at my sister Thérèse and said: 'Poor France, once freed from communism, she will have to deal with a secret society even more perverse: freemasonry.' Then he said to me: 'My child, pray for France, otherwise, it's misfortune for her.' In saying these words he looked sadder than before, but I did not see him cry. I noticed, only, that he looked fixedly at the black flag, which stood there; then, looking at me again, he smiled and recommended that I tell you these things ... (128–1)

(128–2)

During the meditation, which followed, I saw again my sister Saint Thérèse. Her eyes were, first of all, fixed on the black flag then she again looked at me, not ceasing to smile. But, when she lifted her eyes a second time towards the black flag, her face was filled with tears. With her gaze fixed on the flag, copious tears continued to flow. I was so moved that I, also, began to cry. Thérèse continued to cry. It was the first time that I saw her cry like that. Even now, when I think of it, I cannot hold back my tears.

My sister then lifted her eyes towards Jesus but he, not crying, was content to look at the flag. I then heard my sister Thérèse, still crying, speak to Jesus in French. I can only remember a few words and, besides, I cannot write it correctly ... She said ... 'Oh my Jesus!!! ... Jesus ... You kiss ... France ...'* That's all I can remember and I don't (128–3)

---

* This was written in French in Van's text: 'Ô mon Jésus!!! ... Jésus ... Embrasse-toi ... La France ...'

understand any of it. My sister Thérèse looked at me again, her tears having ceased to flow, and she said to me: 'My dear little brother, what do you think of that?' I was happy to answer her: 'All I can do is pray.' She added: 'Yes, dear little brother, pray, do not stop praying.'

Towards the end of prayers, I saw that the black flag was broken and was lying on the ground. Then Jesus leaned again towards me ... as at the beginning ... Thérèse did the same and I saw nothing more, except for my tears, which flowed in the presence of such great love ...

(128–4) When I saw myself seated on Jesus' knees, I was holding a paper and pen in my hand and I was very beautiful, not being my present height but that of a child of four years ... my sister Thérèse was also very beautiful. This time I saw her more distinctly, her smiling and fresh face still adding to my beauty.

When Thérèse spoke to Jesus her voice was trembling and I then understood that she also was very affected. Her face had lost all its freshness. Looking at the pictures that are painted of her today, I find little resemblance.

Each time that I see Jesus, he has no beard; and, normally I say to him: 'My Jesus, your spirit is bearded while you, you have none.' And I have a mad desire to laugh ... one time I could not even sleep during the siesta; there I was on my bed trying hard not to laugh.

## 17 November 1945

(129) *Jesus*: Little friend of my love, it will only be on the day when I see my spouses from Canada arrive in Vietnam that my sighing will be appeased. Then my love will no longer fear being abandoned since the spouses that I have chosen will have a place to stay.

*Marcel*: My dear Jesus, The Carmelites are here, you have only to go to them to find temporary refuge.

*Jesus*: My dear child, I see that you understand nothing of what you are saying. Why do you think that the sisters have the name of 'Redemptorists'? My child, you understand nothing about it. Listen to me and I will explain it to you ... the name the Redemptorists have is my own name of Redeemer. Just as in the world the spouse carries the name of her spouse, it's the same regarding the Redemptorist sisters. If I call them my spouses, they must resemble me and do my will ... (In listening to my words there is no need to laugh or to blush; you must write them
(130) just as I dictate them; then I shall love you. You don't have to blush when you hear me say some strange word. Listen to me, we are alone here,

chatting together; you need not fear that someone will spot us.)

> *On 26 November 1948 Brother Marcel explained to me why Jesus addressed these latter words to him: 'Jesus said these things to me because, on hearing him say that the spouse bears the same name as her spouse, I was ashamed and I did not wish to write the words in the way that he was dictating them to me.'*

I am preaching at this moment. I want my spouses to have a house in this distant land so as to find a place where I can rest and converse, and to comfort me in my sadness; but see, they do not at all wish to follow my will, dominated as they are by fear of this or that. It could be said that they do not believe that I hold all things in my hands. I am very sad; I wish to give souls a dwelling place but I have no home. Is it possible that the words I have said should end up ignored in some corner? (131) My spouses, where are you then? Act quickly, I do not cease waiting for you and souls are waiting for you also. Come quickly, what are you still afraid of? I have no place to find refuge; I have no place to dissipate my sadness.

The duty of the Redemptorist sister is to comfort the Redeemer. I wait for you impatiently, my spouses, come quickly, otherwise I shall be sad enough to die. Come quickly. Truly, my loving spouses, even if I press you unceasingly and the little apostle of my love writes without stopping, I do not see even the shadow of one Redemptorist sister anywhere ... Why do you not come quickly? Why all these delays? When, therefore, will my Canadian spouses bring to me in this land of (132) Vietnam words of comfort? If you love me, if you know how to sacrifice yourselves for souls, it is necessary that you come as soon as possible. My dear spouses, do you understand the feelings of my heart? Come quickly my dear spouses as I am very sad ... That's enough my child, you are tired of writing ... This evening you will write down the words of your sister Thérèse ... Go and rest. I love you ...

## 18 November 1945

***Thérèse***: My dear little brother, I love you very much. The sufferings that (133) Jesus wishes to send to you are already near. Little brother, try to suffer in peace; once the clouds are dispersed you will see the sun of love as I have often reminded you previously ... Dear little brother, are you afraid of suffering? I will be there to help you, and so my love for you will be more and more evident. Listen to me and without allowing yourself to become worried, continue to follow the counsels that Jesus gave you

(134) previously. Even if he adopts an indifferent air towards you, don't doubt his love since the further the love is from its object the closer it is. Little brother you must experience sadness and tears but I will always stand close to you, not allowing any of your tears to be lost but, on the contrary, I will gather them to send them to Jesus; and he will let them fall again as rain on priests and on France. My dear little brother, how these tears will be agreeable to Jesus who will accept them to refresh his heart; and the more he receives, the more will he want. Little brother, all of this dew of the rose that you have, shed it, drop by drop into my hands so that I may offer it to Jesus. Sometimes in the past, I would sit at my table, like you, and shed copious tears, which only increased my sadness and bitterness. But I knew that those tears would console my 'Lover' who stood hidden somewhere and who, later, would fill me with a happiness proportionate to the abundance of my tears ... Little brother, I am content with this

(135-a) advice for the time being; later I will give you more.

**Marcel**: At this point, Thérèse of the Child Jesus composed a poem for me. I have written it down on another sheet of paper where you can read it.

(135–1)
## Peace in Suffering

Remain in peace, little brother!
The dark cloud will one day disappear.
Yes, may your heart stay peaceful
Jesus will emerge one day from his hiding-place.
May your heart be joyful;
Neglected love perhaps fills it to overflowing.
May your heart stay peaceful,
And I will plunge you into the fire of Love.
. . . . . . . . . . . .  . . . . . . . . . . . . . . . . . . . . . . . . . . .

Little brother, remain in peace.
Later, on Jesus' heart
You will see roses, red, yellow and white
That you have gathered and I have offered
... To please the Beloved.
Remember little brother,
That your tears spread like gentle dew,
Like a fine rain you will see them later
Falling from heaven upon the earth.
. . . . . . . . . . . . . . . . . . . . . . . . . . . . . . . . .

Both of us together, little brother,
Let us continue our efforts bit by bit
To lead men to Love.
And by that, do you know, little brother,
What joy we will procure for the Spouse's heart???

***Thérèse***: The words I have just dictated to you form a piece of poetry (135-b) that I have composed for you. Write it on another sheet, otherwise, your director might not understand it. Make two copies of it. You will keep one for yourself ...

Now, little brother, write down what I said to you yesterday; I am going to remind you: Little Thérèse of the love of Jesus, do you love France? Every Saturday, after having recited with me the prayer: 'Dear Jesus, we consecrate France to your love' and on other days, after the *Angelus*, you will say with me: 'Oh Mary, we beg you, be the support of France.' Recite this prayer also in French and I want the Carmelites to recite it in the same way ... When you have time, recount what (136) happened last night. I am giving you a kiss in Jesus' place and I am also giving you mine.

***Marcel***: Father, my sister Thérèse explained to me the meaning of the verses for which you asked an explanation. She said to me: 'In this last verse, I intend to ask you this question: to lead many souls to the love of Jesus, do you know, little brother, how much that pleases Jesus ... If I added several question marks, it is to make you understand that it is a question that I was asking you.'

***Marcel***: My sister Thérèse, I am begging you, come to help my memory, (137) since I just had such a bad stomachache that my hand is still shaking. However, I am able to write.

***Thérèse***: My dear little brother, write as follows:

## Vision

My Father, allow me to recount with my sister Thérèse what happened last night. I was about to make the Stations of the Cross when I saw Jesus seated, looking at France while shedding copious tears. But this vision only lasted a moment.

At the time for meditation, I again saw Jesus sitting alone, looking at France, while crying and he said in a broken-hearted voice: 'France! France!! ... Why are you abandoning me? ... No, no ... May

(138) this misfortune never happen ...' Then, without speaking any more, he remained there, looking while crying. A moment later I noticed my sister Thérèse who was leading me by the hand. This time she had put her cloak on again and I was very small, as on the previous occasion. I then saw her smile, lean towards me and say: 'Let us recite together the Consecration of France to Jesus.' After having said it two or three times with me, she inclined her head on Jesus' breast to cry. At that moment Jesus was no longer crying but he was sad. I was not crying either. I kept my eyes fixed on Jesus who, silently, looked at me with a glance full of goodness and mercy. Then Thérèse, while crying, addressed certain words to Jesus, which I repeated after her. But, as she was speaking French, I understood absolutely nothing and I have forgotten everything. She expressed herself in a shaking but very clear voice, and I had a high and very beautiful voice like a child's. It is actually impossible for me to speak in this manner ...

(139) Then, my sister Thérèse lifted her head up again, Jesus gave her a kiss then pressed her head against his heart as he would have done to a small child. Then Jesus also gave me a kiss but I was so small that Thérèse had to take me in her arms and Jesus leant forward to give me this sign of affection. I was full of joy.

Afterwards I was so distracted that I do not know what happened between Jesus and Thérèse ... In recomposing myself about two minutes later, I opened my eyes and I only saw my sister Thérèse who was leading me by the hand. Jesus had disappeared. At that moment Thérèse gave me a kiss and told me, as she had earlier, to recite the Consecration of France to Jesus. After having said it many times, my sister made a sign inviting me to look towards the sky. Raising my eyes I saw Jesus in a cloud, which was covering him up to his chest, and Mary holding up France in both her hands. She looked at us smiling. Jesus

(140) also looked at France then looked towards us with the suggestion of a smile, which did not strike me as joyful but quite marked with pity and goodness. This lasted a second after which my sister Thérèse invited me to say the invocation: 'Oh Mary, we beg you, be the support of France.' After this prayer, a cloud came to obscure my view of Jesus and Mary. There remained only my sister Thérèse and me in the presence of a figure representing France. We looked at France for a moment while saying: 'Oh Jesus ...'* The time came to recite the Sal ...† a cloud rose again which made us both disappear and, then, my sister Thérèse gave me so many kisses that I could not count them. Finally, the cloud

---

\* This is, in French, the beginning of the invocation: 'Oh Jesus, we consecrate France to your love.'
† *Salve Regina*.

dispersed to leave only the little flower of Vietnam, looking towards France. Once the meditation was over, everything ceased and I saw nothing more ...

I had almost forgotten this vision entirely; my sister Thérèse had to remind me about it today.

*Thérèse*: My dear little brother, I am giving you some words of advice. (141) Do not ever be troubled by doubting the things that Jesus has shown you. Should he notice that, it would sadden him. Even when you feel weak, committing a host of little negligences, do not believe that you have willingly separated from Love. When that happens allow me to offer your weaknesses to Jesus so that he may consume them in his love. If at prayer you feel distastefulness and dryness and you feel neglected, like a poor soul who does not know if love still resides within it; if after communion you do not know what to say to Jesus who remains as mute as you; if finding yourself really very close to the Beloved, you do not receive therein any word of comfort; if, looking at him with love, you reach the stage of not knowing if he understands the feelings of your heart; then you face very painful circumstances, little brother. I myself have had the same experiences. However, in such circumstances, dear little brother, you can only do (142) one thing: resign yourself to remain in this state. For who is to know if you love Jesus your Beloved or in what way you must behave with him. Leave it to me to deal with your other brothers and sisters in heaven; your role consists solely in shedding tears. Do not be sad if I speak to you like this. Later, you will cry a lot but do not forget, little brother, that I shall be there with you, doing everything in your place. That means that, no matter what may be your state of soul, I shall continue always to act this way with you.

In the past I had my Mother Mary to help me; but it is by me that you will enter into relations with all your heavenly brothers and sisters each time you wish to invoke them or converse with them ... I will, therefore, be busier than you, having to run in all directions to connect two loves at a distance from each other ... However, little brother, following the recommendation of Jesus, make known to your director everything that happens; and I will accomplish immediately for you all (143) he decides since he is 'the spirit of Jesus', the love he wishes to give you, to comfort you, his little friend.

Little brother, I am dictating to you a new poem. Write it down as a piece of verse. I want you to give it as a title:

## Waiting for the God of Love
### *(for the Beloved)*

My little brother sitting, wishes to sleep.
I see the sadness pictured on his face.
His steady look expresses an ardent desire,
While uncertainty and distaste reign in his soul;
Love has gone to hide itself afar.

O my little brother, open wide your eyes,
In the light of faith watch attentively;
You remain always in the heart of love.
Little brother, if love's door remains closed,
This door will, later, open very wide,
And then, what happiness for your heart
To be consumed entirely in the fire of love.

(144)  My dear little brother, I am kissing you,
How pleasing to me is your loveable smile,
And how it rejoices the heart of Love.
Little brother, I cover you unceasingly with kisses,
I collect each of your tears,
I run to offer them to the one you love,
In telling him amicably
That these tears have their source in love.

My dear little brother, why such sadness?
I will only be at peace if you give me a smile.
I love you dearly, my little brother,
I will never have the heart to abandon you.

Such are my counsels, little brother,
Do not forget to heed them later.

(145) **Marcel**: My dear sister, why this title: 'Waiting for the Beloved'? Will you allow me to change some of the words? Or better still, do so yourself because I find it is not pleasing to the ear.

**Thérèse**: You are really my cherished little brother. You wish to change the title? I am in total agreement, dear little brother, because I have composed the poem for you. It is, therefore, yours and you are free to make all the changes you wish to alter it to your taste. That will please me provided you still accept my words ... But, dearest little brother, time is up, you will continue in a short while. I wish to remind you now of the conduct to observe in your relations with the brethren ...

My dear little brother, you give the impression of suffering very much at this time. Let me point out to you how to behave towards your brothers in the current circumstances. In public, little brother, never (146) call me your sister but quite simply 'saint' as one would ordinarily do. When someone wishes to make you guess what I have done in the past, it is better that you keep silent since the one who asks you these questions will be the first to contradict your words and you will be disturbed by it. Be content just to smile and reply sweetly: 'I do not know'. In this way you will keep the peace and you will avoid being uncharitable ...

If you hear someone say that such or such a one has entered religion even younger than you, do not reply with a single word so as not to disturb the peace. If someone makes fun of your voice, of your manner of laughing, if one gets impatient with you because you lack refinement or finesse in your language, remain tranquil and recognize that you are truly poor, even incapable of expressing yourself with fine words ... Whatever may be the conduct of the brethren towards you, accept it all with humility. If one has doubts about your feelings, remain calm and (147) keep smiling, showing thereby that you do not wish to offend anyone. If some brother does not cease to mention his misgivings about you, do not answer him but keep smiling all the time; it is sufficient that you do not hold any resentment towards anyone. If anyone suspects that you bear resentment toward him, try to put up with it.

... Dear little brother, I know how weak you are and that it takes nothing to make you cry. Accept all of that cheerfully and be happy to offer your tears to Jesus.

### My Little Brother, Stay Strong in Charity
*(Sung by my sister Thérèse to a Vietnamese tune)*

Even though they may say all that they wish, little brother,
Your role is to suffer unceasingly. (148)
In your pain as much interior as exterior,
Little brother, follow this advice.
Though you may be suffering or disturbed,
Keep smiling and be at peace.
When you are well or badly treated,
Never forget the duty of charity.
I am repeating to you unceasingly, little brother:
Remain in peace in the love of God and of your neighbour.
... But there, because you are still crying, little brother ...

> I am placing a kiss on the pink cheeks of your soul.
> .........................................
> The storm is calming, little brother,
> Sleep in peace on the bed of love.

Time is up, little brother, go and rest. Now, why are you crying so? I love so much, little brother. Try to smile a little and not to blush. I am kissing you, little brother, go and rest.

## 20 November 1945

(149) **Thérèse**: Come on, what's troubling you, dear little brother? Listen, I am going to recite some verses to you. Be happy and look at me; I love you very much, listen:

### My Dear Little Brother

> In the barque of love, you row and I hold the tiller,
> Let us go at full sail towards the heavenly shore,
> What joy for you, little brother, and for me,
> When, arriving at the port, you will spy Love.
> We will then taste happiness unalloyed
> In eternal union with the Beloved.
> .........................................
> However, little brother,
> The barque still fights against the waves;
> Be full of courage! ...
> While you row, I am at the tiller!

(150) **Marcel**: My sister Thérèse, will there be times when I will be even sadder than I am now? I am really sad, my dear sister. I have done nothing to arouse the jealousy of my brethren. I never said that if I eat little it is because I am small; nor have I ever said that I am weak because I am young. What do the brothers know about the health that Jesus gives me? If I eat little I am teased; if I eat a lot I am mocked ... Enough! Jesus knows what I am and you, my sister, you know me also. All Jesus wishes me to do, painful or not, I ask him to help me do it ... Yes, my Jesus, in all you wish of me, so arrange things so that your work may succeed promptly ... Here are my tears, allow me to offer them to you; I love you, dear Jesus, graciously understand the weakness of your little friend.

## 21 November 1945

*Thérèse*: My dear little brother, do you agree to put in writing, for your (151) director's information, the way of perfection by which, until now, I have led you to Jesus? Try to put it in writing, agreed? Jesus also wishes that you do so. Do not neglect to agree to it, dear little brother. So, little brother, be joyful. Were you sad yesterday in seeing that I did not speak to you? I know that you cried a lot; but today, you will be happy all day. It's impossible for you to cry on a recreation day; that would be too tiresome. If you need to cry, wait until tomorrow.

*Marcel*: I am still sad today my sister but only a little. There is only one thing which pleases me; it is to listen to you reciting poetry. Do you want me to listen again? I like poetry a great deal and although I am unable to compose any verses, I love listening to their recitation.

*Thérèse*: I will recite them to you when you are sad. But since you are joyful at this moment, what more would you like? Since you cannot (152) compose lines of poetry, let me compose some for you to recite. Even if you understand nothing, I will compose them, nevertheless, so that in reciting them you will find a soothing of your sadness ... later, when I also will be hidden far from you, what will you do then? Little brother, accept this trial. The day will come when it will be given to you to recite poetry till you are satiated ... Little brother, time is up. There, you are already sighing even though I am still here. Go and sleep, little brother. I love you and I am giving you a kiss. Go and rest little brother, why do you worry? The love that Jesus has left you is still here. That is enough, go and sleep peacefully, I am still with you. Come on, listen to me and go quickly to bed if you want me to love you. Do not cry today, all right? I am always here with you ...

Little brother! How is it that I see you in this state? Why these long (153) sighs? Come on, breathe gently. (I have entirely forgotten what came afterwards.)

> Little brother, the light of the dawn
> Illumines your soul, makes your glance shine.
> Dear little brother, wait patiently for the object of your fervent desire;
> Later, you will see that it surpasses your most beautiful dreams.
> Little brother, your heart, at this moment waiting,
> Will be overflowing with happiness in heaven.
> Oh! My little brother, remain tranquil.
> Exiled far from me on this earth,
> You are suffering in your heart, little brother,

And tears flood your face.
But, once in paradise, dear little brother,
I will carry you in my arms, you will be happy eternally ...!

(154) **Marcel**: My Father, while making the Stations of the Cross, I heard Jesus say to me these few words: 'My child, pray very much for France, without it she is lost.'

## 23 November 1945

*Thérèse*:
Little brother!!!
This land is a place of suffering,
Trials pass and give way to peace.
Today, your heart, troubled and worried
Will recover its tranquillity later, little brother.
Accept suffering in peace,
Love still has need of the alms of your tears.
Resign yourself, little brother, to the absence of Jesus.
Later you will see his love and yours melt into one.
Little brother, such are my exhortations, my counsels,
Always keep the hearth of Love in your barque ...

(155) **Marcel**: My Father, I had completely forgotten something that happened on Tuesday, 20 November 1945.
During the evening meditation, I saw Jesus dressed in priestly garments and he was fleeing while sighing. Having arrived at the place where I was with my sister Saint Thérèse, he gave her, first of all, a kiss, then, taking me in his arms, he gave me one also, saying: 'My child, see how people pursue and strike me; be happy to suffer for me.' I was about to cry and Jesus confided me to Thérèse. I then saw a great number of priests armed with sticks who advanced towards the place where Jesus stood. That lasted about a minute and then everything disappeared.

## 24 November 1945

*Jesus*: My dear little flower, come on, smile and look at me who is about to cover you with my kisses ... Look what is on my heart ... Isn't it beautiful? These flowers you see are your tears of the other day, which have produced them. My child, until now my love has not been able to resign itself to being separated from you for a long time. Having been (156) away for hardly a week, you have already found it too long, is that not so my child? All that your sister Thérèse said to you the other day was that the time of suffering was close, but not that it had already arrived. My dear little flower, I am feeding you still at this time with a mixture of sweet and bitter, but later, you will be fed only bitterness.

Today I am allowing Thérèse to speak to you again to make known to you your destiny but, later, I will abandon you with only the little love I have left you and you must, then, often gaze upon this love. But the time has not yet come. My child, I am giving you a kiss. What you have to write, write it now while you still taste some consolations, since, (157) later, you will not know what to write. My dear child, accept that cheerfully. I am kissing you. There you are, once again a dark cloud is making you feel far from Love ...

*Marcel*: Dear Jesus! Even before I had time to speak to you, you had already left me. Although I am distressed my heart remains joyful. I do not wish to give way to such distaste but to follow your will. It is only because of Love that I must be separated from you. Oh Jesus, I love you, I love you ... Look at me, Jesus, see my tears. Jesus my heart sighs after you. Oh Jesus, I love you ... 'Oh Jesus, we consecrate France to you'.*

My Father, while Jesus was talking to me, I saw him in a white cloud (158) and in a fairly confused manner. His inner vestment was also white while the exterior vestment was brown with a pink lining. I saw a bouquet of roses on his chest that matched the lining of his cloak. Jesus spoke to me again when a large cloud blotted him entirely from my sight and I felt, once again, full of distaste. Since then I have wanted only to cry, and, in fact, my Father, I am actually about to shed tears. O Jesus when shall I see you again?

## 25 November 1945†

*Marcel*: My Father I no longer hear my sister Thérèse speaking to me. (159) All she has done is give me this recommendation: 'From the first of December until the end of the month, you will say with me: "Dear Jesus, deign to wrap in your love the country that you love" and, each time,

---

\* This was written in French in Van's text: 'Ô Jésus, nous te consacrons la France'.
† On the same day in the letter to Jesus: 'Alas! Oh little Jesus, when will the bitterness which overwhelms me at this time come to an end? Ah! This month is the month of **suffering**.'

you will add: "Mary, we beg you, throw your compassionate glance on the priests of France". Concerning the invocation: "Mary, we beg you, be the support of France", you will continue to recite it in French every Saturday and every day after the Angelus. I also wish that priests and Carmelites should recite it.'

The sorrowful child of the love of Jesus. T. Marcel.

(161) **Marcel**: While sweeping the corridor, thinking of the sufferings that I had to endure at the presbytery during my childhood, I said to myself: 'If Jesus had not pulled me from that presbytery, perhaps I would never have known the tenderness of his heart for souls.' I then heard a voice speaking to Vietnamese priests in these words: 'Unfortunate priests, because you have used human malice to hide the tenderness of my heart towards souls, know that it is not certain that you will benefit from this tenderness.' And, as I finished sweeping the corridor, I heard a still more threatening voice which said: 'Put a stone round their necks and throw them to the bottom of hell, to put an end to them.'

My Father, these words disturbed me very much because I have never heard such threats.

*After his work, Brother Marcel came to tell me his concern and his doubt concerning the subject of the author of these words: 'I doubt strongly that these are the words of Jesus because I have never heard him make such threats. Moreover, Sister Benigna Consolata said: "It is only the devil who scolds sinners".'*

*(End of November 1945: great sadness, perspiration, tears)*\*

(162) **Marcel**: I saw Jesus travelling up and down France. He was dressed as on previous occasions. Passing by certain places he was sad, by others he was happy. I then saw him stop, incline his head towards France and smile. Then he said to me: 'I am giving to you all my sorrow.' And I felt as if a weight was pressing on my chest, but that only lasted for a moment.

I saw Jesus walking while looking at France and coming in my direction. The closer he came, the more my sufferings increased. My sister Thérèse was walking behind Jesus and only looked at France. As I could not see clearly, I made an effort to look and I saw Jesus come close to the place where you are sitting, my Father, and he continued looking at France. As for my sister Thérèse, she was looking at me and I saw her

---

\* This was written by Fr Boucher on the back of Van's page 161. (The date 26 November 1945 should appear before entry 161. This was inadvertently deleted.—Ed.)

put her hand over one eye, then stare wide-eyed with the other eye, and laugh with me.

*Brother Marcel was at the time stretched out on his bed and I was in his room two paces from him. His face was twisted in suffering. I saw him look fixedly at something in front of him. Then at a certain moment he tried to laugh but I did not understand why. Once back to his normal state he told me what has just preceded and then I understood.*\*

## 27 November 1945

*In the morning Brother was in a state of distress and oppression and had difficulty breathing, and was tired in his limbs. Communion for the novices in the chapel. He said to me: 'Last night, Sister Thérèse told me to accept many sufferings. I see strange forms: a serpent that creeps to my feet. When I close my eyes I see it and when I open them I see it no longer.'*

## 28 November 1945

*In the course of the day: tired from time to time in his limbs and with a headache.*

## 29 November 1945

*Sadness, palpitations and fever in the morning. Tiredness in his limbs from time to time.*

## 1 December 1945

(163)

**Marcel**: My Father, I have just seen Jesus in a very unhappy state. His hands were clasped close to his chest while his head and his shoulders turned away from a threatening arm, only visible from the shoulder and which I saw from the other side. The fist was clenched and was lifted in front of Jesus' face. The sleeve covering this arm was white and full just like the alb the priest wears for Mass. Jesus did not cease to look at this hand, allowing a great fear to be seen on his face, a fear mixed

---

\* See Appendix, page 379.

with stupefaction. This vision lasted only for an instant; it disappeared as soon as I went out of the chapel.

(164) *This occurred in the novitiate chapel during the short visit which follows the morning conference. Brother Marcel told it to me in an emotional manner before writing it down. And he added: 'My Father, see what it means; for my part I understand absolutely nothing of it.'*

*That afternoon at 3.15:*

*Having returned to his room he was overwhelmed by a great sadness to such an extent that he was unable to come to my room to tell me of it. Trembling all over he began to write to summon me. At 3.30, seeing he had not come to work, I went to his room and I found him at his table about to write to me but hardly able to join together one or two words. I made him lie down. His feet were frozen and his hands hot.*

*He saw Our Lord while I was there reading my breviary. With a great effort he forced a smile. The vision which followed was finished.*

(165) O! My Father! My sorrowful crisis passed although it was not entirely over. At present, my heart has recovered its peace; I no longer feel any fear. Allow me to tell you what just happened.

My Father, you have given joy back to me. This is what I saw. When you were seated close to me, you certainly must have noticed that my gaze was fixed on something. I made an effort to look but without seeing anything outwardly. I then saw Jesus seated on a cloud (the colour of his vestment was the same as the day when I saw the flowers on his heart). And from there he was looking down, smiling joyfully. With his hands outstretched he seemed to want to grab something. I still do not know what he was looking at since I saw only him. At that particular moment I was suffering and I shed tears since I noticed that, in spite of my sorrow which gripped my throat and made me want to cry, Jesus did not even deign to look at me for a moment, his glance (166) remained fixed on some object which I did not see. Then I noticed that you were saying the invocation: 'Oh Jesus ...', 'Oh Mary ...' I then saw the globe of the world turning very quickly and, having arrived at a certain position, as you repeated once again 'Oh Jesus ... Oh Mary ... France,'* I saw a red beam projected on to a specific point and which then enveloped the whole of the terrestrial globe. That lasted until the moment when I turned, smiling, towards you. That is all, Father.

---

\* These last two invocations were written in French in Van's text: 'Ô Jésus ... Ô Marie ... France'.

Father, after having eaten the three bananas that you gave to me, my sadness disappeared; but I still have a pain in my neck. Allow me to wait until tomorrow to continue the story of the little flower of Vietnam.

## 2 December 1945
*(First Sunday of Advent)*

**Marcel**: Father, last night I slept very well. I did not dream as on the preceding ones. At the time for rising I was very awake, hardly feeling any sadness ... after communion, I went up to the oratory altar to serve Mass. Once the prayers at the foot of the altar were finished, I saw, as before, Jesus who was walking very slowly, stopping at each step. His hands were closed in front of him and he looked at France in a pensive mood. As he was walking always like this, slowly, stopping sometimes overwhelmed with sadness without wishing to proceed further, I heard, coming from France, a magnificent chant of which I know only the following words: '... Come. Come ... O Jesus, come here. O Jesus, quickly, quickly.'* I may be writing these words poorly, but I understood them well. On hearing these melodious voices Jesus, with a face full of joy, went closer while walking more quickly. This vision lasted about two minutes after which I heard my sister Thérèse speaking to me. She began by kissing me, then she exhorted me to suffer joyfully and, finally, she dictated to me the following prayer, which she wished to be recited by French priests and the Carmelites during Advent until Christmas: 'Oh Jesus, we beg you, do not delay, come quickly to welcome your spouses: hurry to come to give a broad smile to the country that you envelop with your love.'

My sister asked me also to recite this prayer in French. She has also made known her wish that you take the necessary measures to have it recited by all the people mentioned earlier. She has asked, further, that this prayer be recited after morning communion and at every spiritual communion ... My sister then gave me a kiss, and then everything disappeared. At this moment I am feeling a little joyful; I feel only a little distaste.

(167)

(168)

---

* This was written in French in Van's text: 'Viens. Viens ... Ô Jésus, viens ici. Ô Jésus. Vite. Vite'.

## 7 December 1945

*Around 3.15 he felt tired, he felt ill all over and was incapable of doing anything. Sometimes he must walk, sometimes stand up. He cannot lie down. He hears steps all round him and he is afraid.*

## 12 December 1945

*He is immersed in a great sadness. In the evening he said: 'I do not know if it is I or the devil who speaks. I do not wish to stay in the Congregation because I do not want to do manual work any more. I feel too much disgust.' He is tired. In the evening in giving himself the discipline he felt a pain as if thorns were stuck in the tips of his toes.*

## 13 December 1945

*During the night his feet were hurting a great deal.*

(169) **Marcel**: I feel all the time as if there are little thorns stuck in the tips of my toes. From time to time, on the souls of my feet, I feel heat and a painful sensation as if someone is violently sticking something in them. Sometimes I also, feel in all my foot from the ankle downwards, a stabbing pain in the nerves. Other times again when I walk, I feel such a harrowing pain that I could believe that the soles of my feet have been peeled off. Contact with anything the slightest bit rough just adds to my pain. If I touch anything slightly cold I feel relief; warm things, on the contrary, make me suffer more. When I work seated, I nevertheless feel pain but I can put up with it. When I stand up or when I walk, normally that makes me feel very bad but sometimes not too bad. The heat in the feet is inside and hardly noticeable on the outside. Ordinarily I can stand up well enough but when I suffer a lot I feel something mounting in my throat and my face becomes hotter. At the times of great suffering my feet cannot bear contact with anything whatever except your hands. Also, during these attacks, I like it when you touch my feet because the contact with your hands makes my pain diminish and become more tolerable. The more I suffer, the more disgust I feel; and when the suffering diminishes, my disgust diminishes proportionately. My Father, I am suffering continuously, particularly since last night ...

(170)

*I can only confirm the exactitude of all that he has just related.*

## 25 December 1945

*Marcel*: Little Jesus, I was very sad earlier. During the first Mass I felt (171) full of disgust, asking myself if my soul was going to receive a glance from you or if it would not be able to continue to live abandoned to itself as before. After communion the disgust only increased since, seeing that you were not speaking to me, your little friend, I did not hope to receive the glance that I was expecting from you.

During the second Mass, which I served with my sister Thérèse, I complained that the words that she had said to me several days earlier had no basis in fact. But she did not cease to say to me: 'Be patient. After rising, Jesus must, first of all, get washed and put on his beautiful clothes before coming to give a kiss to his little friend. Stay calm, you will see in a moment. He is very beautiful; do not neglect to look attentively at him.' But, dear Jesus, in spite of this encouragement, I remain deeply sad, without being able to hold back my tears. Have you seen (172) them, little Jesus?

In fact at the third Mass that I served with you, little Jesus, I saw you straight away ... you were magnificently adorned, dear Jesus. But who dressed you in such beautiful clothes? And who made them for you?

*Jesus*: Ah! Marcel you say that I was magnificently dressed? If I was not afraid of making you sad I would have given you a slap ... Who has dressed me so beautiful if not you, Marcel?

*Marcel*: But, Jesus, I have never learned how to make such clothes.

*Jesus*: Then, Marcel, ask your sister Thérèse to tell you who has dressed me so beautifully, providing me with such magnificent clothes.

*Marcel*: My sister Thérèse, is it not Mary who has made these clothes for Jesus?

*Thérèse*: These clothes! Neither Mary nor I have made them. So, guess who it really is. It is you yourself, little brother. As for me, all I have done is help you make them and it is you yourself who has adorned (173) Jesus so.

*Marcel*: My sister, what have I really been able to do to make such a beautiful outfit?

*Thérèse*: Well, dear little brother, first of all let me give you a kiss. Now, here is my reply. Listen to me carefully. Each of the sufferings that have caused you pain, the sufferings endured during these last weeks, each of these sighs sufficed to produce a strand of wool or a flower. I have used these strands of wool that you spun each day by your sufferings, in the same way as the flowers that you gathered, to knit such wonderful clothes for Jesus. Do you understand, little brother? Does it not please you to see Jesus so beautifully clothed? If, today, Jesus' clothes are already so beautiful, they will be even more so on the day of your union with him. Don't worry about where this beauty will come from. Now that Jesus showers you with his kisses, think, first of all of remaining joyful and chase away all thoughts of sadness and disgust.

(174) ***Marcel***: My sister, I am still very sad and not very joyful. Yes, Jesus, I still feel a lot of disgust and a moment ago I said to myself: if Jesus delays any more I will no longer allow him to give me kisses.

***Jesus*** (*laughing*): It is precisely for this reason that I had to show myself to you immediately. Now, Marcel, repeat after me: 'Jesus, I love you', so that I can kiss you. (Jesus did not cease to kiss me while holding my head tightly against his chest.)

Are you sad Marcel? Would you be annoyed with me? Tell me what are the feelings of your heart at this moment. Why do you stay there looking at me? Come on, be happy, don't cry, I am here and if I have shown myself to you it is because I want you to be joyful today. Laugh a little and drive away sadness. Even if during my absence, you feel something lacking regarding me, don't be troubled by it and then these deficiencies themselves will please me.

(175) Thérèse! Marcel is still very sad. Why is that Marcel? Why are you not happy? Your little Jesus is here with you. Come on, repeat: 'Jesus I love you.'

***Thérèse***: Marcel, my dear little brother, what's the reason why you are still so sad?

***Marcel***: Oh, my sister Thérèse, my reply is certainly going to astonish you. Will you please forgive me? I am still asking myself if, really, I am sitting near Jesus or if it is not, rather, an invention of my imagination in order to deceive me. I ask myself if the voice I hear is really Jesus' which speaks to me or that of my own heart.

I ask myself, finally, if it is still possible that I am, on the part of Jesus, the object of such a great love. Whatever it may be, my only desire is to love Jesus. But is it by chance that Jesus does not understand the feelings of my heart, that he asks me to express them?

*Thérèse*: Dear little brother, why would he not understand them? If he acts in this way, it is because he loves to hear you express your feelings. (176)

*Marcel*: My sister, to tell him my feelings I would have to write them in a letter and send it to him; but I do not understand why, at this moment, my heart is full of disgust.

*Jesus*: Marcel, I understand your feelings very well, so I am going to try to make your heart joyful. My lips are on your cheek, I press you to my heart, while waiting for the day when I shall see you in possession of the true joy that I shall give to you.

Marcel, my little wren, sing so that your little Jesus may be happy. Flap your wings so that all the feathers of melancholy will fall and I will give you a new plumage of greater beauty. Oh my little flower, if, until now, you have faded under the effect of suffering, receive, today, all my smiles like a sweet dew that I am sending to you to make you more and (177) more radiant with beauty. Little flower, hold your calyx before me so that I can contemplate it and if I notice a faded petal, allow me to replace it with a new one ... Always keep your freshness ...

My little friend, you who have dressed me in such beautiful finery, believe that I shall not allow you to be inferior in beauty: you will have pink cheeks, a charming face, shining eyes: in a word, there will be nothing in your person, which is inferior to what I myself, your friend, possess. Yes, Love will adorn you with an incomparable finery; and what I say to you now, you will only be able to understand clearly on the day when it will be given to you to enjoy perfect union with me.

*Marcel*: O Jesus! Little Jesus, what are you saying now? And who would be able to understand such figurative language?

*Jesus*: Marcel! There you are again, wishing to understand. How will that help you? Continue, therefore, to write, and there will be somebody else to understand ... You have already forgotten what I said to you before ... it is really unfortunate. And how would you succeed in understanding ... Come on, it is sufficient that you understand these few words: your duty simply consists in writing; in the matter of under- (178) standing, that's your director's business. If you don't understand, that must not trouble you. There is nothing in what I say to you which is beyond the intelligence of your director. I have told you that already many times, but you always forget. Do not be sad. The more you forget, the more you see your weakness and your ignorance, and the more you are dear to me and receive my kisses. So, there are, therefore, hours of suffering and hours of happiness.

***Marcel***: So, little Jesus, I cause you a lot of pain?

***Jesus***: You, cause me pain? I see you are troubled; who told you that you cause me pain, that you dare to say so? Marcel, you are really very inclined to trouble yourself. However you are not any the less my friend, my wren and my little flower. Do not dwell on the thought that this defect of worrying can deprive you of the titles that I have given you earlier, since such preoccupation would trouble you more and spoil everything. Marcel, be at peace.

(179) Marcel! O Marcel how I love you. When I look at you everything about you impels me to show you my love. There are, first of all, your eyes which I see dried up through crying; and the whole of your body, little flower, whose stem has been totally broken by suffering. My dear little flower, do not be angry with me. I ask your forgiveness; it is because I was deeply asleep that I have torn you in such a way. You find me very cruel, little flower. But since I have already asked forgiveness and given you many kisses, what more can you want? Do not forget, little flower, that you rest in my hands and that, any way, you will have to accept the fact that sometimes I will tear you to pieces to see into your depths, which will be worse than you have just been through. Do not think that I am going to leave you in peace.

***Marcel***: Little Jesus, look at you, eight years of age and I see that you are still very mischievous. If I were in Mary's place I would believe myself obliged to smack you. The flower whose beauty you never cease to praise, now you speak of breaking it in pieces ... Really, little Jesus you have no respect for anything; and if you have already thrown the little ball, what will you not do to the little flower which counts for so little?

(180) ***Jesus***: Marcel, can I not do what I wish with what is mine? Whatever it may be, I pay great attention to my childish toys; even if I break them in pieces or throw them here and there, I never abandon them completely.

***Marcel***: Little Jesus, it is necessary that I recount to my director what happened last night. Please remind me so that I may write it down.

***Jesus***: Marcel, you will add this: my Father, little Jesus loves me a great deal. He is very pleased with me, he often gives me kisses and laughs often with me; he is very afraid to see me sad; he is very handsome and walks very softly and speaks with a very gentle voice; he has very curly hair; in fact, he has all the qualities to a superlative degree.

*Marcel*: My Father, after my communion I was still afraid, asking myself if Jesus would come back to me or if he would leave me again for a long time in this state of abandonment. I felt then as if I had some sugar in my mouth and I realized that this sensation, accompanied by a great freshness, only had this effect when I still felt bitterness in times of suffering. When I swallowed my saliva it was not sweet, but each time I breathed I felt something sweet and fresh. As I still felt much distaste, I asked my sister Thérèse: 'Will Jesus come to make me happy?'

*Thérèse*: Certainly little brother, how could he not come to kiss you? But allow me first of all to prepare a place for him. (181)

*Marcel*: Jesus has already entered into my soul, so why must a place be prepared for him?

*Thérèse*: He has not yet introduced himself to you, Marcel, be patient for a little while.

*Marcel*: Then Thérèse was quiet and the vision began.
  I saw, first of all, a very large cradle in which there was enough room for two children. I then saw my sister Thérèse who was carrying a quantity of flowers, which she placed in it very elegantly, then, without saying a word, she placed me in the cradle. I then saw myself as very small, hardly reaching the level of my worktable and dressed in a very beautiful Vietnamese suit. My sister did not cease to stroke my head. I was there for a short while when little Jesus came towards me accompanied by the Blessed Virgin. He was twice as big as I was and wore a very beautiful robe of the most varied colours. These colours took on different shades as Jesus leaned from one side to the other. When he stood still, his robe, without being entirely golden or entirely pink, cast unceasing reflections which made it appear much more beautiful than mine.
  I saw Jesus very well but I was afraid that it was a trick of my imagination; and this fear was such that I dared not look at him. Jesus, for his part, did not stop looking at me while smiling. The Blessed Virgin and my sister Thérèse had disappeared so that I remained alone with him. I forgot to say that his robe reached a little below his knees and that he wore a belt of the same colour as his robe. The sleeves, which covered his elbows, were fuller than was normal. His hair was blond and curly, his eyes were dark and of average size, his lips were fresh and bright red and his face was quite round but not entirely so. Finally, he was barefooted. (182)
  Seeing him like this I found him very handsome but it is impossible

for me to describe him perfectly; all that I can say is that he was of a beauty which surpasses all imagination. However, if at that moment I had been an artist possessing all the colours I could wish for, I would have painted his portrait immediately. But, as I am very clumsy, all I could do was feast my eyes on him ... I stayed there quite dumbfounded, while Jesus sat with me in the cradle, looking at me and laughing, doing everything so that I might understand but he had not yet given me a kiss. My heart, however, was at peace and I had a sweet taste in my mouth. A moment later Jesus took me in his arms, pressed my head against his chest and said to me:

*Jesus*: Ah! Marcel, you say that I was magnificently dressed? If I was not afraid of making you sad I would have given you a slap ... Who therefore has dressed me so well if not you, Marcel?

(183) Afterwards Jesus encouraged me to say: 'Jesus I love you', after which he gave me a kiss. I felt a genuine pleasure and it was only then that I dared open my mouth to speak to him. Jesus, clasping me even tighter, maintained a smiling face and looked fixedly before him, then he caressed me and gave me a thousand marks of affection while Mary and my sister Thérèse stood beside us and laughed together. My Father, that lasted until the moment when I helped you to put away the vestments. Once the vision was over I remained so full of joy that I forgot all my sufferings. And since then, Jesus continues to speak to me.

*All that Brother Marcel related (172-183) happened during the three Masses of Christmas night 1945, when he was serving Mass. Obviously I had not noticed anything special at the time. He then related these facts to me in an excited manner before writing them down. What strikes me about each of these visions is that he remains distrustful concerning them and in no way wants them.*

## 26 December 1945

*Marcel*: Little Jesus, I got up late after the siesta.

*Jesus*: You got up late? Does that concern you? Let me worry about this business and you remain at peace. (Jesus puts his cheek against mine.) So then, have you finally finished being afraid of your director?

Little Marcel, I want to teach you a lesson which will make you understand the kindness of your director towards your little soul. Listen carefully to me, Marcel. It is necessary for you to know that you are indulged in a thousand ways. Why, in fact, has your director not scolded you in knowing that you have extended your siesta without permission? Remind yourself of the facts in order to see: he was standing at the head of your bed and, when you opened your eyes, you saw that he was smiling. Why, instead of scolding you was he happy to smile? In order to make you understand that your little soul is still very (184) weak. Hence, not content not to scold you, he smiled and appeared affable as if he had not noticed your negligence. It's obvious that your director has adopted the same manner of behaving towards you as I do. Marcel, if your director shows himself so full of solicitude for your little soul, why are you still afraid of him? From this moment you must put aside this fear. Since you will still encounter many trials, and in order to get through them, you will need to have total confidence in your director. I have already told you so many times, it is never necessary to be afraid of your director; and if you ever feel yourself dominated by this fear you must tell him frankly: 'My Father, I am afraid of you.' Do not be afraid to speak to him thus; and he, seeing your sincerity, far from being offended will, in recalling the goodness of my heart towards you, treat you with the same kindness. Little brother, remind yourself of this lesson: never be afraid of your director; he will exercise the same kindness towards you as I do.

So, Marcel, give me a nice smile and tell me: 'Jesus, I love you' and, (185) seeing your smile, I will not be able to prevent myself from giving it all my attention. Truthfully, for such a smile to blossom, a heart full of joy is necessary. My dear little Marcel, it is usual that after having smiled in the midst of your tears, you will see other smiles blooming with the freshness of a flower.

Little brother, do you still wish to suffer for me? Even if you did not wish it, it would be necessary for you to suffer nevertheless, since, after having chosen me for your sweetheart, it is no longer possible for you to refuse to suffer. For whoever has agreed to be my little friend, there are three things to do: to love me, to receive my kisses and to receive the sufferings that I send to him. Do not be sad and do not be afraid of suffering. And why would you be afraid of suffering since, by your sufferings you are making me a magnificent outfit and I, in return, will make you one of equal beauty. Oh! Marcel, I would wish to hold my cheek continually close to yours ...

(*Speaking more softly*) Have you finished being afraid of your director? Why were you afraid of him the other day? That's not what I wish. On the contrary it is necessary that you always smile with him. Do you understand? So, today while prolonging your siesta you perceived the (186) kindness and the affection that your director has for you and at the same time you learned a lesson from me. Is that not useful? (*Laughing*) And who would not be able to do the same?

*Marcel*: My little Jesus, it will be necessary for me to suffer more? Will it be soon? Incidentally, little Jesus, how are things in France? I heard the other day that there are numerous parties.

*Jesus*: There is only one party which is really strong and, fortunately, that is the one that wins. Marcel, do you know which party this is? See if you can guess it

*Marcel*: It is the prayer party.

*Jesus*: Correct, but it is not complete.

*Marcel*: I do not know which other party it could be.

*Jesus*: Listen. This party – I must give you a kiss first – this party is that of my spouses. The party of my spouses is very powerful but it must make use of the weapon of prayer to save France. If she did not have this to support her, France would be overcome. Marcel, you also belong to this party and that is why you must pray constantly for France. It is because of this that you will see me give her a smile.

*Marcel*: The month of January is coming and I have not yet prayed for France; my sister Thérèse has not yet said anything to me on this subject.

(187) *Jesus*: I am kissing you without stopping; I respond to each of your glances with a kiss ... Now, go and work with your brothers. It is my will that you do not spend all of your time in your room. My dear little brother, I will hold you close to my heart during all eternity. As for the prayer for France, you will write it in a moment. Now say: 'Little Jesus, I love you', and do not cease repeating it.

*Marcel*: My sister Thérèse, you have recommended that I pray for France, but what intention should I have during the month of January?

*Thérèse*: My dear little brother, are you happy, are you joyful? How many kisses has little Jesus given you already? How lovely little Jesus is. Do you love him, dear little brother? To see you happy is also a great joy for me, but what makes me happier still is to hear little Jesus call me your older sister. Little brother, when I see you happy, my heart also shares your joy; on seeing your smile blossom like a pretty flower, I would wish to pick it, to photograph it and then to show it to you when suffering returns so as to get from you at least the suggestion of a smile.

Dear little brother, think of France. I am giving you a kiss and I am dictating to you the prayer to recite during the month of January. During this first month of the year you will pray for the priests of France: (188)

'Dear Jesus, we beg you, reign in the hearts of the priests of France so that they may be given over entirely to your love. Give to the priests of the country that you love so much a burning zeal for the spread of the reign of your love in the whole world.' Little brother, after your spiritual communion, recite this prayer with me up to the words 'to your love'. But when you receive your sacramental communion, say with me the same prayer in its entirety. Dear little brother, take the trouble to pray for France.

As for your prayer to the Blessed Virgin you will say: 'Dear Mary, protect those whose mother you are, the priests of France. Help them to overcome all obstacles that it will be necessary for them to surmount in order to spread the reign of the love of Jesus in the world.' You can recite this prayer at any time but always in French. May the Carmelites and priests also say it with you.

Little brother, Jesus loves France very much and he is not afraid to make you aware of this love. Yes, he wants you to know it; Jesus loves France so much that he feels the need to show it to the soul of a foreigner like you. You can understand by that the extent of this love ... I am kissing you, little brother, time is up. My dear little brother, I am kissing you, I am kissing you.

*Marcel*: My little Jesus, when my sister Thérèse teaches me the little way (189) along which you lead me, it seems to me that everything in it is joyful and pleasant; is it really thus, little Jesus?

*Jesus*: Yes the spiritual way along which I am leading you is very pleasant; one eats many sweets there, one also receives many kisses and caresses, one finds everything in abundance, as I said to you some days ago. Close to me all is in abundance and even more so.

*Marcel*: However, little Jesus, you are very clever. In your box of sweets there are always bitter herbs mixed with the sweets. Often, when you give me something to eat, I have to eat it completely, without daring to refuse because if I refuse, you sulk and you no longer wish to kiss me. But, when I am helping myself to the box of sweets, if I knew they were bitter herbs that I was holding in my hand, I would throw them away immediately.

*Jesus*: So, Marcel, you would throw them away? If you really did that you would be lacking in the virtue of poverty, you would act against the spirit of the Congregation and certainly your father Saint Alphonsus would not be happy, since the bitter herbs that I give you can still serve for something. It is necessary, therefore, to train you little by little in the practice of poverty since, later, when you will have taken your vows there will still be many things that you will wish to throw far from you but you will not be able to do so. Marcel, if you can still eat of these bitter herbs that I am giving you, continue to do so; try to close the mouth of your heart and to chew. If you happen to make a face, I shall understand then very well all the bitterness of your heart. If I always left you joyful, showering your heart with marks of tenderness, you would certainly end up paying little attention to these favours. In continuously eating sweets this habit would make you forget the sweet flavour. Is this not so, little Marcel? Further, since you are the mother of souls, you need spiritual milk to nourish your children. I am therefore suggesting to you a method which will allow you to produce much spiritual milk and to add to it some stimulating substances. This method consists in eating everything bitter that I offer to you. If you have the courage to impose this sacrifice on yourself, later, your children will be much stronger and robust. Have you understood, Marcel? I am sure that you have not understood clearly; you understand at least that it is at the price of much bitterness and suffering that you will be able to assist a great number of souls.

I am summarizing all that has preceded in a few words which do not contain any image capable of disturbing you ... Remember, Marcel, to reject sufferings that I send you is to well and truly be wanting in poverty. Never do it. Besides this is what your sister Thérèse has taught you: 'Make use of the necessary objects which seem inconvenient to us without complaining, in that is the sign that one possesses a spirit of poverty.' If, therefore, after Thérèse's words you were going to freely reject the sufferings that I send you, you would evidently lack spiritual poverty and then I would not neglect to reward you in giving you some well-deserved slaps whose effects you would feel.

So Marcel, I have not slapped you, why be afraid? I am still here; smiling at you, there's no need to tremble so. Be joyful while I am still playing with you; if I were to go to sleep, with whom would you play? You would have to stay there, crying with your head between your hands without anyone to comfort you. There's certainly your director, but he is busy and can't spend his days by your side. So, be happy. It is not the time for sadness. Now, if you want kisses, let me give you one, and go and rest. You have already been writing beyond the allotted time; nevertheless you can place the fault at my door without troubling yourself any more than is necessary ... Go and rest, little Marcel, I will give you kisses, I will give them to you unceasingly and hold my cheek close to yours for all eternity.

## 27 December 1945

*Marcel*: Little Jesus, a moment ago I had a strong urge to laugh. Even before I finished speaking you did not cease repeating continually: 'All right, all right'. (192)

*Jesus*: So, what is it that you were asking me, Marcel, that I replied thus? You asked to be buried in my heart. It is good, I agree to it most gladly and, even if you did not ask for it I would not neglect to bury you in it anyway ... Come on Marcel, say after me: 'Jesus, I love you.' Little Marcel, why do you not say a word of love to me? Yes, why? Is it that you have already forgotten the word Love so that I must urge you to say it? In order to prove to me your love, Marcel, you have only two things to do: to say to me: 'Dear Jesus, I love you a lot.' Then look at me. Marcel, when you enjoy my conversation, you must say to me: 'Dear Jesus, I love you greatly.' This will be one way of answering me. As for looking at me, you will do so at the times when your heart feels bitterness and is unable to say a word to me. You will use this glance to give me a sign of your love. But you must make use of it only when I am not speaking to you. When I speak to you, don't just be content to remain there, leaning forward open-mouthed listening to me speaking without deigning to reply to me ... My little Marcel, you get younger every day, so much so that I must begin again to teach you even the first words that I have already taught you. Why do you forget so quickly? However don't be sad because you have such a short memory. Even if (193) you forget, you please me nevertheless, on condition that you do not worry about it.

Marcel, I am going to teach you now how 'to sigh with love' for me. Dear Marcel! To sigh with love for me consists in wrapping each of your sighs in all the love of which you are capable in order to then offer them to me. These sighs, flying towards me, release a sweet perfume which intoxicates and attracts me. I then look for the place from where these sighs come to me and when I have found it, I turn in that direction in order to enjoy the fragrance which draws me more and more towards it. Having arrived close, I see the flower with the sweet fragrance. I hurry to gather it joyfully and I take it away to please myself. When it has pleased me long enough I lock it in the bottom of my heart so that this flower will have to stay there in peace throughout eternity. Dear Marcel, look how the simple sighs of love have the power to draw my

(194) heart and to place me as it were outside myself. And if I look at the stem, which has produced this fragrant flower, I see that it is itself completely impregnated with the same perfume. Little Marcel, if only I could find many flowers exhaling such a fragrance!

*Marcel*: Little Jesus, I was a little sad a moment ago because the confreres told me that I was inclined to always judge incorrectly. Doubtless they meant it as a joke but it made me feel ashamed. You can see by that that I am becoming weaker and weaker.

*Jesus*: Why worry about it, Marcel? Come on, give all of that to me and I will accept it. But once you have given something you have not the right to think about it ... In the future, as you are still young, you must allow the confreres to tease you a bit to amuse themselves. You must let them join me for a laugh, otherwise, where would one find something to laugh about? You see that I also like to tease you a lot; however I take care that you should not be sad. Dear Marcel, let me tease you. While teasing you I am giving you kisses and by that I can satisfy my heart without making you cry ... That's enough, go and rest for a while and afterwards you will work with your brothers. You are already very tired: if bearded Jesus knew it, you would not be able to write any more. Enough, go and rest a while. I will give you kisses continually and I am holding my cheek always pressed against yours.

(195) *Marcel*: Little Jesus, my sister Thérèse has given me a song in which she encourages me only to be happy. On hearing it you will certainly not be able to prevent yourself from laughing and from giving me kisses without ever stopping. It is very beautiful, little Jesus.

*Jesus*: It is quite normal that it is like that; the occupation of the wren is to sing every day and to sing for me. Although I like singing myself very much, I also like to hear the song of the wren ... The other day I heard the wren singing but its voice was extremely disagreeable Marcel. On hearing it one would have said that it had a dry throat and an empty stomach; but nevertheless I understood that there were tears in its voice ...

Alas! My little bird, who was this wren? It was you, Marcel. On hearing your voice I was disheartened and incapable of sleeping peacefully. I had to get up quickly to give you something to eat and drink. Now, my dear little bird, if you wish you can eat and drink your fill ...

*Marcel*: Jesus, time is up.

The Song of Thérèse of the Child Jesus (195-1)
(To a tune familiar to Cub Scouts)

One has never seen, seen, seen, one will never see, see see
Be joyful, little brother
Jesus will smother you with kisses.
In your happiness look at him,
Pressing you with delight against his heart.

Be joyful, little brother.
You wish for kisses from Jesus,
Let your heart be happy not sad,
Jesus' only desire is to press you close to his heart.

Be joyful, my little brother.
To be loved by Jesus,
Chase sadness away forever.
It is your smile which makes him happy.

Ah! ... There, now you are laughing ... dear little brother,
By that you fulfil completely my greatest wish;
My happiness is to see you joyful.
... So that Jesus presses you against his heart.

Henceforth, dear little brother
Sing unceasingly for Jesus.
Delighted by your song and your actions, (195–2)
He can only clasp you to his heart.

Sing joyfully, little bird.
So your song pierces the clouds,
To delight the heart of God;
Who will come to you and clasp you to his heart.

## 28 December 1945

*Marcel*: My dear little Jesus, Monday will be the feast day of your Holy (196)
Name.
  On this subject I must ask you a question. This name of Jesus, of whom is this name, little Jesus?

*Jesus*: Marcel, I do not find your question at all difficult; I am happy to

82  *Conversations*

answer it immediately. Pay great attention. Write clearly, I am going to dictate each word separately: 'The name Jesus is the name of the Spouse of Souls.' Is that quite clear Marcel? I wish to choose all souls to be my spouses; that is why I call myself the Spouse of Souls ...

(197) **Marcel**: Little Jesus, today is the feast day of the Holy Innocents. I wonder if, in heaven, these little saints are mischievous like children. They must, without doubt, spend all day playing with you. When I go to heaven it is absolutely essential that I ask you to admit me to their ranks. Indeed they have much time for leisure pursuits doing nothing but playing every day without ever working. Moreover they don't have to be afraid that anyone may come to bother them since no one knows their name and their age. So, since I am very lazy, liking only to play, if it happens that someone asks me to intercede for him with you, little Jesus, I will not busy myself and their attempts will fail. If, on the contrary, I am in the ranks of the Holy Innocents I will have all the time to play with you, to be always at your side and also to tease you freely. Then on Thursdays and Sundays we will have time to go together to see the heavenly countryside, pay a visit to the Blessed Virgin, etc. I will then have everything I could wish for like you little Jesus. It will be very pleasant.

**Jesus**: Marcel, what is it that you just said that gives me an insane desire to laugh? It is really discouraging; you speak without understanding anything of what you are saying. So, listen carefully to me: in the same way that the Holy Innocents had to suffer death for me, you also will have to die for my love. Because of this, you will be admitted to their ranks ...

(198) **Marcel**: Little Jesus, yesterday I heard certain brothers state that they were surprised to encounter many expressions in books which would not be pleasing to you and which, according to them, should not be employed except for men of the world since they indicated a profane love. Have these brethren never recognized you as being their friend? However, I believed that all were your friends. So, why do they find it strange that one uses words that express a deep intimacy with you? Moreover, I notice that you use these so-called unsuitable expressions all the time in your dealings with me.

**Jesus**: My dear little brother, I am covering you unceasingly with kisses and I keep my lips forever pressed against your cheek. Marcel, there is no need for a long speech to reply to your quite natural question. My dear little Marcel, do you know why it is like this? I have already told you that a good number of my spouses do not know what to say to their Spouse and are so ignorant that they do not know that he who is the object of their affection is truly their Spouse. What is even more regrettable is that after having recognized them as my spouses, they, on their part, dare not recognize me as their Spouse, considering that it is madness on my part to act as I do. They also find offensive and intolerable the intimate words which my other spouses address to me ... Finally, I am adding this: the reason for all this is that these spouses do not have enough humility to understand clearly their dignity as children of God and spouses of Christ, since God is at the same time Father, Spouse and Master ... (199)

If all my spouses understood that I am also their Spouse, they would never dare to refuse this dignity of being my spouses; but because they do not wish to humble themselves sufficiently, they never succeed in recognizing the love that I show to them, since this love is without limit ... So Marcel, the only thing to do in order to recognize my love is to humble oneself. Marcel, say this to souls: 'To see my love it is not necessary to analyse it; it is sufficient to humble oneself.'

Little Marcel, do you love me? How do you love me? Tell me what names you give to me. Oh! Little Marcel, love me. Love me just as I love myself, love me madly and all that you love, love it only through love for me. Marcel, call me your little Spouse; call me the butterfly nestled on the little flower of your soul to breathe in the honey and enjoy its fragrance; call me, again, the aeroplane which takes you away to circle in infinite love ... Yes, Marcel, give me all these names. (200)

Now Marcel, do you want something? Do you want me to give you a kiss? I am going to give you one, all right? But Marcel, why are you sad? Tell me quickly so I can kiss you.

**Marcel**: Oh, I only feel a little fed up; and the reason is that, formerly, I had a comfortable bed while now I must lie on this poor bed that you see. It moves and cracks all the time, it's impossible to sleep. It's really detestable!

**Jesus**: Ah! So that's the reason. But Marcel, so you've forgotten? Listen, I am going to refresh your memory. If you accept cheerfully this uncomfortable bed, you will be able to practise in one fell swoop three virtues ... And what did your sister Thérèse teach you? When one is poor does one complain at having an uncomfortable bed? However Marcel, I do not wish to scold you; I simply want to teach you a lesson. (201) Be happy to sleep in this uncomfortable bed. I will so arrange things that it will cause you less discomfort. Remember the three virtues that you must practise: obedience, self-denial and poverty ... In the past, precisely at this time of year, I also had to lie on the straw of little lambs. It felt very bad; there was only a little straw and the straw also was damp, so much that I felt very uncomfortable. If, then, I had complained to the Blessed Virgin, nowhere could she have found me a more comfortable bed ... now, my little friend you also must do the same. It is because Father Master has not been able to find a better bed that he has had to resign himself to giving you this one. However, Marcel, believe that you are much luckier than I because you have a mosquito net and woollen covers. Spoilt as you are, what reason would you have to complain? Offer me all of that and I will give you kisses! ...

Marcel, it is necessary for you to realize that you haven't yet the least virtue. If, in these circumstances, I had not spoken to you, I do not know when you would have stopped having red eyes.

(202) Little Marcel, you have not the slightest virtue. And, to speak frankly, in your case there is nothing; one finds there nothing of beauty. But do not be sad because of it. Do you understand? Look at the flower which is your sister Thérèse; she recognized that she possessed nothing but in reality she possessed everything because, in possessing nothing, she obtained everything ... Do not be discouraged, Marcel, all you will ask for, all you will wish for, I will grant to you. Do you now wish that I give you some kisses? How many do you want? But it is first necessary that you tell me: 'Dear Jesus, I love you.' Without that who would wish to kiss you? When you have said: 'Jesus, I love you', I will give you as many as you wish for.

## 29 December 1945

*Jesus*: Oh! Marcel, do you want to speak to me, do you want to call me in French? Let me teach you a very easy phrase that your sister Thérèse normally repeats to me all day long. Write this down: 'Dear little Jesus, come to me'. Another time: '... to France'. Another time: 'to the priests of France'.\*

Do you understand that Marcel? I will explain it to you:† 'Dear little Jesus, come to me ... come to France ... come to the priests of France'. You will recite these invocations with your sister Thérèse. She is already quite used to doing so. And I, on hearing this call, I shall rush to come to you without delay; assured of meeting there at the same time your sister Thérèse.

---

\* These three invocations are in French in Van's text: 'Ô petit Jésus, viens avec moi' ... 'ave la France' ... 'avec les prêtres de France'.
† Jesus repeats the same three invocations in Vietnamese.

*Marcel*: Little Jesus, is my sister Thérèse with me at present? I notice (203) that, since yesterday, she has not said a single word.

*Jesus*: But yes, she is always at your side; if she does not speak to you it is because she gives way to me. When you sleep at prayer, she speaks in your place so as not to leave me alone with nothing to do, or of falling asleep meself; since if it were necessary that I sleep, even a million Marcels would not succeed in waking me. I am very inclined to sleep and if I have no one to chat with me, I fall asleep immediately and, once asleep, I awake when I really wish to. No one is capable of dragging me from sleep. You yourself could cry loudly and it would be in vain. This is to say that Thérèse loves you greatly, you, Marcel, her dear little brother, since she looks after everything in your place. She doesn't want to see you lose your smile ... Time is up ...

*Marcel*: Little Jesus, there is one question I wanted to speak to you about but I always forget it. Now I remember and I will speak about it. The year 1945 is approaching its end. In a few days time I will receive a patron for the New Year.* This year it was little Thérèse who was given to me for my patron. I was very happy and, in fact she has spared nothing in order to help me during this first year of my religious life. From my entry into the monastery she has adopted me as her little brother, not wishing to leave this to any other saint. Seeing that I would wish to have her as patron to the exclusion of all others, she gave herself (204) over to my desire joyfully ...

Next year I do not wish to give up the name of my patron of this year; I want only the name of 'Thérèse of the Child Jesus'; or, if you wish to change this name for another, may it be yours, little Jesus. If I lost the name of Thérèse of the Child Jesus without you replacing it with your own, I would be very sad and the sweet that we eat on the occasion of the drawing of patrons would appear to be totally insipid. And even if you then gave me kisses, it is not certain that these kisses could make me happy ... Little Jesus, the name of Mary, that would do also; I love the name of Mary very much: she is my Mother and, usually, she tells me that in heaven she will sit me on her knees to allow me to converse with you. Ah! Yes, I would also accept the name of Mary. Therefore,

---

\* It is a Redemptorist custom, provided for in the Constitution: Every year, a patron saint will be assigned to each religious by lot, with a special virtue to practise and a prayer intention for the year for a pagan nation or for the needs of a particular group of faithful. This drawing of lots will take place on the eve of the Circumcision of Our Lord (1 January) in the evening.
Cf. Constitution of 1933, III, 9.

little Jesus, you must make sure that I draw one of these three names. If that does not happen, I will cry, you will see ...

***Jesus***: Marcel, what are you saying? It is not very nice. If you follow your self-will like this, who will wish to kiss you? And what good would it be to you to choose a name and then discard it?

(205) (*Smiling*) Ah! I see you are sad. If I speak in this manner it is not with the intention of scolding you; leave this business to me. I will choose the name of a patron for you, which will appear very strange for you. What is this name? I am not telling you yet, but whatever it is, you must accept it, joyfully. You say you are sad for the smallest thing; when you give way thus to sadness, that saddens even more your sister Thérèse since her only wish is to see you happy. Therefore, never be sad, Marcel. If by some misfortune your sister became angry and left you there all alone, what would happen? Even if you cried a lot and pulled a face you would no longer find anybody to wipe your tears. It would be a great pity. So be happy always and then you will receive affection and kisses; in a word you will obtain everything. What more can you wish for?

Marcel, you already have a red face. I am kissing you and embracing you, if that's all right? Go and sleep peacefully, time is almost up. Come on, go and sleep. If you don't you will go to bed late and you will lay the blame at my door. Even if bearded Jesus does not scold me, I still will have to accept the responsibility. That's enough Marcel, go and sleep. Your face is quite red and there you are still ready to write ... I am speaking to you no more.

Marcel, have you finished your work? Since it is the recreation day and you have some free time, I am now going to speak to you so that you can write. Are you still experiencing disgust?

***Marcel***: Yes.

***Jesus***: You must tell me so that I can find a way of making you happy.
(206) This disgust takes away the wish to work, does it not? So, what work would you like to do?

***Marcel***: I only want to play.

***Jesus***: But Marcel, how would you be able to play? Since you are a religious and furthermore a lay brother, how would you be able to do so in an appropriate manner? When you are in heaven you will be able to play as you wish ... However, Marcel, when you are working it is not necessary to do a lot of work; it is sufficient to do small things as your sister Thérèse has taught you: 'Even if at the end of a whole day you have not succeeded in dusting a single chair, you must not worry.' Marcel, it is not the amount of work which pleases me; Thérèse has already told you that and you have forgotten. Let me remind you; your duty is to love and to work. Yes, to work for love of me. There you have it, your duty as a religious ... if some work appears difficult to you, you must tell your director frankly, just as if you were telling me. If he judges it worthy of attention he will attend to it; if, on the contrary, he leaves you with the same work, you have nothing to fear, it is my spirit which will have wished it so. For me, Marcel, I do not wish to cause you the slightest pain since you do not have the strength to put up with even the slightest trial. As soon as the slightest difficulty presents itself, let your director, who like me loves you a great deal, Marcel, know about it immediately. As you are very weak I cannot keep myself from spoiling you. Marcel, be happy with the crosses I send to you spontaneously without taking up others which you would not be able to carry and that you would have subsequently to abandon. You do not have to try to keep up with your brethren; you must understand that your strength is quite limited and that you need to be supported by me in everything ... (207)

## 30 December 1945

*Jesus*: Marcel, did you understand what I said to you yesterday? Try to remember. Never dwell on thoughts like this: 'This cross would be preferable; I would be able to carry it without difficulty since it is small.' My little Marcel, never dwell on such thoughts. Such a cross seems light to you but, in reality, it is very heavy and you would not have the strength to carry it. You must always, always, recognize that you are very weak; it is because of this that I will give you kisses, that I will clasp you to my heart always, always, always, always, always.

*Marcel*: Oh little Jesus, I have a strong urge to laugh, why repeat so many times the word 'always'? ... My feet itch a lot. Even if I scratch non-stop, they itch all the time. Do something to reduce it so that I can write in peace; if not I will lose a lot of time. Little Jesus, I love you very (208) much. As I am smaller than you, little Jesus, I am going to climb on your shoulders and you are going to take me to paradise. It must be very nice to be seated on your shoulders. What I always used to do, being small, allow my little soul to do it again now, all right?

Oh! Regarding this morning's communion, little Jesus, why have I felt this fragrant warmth in my mouth? It was really delicious to eat you then. What happiness if that was repeated every day. Yes, it was really

88     Conversations

delicious, little Jesus. But you made me taste this flavour for only an instant and now, when I think of it, I have a strong desire that it should happen again.

(209) *Jesus*: Now Marcel, allow me to speak and listen carefully. Today, Sunday, I wished to spoil you still more ... But, once these sweetnesses are gone, there will come a time when you will have to accept bitterness. If I tell you these things, you do not have to be saddened by them, do you? Later, there will be occasions when you will no longer wish to eat me; you will feel such a disgust that you will no longer wish to swallow. Why, Marcel? You do not understand now, and furthermore, I do not wish to tell you too soon. But, once the day has come, you will be able to see and understand. For the time being remain, most of all, happy, since the more joyful you are, the happier I am, the more I love you, the more I shower you with kisses and the closer I clasp you to my breast ...

Marcel, don't you find it blissful to be loved by me, to have been chosen to be my little friend, my spouse, the mother of souls and the apostle of my love? Marcel, what greater happiness would you be able to wish for? However, Marcel, how numerous still are the souls who should have accepted the same duties as you, duties that I reserve for my most cherished spouses, who do not even deign to pay any attention to them, and thus cause a delay in the work of my love. These duties are, at this time, still abandoned in some corner because no one can be found to accept them. I am still waiting and if a soul presents itself ready to accept them, I will confide them to him without delay ...

(210) Marcel, I am at this moment very sad in seeing myself abandoned thus by souls; that goes without saying. But there is still one more thing that I am afraid of: it is that a number of souls that I have chosen to be my spouses do not come forward, they also abandon me. Neglecting the duty that I had given to them, they will return it to me, then, becoming like other souls, they will take revenge on me in a very cruel fashion, regarding me as a simple stranger and acting towards me as if they had never been my spouses. Oh! What can I do Marcel, before this immense task which is demanded by my Love? To what spouses shall I now entrust these functions so necessary for the good of souls?

*Marcel*: Little Jesus, entrust these functions to priests, to the priests of France.

*Jesus*: But is it possible, Marcel? Will they accept these responsibilities? Pray a lot. Pray that my spouses accept these responsibilities without ever being discouraged or abandoning them in the face of difficulties, but carry them out zealously right to the end ... If it were so, I would be very happy. I would be smiling always, I would give you many more kisses, I would make you more joyful and all would be for the best.

***Marcel***: Little Jesus, what is it you said to me last night after the Way of the Cross? I have forgotten everything. Do you want to remind me so that I can write it down? (211)

***Jesus***: Last night Marcel, seeing you sad, I took the opportunity to remind you that the day will come when, without knowing why, you will feel sadness and disgust as you did the other day, but even more so. There will also be times when it will be impossible for you to cry. I shall then be very happy because I will no longer have to be near you to wipe your tears and I will be able to sleep in peace ... However, Marcel, do not be misled by my words since, in reality, I will never separate myself from you; my glance remains fixed on you ... And if, then, you do not feel any consolation it is precisely because my love wants you to be in that state. Sometimes, also, you will face another kind of suffering that you will never have experienced before that day. This form of suffering is completely modern; it is a 'new fashion' that I have created just for you. I save it for my most intimate spouses: it is something very good that few souls know ...

Marcel, do you want me to let you know about it now? I think it is good to speak to you about it in advance, so that when the time comes, you will understand more easily. Marcel, it will not be necessary to scold me then, all right? Here is in what this kind of suffering consists, the suffering that I save especially for my closest spouses: just simply hearing my name pronounced, the name of Mary and of the saints, for example that of your sister Thérèse, will be enough to make you shed all the tears you have; and you will then wish, if such a thing were possible, that you had never known these names which will only add to your torment. The more you think of them the more you will suffer; and this suffering will be so much more painful since it will be impossible for you to make it known either by words or actions ... It will be like the other day but of a greater intensity, so much so that if you were able to die of this torment you would die of it immediately. However, I know a wonderful recipe which allows me to keep the flower always very fresh and thanks to which I can freely amuse myself with it and even reduce it to pieces without it losing anything of its customary freshness ... (212)

Marcel, seeing me amuse myself in such a cruel manner, are you afraid? Oh Marcel! Do not be afraid since you will always remain for me the little flower that I can play with. And why would you be afraid? When this time of trial has passed, I will have grown and I will know (213) how to distinguish between good and evil and you, little flower, in the arms of my Love, you will know a much greater peace. So, there is no reason to worry or to be afraid ... However, Marcel, it is necessary that you understand that I speak to you figuratively, using concrete words to help you better understand my thoughts. In reality you will feel nothing except interior pains ... Marcel, allow me to entertain myself quite freely. And so your sole comfort will be to conform in all things to my will. The flowers that I crumble, Marcel, are precisely those that I am happy with. Perhaps you are thinking that it is easy to entertain oneself with each flower. Think again. Do not believe that they all please me equally.

(214) **Marcel**: Little Jesus, did my sister Thérèse know the kind of suffering you have just spoken to me about?

*Jesus*: Your sister Thérèse? Marcel, she has suffered a lot; yes she endured great suffering and only sufferings that no word could describe. Only the soul who has experienced this kind of suffering is capable of understanding it, but without being able to make it known.

**Marcel**: My sister Thérèse, did you endure this kind of suffering for a long time?

**Thérèse**: Dear little brother, why do you want to know everything? Is it in case you might be afraid, by any chance? Yes, I have suffered, as little Jesus has just told you and my sufferings were the same as yours. I realized that I was suffering, but without being able to give expression to it. My only hope was in God who alone was able to understand my sufferings. It will be the same for you, little brother; nevertheless, given your great weakness, I hope that this time of trial will be of very short duration. So, chase away all your worries. Jesus, in sending suffering to you, will certainly give you the strength to accept it cheerfully and with joy.

(215) Look at me little brother. In the past, I suffered like you, my sufferings lasted even longer than yours. However, I was able to get through it since the suffering, not being our work but that of Jesus, it is he, himself, who must take charge of everything ... Little brother, keep your soul in peace, and, in the time of trial, I also will be able to help you, at least a little ... dear little brother, how weak you are! But thanks to your weakness, you will be spoilt all the more, and you will receive greater signs of love.

**Marcel**: My sister Thérèse, are you weaker now than me?

*Thérèse*: Naturally, little brother, we both belong to the category of the weak; but since I am in heaven now, no longer able to lack anything, why do you ask me such a question? We must always, however, accept our humble state; to which few pay any attention.

*Marcel*: My dear sister, I am very sad at not being able to mortify myself as you did. I heard a brother say the other day that each year, during Lent, you only took one meal per day, in the evening, and that at this meal you did not eat your fill. He added that you also gave yourself the discipline every evening ... Concerning mortification, I do not even do a thousandth part of what you did. I eat my fill three times a day; I only take the discipline twice a week, in addition to those that I draw by (216) chance during the novitiate. As for chain bracelets I only wear them for a few hours and still, I find it very painful ... So, what am I to do, sister?

*Thérèse*: You are truly my dear little brother. Listen, I am going to answer you. When you hear the brethren say this and that, do not trouble yourself. Dear little brother, remember what I have said to you many times, but which you always forget from one time to the next. It is necessary not to forget it again and, for that, ask little Jesus to give you a little more memory. I have never mortified myself outside the Rules of the Carmel. Understand, although I was bound solely to follow to the letter the prescriptions of the Rule, outside that, it was impossible for me to mortify myself as my companions did. You must do likewise. Try to keep perfectly your Redemptorist Rule which contains nothing beyond your strength. If you had been stronger than me, God would certainly have called you to enter a more austere order. but because you are very weak, he has chosen for you a congregation (217) proportionate to your strength. Little Jesus is very wise, he does not easily deceive himself as you do. Dear little brother, don't be discouraged, all right? Keep perfectly the prescriptions of your Rule concerning mortification and ask little Jesus to guide you according to these prescriptions, without wishing to impose on yourself extraordinary mortifications which are not necessary. Since little Jesus has wished to choose for you in advance mortifications which conform to the Rule of the Redemptorists, why do you wish to mortify yourself like the Carmelites?...

Ah! I see you are laughing, little brother. You remember the previous story? It was very amusing was it not? A boy who asks with insistence to be changed into a girl in order to enter Carmel ... Now, although you are a Redemptorist Brother, you can, however, be called the 'little spouse' of little Jesus and be at the same time my dear little brother. Is that not a great happiness? I am giving you a kiss; it is already almost time to go to bed. 'I wish for you to sleep in peace on the bed of Love.' That is a line that I dictated to you previously ...

(218) **Marcel**: My sister Thérèse, I have a problem to tell you. You will certainly wish to tell me what to do. I have a pair of socks that I can no longer put on because they are too tight; in putting them on I am afraid of tearing them. Consequently my feet are cold and I dare not put on these socks, which are still in good condition, for fear of tearing them and thus failing in poverty. On the other hand, if I return them to Brother Tailor, it will be a total lack of abnegation on my part since, naturally, I do not like these socks which are too small and not very nice.

**Thérèse**: Marcel, my dear little brother, your question does not really make any sense. You must admit, first of all, that you demonstrate a profound ignorance. If you are incapable of making a judgement on something so minuscule, then what are you capable of? However, little brother, the greater your ignorance and the more you give that impression in the eyes of your brothers and sisters (the saints in heaven), the more it will be given to you to understand clearly and with certitude. Supposing even that you know something or other, pretend to know nothing so as to understand more clearly. Now, dear little brother, here is my answer. But I demand payment in advance for your debt. Put down your pen and recite with me the prayer that I dictated to you for France (...) You are very good, little brother, I love you very much and I am giving you a kiss. Now, listen to my reply.

(219) Little brother, here is how you must keep the vow of poverty according to the Rule. My instruction is based on the Rule. Objects made available for your use, even if they are not very beautiful and are of poor quality, nevertheless be happy to use them. Concerning your socks, because they are too small you can no longer make use of them; you must, therefore, give them back to the tailor in case someone can use them. But if, with the intention of practising self-denial, you put on these socks and tear them, then you really are lacking in poverty. On the other hand, if you avoid this clumsy act of renunciation, these socks which are still in a good state will be useful to someone else without the need of wasting time and thread to repair them ... do you understand? That is the virtue of poverty.

As for your question on the subject of self-denial, suppose, little brother, that after having given back the too-small socks, you are given others which fit you well but which are ugly and badly darned ... if you accept them and wear them joyfully, you will then practise self-denial without neglecting poverty. On the other hand, if in making use of an object, while practising a certain self-denial, you are lacking in poverty, that is a pity which, no matter how minute, redounds not only on you but also on the whole community. That's clear, is it not?

I do not know if your Father Master will be happy with the instruction I am giving you here. Anyway, he will be able to read these things himself and he will certainly be content with them. Is that not so, little brother? My dear little brother, first of all ask of him the permission indicated here: when you do not understand a point of the Rule and (220) you cannot question him, that he allows me to explain it to you. He will certainly agree since, after all, I am your older sister and you are my dear little brother. If he will not allow it, he will have to waste much more time in answering you while if he allows it, besides wasting less time replying to you, he will also be able to read the explanations that I am giving to you. If there is some error there, he will spot it and he will point out to you what needs correcting. If it is correct he will encourage you to conform to it. Faced with such advantages bearded Jesus will certainly be happy ...

That's enough little brother, always keep smiling; I am giving you a kiss. It's already nearly time for walking in the garden. Enjoy your rest.

**Marcel**: My sister Thérèse, shortly after your lesson (*on poverty*) I received another pair of socks which does not demand from me the smallest act of self-denial. If bearded Jesus spoils me to this extent, he will agree also, without any doubt, that you should explain to me the points of the Rule that I do not understand.

Listen, little Jesus, I am going to sing something to you. And my sister Thérèse is going to sing with me also. It will be very beautiful, you will see, and you will not be able to keep from smiling.

## Jesus, I Love You

Jesus I love you, I love you ...
My Jesus, I love you, I love you.
Jesus, I love you with all my heart.
Jesus, I love you with all my mind.
Jesus, lend an ear to my song: (221)
Jesus, I love you, I love you, I love you.
Dear Jesus, will you please laugh loudly?
I am mad for love of you, Jesus.
Yes, Jesus, my heart is drunk with love,
It would wish to cry unceasingly: I love you, I love you;
Jesus, listen to me say again to you:

I want to love you, to love you always.
Jesus, even if you gave me a thousand lives,
I would not cease to cry: I love you, I love you ...
But who is he that I love, to love him to such an extent?
It is someone certainly worthy of being loved.
Come Jesus, give me a kiss.
I never cease from saying: Jesus, I love you,
It is necessary that you give me a kiss.
I have finished my song ... Drunk with love for you, Jesus.
Jesus, love of my heart,
This is the end of my song but not my love.

(222) Little Jesus, are you pleased? I have not ceased to repeat; 'Jesus, I love you', are you satisfied? If you wish still more let me ask my sister Thérèse for another song that I shall make you listen to, to please you. Little Jesus, are you happy? What is there to compare with love? What is more agreeable to the ear? But I see that you are still sleeping; which is, doubtless, a sign that you prefer sleep to love. Whereas you should stand beside your little wren to feed him, caress him and listen to his songs of love. I see that the more he sings, the more deeply you sleep when you are not going so far as to run away. Little Jesus, you certainly understand then the fate of your little wren ...

Little Jesus, nothing is as painful as to be your little friend. However, a single one of your kisses, a single glance suffices to chase away the sadness and intoxicate with a perpetual joy. So, therefore, beside great suffering, indescribable joys are also found.

## 31 December 1945

*Jesus*: Marcel, what are you saying? There you are, about to reproach me. Don't you remember all the times when you have slept or been distracted at the time when you were talking with me? I myself was very sad then and all the times that you slept, I had to stay there and wait until you awoke. I remained calm, not daring to cry, so as to allow you to sleep.

*Marcel*: But little Jesus, you had my sister Thérèse to speak to you in my place!

(223) *Jesus*: Whose concern is that, Marcel? When I am sleeping, bearded Jesus is there who caresses you in my place, little bird. What more do you want?

*Marcel*: Little Jesus, I still have my mother Mary with me and my brothers and sisters, the other saints while you, you have only bearded Jesus: you are, therefore, far from competing with me.

*Jesus*: So, little Marcel, one more question. The matters that you must discuss with me, are they the affairs of your mother Mary and of your sister Thérèse? In the same way, when it is a question of suffering, my little friend, that is a duty which comes back to you. Your Mother Mary and your sister Thérèse being in heaven now can suffer no more for me; but you, my little friend, as you are still in this world, it is necessary that you suffer for me ... I intend to hide my love from you a little so that yours may become stronger and more intimate from day to day. Do you understand, Marcel? My gaze is constantly fixed on you.

*Marcel*: Little Jesus, I love you very much. Now I wish to ask you a question. How is it that I hear certain brothers say that they have a great fear of you? Little Jesus, how do you behave toward other souls (224) that they are afraid of you? If you acted with them as you do with me, I ask myself who could be afraid of you, since you are so good, so sweet, only finding pleasure in love. That there can be souls who are afraid of you is something I find very strange. It has never happened that you scold me and yet there are souls who are afraid of you. Could it be because you treat each soul in a different manner? That being the case, what use will the words that I am writing here be for souls?

*Jesus*: Yes, Marcel, it is very strange. I find it strange myself and I do not understand why a good number of souls have such a fear of me. They are so afraid that they dare not even open their mouths to say a word of friendship to me. However, I conduct myself towards these souls just as I do towards you. But, Marcel, so that this does not surprise you unduly, the explanation for the attitude of these souls is that they do not have enough love for me, that they do not wish to listen to my words nor receive my kisses. If they really loved me, they would have (225) no reason to be afraid. In fact, it is simply because they compare my love with that of earthly creatures, that they fear in that way. If, on the contrary, they used the glance of love to probe the depths of my love, their fear would disappear. And, to be even more precise, Marcel, listen well: one is afraid because one wishes to be afraid since I do nothing that is of a nature to frighten anyone. And if my love ever wished to sow fear among men, it would no longer deserve the name 'Love'. If, in the presence of love, these souls continue to fear it is because, for them, my love is not love ... My conduct towards all souls is the same as towards you, Marcel; I wish to give them my kisses and give them evidence of my love; but because they do not cease to be afraid, I cannot give them these kisses, nor even address a single word to them ... Marcel, tell these souls this thought: 'Be afraid of sin, but do not be afraid of God.' Only sinners are afraid of God; but those who really love him never say they are afraid of him. When I exercise my justice, it is not to punish souls who love me, but only those who do not love me. When these latter affirm that they are afraid of God, it is because they consider God as being sin.

(226)

*Marcel*: Little Jesus, I understand absolutely nothing.

*Jesus*: Marcel, who is obliging you to understand? Ignorant as you are, how would you be able to understand? If you have not yet understood what it is to lack poverty and to renounce yourself, you will understand even less what I have just said ... Besides, I have not said these words for you, but really for souls who are afraid of me. Since you are not afraid of me, it is not necessary that you understand. Since you already love me, what would you be afraid of? Till the day you die you will only love me; consequently, you have no reason to be afraid. Marcel, how I love you. I would wish to hold you close to me always and cover you with kisses, and this desire will remain unchangeable for eternity. Yes, Marcel, my little friend, I will love you, I will give you kisses, I will hold you close to my breast, and you will be filled with delights. Then all that you wish for, I will gladly grant you ... Marcel, may your love melt entirely into mine and then you will possess exclusively all love.

(227)

*Marcel*: My Father, my heart beats so strongly that, perhaps, I am going to die at this moment ... I do not know what power has gripped my soul; but that has only lasted an instant and I have recovered my habitual calm. Only two words remain for me: 'Love and to love'.

# 1 January 1946

*Jesus*: Marcel, for the new year I wish you an abundance of everything: much love, much joy, much suffering. I wish that you eat a lot, that you have a lot of fun, that you sleep a lot, that you work a lot ... in a word, I wish everything for you in abundance.

Were you surprised yesterday to receive Saint John Eudes, of whom you had never heard, as your patron for the year? It's very strange is it not? Is that what has made you sad?

*Marcel*: Yes, little Jesus, I am very sad. After having asked you insistently, you have given me neither your name nor that of Mary and you have not even left me that of my sister Thérèse. You always tell me that you give me all I ask; and yet, after having begged you so much, you have not given me what I desired. Truly, you do not keep your word. I am very sad because of it, little Jesus.

*Jesus*: Come, come, Marcel, what did I say to you the other day? I told you that I would choose a very strange patron for you. So, how can you reproach me for not having kept my word? This year, as I really wish to sleep, I will, therefore, be busy sleeping. Mary, my mother, will have to cradle me to get me to sleep and your sister Thérèse, she will have to love me in your place. We are all three very busy, and if, by chance, you called us, we would have to leave our occupations, which would be very annoying. That is why I wished to give you this year Saint John Eudes so that you focus on him. Moreover it is necessary that you enlarge the circle of your relations with your brothers and sisters, the saints. If you always keep, jealously, your sister Thérèse, always concentrating on her, perhaps one day the work of my love would end up being disclosed. (228)

*Marcel*: So, Jesus, why have you not given me my father Saint Alphonsus? And who, therefore, is Saint John Eudes, little Jesus? I know absolutely nothing about him; I only heard of him for the first time yesterday.

*Jesus*: Saint John Eudes, Marcel, is Saint John Eudes, that's all. He is a saint who loved me a lot during his life, after his death he ascended to heaven with me and then the Church canonized him ... And now, I want to give you him as your patron for the year. Marcel, you are too fussy; even if you know nothing of Saint John Eudes, that's of no consequence and I am not obliging you to know any more about him. The only thing that you must know is that I have chosen him for your patron of the year. And since I have chosen him for you, why would it not be as suitable as another. Do not be sad, Marcel. And even if you were sad, you would not be able to change it since you have already eaten some sweets in his honour; if you were going to change, all the saints would make fun of you and you would be very ashamed. (229)

*Marcel*: My sister Thérèse, why did you not present yourself last night to be my patron for one more year? It is not that long.

(230) ***Thérèse***: My dear little brother, what has little Jesus just said to you? Pay attention to my reply. If I have not agreed to be your patron for the year, do you cease by that to be my dear little brother? Not at all. You remain always my dear little brother and I, I continue to teach you to love Jesus. You do not have to worry about being abandoned by me. Be at peace. Remain joyful and smiling since seeing you sad makes me sadder. When it is time to be joyful, why be sad over nothing? When little Jesus decides something concerning you, is it not by love that he does it? Little Jesus loves you a lot. He never wishes to see you sad; and if you are sad, he no longer knows who to laugh with. You are like me, the plaything of little Jesus; you must therefore behave in a way to make him joyful, without ever allowing any sadness to appear. If he sees you sad, he is very upset, believing he has hurt you in some way and being himself the cause of your sadness. When he sees your tears flow, it is impossible for him to remain tranquil. My dear little brother, I must always stay near you and when I see you a little sad. I must do all I can to hide your sadness and your tears from Jesus, to spare him a much greater sadness. Indeed if your sadness adds to his, Marcel, what could please him?

Little brother, never be sad. Keep smiling so that little Jesus might be more joyful. I love you little brother, I am giving you a kiss; my only wish is that you remain always happy. That is something that I have repeated to you many times, little brother, do not forget it. And if you happen to forget it, I will remind you of it. So, little brother, smile, smile, come on, smile! Do you remember that time when I put my hand over my eye to make you laugh? It worked, didn't it? Dear little brother,
(231) I love you a great deal; my only wish is to see you always smiling ...

Incidentally, dear little brother, during this month, do not forget to pray especially for the priests of France, above all for those who at this moment are persecuted in your country of Vietnam.\* Although that may not have serious consequences, it is a painful trial for them. So pray that they are never discouraged. A time will come when Jesus will return to put an end to their sufferings.

Oh! Priests of France, my brothers, be brave and redouble your efforts ... On this earth who does not know suffering and scorn? You above all, my brothers, it is only at the cost of hard sacrifices that you will succeed in establishing the reign of Jesus' love in this world. It is only at the cost of hard sacrifices that you will succeed in plunging the whole world in the brazier of Love ... O my brothers, it will be neces-

---

\* On 2 September 1945, Ho Chi Minh had proclaimed in Hanoi the Democratic Republic of Vietnam.

sary for you to suffer much since it is to you that the love of Jesus wishes to confide the expansion of his reign throughout the universe. Be faithful and constant, welcoming with joy all trials and, later, in the kingdom of Love you will see the result of your work ...

As for me, your little sister Thérèse, from the heights of heaven I am going to enlist an army of little souls to help you. They will be your breath, your nerves and bones guaranteeing always union among you for the prosperity of the reign of the love of Jesus ... (232)

Priests of France, my brothers, be convinced that the words which fall on this paper have not for their author the little soul who transcribes them but really your little sister, the little flower of heaven. Remind yourselves that, from on high, your little sister Thérèse never abandons you, since she still continues to fulfil now in heaven the mission that she had on earth.

Thérèse of the Child Jesus<br>To my brothers, the priests of France

*Jesus*: Marcel, are you happy now? Are you pleased with me? Do you wish me to kiss you? Say to me: 'Little Jesus, I love you'. Recite also the invocation I have taught you: 'O little Jesus, come with me.' Chase away all sadness, Marcel, I do not ever again wish to see you sad. As your sister Thérèse has just said, to please me, you must always be joyful.

*Marcel*: Little Jesus, is it really true that the female saints love you with a more ardent love than their male counterparts? I have heard some brethren say it is because ordinarily the female saints love Jesus with a more ardent love that many among them receive extraordinary favours from him. Is it really true, little Jesus? If this were really so I would demand to be a female saint since if, in being a male saint I should love you less than in being a female saint, I would not like to become a saint. (233)

*Jesus*: Marcel, are you asking again to become a female saint? How could that happen? Allow me to give you some explanations. It is not true that the female saints love me more than the male saints nor is it for this reason that I show myself to them. If it were so, how can you explain the fact that there are many female saints to whom I have not shown myself and who, in fact, love me more than the others? There you have a general reply which will help you to understand. When it is a question of souls, remind yourself Marcel that it is not a case of distinguishing between man and woman; as I have already told you, each soul loves me with a different love. Those who love me with a forceful love, even if I do not give them any external sign of love,

(234) never abandon me, since they know me sufficiently and are always disposed to act with courage ...

However, Marcel, it is another thing for the weak souls like yours. These souls love me with a really ardent love but lack constancy, so that, if at the time of trial, my love did not show itself to them, these souls might not have the strength to love me. I am, therefore, obliged to show my love to these weak souls. Without that they would fall and, once fallen, in spite of all of their efforts, I do not know if they would be able to rise again. Do you understand, Marcel? Normally it is to these little souls that I must show my love; and it is precisely because they are weak that they give greater glory to me in making my love shine forth more each day. It is for this reason that your sister Thérèse has taught you to accept your weakness with joy; the greater is your weakness, the more love supports you. And if anyone recognizes his weakness, this is not a reason for me to abandon him; since, for me, the essential thing is that one loves me with a sincere heart.

*Marcel*: So, I am very weak then?

(235) *Jesus*: Yes, Marcel, you, the first little flower of Vietnam, you are very weak. I have never seen a soul weaker than yours. However, Marcel, this must not discourage you. It means little that you are weak. After having put everything into my hands, why would you be afraid of your weakness? All that remains for you to do is to love me. As for the rest, I will take it upon myself. Indeed, what can little children know? To love: there you have it, their sole occupation.

*Marcel*: So, I am weaker than my sister Thérèse? Nevertheless, my sister Thérèse, being French, certainly had better health than me. Is this not the case, little Jesus?

*Jesus*: Oh Marcel! What a question! When I am speaking of the spiritual soul, here you are measuring the health of the body. It is not the fact of being French that makes the soul strong. Really Marcel, you know nothing. Not only are you weak but also you know nothing of your weakness. However, remain in peace; if you know nothing of your weakness, I know it very well and that is sufficient. For yourself, be happy to love me. 'My Jesus I love you', these are the words you must know.

Concerning your sister Thérèse, she recognized her weakness, since she was truly weak, and this weakness led her to give herself up totally
(236) to the action of my love. It is thanks to her weakness that she has been able to lead many weak souls to recognize their weakness and teach them the conduct necessary in this state of weakness. Marcel, don't go

so far as to believe that the French are not weak. You are too meticulous. But don't take that as a reproach. Say to me: 'Little Jesus, I love you.' The time is up; I will speak to you again later.

*Marcel*: Little Jesus, now that I have the time, there is something I wish to say to you. Is that all right? I do not yet understand what you said to me earlier. Do you wish me to understand?

*Jesus*: Yes Marcel, I do wish you to understand but it is bearded Jesus who will make you understand. But you seem to be very tired. That's enough, go and rest; I do not wish you to tire yourself by writing. You please me just as much by taking a rest. Go and bathe your head to soothe your itchiness and, when your fatigue has disappeared I will speak to you again. Marcel, I love you very much. I do not cease giving you kisses and embracing you in my arms. I look at you all the time and I smile on you and I am always pleased with you. So, therefore, because of the single fact that you always recognize your weakness, you receive from me perpetual support. That is enough. You are very tired Marcel, very tired. I am giving you a kiss and I hold my lips close to your cheek for all eternity. (237)

*Marcel*: Little Jesus, I have some time now and I feel less tired; after more than an hour of recreation, how could I not be rested? You spoil me a lot, little Jesus. A moment ago there was no electricity; I asked you for it and you gave it to me immediately. The only drawback is that you amuse yourself a little in not ceasing to make my light blink instead of leaving it steady. So, little Jesus, speak. You suffer from the defect of giving me too many kisses. Before I have even finished saying: 'Jesus, I love you' and from the moment that I appear a little joyful, you do not cease to cover me with kisses as if you had never given one to anybody.

*Jesus*: Marcel, be happy. You have spoken long enough, it is now my turn. Really, Marcel, I indulge you in everything and I love you dearly. My only wish is to converse with you, to take delight in you and to joke with you, in a word, to do everything with you. Marcel, does this thought not please you? You always receive my kisses and my smiles; to each of your sighs I respond with marks of my love ... Marcel! If you (238) did not love me, whom would you love instead of me, your little Jesus? Marcel, think only about loving me; love me with all the love of your heart since only love is eternal. In heaven only the love to love me will remain in you, as your sister Thérèse has taught you.

Go now to meet your director.

## 2 January 1946
### *Meditation on Jesus crying in his crib*

***Jesus***: Marcel, do you love me? Why did you laugh last night while meditating on the tears that I shed in the crib? At my birth I found myself in the same situation as other little babies; I suffered from the cold and felt sad. If, at that particular time you had been there to talk to me, I probably would not have cried. If I had heard, as I do now, words of love, I would, doubtless, have forgotton the cold completely. Not only was I cold but I was very sad, not having anyone to chat cheerfully with me and to dissipate my sadness. The sadder I was the more I felt the cold and, finally, I was so cold that I cried …

(239) The Blessed Virgin, seated close to me, cradled me while wiping my tears; however, I was thinking then of someone and, in spite of all my mother's care in soothing me, I did not cease crying … I wanted to have a puppet, a car, a ball or some other toy to distract me; but, at that time, people had not yet invented these toys, which did not exist, but that I would have liked a lot. Now that these toys exist, I can amuse myself at my leisure.

Marcel, it is your sister Thérèse who was the very first to agree to be the little ball as my toy; now there are a great number of souls who equally have agreed to be such or such a toy with the intention of offering it to me to please me. It is the same for you, Marcel. You are the little flower that I gaze on and with which I amuse myself. I love dearly the little flower of Vietnam. Marcel, when I entertain myself with my toys, I bring to it plenty of spirit; the more I amuse myself, the more boisterous I become and the more I am happy with my toys, so much so that I would wish never to leave them. There are, however, times when I must separate myself from them. This separation is painful and it is so, not only for the toy but for me also. It is painful for me since I can no longer play freely, love forces me to suppress my passion for games. It is also painful for the toys since, the game being over, they cannot find anyone to play with them so that they must always stay in the same corner, which is very tedious. Yes it is very painful for them but it is even more so for me since I must stand before these toys and (240) be content to look at them, without being able to touch them. I would want very much to play with them but my love compels me to impose this sacrifice on them …

Marcel, my little flower, I am inclined to be very inquisitive concerning you, wishing only to tear you in pieces to see what you are made of; but I have not yet found a means of satisfying my curiosity. I am waiting for a propitious time to do it. Little flower, a day will come when I will tear you in pieces in order to find out.

Marcel, do not be sad about this. Even if I pluck you to little bits, even if I cause your petals to fall one by one, fear nothing since these petals will fall nowhere but in my hand. And after having satisfied my curiosity, I will reassemble them again and, then, the little flower will only become more beautiful. Then, because my childlike nature likes change, each time I repeat this action, I will enrich the little flower with a new colour. Isn't that fortunate, little flower? You have, therefore, no reason to be concerned. I have not yet torn you to pieces. On the contrary, I smile on you always, I hold you in my hands to contemplate you and to bring you to my lips. What reason could you have to be sad? (241) Come, little brother, keep smiling. Since you are my toy and my possession, allow me to do with you all that I wish; it is on this condition that I shall be happy. If, as soon as I speak of plucking you into pieces, you adopt a sad demeanour, how will it be possible for me to remain joyful with you? And if Thérèse knew that you acted in this way, she would reprimand you, she who does not cease to remind you that, even in difficulties, you must never be sad but always joyful. I myself have just told you the same thing, assuring you that I continue to smile on you and to give you kisses and, consequently, you do not have to fear that I will put into execution immediately what I said earlier. So, Marcel, be joyful and say again to me: 'Little Jesus, I love you. O little Jesus, come with me.' I love you very much, Marcel, I am very happy with you and when I see you joyful, I am happier still.

**Marcel**: Little Jesus, why am I so sad this evening? I feel absolutely no joy. It is, without doubt, because you have decided to leave me alone very soon. I feel full of disgust. It's so already; look at you, you are asleep, you no longer speak to me. Come, little Jesus, speak. How can I be happy if you do not speak to me? I feel myself overwhelmed by distaste; your little flower is abandoned once again. Little Jesus, why do (242) you go to sleep so quickly? Are you really asleep or do you simply wish to tease me? My sister Thérèse also keeps silent ... It is a fact, little Jesus, from now on your little flower will have, once again, to bear the burden of his sadness ... However, little Jesus, even if I must die under this sorrowful yoke that you impose on me, I give myself to you in total confidence, wishing only to love you alone ...

Little Jesus, are you asleep already? If you really are asleep, try to make an effort to wake up so as to hear the words 'O little Jesus, come with me' which I have just said to you. But, little Jesus, that's how it is, you are leaving me full of disgust. I am stopping here, the time is up but I am still feeling disgust. If at the evening's meditation you do not speak to me, I am going to cry so that you will hear me, and cry in such a fashion that you will be dragged from your sleep and unable to go back to sleep. You will then have to speak to me. But, unfortunately, if you are truly asleep, it is not easy to wake you. Nevertheless, I still hope that you are not asleep because how can you explain that you have fallen asleep so quickly without even saying a word to alert your little friend?

## 3 January 1946

(243-a) **Marcel**: Little Jesus, it is true then you are speaking to me no longer. If you speak to me no more, I, for my part, will no longer write and it is you who will be the loser, not me. That's the truth of it, little Jesus: 'Whoever sleeps for a long time cannot grow rich.' You have no great reason to sleep like this; souls deprived of your words will not love you as much yet, in spite of this, you still like to sleep ...

Little Jesus, I can now speak to you as I wish; I feel a lot of disgust, but I have the Blessed Virgin to chat with me. Little Jesus, the Blessed Virgin loves me very much.

## Vision of the Blessed Virgin

(243–1) **Marcel**: That evening, during meditation, I felt myself overwhelmed by disgust; my sister Thérèse no longer spoke to me and little Jesus was asleep. I turned, therefore, to my Mother Mary to converse with her. I had hardly spoken a few sentences to her when I noticed her, standing at my right, dressed entirely in white. Her inner clothing was a long white dress, with a narrow belt of the same colour. Over that, she wore a large cloak, almost as long as her dress. Her head was covered with a white veil which reached to her shoulders, and this veil was held by a headband, also white. Beneath this simple exterior the Blessed Virgin was very beautiful. Her face was very similar to that of Jesus, but a little less chubby (little Jesus was more podgy than she). At that precise moment I saw myself as the same size as before ... My Mother Mary
(243–2) leaned towards me, she looked at me smiling. Looking steadily at me, she, first of all, made my sadness disappear completely. I found myself at the Blessed Virgin's left; with her right hand she held my right hand while I looked all the time at the Child Jesus in the crib. Mary spoke to me in these terms:

**Mary**: Little Marcel, do you wish to see paradise, little Jesus and also your sister Thérèse?

*Marcel*: Mother, I dare not, but I am ready to follow your will.

*Mary*: My child, do you want the happiness that I have promised you? (I did not reply.) However, my child, you must suffer some more before I give you this happiness.

*Marcel*: During the *Salve* …* Mary gave me a kiss, then, drawing me towards her, she wrapped me in her cloak while saying: 'In spite of sufferings, you will always remain sheltered under my cloak, in company with little Jesus. You have nothing to fear. It is my cloak, also, which will collect your tears.' I saw nothing more then than my two feet which stuck out from below the cloak. And during the Angelus I no longer saw anything.

Yesterday evening, she promised me, her little child, to let me see paradise with you, Jesus, and with my brothers and sisters, the saints. She asked me: 'Do you wish that my promise should be realized?' I replied to her: 'I do not wish it but if you and little Jesus wish it, I agree.' (243-b)

*Mary*: It will be necessary first of all that you suffer a lot.

*Marcel*: Little Jesus, this promise of Mary, I do not know when it will be realized. I also asked her for the grace to love you still more. Then, during the *Salve Regina* she gave me a kiss and, wrapping her cloak around me, she said to me: 'In spite of sufferings, you will always remain sheltered under my cloak, in company with little Jesus. You have nothing to fear. It is my cloak, also, which will collect your tears.' She said, again, other things to me but I have forgotten them. However, little Jesus, I am still joyful. (244)

Yesterday, my sister Thérèse said to me simply this: 'Little Jesus is still asleep; he will not wake up until *Têt*.'† That is all. Little Jesus, how can you make yourself sleep for such a long time? It was only a few days ago that you were awake and, here you are, asleep once again. Are you not afraid that your little wren will end up getting tired of seeing you sleeping? Little Jesus, continue to sleep. As for me, I am about to take a siesta; since you are sleeping, I am going to sleep also. You are sleeping in Mary's arms and I will sleep in your heart. During your sleep you hold a toy in your hand but I, I must hold the cross. Tell me, little Jesus, which of the two is the more privileged? However, little Jesus, you may

---

\* The *Salve Regina*.
† *Têt* is the Vietnamese New Year's Day. In 1946 it fell on 2 February.

continue to sleep in peace; as long as the little flower will remain in your hands, she will never fear of losing the colour of 'Love'.

(245) As long as Love lasts, I will not cease to give it my love. Your love and mine will be united together for eternity. Your lips eternally pressed against my cheek are the symbol of this union. Dear little Jesus, you say that you love me dearly, that you are always giving me kisses, that you look at me, that you smile on me and that will last eternally. Remember these words and never allow my cheek to be far from your lips ... Little Jesus, dear little Jesus, continue to sleep in peace. As for me, I am also going to sleep; the time is already up. 'Dear little Jesus, come with me, come with France, come with the French priests.'* That's enough, little Jesus, I wish you a peaceful sleep and I also am going to sleep.

## Mother Mary

*Marcel*: My Mother Mary, little Jesus sleeps, but you, you remain with me. I love you very much and, in union with your loving heart, I love little Jesus. Dear Mother, all the saints know how to give you various titles but I can only give you, quite simply, the name of Mother, Mother of souls. Mary you are my mother, and in heaven as on earth, I will give you the name of Mother. I do not wish to call you 'Queen' or 'Our

(246) Lady'. To speak to you and to give you a name, I only know how to use simply, 'Mother'. Dear Mother, I am suffering a lot at this time: my sister Thérèse no longer speaks to me, little Jesus is asleep, I feel full of disgust and added to that I am pestered with thoughts of women. When I am with you in heaven I will no longer think of women, isn't that so? Dear Mother, graciously love me, give me kisses and, like yesterday, hide me under your cloak. Mother, I love you dearly; you are truthfully my Mother, and eternally you will be my sole and real Mother. Dear Mother, condescend to love me and kiss me. Look after this little flower as a plaything for Jesus. When I am in heaven I will be able to love you much more; in union with little Jesus, I shall be able to show you much more love. As long as I remain on earth I have the feeling of being very cold, very dry in my relations with you. I want to love you as much as

(247) you love little Jesus; and so I already love you twice like him. Let me do the sum in order to see. First of all, little Jesus loves you, and that is my first part; then, my wish to love you as much as you love little Jesus makes up my second part. Therefore, that makes two parts: Jesus' and mine. Dear Mother, I will do the same thing in heaven ... O Mary my Mother, give me your compassionate glance. Have pity on the priests of

---

\* This was in French in the text.

France and Vietnam; have pity on those souls who do not yet know how to love Jesus; have pity on my little sister who is also the little spouse of little Jesus; and do not forget my little brother. May they both always keep simplicity of heart so as to be loved by little Jesus.

Dear Mother, that's all I have to say. I am saying goodbye to you; I am asking your blessing for me and also for my bearded Jesus. Finally, I send my greetings to little Jesus and my wish that he sleeps peacefully. Greetings also to my sister Thérèse and to my father Saint Alphonsus. I ask of the latter to obtain a miracle to cure Brother Bảo who is the youngest of the choir brothers as I am of the lay brothers. On this subject, condescend, dear Mother, to ask little Jesus to cure this brother so that, later, he can preach to make you better known. As for me, I must be happy to love you. Yes, my Mother Mary, I love you. Allow me (248) to love little Jesus with you and deign to present my greetings to all the saints, my brothers and sisters in paradise.

Your child, J. M. T. Marcel

*Mary*: Marcel, my child, I acknowledge you as my child, my dear child. Love me. Do you understand? Marcel, I, your Mother, I love you and I have pity on you more than I love and take pity on little Jesus. Towards little Jesus my heart feels only love while towards you it feels love and pity. Only little Jesus can be loved purely and simply; as for you, you can only be loved with a love mixed with pity. My dear child, nothing is sweeter to me than to hear you call me your Mother. Yes, truly, I am your Mother, and nothing pleases me as much as to note that you really love me with a simple and sincere heart. I acknowledge you as my dear child, I carry you in my arms. I offer you to little Jesus and he will consume you in the fire of love, so that my hands will be like the sacrificial altar while you, following the example of little Thérèse of the Child Jesus, will be the holocaust victim offered in love and this holocaust, little Jesus will accept. My dear child, what happiness can equal (249) yours?

*Marcel*: But, dear Mother, what will my sister Thérèse be to me?

*Mary*: She will be your sister, she will take you in her arms to place you on my knees with little Jesus, and with you she will tell stories to little Jesus.

## 4 January 1946

(250) *Marcel*: Dear Mary, my Mother, little Jesus is well and truly asleep. Let him sleep and let us chat together ... Tomorrow, dear Mother, is the first Saturday of the month. Would you wish to indicate some intention for which you would like me to pray? I love you a lot. I love you twice as much as little Thérèse loves you, I would even say three times since I love you also with my sister Thérèse. Mary my Mother, I wish that in heaven you call me familiarly your little Marcel as you do for my sister Thérèse. I used to believe that you gave to her the name of 'Saint Thérèse' as people do ordinarily. But, one day, I heard you call her 'little Thérèse'. Do you remember, dear Mother, that day when you said to her: 'little Thérèse, make sure you tell this to Van: Van you will enter a Congregation where you will be Jesus' little brother and where Mary will call you her special child, her dear child.' And other things still that I have entirely forgotten. So, in heaven, in our relations with you, as in your relations with mankind, the manner of expression will remain the same as on earth. On that score, once arrived in heaven, I will always call you by the name of Mother as my sister Thérèse does. And if the saints are singing some canticle in your honour in which they give you the name of 'Queen', for my part, when the word 'Queen' is reached I will replace it with the word 'Mother'. Yes, this name of 'Mother' is the only one that I like to give you. I do not like to call you by the name of 'Queen' or any other name. Dear Mary, you are Mother, simply Mother, not anything else. For me you are Mother and the only one to be really my Mother.

*Mary*: So, my child, what is the name you wish me to call you?

*Marcel*: I would like you to call me, simply, 'little Marcel' as you do for my sister Thérèse. That is what pleases me most

(251) *Mary*: My little Marcel, here is something I am recommending and that you will put into effect tomorrow. I am also making the same recommendation to your director. Tomorrow, the first Saturday of the month, the day which is dedicated to me, I am not asking you to do anything extraordinary; I am simply asking you to offer all your works of tomorrow for the intentions of all my little apostles – those who, according to Jesus' words, must later establish my reign on earth – so that, full of zeal and courage, they can stand up to the devil. My reign will come after that of the love of Jesus; and this reign will be more or less stable here below according as there will be more or fewer prayers. If one prays little, it will last a short time; but the more one prays, the

more firm and long-lasting will be my reign. As my reign will come after the reign of the love of Jesus, it will be only the sign that will reveal clearly to men the reign of the love of Jesus, and will lead the world to recognize clearly that I am truly Mother.

My child, pray, go to communion; sacrifice yourself for those who, later, will be my apostles.

Little Marcel, do you not know that later, in heaven, you will have a mission similar to that of your sister Thérèse? You will be like a second Thérèse of the Child Jesus. The first taught you the manner of entering into relation with the love of Jesus; as for the second, she will teach souls the manner of entering into relation with me and to expand my reign in the world. However, you will already be in heaven at that time, so your role, my child will not consist in being the apostle of my reign but rather in coming to the aid of the apostles of this reign. That is the mission I wish to give to you later. Nevertheless, you will remain always the little apostle of the love of Jesus. Marcel, my child, I am repeating my recommendation again. Every first Saturday of the month offer your actions for the intentions that I have just recommended and pray a lot just as I have asked you to do. (252-a) (252–1)

*Marcel*: But, dear Mother has my sister Thérèse no role to play in the expansion of your reign?

*Mary*: She has one, but it is not necessary for you to know it. The first Thérèse will help the second; you will know that in heaven. For the time being, continue to follow my teaching.

## 5 January 1946

*Mary*: Are you sad, little Marcel? Little Jesus is fast asleep ... My child, if you are sad, pass your sadness to me so that I can hide it; otherwise little Jesus would notice it, he would feel sadness and he would be disappointed. Yes, I am going to hide your sadness; my only wish is to see you always joyful. I want you to love little Jesus always but, in your love, I wish that there will be joy, a joy that shines out. You must, therefore, love little Jesus in joy. Yes, even in difficult moments, joy should always accompany your love. The word 'joy' must be attached to the word 'love'. (Joy and love, love and joy.) (252-b)

Remember these things. Yes, I recommend it straight away, remember these things because the day will come when you will no longer hear my voice; you will then have to resign yourself to remaining alone in this room with the words 'joy and love'. That's enough. Do your spiritual reading. I am giving you a kiss in the hope that it will be always in joy that you will love little Jesus.

(253) **Marcel**: Dear Mother, I see that previously my sister Thérèse wished to be a priest in order to preach and to make you known; she obviously loved you a lot. Consequently, later in heaven, when your reign spreads throughout the world, you will have to assign a role to her since, without that she will certainly be very sad. Unless her role consists in teaching me how to behave in my relations with you. Mother, it would not be that? ... As for me, following my sister's example, I love you a lot and I would wish to be a priest in order to preach on Saturday in your honour; but neither is that for me. Nevertheless, once I'm in heaven, I will ask my father Saint Alphonsus for permission to come back to the monastery to speak about you, dear Mother. Or still, since I am a man, I will be able to disguise myself as a priest in order to preach and teach people to love you.

(254) Dear Mother, I love you dearly and I would wish that all men also learn to love you. It is very easy to love you, Mary. You are happy with a simplicity of heart without demanding anything out of the ordinary. Later, in heaven, I will realize my desire to make you loved. Knowing then all languages, I will be able to speak as I wish and teach the entire world to love you, you, Mary, the all-loving Mother. I will say to men that, to please Jesus and deserve his love they must love you. I will say to them that it is in loving you that they will hear clearly Jesus' voice. Indeed , if they love you, you will carry them on your knees with little Jesus, you will shelter them with him under your cloak so that they will hear everything he will say ... Dear Mother, later in heaven, I will love you even more ... Dear Mother, it is almost time to lie down; I cannot write any more. Deign to bless your second little Thérèse.

(255) **Mary**: Marcel, my child, listen to what I am saying to you now. Later, when you are in heaven, you will be able to honour me in all the ways that you wish; but, remember always that I have already assigned to you a special mission to fulfil towards me as I told you yesterday ... So, my little one, I love you dearly, my little one, and you, you must pray really hard for the apostles of my reign. Prayer will serve them as arms and food; and before engaging them in the battle against the powers of hell, it is necessary that I prepare for them these arms and this food, which will be at their disposal later. It is to you that I am confiding this mission, which you must accomplish while you are still on earth. Afterwards, when you are in heaven, I will confide to you another mission.

Listen to me. As Jesus told you, at the beginning of the battle, my apostles will appear very weak, so weak that one will believe them unable to face up to hell ... But, my child, for what reason will my apostles be allowed to submit to this humiliation because of me? I will have to allow it for a certain time so that my apostles will learn to be more humble ... However, my child, the more the devil is victorious in the beginning, the more he will be shamed afterwards. It will no longer be me in person who will crush the head of Satan; but I shall be happy to let my children accomplish this work on my behalf. Seeing me use my weak children as many feet to crush his head, Satan will be completely disgraced ... Then my reign (Mother, there is a power cut, give me ...) will establish itself in the world little by little as Jesus told you. I shall be greatly honoured on this earth; but my child, it is necessary that you pray, pray a lot. Prayer, that is the work you must accomplish in order to glorify me on earth. Offer to Jesus your breathing as so many acts of (256) love; ask him to give to my future priests hearts full of courage and zeal since it is his intention to glorify me on this earth, and it is for this end that he wishes to establish my reign after the advent of the reign of his love.

Finally, my child, allow me to give you a kiss and wrap you in my cloak with little Jesus; and, later, you will be able, as you wish, to glorify me according to the desire of your heart ... Once again, my child, I recommend this to you: love little Jesus in joy and pray for my little apostles. Pray with words, pray with your sighs, pray with your desires. Of these three ways of praying you will be able to use the latter two more easily. My child I love you (with a compassionate love) more than I love little Jesus. All I ask of you is to pray, to pray a lot and to make your prayer become food and arms at the service of my future apostles.

**Marcel**: Mary, my Mother, I love you so much. He who does not love you, dear Mary, he's a devil is he not? Because the devil does not love you and (257) only those who do not love you are devils, is that not so? Dear Mother, suppose that one day I am in hell, I am sure that even the devils would be afraid of me since I would continue to do what I do now, not ceasing to repeat: 'My Jesus, I love you. Mary I love you.' Then the devil, hearing the names of Jesus and Mary, would flee terror-stricken. Dear Mary, allow me to go quickly to heaven and when I am there I will be able to love you much more and glorify you more. Yes, when I am in heaven I will be able to work with total freedom to please you. I will then be able to sing and dance with little Jesus and, when we are tired, you will take us both in your arms and there, on your breast we will rest while chatting together. As long as I am on this earth, you know very well, little Jesus is very mischievous with me; more than once already, as you know, he has hit me and torn me up. But when I am in heaven, he will certainly be better behaved, because then only love will remain without any suffering, is that not so? I will then be bursting with happiness; you will love me, Mother, little Jesus will love me, my sister Thérèse will also love me. And finally, in the same way, all the inhabitants of heaven will love me. Dear Mother, what delights I shall taste at that time. It will be a compensation for the sufferings I am now enduring.

(258)

## 6 January 1946

*Marcel*: My Mother Mary, is it really true that the end of the world is close? I have heard people say that. Is it really true? They say that in the year 2000 it will be the end of the world, that after the reign of five other Popes the Antichrist will appear. But, dear Mother, under what form will the Antichrist appear? Is it true that he will kill your apostles? Will he be black with horns and even a tail? Dear Mother, the Antichrist will certainly be very nasty ... But, as I will be in heaven, there is no reason why I should fear him. As for your little apostles, if they must be witnesses of his coming, they will without doubt be very afraid. As for me, I no longer fear anything concerning that time; and as I have already prayed for your little apostles, they will certainly be more courageous than I am myself at this moment. Is that not so, dear Mother? Yes, I am very weak; as soon as I feel a little distaste I shed tears. In spite of this little Jesus loves me still, he is happy with me, he has even said that if I always recognize my weakness, he will love me even more.

(259)

*Mary*: So, my child, my little Marcel, do you love me? Concerning your question about the end of the world, I know absolutely nothing. I know neither the day nor the month when it will happen. Only the Holy Trinity have knowledge on this subject. For me, all I know is that Jesus wishes to re-establish the reign of his love in this world. It is by the bond of love that he wishes to bring unity back to the world; to make the world a kingdom that belongs to him alone. The reign of his love will be like a column of fire which will support the world when it is on the point of being destroyed. Little Marcel, my child, it is through compassion for the world that Jesus wishes to sustain it with the fire of his love. And if the world comes back to life, it will owe it to this flame of love ... My little child, the world will be able to live in this flame of love, it will become like a globe of fire in the hearth of the love of Jesus, and all on this earth will advance in the radiance of love ...

That's enough. That's all I wish to make you understand. The most necessary thing for you is to pray a lot, to pray for the world ... Then all will be transformed on this earth; a living flame of love will form (260) in the world to support it. My child, pray, pray a lot so that the reign of the love of Jesus may be solidly established on earth in all its beauty, and it will also be the same for my own reign. The entire world will recognize me as its real Mother, and it is then that it will understand, clearly, the compassion with which my heart overflows for it. Pray, my child, the reign of love will soon arrive in the world and my reign will soon follow it. Pray my child. But concerning the end of the world, leave that to the Trinity. Your role is to love Jesus in joy, to pray very much for the apostles of the reign of love and for those of my own reign ...

My second little Thérèse, listen to me; each time I speak to you, I can only suggest the same thing: prayer. Prayer of the will, prayer of works, prayer of feeling. Do not forget that there are many means which can help you to pray without tiring youself. You must not be afraid of prayer. The first Thérèse of the Child Jesus has taught you the easiest (261) method of prayer, which does not require any words. Since you are very small, continue to follow this method just as she taught you. Little Marcel, my child, pray a great deal for my apostles. Prayer is the weapon and the food that will later serve my favoured children. I wish to have a great supply of it in reserve that I will keep at their disposal. When you turn your glance in my direction, remember what I am saying to you now; that will be a very easy manner of praying that you will be able to use many times a day. My child, continue to follow the method that your sister Thérèse has taught you; I am only reminding you of it now so that you may remember it more easily.

**Marcel**: Dear Mother, which country will be specially the apostle of the expansion of your reign in the world? Will my country of Vietnam have a part? I, myself, would really wish to be your apostle but I will already be in heaven. Anyway, even in heaven I will have to do all that I can, with little Jesus, to love you perfectly. At this time, dear Mother, my love for you can only be expressed by great desires; but, in fact, it remains quite inferior to that of my brothers and sisters (*the saints*). I will have to wait until I am in heaven to learn how to love you more (262) perfectly. My dear Mother, it is always there, the object of my desire, but I still have to wait a very long time before I will see this desire fulfilled.

**Mary**: My child I want you to go and rest now. Go and sleep. What pleases me the most is to see you do my will; and, while pleasing me you make your beloved Jesus happier ...

Little Marcel, now listen to my reply to your question. I do not choose my apostles exclusively in one particular country; I choose them in all the countries and there are some in every country. The army of my apostles is divided into two groups which accomplish the same mission and pursue the same end: the spread of my reign throughout the universe. One of these groups takes it upon itself specially to pray and the other to announce to the world the coming of my reign. Thus, little by little my apostles will become more numerous each day and, thanks to their always-increasing number, they will succeed little by little in establishing my reign. I am pleased to tell you this: I will choose the apostles who will work for the spread of my reign exclusively from the kingdom of the love of Jesus since, at that time, the world will become the special kingdom of Jesus. For the rest, I do not wish to make it

(263) known to you now. When you are in heaven, I will let you understand things more clearly; but, for the present, I am happy to point out to you the most necessary thing: that you must pray and pray a lot. If you want my apostles to be brave and faithful, store up plenty of prayers to defend those who are your brothers.

My little Marcel, if I make these things known to you, it is with the sole intention of exhorting you to prayer. Pray, my child, since prayer is of the greatest importance. I want you to apply yourself to it from now on, above all on the first Saturdays of the month. Tell the world clearly that it is on the solid foundation of prayer that my reign in this world will be established. If one prays little, my reign on earth will be of short duration; on the contrary, the more one prays, the more will

(264) my reign be solid and durable. My dear child, if my reign lacks solidity in this world, the reign of the love of Jesus will not be solid either. Little Jesus wants me to stand on the same side as he to witness his real love for the world. My child, is it possible for the world to have any happiness comparable to that of possessing a Mother with a heart full of compassion such as mine?...

My child, give me the name Mother of the Universe. My children, I love you more than myself, more even than little Jesus. Indeed, if I had not loved men more than Jesus, what would have obliged me to accept you as my children, you, sinful men? If I was happy to accept only Jesus as my child, nobody would have been able to reproach me. However, through pity for you, mankind, I have not disdained to accept you also for my children and it is with all the love of Jesus that I myself have loved you. Suppose that Jesus is not God and a God infinitely just, he would certainly reproach me for not loving him alone but, instead,

(265) lavishing all my love on men. If Jesus, who is incidentally a jealous God, does not show any jealousy, when will he? I add also that God has not obliged me to accept the role of being the Mother of men but only that of cooperating in the work of the salvation of the world, in such a way

January 1946  115

that if I had not wished to accept mankind as my children, I would have been lacking in nothing before God ... My dear child, if you do not understand anything of what I am saying, it does not matter. Your personal role is to write it down; content yourself with writing and that is enough ...

In order to show his mercy towards the human race more clearly and wanting me to cooperate in a more obvious manner in the work of the Redemption of men, God has bequeathed me to you as Mother so that you understand that his love for humanity is truly without limits. Therefore I have agreed to be the Mother of the world so as to make known to men the love which God has for them, in such a way that the love I carry for Jesus, unites with the love I have for men, my children (266) ... And if Jesus wishes to establish my reign in the world, following the reign of his love, it is equally so that the world clearly sees his great mercy towards men.

My child you don't have to worry if you do not understand anything I am saying. Bearded Jesus understands very well. Furthermore, your function is not to understand. Remain joyful. Love little Jesus well and pray ... Much. Let me give you some kisses and cover you with my cloak with little Jesus ... It is time. Go and amuse yourself. I am really your mother; I am always pleased with you ...

*Marcel*: My Mother, Mary, I cannot recite many rosaries in your honour every day. Does that sadden you? And when I recite the chaplet in community I am very distracted; does that make you sad? For my part, dear Mother, I am very sad since externally I only do a few things to show you my love and, again, what I do is worth nothing. I really beg your pardon ... Later, in heaven, I will make up for it by a greater love. (267) Mother, I am very sad that I love you so little; but I know that you understand me perfectly ...

But, dear Mother, I was forgetting one thing. I love you dearly; I love you three times as much as little Jesus, yes, three times as much as he. And to tell the truth, I show you externally more love than he. I am sure that Jesus, when he was still young, remained snuggled up against your breast and repeated unceasingly: 'Dear Mary, I love you, I love you dear Mary.' That is all he knew how to say. He was quite lazy, little Jesus. He slept all day; he did not even know how to recite the rosary in your honour. As for me, I repeat several times a day the same words as Jesus, and, what's more, I can say at least five decades of my rosary in your honour. It is obvious that on this point little Jesus is inferior to me. That being the case, it is not surprising that you do not love him as much as me ...

Little Jesus, are you still sleeping? You only know how to play and sleep, sleep and play ... Later, when I will be in heaven, I will not tolerate your sleeping in this way for a single second.

(268) Little Jesus, this evening, during Benediction of the Most Holy Sacrament, I had a strong urge to laugh. The young member of the juniorate* who was holding the thurible was acting in a very nonchalant manner and, on the surface, it looked as if he had no love for you and, by his attitude, he must have caught your attention. If I had the urge to laugh it is because this little young aspirant, by his completely natural manner, gave me a strong wish to do so ...

Little Jesus, in my behaviour towards you, I also wish to act like this little junior; I wish to be like him so that, seeing me, you want to laugh. I want by my manner and my innocent gestures to attract your attention and make you want to laugh. Yes, little Jesus, may I become a comedian who always makes you laugh with me. But what comedy shall I play to make you laugh a lot? I will imitate this evening's little altar server; by my innocence, I will catch your eye and make you laugh a lot ...

(269) Little Jesus, I am thinking at this moment of the souls of children. Children are really happy, aren't they Jesus? You, who were at one time their age, without doubt you understand them perfectly ... You have never been angry with them since their simple defects cannot cause you the slightest distress. In spite of their defects, in the presence of their simplicity and candour, you cannot prevent yourself from loving them a lot. What I think, dear Jesus, is that you understand perfectly; what is it that children could really offer to you to please you? Having only their simple and pure hearts, they would not how know to find anything better to offer you ... And is it not for this reason that the kingdom of heaven belongs to them; although their hands are empty ... That's enough. I am speaking no more on this subject here since I must write these things in 'the way of spiritual childhood in order to lead these children to perfection'.

(270) Little Jesus, sleep in peace. I am still joyful, your little wren can still sing and your little flower give her smile. These days my sister Thérèse no longer speaks to me. Where has she gone? Only my Mother Mary remains here to speak to me ... I am thinking a lot about you, little Jesus ... My only wish is to see this month come to an end very quickly so as to celebrate Tết with you. Little Jesus, continue sleeping peacefully ... Later, in heaven, we will be able, at our leisure, to play together

---

* The juniors were the students of the Juniorate, the school of general formation for the young aspirants to the Redemptorist life. At the time of his first interview with Van, Father Couture had suggested that he join the Juniorate at Huế. *Autobiography* (759)

under Mary's cloak and sleep in her arms when we are tired. We will also be able to listen, as we wish, to my sister Thérèse recite poetry to us ...

Little Jesus, time is up ... You see, I keep smiling; continue to sleep in peace. I am going to have my meal.

## 7 January 1946

*Marcel*: Mary, my Mother, you are not speaking to me any more? In (271) spite of your silence I am not really sad. Today I slept right through meditation. Mother, is it because of that that I have offended little Jesus? Since he is asleep, I sleep also and if I am sleeping it is because you are no longer talking to me. Besides, I no longer know what to say to you, if not these simple words: Mary, Mary, you are my Mother; you are my Mother, dear Mary. I love you dearly. Allow me to join myself to you to love your little Jesus. My Mother, your name is Mary; I am so accustomed to this name that if, now, you took another, I would no longer recognize you as my Mother. You alone, Mary, you are my true Mother. Mary, you are my Mother, my true Mother. In heaven I will be able to love you as I wish. Dear Mary, you are my Mother, my Mother and I do not tire of repeating it, since your name of Mary is the name of my true Mother. Mary, I love you ... However, dear Mary, whatever the situation, I do not love you as much as I love Jesus.

*Mary*: Come, come, little Marcel, I have never obliged you to love me (272) more than you love Jesus. He, alone, is worthy of being loved, you understand, my child? As for me, I am only the intermediary between Jesus and you, and my role is to act in such a way that your love for him may become, each day, stronger and stronger ... I dearly love little Jesus, I also, however have less compassion for him than for you. Nevertheless, in justice, Jesus and you must both love me since I serve as the intermediary between you both. If I were not there what would you do to understand? Thus if you wish to act in conformity with justice, you must both love me. Little Jesus is very good.

*Marcel*: Tell me Mother, what pleases little Jesus the most? I am asking you this so that, knowing what he likes, I can try to please him.

*Mary*: Could you have forgotten already? Even though little Jesus has told you already ... What Jesus prefers above all are the roses of suffering; and your preoccupation must be to collect many of these roses to offer to him. My child, I am going to tell you a secret so that

(273) little Jesus will prefer your roses above all the others: each time that you pick a flower, do it always in such a way that there is in it nothing lifeless or faded; take care that it is always very fresh ... My child, I mean that at times of suffering, of whatever nature, you must remain always joyful. Should it happen that you shed tears, that is not important. On the contrary if, possessing a beautiful flower, you were to make it lose its freshness, little Jesus would certainly reject it. Now, my child you must always love little Jesus in a joyful manner. If you love Jesus in peace and joy, the flowers that you will gather for him will sparkle by their beauty and their freshness. What is more, these flowers kept in the fire of love will last a long time, and little Jesus will be able to make use of them when he wishes to enjoy them. My child, is that not worthwhile?

**Marcel**: Little Jesus, you are still asleep? It is still more than twenty days before Têt. Really you are sleeping a long time; I sigh after you all day,
(274) each hour, each minute, each second, and you still sleep.

*What follows is a description of a picture of Jesus sleeping: 'The Dream' that he is looking at on his table.*

Jesus, I see that you are holding a bunch of grapes and that you are deeply asleep. With two pillows what more could you wish for? You are certainly not afraid of getting a headache. Little Jesus, tell me what you are dreaming about at this moment? Do you dream only of smiling at me? May it please heaven that that is the object of your dream; and in that case, even if you slept for a whole month I would not feel any sadness because of it. I see that my sister Thérèse is there to chase away the mosquitoes from you; so you are no longer afraid that they might sting you ... So, little Jesus, sleep right up to Têt. I wish you a restful sleep. As for me, your little friend, my sole occupation is to gather a quantity of very fresh flowers and keep them in reserve, waiting to offer them to you as a present for Têt when you awake.

That's enough. I am also going to sleep because, last night I watched a play which made me lose more than an hour's sleep. Goodbye, little Jesus. Always united in mutual love.

(275) Little Jesus, are your eyes not satiated with sleep? I feel a lot of disgust at this moment: my Mother Mary speaks to me no more and, added to that, no trace of my sister Thérèse ... It is a fact, now I remain quite alone and I feel a deep aridity. However, little Jesus, I beg you not to worry about it. Continue to sleep in peace since I still love you joyfully, and willingly walk on thorns to gather very fresh flowers to offer to you. And I also willingly force myself to let you hear my most

beautiful songs to charm your ears and help you to sleep in peace.

Dear little Jesus, 'to love you in joy', such is the last recommendation that my Mother Mary gave to me in the course of this trial ... Oh little Jesus, from now on only words mixed with tears coming from the heart of your little friend will fall on this paper ... Oh! To love, to love. My beloved Jesus, even if I must suffer unto death, it is with a joyful heart that I wish to love you alone, my dear little Jesus ...

Little Jesus, are you having a good sleep? And what are you still (276) dreaming about? You are dreaming, doubtless, of a certain little flower that you played with in the past, which explains, perhaps, why you are always smiling while you sleep. Little Jesus, the flower that you are holding in your hand is not at all crumbled or faded; it always keeps its freshness ... Continue, therefore, to sleep in peace, continue also to dream that you hold the little flower in your hand, like a toy, but don't dream that you tear it to bits because, when you wake, seeing yourself deprived of your toy, all you could do is cry.

Little Jesus, do you hear me speaking? Continue to sleep in peace. Time is up; I am stopping while greeting you in Mary's arms. United in a mutual love, remind yourself, little Jesus, that 'Love is never far from love.'

Little Jesus! ... I feel myself invaded already by disgust and sadness; but I can still love you in joy. Dear little Jesus, do you still dream that you are playing with your little flower, or has this dream ended already? I feel myself filled with great distress in thinking that I will (277) have to wait for you for twenty-two or twenty-three more days. What could I do during these days of waiting? ... Oh, I already have some work. Yes, I have found an occupation, a single occupation, that seems easy but which is at the same time difficult; an occupation which, although difficult, remains, all the same, relatively easy, is that not so, little Jesus? This occupation consists in loving you joyfully. Oh! I still have another occupation: that of gathering roses, which would accompany my wishes for a happy new year. This is very good. Little Jesus, continue to sleep well. As for me, I continue to sing and to love you with a joyful heart. However, whatever I do, I feel disgust.

Today, little Jesus, I found a paper written by Brother Mark on the subject of vocation and which made me want to laugh. It is nothing great: only two or three sentences but each time I see Brother Mark, I want to laugh ... On the other hand, little Jesus, is it really you who has allowed it? But, concerning my relations with Brother Mark, the thing is not important. Formerly I would go to him to let him know what was on my conscience, as you know little Jesus. It was also a time when, and I do not know why, I felt a strong aversion towards this brother, although nothing that I saw in his behaviour gave me any wish to

(278) reproach him. He, however, was always smiling at me. Little Jesus, I have been able to see by this how weak I am in everything ... Currently, I no longer have any aversion towards this brother; on the contrary, I love him as before. Yes, little Jesus, this confrere is my spiritual brother since he has taught me the way to behave towards my spiritual director. Nevertheless, I have been very ungrateful towards this spiritual brother. Little Jesus, will you please forgive me? In the future I will correct myself and no longer have any voluntary aversion towards him.

Little Jesus, my disgust is growing from day to day. Nevertheless, sleep in peace; it is in joy that I wait for you to wake up. I do not cease to love you alone, little Jesus. This little flower only exists to be offered to you, to you alone, so that you can crumble it, play with it, look at it; she does not wish to exist for any other. Little Jesus, I love you a lot, a lot. I know, truly, that the only thing capable of giving you peace, is to see that I love you in joy. And since at this moment I am loving you joyfully, it is impossible that you should be sad because of me. So, little Jesus, what more could you wish for?

(279) Here I am reduced to talking alone to sheets of blank paper; and, after having posed the question, I must answer it myself ... Little Jesus, sleep peacefully, but remember the little flower that you are holding in your hands. Never allow her to cause you the slightest displeasure. Keep her intact; wrap her in the flames of your love according to the promise that you made to me.

My little Jesus, I no longer taste the slightest joy. Honestly, everything appears difficult to me and the only joy remaining to me is the one I taste in recreation with the brethren twice a day. And to think that this sadness and this disgust will continue until Têt ... Dear little Jesus, I want you to continue to rest peacefully in the midst of the sighs of love that I offer you every day; and I am sure that you find it very agreeable to sleep among these modest flowers ... Mary, my Mother, graciously hide my sadness from little Jesus and do not allow him to see it. Arrange things so that I always love little Jesus joyfully ... And you, my sister Thérèse, you too come to my aid.

## 12 January 1946

(281) *Mary*: Are you sad, my little Marcel?

*Marcel*: Yes, my Mother, I am very sad.

*Mary*: So, what saddens you so? Tell me.

*Marcel*: I am sad because little Jesus is sleeping and has forgotten me completely; he is no longer interested in me, he no longer even deigns to speak to me. And you, Mother, you have done the same thing, in maintaining silence towards me since the other day. And my sister Thérèse has done worse still: she has abandoned me, I, her dear little brother, not paying any attention to me ... I really wish to repeat often: 'Jesus, I love you' but I feel such disgust that I cannot do it. I also feel a certain reluctance in reciting the Hail Mary. I can say easily: 'Mary I love you', but as soon as I recite the Hail Mary I feel an immense disgust, sometimes I do not even know what I am saying; I am reduced to repeating 'Hail Mary' without ever finishing the prayer. My dear Mother Mary, I love you a lot, please pardon me. When I am in heaven, I will, without doubt, be able to love you more. But the fact remains that I find it very painful to continue to live on this earth ... Dear Mother, as I still have much to suffer, have pity on me.

*Mary*: Little Marcel, my child, if I gave you a little more joy today, would you be happy to accept it? I would never have the heart to (282) abandon you, my favoured child. My dear child, if you do not feel the fervour of your love, do not worry about it. Indeed, what has your sister Thérèse taught you and, I, what have I repeated to you on this subject? Remain at peace, your good will is enough. The sufferings you are now bearing are the best proof of your love for Jesus. And if you do not feel this love, it is because you have offered it entirely to little Jesus. It is the same in regards to me; I am not reproaching you in any way if you do not feel any fervour in loving me. Feelings of fervour and love are two different things. When you feel joy in loving, supposing that you are capable of expressing your love, certainly you would do it as much as is possible. This is what one calls the fervour of love. On the other hand if, in loving, you only feel distaste and sadness, without feeling anything of the fervour of your love but that, nevertheless, you keep in your heart the desire to love, come what may, even were it necessary to die of it, that is to love with all your heart, with all your strength ...

My child, for the moment, offer to little Jesus all the love of your heart, offer him equally, the fervour which you formerly enjoyed. In (283) that way, whatever the fervour of your love might be, Jesus will accept all and you will not cease loving with all your heart and with all your strength ... My child, do not forget what I have just reminded you of, retain it with care. And if you feel yourself incapable of expressing your love to little Jesus, do not worry about it unduly, accept this trial and in doing so you will give to him double evidence of your love. And I, in seeing you so unhappy, how would I be able not to love you more? Therefore stay peaceful; it is sufficient that you have the will to love

Jesus. Regarding your relations with little Jesus, in all that you have done until now, allow me to concern myself with it in your place. It is sufficient for you to accept this trial with a joyful heart.

Your love, it is me, myself, your Mother. Be happy to offer your love joyfully to little Jesus, that is to say, myself, and that is enough. With regard to your conduct towards me, I have nothing to complain about. The only occasion when I would complain would be when you do not accept joyfully the sufferings that Jesus sends you ...

Your sister Thérèse always has the same affection for you. Leave to her the task of being concerned for you about your relations with me. Your only occupation should be to love in joy. You can cry when you are sad and laugh when you are joyful, but your heart must love little Jesus always in joy ...

My dear child, I am again giving you this advice: the prayers and ejaculations that you can say aloud, say them. If not, be content to think of them and to offer them to Jesus and that suffices. That is a method that your sister Thérèse has taught you; could you have forgotten it already? Continue to follow this method and, by that, you will practise prayer of the will.

(285) If there is anything else, let your director know of it without being afraid. Just as little Jesus is able to spoil you, he will also allow bearded Jesus to treat you benevolently. Tell him frankly all your trials without fear of displeasing him or of following your self-will. In fact you are not following your self-will if, after having made all known to your director, you put into practice exactly what he says to you. By that, you are following little Jesus' will. On the other hand if you do not speak to him about what increases your sufferings, you are following your own will, taking on yourself useless crosses which do not come from little Jesus.

Although little Jesus has told you not to be afraid of your director, why are you still afraid? Little Jesus cannot then sleep peacefully. Now if you do not want to speak of them to your director, have, at least, the humility to say to him these few words, or let me say them in your place; all right? 'My Father, I no longer wish to sweep the corridors ... There are many things which contribute to my sufferings ... ' Remain now in peace; your director understands you and he is the one who must attend to your external work, since little Jesus wishes it to be so.

(286) You will still have much to suffer. But if you do not speak of it to your director, you will not be at peace. Tell him everything, frankly, even if you believe that it is laziness that makes you speak so. You think it is laziness but your director thinks otherwise. Since you are not, yourself, Jesus' spirit, the spirit of Jesus will not judge as you do. Why are you still so troubled? So, let us concede that you act thus by laziness. In this case, I wish to favour your laziness otherwise you would become

discouraged. Since you admit to being lazy, I wish that you were even more so, provided that you always follow the directives of the spirit of Jesus.

You will have to do a less difficult work and thus you will be less troubled concerning your daily exercises of piety ...

I want you to love little Jesus in peace and joy. I love you, I feel compassion for you, I am smothering you with kisses, I am wrapping you in my cloak. So, remain peaceful, I will hide your sadness so that little Jesus does not see it, nor others either, except your director. I want you always to let him know clearly the feelings of your heart.

## The end of January 1946

*Marcel*: My Father, this morning it seemed that I heard my sister (286-1) Thérèse speaking to me, but it was not very clear. All she did was give me some prayers to recite for France. This is what I believe I heard:

'Dear Jesus, may your love become the pillar that supports France. It is on this love alone that we wish to lean.'

'Dear Mother Mary, true Mother of France, graciously strengthen it, in assuring it a true peace. Now dear Mother, maintain social order in its breast, obtain for it a true peace and may it live always in the love of Jesus your Son.'

My sister Thérèse again addressed to me some words of comfort but I no longer remember them. As for the prayers for France she did not (286-2) tell me at what time to recite them. Today, I feel more disgust than ever; that is why I did not hear very clearly the words I have just reported. I will ask my sister Thérèse about it. It is probable that I must recite these invocations as normal. She has, moreover, given me two invocations to the Blessed Virgin and I do not know when precisely to recite each of them. My Father, see to it yourself what must be done. I feel completely dry; it is impossible to write any more.

## 2 February 1946
### *Têt*

*Marcel*: Dear little Jesus, it is Têt! And here I am seated all alone, letting (287) long sighs escape, not having anyone to play with and not even hearing one word from your mouth ... However, dear little Jesus, if I love you, it is not with the intention of tasting joy, sweetness, consolation, but solely to please you ... I am certain that seeing my smiles mixed with tears gives you great joy ... At the sight of the drops of dew that weakness allows to fall from my eyes, without doubt you are not able to prevent yourself from having great pity for poor sinners, above all in these days of rejoicing ...

O little Jesus, all the pleasures, all the moments of sweetness, I offer them to you; as for the sufferings that you send me, I accept them and I offer them to you once more as a spray of spring flowers intended to divert you, to enchant your glance, to rejoice your heart, and at the same time to make you forget the blows that sinners rain down on you today ... People stop working on the day of Têt in order to have fun. (288) But I, I do not rest; I want, unceasingly, to gather a great number of very fresh flowers for your delight.

Little Jesus, since you and I make but one whole, it is sufficient that you alone are joyful; I am not obliging you to pay me back in return: the sentiments that you feel are mine also. Little Jesus, I will never abandon you. The sight of crosses (that you call roses) will never make me withdraw. When I see that you are happy and joyful, the more I wish to please you, the more I wish to drown you in my smiles of love ...

O little Jesus, the spray of roses in question is truly difficult to gather, however my sister Thérèse and I will never allow ourselves to be overcome by difficulty. We will each make a bunch equally abundant to offer to you as a kind of plaything. Little Jesus continue to play, continue (289) sleeping. Even if the present trial lasted until the end of my life I would gladly accept it and would put up with it joyfully to please you. All that comes to me from your hand, sweet or bitter, I accept with joy to please you. Concerning my tears, they are hidden completely. Little Jesus, I wish you peace. In spite of my sufferings I wish to love you in joy.

## 3 February 1946

*Marcel*: Little Jesus, it is already the second day of Têt. Your frail little flower is still torn and crumbled ... Who would be able to understand my feelings in view of so many spring flowers which, full of freshness and beauty, are vying with one another to blossom! It seems, Jesus, that your little flower is the only one to be sad; even the aspect of spring, far from bringing it a little joy, only makes its sadness increase ... Alas! Little Jesus, when you see your little flower in such a miserable state, (290) you also must sigh a bit. Compared with other flowers she is only worth being abandoned in a corner, in the corner of a room in the novitiate .... She has plenty to moan about, your little flower, left to herself, sighing long sighs, in the middle of a swarm of buzzing mosquitoes but forcing herself to smile in spite of her tears, her eyes focused on the distance in sad expectation. However, although sad and faded, your little flower asks unceasingly to keep her freshness in order to offer it to you, little Jesus. Yes, little Jesus, despite suffering, I wish, nevertheless, to love you in joy, you, my sweetheart ... Do you understand me? Mary, my Mother, I beg of you, always remain close to me to hide my sadness from little Jesus. Do not allow him to see it lest, in seeing it, he would become sad and that would increase my own sadness ... I am stopping here; I am full of disgust. Mary, my Mother, I salute you and I love you.

My Mother Mary, even if I raise my eyes towards you, I see that you still remain silent. Dear Mother, graciously send a glance of compassion on your poor child. Seeing the feelings of my heart, I am sure that you will not be able to stop yourself from having more pity on me ... Dear Mother, when I open my heart to you in all sincerity, do you understand what I am saying to you? Dear Mother, look at my heart, it is immersed in disgust and my soul is overwhelmed by suffering. In this state, what can I say to you to open up your heart? In reality I know that you understand my feelings better than I understand them myself. Dear Mother, deign to stem my flowing tears and hide my sufferings, which reveal themselves a little on my face. Alas! O Mother, how I am suffering at this moment! If, previously, you had not suffered yourself, you would not be able to understand me today; but since in the past you have very often known bitterness, it is a fact that now you understand me better than I understand myself. (291)

(292)

O Mary, O Mary my Mother, see my heart, see how its wound has become very serious ... However, Mary, love will cure me of this wound ... Mother, deign to hide it from little Jesus for fear that he will be sad on seeing it. Better to suffer alone for little Jesus than to see him sad because of me. It is sufficient that I endure this sadness all alone, without little Jesus knowing it, since I am his spouse ... That's enough Mother, time is up. See you tomorrow! Take pity on your poor child, your little Marcel.

## 4 February 1946

*Marcel*: Dear Mary, my Mother, although I made this rendezvous for today, now. would you believe it, I no longer know what to say to you ... Dear Mother, dear Mother, do you have pity on me? On seeing my suffering, you certainly have more pity for me. Yes, I do not doubt it; you have more pity for me now than before. (293)

Dear Mary, my Mother, if you had not experienced suffering, I would not be sure that you understand me at this time ... Dear Mother, have pity on me. I am at this moment feeling almost inexpressible sufferings.

(294) Mother, take me by the hand and lead me. Do you feel pity for me? Oh! I know well that you feel more pity for me than for little Jesus. Therefore, I raise my eyes towards you. Mother, where are you? Graciously glance towards your child who is suffering so much ... Mother, Mother, Mother, Mother – Mother – Mother, I am suffering a lot, it is not certain that your second Thérèse can ever see little Jesus again ...

Mother, yes, yes, whatever are the vicissitudes of my life, even if it were necessary to live eternally away from little Jesus, I would not continue to love him less ... Mary, Mary, my Mother, look on your poor Marcel ... Mother, I am going to die of sorrow.

Alas!!!! Mary, Mary, I do not cease to call you and you do not answer me; I lift my eyes towards you, deign to welcome me ... Mary, Mary, Mary, Mary, Mary, Mary, Mary, Mary, I will recognize you eternally as my Mother and I will call you my only true Mother. Mary, remember me, for fear that I succumb under the blows of suffering ... Mary, I will die on your breast in little Jesus' presence.

(295) Dear Mary, I love you dearly, yes, dearly. Mother, keep me warm under your cloak. I can speak no more. Condescend to throw a glance on your child, Mother, my Mother ...

Little Jesus, I love you dearly. At this moment I have nothing more to offer you except my sighs; I therefore offer them all to you. I still remain joyful; however ... There is one thing I am not telling you. If I told you in what situation I actually find myself, that would plunge you into sadness; therefore, I do not want you to know it. Or, if by chance you know it already, pretend not to know anything so as not to be sad in seeing me in this state ...

(296) That's enough, time is up already. When we are together in heaven we will be able to chat longer. It will no longer be as it is now ... Little Jesus, I wish that you remain in peace. Mary, graciously glance on your little Marcel ...

Mary, my Mother, time passes but suffering remains, not ceasing to torture my heart. However, until now I have not dared say to little Jesus that I am suffering a lot. I have spoken of it only to you, dear Mother, knowing well that, any way, you will hide my sadness from little Jesus and my disgust. Always remembering the advice that you have given me, I remain joyful; I continue to love little Jesus in joy. I often find that very painful. Also, try to understand me and if it happens that accidentally, I neglect something, I beseech you to act in my place ... At this moment I no longer find any consolation in looking at little Jesus.

(297) Besides, dear Mother, if I love little Jesus it is not at all with the intention of seeking my own consolation. You know that all that pleases little Jesus, I do gladly for his pleasure.

Mary, look at your little Marcel. I am full of disgust and, yet, you remain my true Mother. I firmly believe that little Jesus is concerned about me. It is, without doubt, because he thinks that I do not have enough confidence in him that he tests me in this way. Is that not so, Mother? Yes, all that little Jesus wishes to do to me, he does. He can send me the trials that he wants, my love for him will never lose its ardour. On the contrary, the longer the trial lasts the stronger will be my confidence in him ... Oh! Mary, my Mother, what joy you taste in heaven. It seems to me that I am alone, exiled on this earth. However, I hope, one day, to be eternally happy with you in the company of little Jesus and of my sister little Thérèse ... But, dear Mother, that day, is it far off or near? Will it be in reality what I hope it to be? Is it not, rather, a vain dream of my imagination? Whatever might be, dear Mother, I do not stop hoping that this happy day will certainly come. Still, at this time I am suffering a lot, asking myself when will this day of happiness be given to me. Anyway, I do not continue to love Jesus less and continue to call you my true Mother for all eternity. (298)

## 11 February 1946

*Marcel*: Jesus, there is nothing extraordinary in the fact that I recognize my weakness; in fact you already know the state of my soul. My confidence, however, is far from being weak. I know with certainty that only confidence is capable of attracting your heart to me ... Jesus, I am very wretched and, when I think of my weaknesses, this thought only leads me to discouragement. One thing comforts me, however: it is that by a simple glance thrown at your love I can fascinate you, dazzle you. I cast my glance, therefore, on your love, I confide myself to your love. I am certain that your love will never abandon me, that it will never be saddened by my weaknesses. Love knows me, Love understands my feelings thoroughly. (299)

O Love, there is nothing but that. Sometimes, in thinking of my fate, I feel overwhelmed by fear and I do not know how to defend myself against these feelings. I have only one means which my sister Thérèse has pointed out to me and which consists in going to hide myself in Love's shadow, to confide everything to Love. Yes, yes, I continue to act in this way; I deliver myself to Love with the certitude that Love will never refuse to welcome the glance of a little weak soul like mine since it finds condensed in this glance all the love and all the confidence of which my heart is capable. So, therefore, dear Jesus, graciously accept this glance of my weakness. Little Jesus, is my trial going to end soon? Why do you make me wait so long? (300)

(301) Dear Mary, these days I do not know what to say to you. My soul is truly like an abyss filled with sufferings and my heart like uncultivated land ... this land previously received the warm rays of the sun of love but at this time it is covered by a cloud which hides from it the influence of these rays; it only receives a little warm air coming from the sun of love. The landscape of my soul presents a very sad aspect. It no longer merits the name of flowerbed; the only appropriate name is that of uncultivated land that no one wishes to look at ... Alas! O Mary, you know that, previously, my soul was really only an uncultivated plot; but, transformed by Jesus' hand it became his flowerbed, his place for rest and for walking ... But Jesus has now distanced himself from his bed of flowers, leaving it, once again, to adopt the features of uncultivated land. Dear Mother, I am not sad myself because of this situation since I know that my soul, which has become uncultivated ground, always carries the imprint of the step of my Beloved. This imprint remains a cause of comfort for my heart. Although I can no longer see Love in

(302) person, I can, at least, see the traces of this Love, and that is sufficient for me. Indeed, according to Thérèse's words, if I love Jesus, it is not for the consolation of being loved in return.

Dear Mother, in seeing the state in which I find myself, you must certainly be distressed ... Dear Mother, do you understand the depths of my heart? As you have suffered greatly in your heart, I am certain that, at this moment, you understand my personal feelings. My sole regret is that in the past, you did not have a mother to hide your grief as you do at this time for me. Mary, dear Mary, here is my heart, deign to understand its depths ... Dear Mother, when will it be allowed for me, your child, to see Love again? When will this uncultivated soil which is your property once again see the sun of Love shining? ... Alas! Mary! Mary! Mary! Mary my Mother, it will be necessary for me to be

(303) crushed under suffering until I die of it. Nevertheless, even if I die, at least it will be under your cloak with little Jesus. Dear Mother, how I feel this disgust! Dear Mother, I am suffering, I am suffering ... I am suffering. I beg of you do not let little Jesus see my suffering so he will not be sad because of me ...

Mary! I ask myself if I will be happy after my death??? ... Little Jesus never stops telling me that I will be but, at this time, these words are to me nothing more then a gust of wind, which passes quickly leaving me only a feeling of coolness. But I really believe that Jesus never deceives me, since he is the Truth. Supposing, even, the impossible, that this promise were not true, I would not be discouraged and my love for

(304) little Jesus would be in no way diminished, as the teaching of my sister Thérèse reminds me ... Dear Mother, whatever might happen, I wish to continue to love Jesus and, if my love for him is too weak, you will

want to love him with me. And if that does not yet suffice, I ask Jesus to love himself in union with me. Dear Mother, the flame of love that burns in your heart as in mine, comes in its entirety from the hearth which burns in the heart of Jesus. Let us unite ourselves therefore to this fire of infinite Love in order to love Jesus eternally. Yes, eternally, I will continue to love Jesus and, even if during eternity I cannot see Love, I will not continue to love him less than eternally.

Little Jesus, if I love you, it is not for your kisses, but with the sole intention of pleasing you. Do you understand me?

Mary! My Mother, Mary, after having tasted the suffering that I am (305) now enduring, I can understand a little what your sadness must have been when you lost little Jesus ... Dear Mary, dear Mother, it seems to me that you must have been very unhappy at not having at that time a mother to comfort you and hide your sorrow as you do for me. However, dear Mother, I am still suffering a lot, and I have the feeling that it is nearly impossible that I can suffer more. Nevertheless, I keep my glance fixed on you in the certainty that you will understand me ...

Mary, Mary, Mary, Mary, Mary, Mary! Shelter me under your cloak with little Jesus. We are both held tightly against your heart but I feel like I am a thousand miles from Jesus. Oh! My Love, I love you, I love you, I love you. Deign to accept my love.

Little Marcel

To Mary. My Mother, you tell me that you have more pity for me (306) than for little Jesus. So then, I have need of your pity? Dear Mother, at this time do you understand the feelings of my heart? I feel an immense disgust and it seems to me that little Jesus is quite indifferent towards me. Mary, I love you and I ask you to unite me to yourself in order to love Jesus. When I look at him I can only sigh deeply; and it is the same when I look at you, dear Mother, or when I look at my sister Thérèse. I am stopping now, dear Mother, it is already passed the time. I love you dearly. Graciously bless me, Mother, me, your child, immersed in disgust.

My dear Mother Mary, ever since the other day, it seems as if I no longer know how to speak to you, to you dear Mother. Although, during these last few days, I feel a little less disgust, I think that Love is still far from me. I know that this time of trial imposed on me by Love is truly very beneficial for souls but it does not remain less hurtful for me your poor child ...

Mother, I thank you for having compassion on me. It seems that your cloak has absorbed all my tears. Dear Mother, I am not sad at having (307) shed them so abundantly and, if little Jesus wants me to shed even more, all I ask is to follow his will joyfully, to please him.

Mother, you know my great weakness; however my weakness and my misfortune will be a reason for unshakeable confidence. Yes, dear Mother, I hope, I hope always and, even if I should not see little Jesus again, I would still hope nevertheless. You doubtless understand very well also that little Jesus, being more mischievous than me, likes this game of hide and seek a lot. Where, therefore, is he hiding so well? However, where else would he be able to hide than under your cloak? One thing is certain; I will end up by finding him one day. Little Jesus must find it very amusing to be so well hidden; and when he sees me looking for him everywhere without succeeding in finding him, he must find in that a greater joy, thinking himself very skilful. However, dear Mother, since you doubtless know where little Jesus is hiding, I am (308) asking you to pass on to him this advice: 'Little Jesus, be careful; don't rejoice too soon, you could regret it. The day will come when you will have to take the initiative and come to me. I know you very well: if I am not there to play with you, you will be very bored even if the game, in itself, is very interesting.'

Mother, all that remains for me now is to wait. Although it may be very painful for me to be separated from little Jesus, I am, nevertheless, sorry for him who must be sadder than me. I do not cease, therefore, to wait for him and when he comes to me, he will make up a new game ... But, alas dear Mary!!! It will still be necessary for me to wait a long time ... Nevertheless, the anchor of my hope always remains secure in the Love of Jesus.

Dear Mother, a moment ago, because of lack of time, I had to interrupt my conversation with you. Allow me now to continue. Mother, it seems to me that my words are very difficult to understand since I speak in such a disjointed manner. I see, however, that you do understand me. Yes, dear Mother, what I say you already understand. I love you dearly. You know that I am here feeling absolutely alone. It is very easy (309) to understand, is that not so Mother? Little Jesus and I, we play together both of us. Now, little Jesus has gone to hide, and I, here alone, I have to cover my eyes to go and look for him; but in spite of all my searching, I have not succeeded in finding him and I have had to resign myself to being all alone ... So, dear Mother, that explains why I am here all alone. You know, dear Mother, that when little Jesus is absent, it seems that my least movements are marked with a stamp of sadness.

Mary it is a great pity for little Jesus since if I am so sad, who can describe what little Jesus must suffer??? ... Unless, perhaps, he has found other playmates. Yes, that's possible. Mother, I am sure of it: little Jesus must have already found one or more companions, and it is probable that because he plays with them (*his spiritual friends*) he has forgotten me and the game of hide and seek that we had begun together. Yes, it's highly likely and my supposition may well be true. I am not sad at seeing that little Jesus acts in this way with me. On the contrary, I am happy, dear Mother, since I know that the Spouse of my soul finds comfort in conversing with new spouses. If he played with me all the time, what new consolations would I be able to obtain for my beloved Spouse? Yes, dear Mary, the Spouse of my soul is currently receiving comforts and I am glad of it. I accept sadness and dryness so he is consoled, even if this state of sadness and bitterness must last until the end of the world. (310)

Oh Mary! My dear Mother, I am certain that, later, little Jesus will be concerned about me again and that I will be allowed to see the new spouses that he will have found ... Dear Mary, then, without doubt, I shall taste complete happiness ... For the time being, I must live in the expectation of that happy day which is surely a long way off. There is one thing, however, which comforts me, it is the conviction that the Spouse of my soul does not utter deep sighs like me; this makes me very happy Mary ...

That's enough. I look fixedly on you. Today, it is possible for me to speak to you but I do not know if I will be able to do so tomorrow. So, I am saying goodbye to you and, even if I cannot speak to you, that's not really important since it only takes one of my glances for you to understand the depths of my heart.

## 3 March 1946

*Marcel*: Mother, the time is up, it's now my turn to go and visit Jesus and to comfort him.* I beg you to come and help me. I am sure that my tears are going to flow; will you please wipe them with your cloak? Do not let Jesus see them lest he become even sadder. To cry in his presence would not be the right thing to do. It is true that he already knows my great weakness, this weakness proper to a child but, even so, I do not want him to notice it since the visit that I am going to make to him to comfort him would only sadden him more, which is not appropriate. Having arrived in Jesus' presence I will say to him: (311)

'Jesus, I bring my sighs of love to you and I wish them to be placed on the altars of Europe, since, in these days of carnival your tabernacles are certainly neglected. You hear only few words of love, and still these words are drowned out by many blasphemies. I wish to send my heart to you to comfort you because in my country this custom of carnival

---

* Adoration during the days before Ash Wednesday, 6 March.

(312) does not exist. I wish to send it above all to France, the country for which I must pray in a very special way at this time. I wish to send it also to Canada where our Vice-Province of Indo-China has many benefactors. Today, the first day, I will therefore pray for France, tomorrow for Canada and Tuesday for Vietnam and for the countries where the carnival tradition exists.'

Dear Mother, that is what I will say to Jesus; I am sure that he will welcome my words with joy. My greatest happiness during these three days will be to have been able to visit Jesus in the tabernacles of the whole world ... Mother, the time is up, I am saying goodbye to you.

## 10 March 1946

(313) *Marcel*: Mary, my Mother, today allow me to write another letter to you. Dear Mother, if, at this moment, you look into the depths of my soul, you will see that it is truly desolate. And in this state how could I express to you the bitterness of my heart? However, I really believe that you know my feelings, and more clearly perhaps than I know them myself ... Mary, Mary, my Mother, yes I know that truly you see more clearly into my soul than I do ... Mother, I no longer know what to say to you but I am absolutely certain that in looking at my soul, you already know what I want to say. Dear Mother, you already understand. And that you understand is enough for me; I do not ask you to let me understand, for fear that I should die before having received the last kiss of Jesus ... But, my true Mother, what are my feelings at this moment? It is difficult even for you to reply to this question. In fact, I do not know what human word could express what I experience just now. I can only repeat the words of my beloved sister: 'There are many (314) kinds of suffering that are impossible to describe in this world.' It is really true, dear Mother. The world is so lacking in words that one does not know what words to use to make people understand the nature of interior sufferings. Only those souls who have experienced them are in a position to understand them.

Mother, how stupid I am! I heard my sister explain these things to me, before; but it is as if I had found her lesson too hard to comprehend, so much so that I have not been able to understand. I understand now but without being able to express it. Anyway, dear Mother, that is not necessary. No, it is not necessary that the world knows that I suffer; it is enough that you know it, my beloved Mother. As for me, I don't need to know either. You are there, dear Mother and it is for you to take care of everything in the place of your child. And I, I am happy to look at you, to squeeze myself into your arms, to hide myself under your cloak.

Mary, my dear Mother, at the moment I am enduring a pain which is capable of killing me. But, when I see you at my side, my Mother true and very dear, I can smile again, and be joyful. Alas! Dear Mother, perhaps there is no more hope that I will ever see the day that Jesus promised me. In spite of all, I hope that you will not let me die under the yoke of the suffering which overwhelms me at present ... Alas! O Mother, I am suffering a lot ... Dear Mother, condescend to look at your poor child ... Held tight in your arms I do not stop looking at little Jesus while he does not cease looking elsewhere ... Mary, I ... It is time already. (315)

## 14 March 1946

*Marcel*: Mary, my Mother, I would wish to speak to you but I do not at all know how to express myself. All I can say, in using a new way of speaking, is that I am changing suffering into a cross. Yes, my Mother, sufferings are crosses and crosses are roses. For some time, it seems to me that the cross has never left me for a single moment; it is always there at my side. No matter in what direction I look, I see only crosses, nothing but crosses ...

Dear Mary, these crosses, I accept them all. I know that I possess a special talent that gives great pleasure to Jesus; it consists in receiving all crosses, and once they are in my hands, I throw them in the air where they change into roses ... I also know that Jesus loves flowers a lot; and when he sees that I possess the talent of changing crosses into roses, it seems that he forgets even my pains and fatigue to continually send me crosses ... (316)

Jesus, does that console and please you a lot? Fair enough, I sacrifice myself willingly to give you this pleasure.

## 15 March 1946

*Marcel*: It seems to me that during these past few days I taste a little consolation but, from time to time, I still notice one cloud or another that comes to darken the sky of my soul.

Mary, I love you dearly, yes, I love you dearly because you are my true Mother. Allow me to speak today of the sufferings I have endured during these past few days. Mother, look at me. I have just said that I will speak to you of my sufferings but, in fact, I do not at all know how to speak to you of them. I cannot do anything but show them to you. Truly, dear Mother, during these days I have suffered a lot and without (317) the slightest consolation. What is more, I have had to accept food that I did not like, so I could only cry secretly in a corner of my room. Mother, you know that I am very weak. You also understand, without doubt, that faced with trials, I have shed many tears. I have, however, also obtained a favour; after each suffering I understood more clearly Jesus' conduct toward me ...

(318) My Mother, during this Lent, I have again received a grace similar to that of Lent last year. Is it necessary, dear Mother, that I tell you? I know that you know it already; however it is necessary that I tell you nevertheless, to please you. Mother, this grace consists in accepting suffering with joy in the firm hope that suffering will come to an end one day, that the storm will dissipate, and that it will be granted to me to see again the sun of love ...

However, dear Mother, there is still one point on which I seem not to have obeyed you as I ought. I do not understand why, but I wanted to go and find my spiritual director to make known to him all my trials; I wanted him to see all my crosses so that he could console me but each time I set out to do so, my heart recovered its peace so that I did not go to meet him. And after a short while, it began again. I do not know how to tell these things to my director and he, on his part, does not understand the emotions my heart, so that I feel an even sharper pain. Nevertheless, this crisis has now passed, although it was hardly two days ago. It is also possible that, once these two days of recreation have passed, things will begin again, even worse, after tomorrow ... However, Mother, that has little importance. My sister Thérèse has given me the talent of changing crosses into roses for Jesus. Thanks to

(319) this gift, Jesus knows that I love him a great deal. Dear Mother, isn't that wonderful? ... Self-sacrifice ...

Self-sacrifice, a word that I learned during my visit to Quảng-Uyên. This word is for me, perhaps, the most important and it is why my sister Thérèse taught me it so early. Is that not good, Mother? Also, when I am on the point of forgetting it, I see this word 'self-sacrifice' spring up from somewhere, which reminds me again of my duty ...

But, Mother, if I am not mistaken, it is time already. I cannot speak to you any longer, will you please excuse me. In fact the time has already passed. I have gone over the time by a few minutes ... Mary, my dear Mother, I am saying goodbye to you.

Dear Mother, dear Mother, dear Mary my Mother, the recreation days are almost over, and here we are. Once again I see only crosses around me. What can I do now, dear Mother? Tell me what were the nature of your sufferings? ... Dear Mother, after a short while the image of the Infant Jesus fled away carried by a single one of my sighs. Little Jesus still sleeps in front of me and I do not know what he is dreaming about at this time. He still holds a bunch of grapes in his hand (320) and an ear of corn. Mother, Jesus' sleep is much different from mine. While he holds in his hand the bunch of grapes and the ear of corn, I must hold the cross ...* It's very different, is it not, dear Mother?

My suffering Jesus seems to smile; my sister Thérèse does not stop throwing flowers at him; the saints, and in particular my father Saint Alphonsus, are busy looking at the flowers thrown by my sister Thérèse, so that nobody pays attention to me or feels a little pity for me. You are the only one, dear Mother, who still seems to glance slightly in my direction ... And this is only right since you are my Mother, my true Mother. If you also were going to pretend not to pay attention to your unhappy child, that would be very cruel on your part. Dear Mother, I am kissing you. When I am in your arms I no longer fear anything. Mary, I do not cease to cover you with my kisses, I love you dearly. Dear Mother, do not stop looking at me; it is sufficient for me that you alone understand my heart's feelings. Later, in heaven, I will have the happiness of seeing you; and, if you were not there, beloved Mother, it would be preferable that you do not allow me to enter. These words may (321) sound hurtful with regard to the Blessed Trinity, but that is not so. Indeed I know that the Blessed Trinity, whom you love greatly, has made you Mother of saints, Mother of souls. Now, without you, it is certain that one would only see hatred and discord among all of us, which would only degenerate into blasphemy, even against the Blessed Trinity, as happens in hell which is deprived of your presence. If you were there among the damned, it is certain that one could no longer call that place hell, but, rather, a second paradise.

Dear Mother, you are truly fortunate. The Trinity loves you with the intention of making us understand clearly the love that the divine Persons have for us and also to make easier our relations with the Love of the triune God. However, dear Mother, one cannot be mistaken about you! Since your happiness is far from being comparable to mine. Indeed, Mother, would your happiness win over mine (322) even though I have the good fortune of having you for my true Mother? ... Dear Mother, how happy I am ... Yes, what happiness for me to have you for my real Mother. The happiness of being your child outmatches yours of being yourself, Mother. Is it not for this reason that my sister Thérèse has exchanged the dignity of mother for that of being a child ...

Mother, later in heaven I will sing with you the canticle of Love in honour of the Blessed Trinity. What happiness is sweeter than to rest in

---

* This alludes to a picture on his table.

your arms in order to love ... No words can express the intensity of this happiness.

Time passes very quickly in this world. It is nearly time already for Benediction of the Blessed Sacrament. I cannot speak to you much longer, Mother. Please understand me ... I am stopping here, I am replacing my pen without knowing when I will be able to take it up to express to you on this paper the feelings of my heart ... Dear Mother, graciously have pity on me, your poor child. When my hand puts down the pen, it will, instead have to hold the cross ...

(323)

O Jesus! Jesus! Jesus! Jesus! Jesus! Yes, I accept ... As long as you wish ... O Mary! Mary! I never stop looking at you!!!

## 17 March 1946

*Marcel*: My Mother, Mary, I am very tired; I no longer wish to write. Dear Mother, I have a great desire for heaven, and when I am there, little Jesus certainly will not be able to treat me as he does at present, is that not so, Mother? Because of my sufferings, God will certainly love me more. Instead of calling him by the name of God, I will give to him only the name of Father. It has been granted to me to understand something which comforts me a lot: it is that, later, in heaven, in order to express his love for souls, God will use towards each one the very manner that this soul used for dealing with him on earth. It will be the same with you, dear Mother. I am certain, therefore, of being loved like a child since I do not wish to deal with God as my Lord, but only as my Father; I do not wish to give him the name of Lord, but only that of Father. Later, in heaven, what happiness to give to God the sole name of 'daddy' and to you, Mary, only the name of 'mammy'.

(324)

> *Brother Marcel told me himself with joy that he found these names of 'daddy' and 'mammy' (that he said in French) given to God and the Blessed Virgin, very beautiful.*

But, in fact, I do not know what words to use to describe this happiness to come since the language of this world is so poor that it cannot describe the things of heaven. Oh! How unfortunate this world is! When will I be able to leave it? However, I am certain that this day is not very far away; I even believe that it is close since, during these recent days, I have felt something like a foretaste of heaven. Yes, it is possible ... But why? I do not understand ... Mother, a simple sad sigh seems to me to last a thousand centuries. However I must continue to breathe without stopping. in spite of the sadness and distaste which accompanies each of my breaths

Mother, this earth is the place where one shows one's love, while, in heaven one will be content with simply loving. Mother, is there yet another means which allows me to show my love towards my Father? If (325) such a one exists, deign to teach it to me so that I can use it to make him understand that I love him a lot. But, in the sad situation where I find myself it is obvious that I can do nothing if it is not to express to him my love by means of my sorrowful sighs and to please him by offering to him the flowers of my tears. That is all that my little soul can do; but that suffices for drawing my heavenly Father's attention ... Mother, I am speaking in a disorderly and disjointed manner but I am sure that you understand me better than I understand myself. Dear Mother, I love you dearly and I wish only to call you by the name of Mother. I love you a lot but it is only in heaven that I will be able to show to you all the love of my heart ... Mother, I am tired and I do not know what more to say. Later, in heaven, I will know how to compose verses like my sister Thérèse of the Child Jesus. She will certainly teach me to do it, and then I will compose a poem on love and another on your name of Mother. I will also know French ... All my wishes will be fulfilled. (326)

When I was little, I asked you to take me to heaven with the Holy Innocents, in order to go by aeroplane; but now, I no longer wish to go to heaven in an aeroplane, I wish to go there simply to love ...

That's enough, I'm tired, Mother. My sole occupation in heaven will be to love; I will do nothing else but love, is that not the case, Mother? I am saying goodbye, I am giving you a kiss, never separate yourself from me. Dear Mother, Mother! Mother! There! The name I want to give you forever; even in heaven I do not want to exchange this name of 'Mother' for that of 'Queen' because in the word 'Queen' there is less love than in that of 'Mother'.

## 22 March 1946

*Marcel*: My dear Mother Mary, I have the cross in my hand still. But I love Jesus dearly and, in loving him, I also love the cross; in loving the cross I must, necessarily, love him also. It is good, dear Mary, my Mother. If I did not have you for my Mother, my sighs would not be transformed into roses. Mother, is that not true? There is nothing (327) astonishing in that since I know that nothing passes through your hands without acquiring a new beauty. Accordingly, I can, without blushing too much, recognize myself as Jesus' little friend ...

Incidentally, dear Mother, a moment ago I ardently desired that

(328) Lucifer recognize you as his Mother. This is what I said to him; but I do not know if he took pains to listen to me. Mother, allow me to tell it to you. I love you dearly and although, at present, I do not taste any consolation, I believe that I am still in your arms and I feel a great peace because of it. Mother, here, therefore, is what I said to Lucifer: 'Lucifer, I know that, in truth, my Mother has more pity for you than she has for me. Supposing that I am a devil even more unhappy than you and it is possible for me to tempt you. I would suggest you recognize Mary as your Mother ... Lucifer, I am very envious of the pity that my Mother has for you. Understand well that the greater your misfortune is compared with mine, the more my Mother will have compassion for you. Mary remains your Mother even if you do not wish to recognize her as such. Lucifer, what still frightens you? You would only have to say these few words: "I acknowledge that Mary is my true Mother". Nothing but that and my Mother would have immediate pity on you. And afterwards, in heaven, she would love you more than she loves me. There is no mother to compare with our true Mother. Why do you not recognize her as your mother, whereas I recognize her as mine? It's a great pity! And what shame is there in recognizing yourself as a child of Mary? You are now as black as coal but if you made the slightest sign acknowledging that you recognize Mary as your mother, that would be enough for Mary to give you her love and make you as resplendent as an angel.

(329) But alas! Alas! Lucifer! If that were possible! If that were possible! If prayer were capable of breaking the hardness of your heart I would prefer to stay on this miserable earth and pray for you until the end of the world so that you might recognize Mary as your Mother. Yes I would prefer to live without enjoying the vision of my Father and my Mother in heaven so as to pray that you acknowledge Mary for you true Mother.'

Mary, my Mother, I love you dearly and I wish that everyone recognized you for his or her Mother, without even exempting the devil. My Mother, will the devil ever agree to recognize you as his Mother? Probably never! Then why do you remain compassionate towards him with a pity greater than you have for me? Enough, Mother, save this pity for me.

(330) Let us suppose that I had to go to hell to exhort Lucifer to recognize you as Mother. I would consent gladly. But it is probable that I would die there since I would have to hear blasphemies against my Father and my Mother in heaven. If the damned in hell recognized you as Mother, what happiness! Because of this, it would be preferable that no more people fall into hell.

Mother, why is it that in writing the preceding lines my hand trembled? Are you satisfied with what I have written? In my opinion, in all that I have done there is nothing of a nature to displease you. It is probably the devil who was troubling me to prevent me from saying anything bad about him. Is that not true, Mother? He can do anything he wants, but I will always believe that divine mercy, just like yours, does not cease to wait for Lucifer. And by that the world will know that God's mercy is limitless. And when he is plunged in this ocean of Love, he will see that it is infinite. Therefore, dear Mary, my Mother, as I am already immersed in this ocean of Love, no force is capable of pulling me out of it; even the efforts of a hundred thousand worlds would not succeed in doing so. Furthermore, God himself would not be able to succeed in throwing me out of this ocean of Love.

Dear Mother I dare, again, to throw you a challenge; yes, I challenge you to dare to show me an angry face ... Mother, what have I just said? (331) My words are much too aggressive. Dear Mother, I beg God's pardon and yours also. If I dared to speak so, it is because of the certainty I feel that the Love of God will never be able to abandon me.

Jesus, you really love me excessively, with an eternal love, without end, without measure and which no tongue can perfectly express. So, all I can do is to deliver myself entirely to your Love, and to love no one but you.

## 25 March 1946*

*Marcel*: Today is the 25th of the month and Jesus does not condescend to open his mouth to say a word to me. In conducting himself thus, can it be that he still has a little love for me? Or could it be that he is angry with me? Would it be possible, Mother? I am almost certain that it is not so since I am convinced that there is no reason that Jesus, in his love, is annoyed with me. Supposing even that my heart is full of sin, it would still not be a sufficient reason for Jesus' love to be annoyed with me. Oh Mother, there, that's all I can say, and yet these simple words make tears come to my eyes. At this time my soul is plunged into sadness but (332) I do not wish Jesus to know it. Mother, I love you dearly.

---

\* In a letter to Jesus of the same day: 'I offer myself to the fire of your Love'. It is all I have to give you. Deign to accept it and bless me, your little Marcel. Love.

## 26 March 1946

(333)

*Marcel*: Mother, I am very sad. Brother Basil already knows how to sew better than me. He has just begun to learn but he is more skilful than me. I like working at the sewing machine, however I am rarely asked to do it. I see that from day to day Jesus treats me less well. He has even taken back all the little things that pleased me; nothing remains for me. So, that's fine, I will cry so that Jesus hears me.

Mother, in such circumstances I suffer a lot. And usually, all I do now fails; it is rarely that I succeed as I would wish. For example, I sewed some pillows on the wrong side and Brother Basil had to undo them so as to sew them again, Whenever I want to do something beautiful, the opposite results. Mother, you can imagine the tears I would shed if, in similar circumstances, I was left to my own weakness ... But, dear Mother, you are there to hide my tears and if it happens that I shed some, I am sure that you would not allow anyone to see them since these tears are very precious. You love me a lot, dear Mother.

I am stopping here. Time is up already; I must go to say my rosary. I am giving you a kiss. Mother, are you giving me one also? Continue to give me a dozen of them immediately so as to take away my sadness; but say nothing to Jesus, all right? I love you, dear Mother.

## 27 March 1946

(334)

*Marcel*: Oh Mary, my Mother, I am really sad. I had thought, at first, that when Jesus and I play together, your presence was not necessary, and that it was enough, to reassure us, that you remained seated at a distance watching us at play. But, Mother, you see where my Jesus has gone now. While we were playing happily together, my companion suddenly disappeared. Mother, judge for yourself what my sadness has been; it was precisely at that moment that I began to feel this interior pain. And my sadness has been all the greater as the game had, at first been joyful. Mother, I looked into the distance, to see if you were still there, since I was certain the only means of my being at peace was to go and rest on your heart. Yes, that is very true. But, dear Mother, how many days have you allowed me to rest on your heart? If I remember, that lasted a little more than a week, after which you disappeared in your turn, making the emptiness around me complete. Truthfully, Mother, it was very sad and it is this which has compelled me to complain to you as I have just done. However, I remained convinced that, in spite of all, you always remain my Mother. Oh my Mother, I love you dearly ...

A spirit of gloom comes, unceasingly, to trouble me; but I am not afraid since the little love that Jesus has left to me remains by my side; his room is just opposite mine. But, this little bit of love, it happens sometimes that Jesus demands it from me also ...

*I was on retreat for five days.*

Yes, it is quite true, Jesus asked this sacrifice of me at one time, and I, I have promised as well to give him all, accepting the fact that he takes from me, if it is necessary, even the small amount of love that he has left (335) to me.

Dear Mother, I am suffering a lot ... Today a brother said that I was virtuous in word only ... It is quite true, Mother, I do not possess any virtue worthy of notice. The virtues that Jesus decorated my soul with previously, he has now taken away from me, in such a way that my soul has become again what it was: weakness, pure weakness ... Furthermore, I notice that, ordinarily, the words of men do not conform to the truth. I have an example of this in this very brother who, formerly, congratulated me on having much virtue and, in particular, much patience ... There you have the words of men: at first very flattering, afterwards fairly caustic ... If I had paid attention to the words of men, I am certain, dear Mother, that now I would no longer be able to converse with you ... Mother, I am very sad; continue to love me always. For my part, I love you dearly and, in all justice, you must also have pity on me.

## 28 March 1946

**Marcel**: Mary, my beloved Mother, now is the time to open my heart. I (336) love you dearly and you are the only one whom I recognize as my true Mother. Mother, while out walking today, I saw an A.F.A.T.* serving in the French army. Each time I met a French person, I wished that these French loved Jesus. Indeed, knowing that Jesus particularly loves France, it is appropriate that the French love Jesus as well with a special love. I then saw a car that was carrying a group of French children; they looked very happy ... Yes, my heart, just like the hearts of these children, is still joyful. However, my most ardent wish is that there may be someone to teach them to love Jesus ... To imprint in their hearts the seal of Jesus' love. Dear Mary, please do this work in my place. I know

---

\* Womens Auxiliary Army.

(337-a) that my special mission is to teach souls to love Jesus and that I must exercise this mission especially on the souls of children. As for the souls who imitate the virtues of children, they will have other apostles. Nevertheless, it is only in heaven that I will be able to accomplish my mission.

Ah! I note Mother Mary, that I should not have spoken of those things; that escaped me ... Besides, you will be the only one to know about it ... I do not understand why; I intended to say more about it but I have forgotten everything. It is probable that the time has not yet come for me to speak of it. Is that the case, dear Mother? Probably it will only be permitted to me later to reveal that I am an apostle of the love of Jesus and the apostle, especially, of children ... I am stopping here, I have forgotten everything. Dear Mother, I love you dearly. Please bless me and bless also the souls of children.

(337–1) I notice, today, that my sister Thérèse is speaking to me again. But she only says a few things and tells me to pray for France.

'Dear beloved Jesus, make France love only the truth.'

With Mary: 'Oh true Mother of France, remind Jesus that France does not yet have true peace ...'

Thérèse adds: 'Little brother, tell your Director that when he sends these words to souls, he must also write them in Vietnamese, they must not be read only in French. And do this on each occasion.'

(337–2) **Thérèse**: None of the little things that you do cause Jesus any pain. Remain in peace. Jesus is always happy with you. I have the feeling that Jesus is going to give you peace. But I cannot tell you when, otherwise that will trouble you. Remain peaceful. I am embracing you. It is very necessary to pray for France and later, I will tell you how to pray for Vietnam.

**Marcel**: Concerning my soul, since last night, I am no longer troubled. Right now my soul seems to be very light. I only feel lonesome. I no longer feel any other suffering. But I do not know when it will return. This time I heard Thérèse much better than the last time. The last time I was very happy but that did not last ... That is all there is. I am asking you, my Father, to pray for your little child ...

What I wrote the other day on the subject of giving, it was Thérèse who told me that, but I do not remember all of it. I simply remember that she had spoken about it, but I forget when she said it. So I ask you not to pay attention to what I wrote, since that came from me ...

## 29 March 1946

*Marcel*: Dear Mother, it is free time now. All I want to do is to come and snuggle up against your heart. Mother, I love you dearly. Please listen to me. I am going to speak to you of my concerns. How fortunate I am to have you as my true Mother. Every evening I am able to rest on your breast to express my feelings, what joy for you, Mother, and what happiness for me. Alas, these happy soirees are quite rare and it does not happen often that I enjoy a day like today. Although I can express my feelings, suffering does not leave me. And if you feel joy, for me there is hardly any change. Dear Mary, I love you. You are my true Mother, I love you dearly. (337-b) (338)

Mother, this evening I suddenly recalled the time when I was your cub scout at Lạng-Sơn ... Oh! how quickly those joyful days passed! Mother, when I was your cub scout, I loved to play and to sing and it is still the same today. I remember in particular a game which consists in finding an object, no matter what, by following certain signs marked by the Chief. I really loved this type of game, which reminds me now of the way in which little Jesus acts with me. Indeed, what I did outwardly in playing at Lạng-Sơn, little Jesus now does in my soul. I know that little Jesus wants me to take pains to look for souls for him and he has traced out easily-understood signs that I must follow to reach this goal. I know too that to follow these signs and to succeed in the search for souls, it is necessary to pay great attention and be joyful in a natural way. Crosses are the spiritual signs that Jesus has given me. Wishing that I follow the path exactly, he has sown it with a great number of crosses ... Mother, having arrived at this point; I no longer know what to say. All I remember is this: what I used to do, outwardly, while looking for such or such an object, I understand that Jesus now does in me. But, to find souls for Jesus, what crosses I must meet! And it is so much the better since, the more crosses there are, the less chance I have of following the wrong path ... And I am certain that later, on arriving at the country of Love, I will meet there an innumerable crowd of souls. I will have no more need to look for them, I will only have to take them and offer them to Jesus ... dear Mother, time is up. (339) (340)

## 30 March 1946

*Marcel*: My dear Mother, I always feel some distaste, but during these latter days, and today particularly, I seem to taste in my soul a little joy. Mother, reminding myself at this time of the method that I use ordinarily to ask something of God, I feel an immense joy. Later, in heaven, I will continue to use the same method without changing anything. God is my true Father. Now, to please him and to act in such a way that he is always pleased with me, I will not cease to keep close to him and to ask him for graces in great number. One might think that this will be very boring for him, however, I know that his Father's heart is not like that of earthly parents. Yes I know that he is a Father with an infinitely kind heart, that he leaves his children completely free to come and importune him unceasingly, and that he finds his happiness in this since he can then show them his goodness and his mercy ... As for me, little Marcel, when I speak to him, my Father, I will know how to behave like a skilful and importunate little child. When I want to ask him a favour, I will present myself first of all before him, or rather, kneeling before him, I will place both my hands on his knees and I will speak to him in these terms: 'Father, I love you dearly. At this time I have need of a favour, be it for me or for another. In the name of "your merits" and of "your love" I beg you to grant me this favour.' Dear Mother, I am sure that my Father will take pleasure in granting it to me, since I will have prayed in the name of Jesus who is 'Merit itself' and in the name of the Holy Spirit who is 'Love'. I am absolutely certain therefore that he will give me a sign to go and find you, dear Mother, and when I do, I will speak to you like this: 'Mother, through pity for me, grant me this favour.' Surely, Mother, I will then be comforted. Yes, I will be greatly comforted; however, dear Mother, it is only in heaven that I will enjoy perfect consolation ... Dear Mother, I love you dearly. Time is up.

## 31 March 1946

**Marcel**: Today the month of the Holy Spirit ends.

> *The month of March was, formerly, especially dedicated to the practice of charity towards God=Love=Holy Spirit.*

Dear Mother, yesterday when I was conversing with you about my relations with my true Father in heaven, I had to interrupt myself because the time was up. I regret it very much because once the opportunity has passed I forget all I intended to say to you ... Incidentally, dear Mother, you are truly more meticulous than I, obliging me to write down even disjointed stories. Really, it is difficult for me to respond to your wish. But, Mother, I love you dearly and I understand that these childlike stories will be useful to all the souls of children whom my sister Thérèse has asked me to watch over, in her place, in a special manner; and by that, I will give more pleasure to my Father in heaven.

Mother, later in heaven, I will be seated on your knee and I will look at children. Then, I will give them a sign to look at me and, I am sure that, in looking at me, they will see you about to rock me gently with little Jesus. Seeing that, they will come close to you so that they may enjoy the same happiness. And, once close to you, it will be easy for them to get close to my true Father ... Mother, who knows if children will be your little apostles? It is a simple hypothesis that I am expressing since, in fact, I do not know your intention. I am only surmising; it is for you to see if it is true or not. Whatever it may be, Mother, I beg you to have pity on children. My feelings are similar to theirs, so that, understanding my own feelings, you understand as well those of children.

Mother, I think continually of the souls of children. It is impossible for me to banish this thought. In my opinion, if my Father in heaven revealed to the world how much the soul of a child is pleasing to him, (344) it is probable that the world would recognize that child as king of the universe. If there were no children in the world to delight the eyes of our true Father in heaven, it is certain that he would no longer wish to gaze on this earth. In former times, Jesus never scolded the Apostles, except on one occasion, when they prevented the children from coming to him. Mother, blessed are the children because Jesus loves them more than all the others! While he was on earth, he did not hesitate to take them in his arms and kiss them. And among those favoured by Jesus, no one has had the privilege of being held close to his heart and receiving these marks of love except children. Dear Mother, we are truly very privileged, we the children ...

Mother, I am at the end of my paper; only a few lines remain. Please give me a kiss and give one also to the souls of your dear children ...

My Mother, Mary, I always think a lot about children. They are like (345) open books where all men can learn the correct behaviour towards their true Father in heaven. Is that not so, Mother? That is something you understand perfectly. After many years spent in the company of little Jesus you understand so well the character of children. It is the same for little Jesus; after having been a child, he also must understand the life of a child ...

My Mother, in past times, little Jesus did not have the slightest defect; there is nothing astonishing in that, since he is true God. However, he also knows one thing: that the natural defects of children never sadden him since we, the children, are all descendants of Adam.

Dear Mother, how is it that I understand these things? Truly it is the work of my sister little Thérèse. Because Mother, she did not have enough time to speak to children about you, she wishes to make use of me now to do it in her place. If I speak in this way, it is not at all with (346) the intention of my making it known to all men, but because Jesus has made these things clearly known to me about the time of Lent, last year, when I was seated on his knees ...

Dear Mother, I recognize further that I have no talent that makes me worthy of being the apostle to this group of pure souls. But because I am part of this same group and perhaps because I have a sensitive ear, I can grasp more clearly the words of my sister Thérèse ...

Oh Thérèse, if you had not had to look after two orphans in the past, I am sure that, now, you would not understand the souls of children. I beg you to remember what you asked of God in favour of children, since that is your work and not mine. However, since you asked Jesus to make use of me to accomplish this work, you must watch over it yourself; as for me, I am simply like the humble pen of Jesus ... If you wish to make use of me to write something, I can only follow the impulse that is communicated to me by you ...

(347) Mary, my own mission is to be the apostle of souls, and the special apostle of children. If such a thing were possible I would wish to leave this room to go to preach to children; but my humble condition as a Brother of the Congregation of the Most Holy Redeemer does not permit me to immediately accomplish this mission. It will be only later, in heaven, that I will be able to accomplish this mission perfectly. The time is up. Dear Mother, please bless me, since my soul is, in all things, like those of the children of the whole world. Allow me to go and rest in peace in your arms ...

Mary, my Mother, since I am still allowed to chat with you at this time, I am going to speak with you, if you want to. Will you listen to me, dear Mother? Even if you did not wish to listen to me, you must, nevertheless hear me, because in hearing me whispering in your ear unceasingly, even if you did not wish to answer me, at least you would have to resign yourself to listening to me.

But, Mother, what foolishness I have just said there! How could it ever happen that you were not happy to listen to me? I know very well that my true Father and my true Mother are always ready to listen to all my stories in all their detail.

(348) Mother, I love you dearly. My greatest happiness in heaven will be to hear my real Father and my true Mother both call me their child. As for my father Saint Alphonsus, he will do the same thing. In this regard, I recall a story and I am asking myself if my sister Thérèse has spoken of it to my father Saint Alphonsus. Formerly, I did not wish to give to Saint Alphonsus the name of father; I wished to call him, quite simply 'saint' since I believed that it was only appropriate to give to God alone the name of Father. In spite of this I often made the mistake, using the word 'father' instead of the word 'saint'. It was only later that my sister

Thérèse taught me what was necessary to say. I was then very ashamed, but perhaps my father Saint Alphonsus paid no attention to it. My sister told me that I had to call him 'father', not because he is the father of all men, but the common father of members of the Congregation. Now, being a child of the Congregation, I must call him 'father'. Ever since then I have corrected myself and I even love to call him my father since he, himself, calls me his child ...

Mother, my father Saint Alphonsus loves me a lot, doesn't he? I am sure that in heaven he will love me even more, because, like him, I have a great love for you, dear Mother. However, one thing is certain, it is that in my relations with you I will be more powerful than my father Saint Alphonsus. Since he sometimes calls you Mother, sometimes Queen; in calling you Queen, he must recognize himself as being of the people. For me, in never calling you Queen but only Mother, I am always your child and never someone 'of the people'. So, therefore, I will be called 'Son of the King'; now the son of the king has more power than a man of the people. Is that not so, Mother? However, he is still my father ... Also, I will make use of my power to oblige him to love me, since I am always his humble child ... (349)

My father Saint Alphonsus, I love you a lot. In heaven I will be close to you. You are very old; your back is bent like Brother John Baptist's. My father, I love you greatly and to prove to you my love, I wish to do all in my power to observe the Rule of the Congregation perfectly, so as to please Jesus. My father, the time is already up; please bless me, I am going to walk in the garden ...

## 2 April 1946

*Marcel*: Little Jesus, the thought has come to me that you are not very just ... Without reason, you left me alone for nearly three months, to the point of depriving me of all joy, even on the day of *Têt* ... but, you do not cease to repeat that you love me a lot, etc. (350)

*Jesus*: What! Marcel, what did you say? Are you not afraid that I might scold you? What you say is quite right, but the souls, what do you make of them? Did you not say, previously, what your mission was? ... In speaking as you do, you show that you do not have much love for souls. And, what's more, this month you devote yourself to the practice of charity; I am exhorting you, therefore, to practise it again. Be always ready to sacrifice yourself to win a great number of souls to my love, otherwise my love is very sad.

## 3 April 1946

*Jesus*: Little Marcel, do you love me?

*Marcel*: Yes, I love you.

*Jesus*: But, how do you love me?

(351) *Marcel*: I love you so much that it is impossible for me to express it.

*Jesus*: In that case, you must never worry. When I say something to you, you must listen straight away.

*Marcel*: But, little Jesus, why does Brother Mark behave so harshly towards me? Do not forget that I can place the fault at your feet since it is you who lives in Brother Mark; it is you who allows him to make me suffer. Little Jesus, before accusing me of lacking in charity, see what virtue you yourself are lacking in acting as you do. Enough, this month, the month of brotherly charity, I beg you in my turn to devote yourself again to the practice of this virtue. And we, in practising it thus, both of us together, we will certainly make rapid progress and Mary will be happy ... That's enough; time is up. See you soon ...

(352) Little Jesus, here we are now well into Lent and, lo and behold, you are sending me delights. It seems to me that acting so you are behaving against the spirit of the Church. Is that not the case little Jesus?

*Jesus*: Come, come, Marcel, you are speaking as if you do not know how to reflect. If you were to speak that way to someone who was about to do you a favour, the person would not be able to stop himself from scolding you. But I, far from scolding you, I still love to hear you speak in this way, since you do not intend to reproach me and, furthermore, it gives me an opportunity to make you understand something about grace. Marcel, listen carefully. In order to give grace to men, I do not need to wait for a particular season or to pay attention to the temperature because, in that case, there would be times when men would be deprived of the grace necessary for the life of their souls. Marcel, your question is very clumsy and proves, furthermore, your great ignorance. Remind yourself that my Love never acts in that way. It knows the moment when it must show itself and when it must be hidden. Will you remember? And never ask me that question a second time.

(353) *Marcel*: Little Jesus, you treat me like an ignoramus, but perhaps you

are even more so than I. In fact you do not know how to sew, you only know the trade of carpenter.

*Jesus*: Who told you that? Ask Mary if I did not know how to knit clothes with her. It is only after having grown up that I became a carpenter. But when I was small, I sometimes spun the wool so that Mary might knit clothes and Mary also taught me to knit them myself. She loved me very much.

*Marcel*: But at that time there weren't any sewing machines. That is why I am saying that you do not know how to sew with a machine!

*Jesus*: And yet, Marcel, if I were not there to guide your hand, you would still be crying. And in boasting that you know how to sew, are you not afraid that your sister Thérèse might make fun of you?

*Marcel*: I have never cried in that way, or if I did I have forgotten completely.

*Jesus*: It is true, little Marcel, you have not cried a lot, but you have at least blushed and I, seeing you in this state, I really wanted to laugh. Nevertheless, I dared not let you see for fear of making you sadder still. (354)

*Marcel*: I am not at all worried. If you allow your work to fail, the damage is yours alone. It is you and not I who carries all the responsibility. Later, in heaven, I will tell Mary. However, I will also ask her not to punish you, since I love you dearly, little Jesus.

Yes, we love each other a lot, but our love remains very secret; it is only, probably, in heaven that our mutual love will be able to show itself externally. Ah! Little Jesus, I love you; graciously concentrate your attention on children. You have already promised to them the kingdom of heaven. Now, I clearly see what you say in the Gospel: 'The kingdom of heaven belongs to children'.* But then you did not add anything to teach them what they must do to obtain this kingdom ... By that, you (355) clearly allow it to be understood that you do not oblige children in anything in particular, that it is solely by love and by virtue of your merits that you procure for them the kingdom of heaven ...

However, Jesus, it is necessary to teach children to love you, so as to make them know of the kingdom of heaven. Since if they do not love you, they would not know what the kingdom of heaven is ... It is time now Jesus.

* Luke 18, 16–17.

(358) Little Jesus now is the time to satisfy my curiosity. For more than two months you have remained hidden, amusing yourself somewhere in a very secret place and allowing me to shed abundant tears ... Now, I am going to ask you many questions that you will not know how to reply to. Dear little Jesus, when you were with Mary, in Nazareth, what did you do? Did you play with the other children? Did Mary, your Mother, spoil you?

*Jesus*: Come, come, Marcel, slowly! Listen to me, first of all, speaking to you. If you ask me question after question without allowing me to speak, how will I be able to answer you? It is true that your questions are very detailed, but I am, however, happy to reply to them to please you, and also with the intention of showing that there are very impor-
(359) tant connections between my childhood and the souls of children. Furthermore, if previously, I have shown my love as a Father towards his child, I will now do it as a friend towards his little friend ...

Little Marcel, be happy to write the following, so that children also can understand the love which their Father in heaven has for them. Marcel, even write the words which seem to have no importance and I will place my lips on them as I do on your forehead ... Yes, little bird, sing out loud, so that other little birds know that the nest where you now rest is a very sweet nest.

*Marcel*: Time is up, what shall I do, little Jesus? That's enough, let me give you a kiss.

## 4 April 1946

(360) *Marcel*: Little Jesus, the other day I questioned you on what you did at Nazareth. You replied to me on that day, but I have now forgotten everything. You will, therefore, have to reply to me again so that I can write it down. If not, I will no longer say to you: 'Little Jesus, I love you.' But I am saying that as a joke, little Jesus, since, if I did not love you, whom would I be able to love? So do not pay any attention to this foolishness ... That's it, time is up. See you soon. This evening, if I have some free time, we will chat longer. I will then have all the spare time to ...

At midday, little Jesus, I ate some rice with fish. It was very tasty and while eating I thought of saving a mouthful for you ... Yes, little Jesus, we love each other and we love each other at all times. Incidentally, little Jesus, when you were on earth, did you ever eat fish? Did you eat dishes similar to those that I eat?

*Jesus*: Obviously, I ate dishes similar to those that you eat. I sometimes ate meat, sometimes fish, sometimes vegetables; but Mary prepared these dishes in a very mouth-watering manner, it was not at all like that which you eat. (361)

*Marcel*: Why do people say that in your time, roast dishes were the best and that many dishes were not served then as they are now? One would soon get bored with such a regime. When I will have to do the cooking, tell Mary to teach me how to prepare many excellent dishes. And you, little Jesus, do you know how to cook?

*Jesus*: Yes, I do. When I was still small, ordinarily, I did not go to play with the other children. I remained by my Mother's side whom I loved dearly and my intention in staying close to her was to make her understand better many things about God. Mary also loved me dearly and, normally, all that she did, I also knew how to do.

*Marcel*: However, little Jesus, you did not know how to cook rice since there was no rice in your country.

*Jesus*: I know how to do so now, but you, Marcel, you do not know how to make bread. And if I had not made it in your place, you would certainly have been on the point of crying. Weak as you are, you still dare to boast. However do not be sad. If you are weak, I am there to support and guide you. Do not be afraid when I am asleep, since our Mother Mary is always at our sides accompanying us.

*Marcel*: In the past, little Jesus, what did you call your Mother Mary?

*Jesus*: I called her 'mammy' and I gave Saint Joseph the name of 'daddy'.

*Marcel*: To indicate yourself in speaking to Mary what terms did you use, *tôi* or *con*?* (362)

*Jesus*: I used neither the one nor the other; I referred to myself simply by the words: 'your little one'. I spoke to her as you yourself speak to her. For example, I used to say to her: 'Mother, today you served some-

---

\* The hierarchy among people in Vietnam is very marked, even in the heart of a family. Thus older brothers and sisters have a different designation than their younger siblings. *Tôi* is the same as 'I' and is only used among equals. Children do not use it but rather *con* indicating child.

thing very good to your little one.' 'Mother, why do you shower your little one with kisses?' ... 'Mother, do you love your little one?' Often, also, I told her childish stories as you yourself do ... Yes, that is, for us, the only way to behave towards her, to please her.

*Marcel*: Dear Mary, my Mother, does your 'little one' love you well? When he was a child did you spoil him as much as me? I think, and with good reason, that you spoiled him more than me since he was much better behaved than me. I do not understand why 'your little one' loves me so much. He takes pleasure, even, in telling me insignificant stories ... It is true that I have a very inquisitive mind yet I am loved by little Jesus and by you also, dear Mary.

(363) Dear Mother, I am so happy that I ask myself if I will be more so in heaven. Judging it in accordance with my natural limitations, I think that if, in heaven, I have but a degree of the happiness equal to that I taste now, I will find that sufficient. Nevertheless, it is impossible, of that I am certain, that your 'little one' could not give me more ... But, Mary ... that will be enough. The only thing necessary is the love that joins me intimately to little Jesus and places me on your knee, dear Mother. I think, also, that no greater reward exists than 'Love' ...

*Jesus*: Why do you trouble yourself so, little Marcel? That is something I do not wish. Write down what you can remember, without always trying to retain all that I say to you. Have I not previously advised you on that? Could you have forgotten already? Neither have you to scrutinize my words; let my spirit do so instead of you.

This morning you asked me this question: 'Jesus, what is it about the flower that you concern yourself with it to the extent of decorating her with all the colours?' Little Marcel, what was my reply? Come on, do not be sad, I am going to say it again so that you can write it down: 'I interest myself in the flower and I clothe her in beauty so that, by her beauty, she may lead you to think of my love.' Little Marcel, the flower does not think of itself; she is happy to remain as I have made her, without perplexing herself as you do, since she does not know how to examine where the beauties which are in her come from ... How she received them ... And what to make of it ...

(364) Marcel, you do the same ... You do not have to fear that my love will ever allow you to fall into error. My 'spirit' still remains for you. You will have reason to fear only the day when you will see that my Love has disappeared and with it my Spirit. But will that ever happen? No, be absolutely sure, that will never happen. Little Marcel, be happy. Do you want that? Give me a big smile. Now, when you are allowed to smile, you do not smile; on the other hand, when the time comes to shed some

tears, you feel like laughing ... That is truly something more opposed to the spirit of the Church than what you dared to reproach me for earlier. Oh my little one, my little Marcel, I love you dearly ... Go and ask for a sheet of blotting paper and then come back and write.

Little Marcel, did you hear the shot a short time ago? Like the bullet in the rifle, you also must deliver yourself into my hands, allowing me to aim you where I wish and only seeking to please me. Try to act in this way.

*Marcel*: For a long time little Jesus I have wanted to ask you a question. Do you wish to answer me? People say that during your childhood, you never laughed or cried, that you remained peacefully wherever the Blessed Virgin wished to put you, and even when you were hungry ... Is that really the case?

*Jesus*: Marcel, your question seems to betray a certain confusion. Because of your childish nature you seem to like to see me only as people assume me to be. However I am going to answer you clearly. Be (365) calm and continue to write, while listening.

Above all, little Marcel, you must understand that, in accordance with my Divine Nature, I am the second Person of the Trinity and that, as a consequence, I am one with the Father and the Holy Spirit. However, as a man, I had in me the weaknesses of childhood. Now, supposing that even outwardly I was only one with the Father and the Holy Spirit, I would have had need neither to eat nor sleep ... etc. Consequently, from the moment when I took on human nature in the womb of Mary, I had, in the same way, taken on myself the weaknesses of humanity. By that, you must understand, little Marcel, that the weakness of infancy had been mine also, with this sole difference, that I had no failings as you have. I was neither greedy nor unruly like you. I cried but when Mary comforted me, I understood immediately ... What is more, if a child never smiled, it would make the family lose its joy. If, therefore, in the midst of the Holy Family, I had always kept a serious face, without ever laughing, it is certain that Mary would not have dared to call me her child. Then the mystery of the Incarnation would have been unveiled and the Blessed Virgin would no longer have even dared to indulge me freely as she wished to do ...

At that time I acted in everything like other children. When relatives, on a visit, gave me cakes, I accepted them gladly and I ate them quite (366) simply. I also thought then of the sprays of sweet-smelling flowers which would be offered to me later by you, little Marcel, and by other souls; and this thought made me much more joyful, even making me forget the sufferings that I endured because of the sins of men ... Oh!

Little Marcel, it was also for love for you; and tell it too to the souls of children so that they know it: I have, like them, passed through a state of infancy ...

Later, little Marcel, when the children of the village came to play, I played gladly with them and I profited from the opportunity to make them understand the kingdom of heaven. These children were also very happy with me. However, I never went to play far from Mary; I always stayed near her. At that age, Mary did not spoil me and I behaved like the other children. Mary always called me child, but in her heart, she lived continuously united to me ... After the death of Saint Joseph, I spoke to her often of the sufferings I would have to endure later ... Then, Mary cried a lot and I cried with her ...

Enough, little Marcel, you are already too tired; go and rest. You will write another time. If you are too tired bearded Jesus will certainly not be happy.

***Marcel***: Little Jesus, a moment ago, when we went to make some hosts, Brother Anthony scolded us and it was your fault. Who have you told not to warn me? You once again lacked charity. Indeed since you live in Brother Anthony, it is therefore you who have scolded your little Marcel. During the holy hour which will take place in a moment I am going to tell Mary ... In the future I do not want Brother to act in this way. If he had spoken in a more agreeable manner, wouldn't that have been better?

***Jesus***: Come on, my dear little one, you make me want to smile. I did not wish to come down to this world and yet I came down through love with the intention of redeeming it. I have suffered here also for you, little Marcel ... Now this Brother addressed only a few words of reproach to you. It is not a sufficient reason to make you sad. Also I am not giving it any attention, considering this sadness as a simple wish to smile ...

But, little Marcel, you said that in a moment you are going to tell Mary of my negligences in your regard ... I couldn't ask for anything better. And I, on my part, will let her know all your lapses in my regard so as to see which of the two is more culpable ... Is that to your liking?

***Marcel***: Regarding that, little Jesus, I beg of you to settle the business in a friendly manner. Do you agree? Anyway, I am not afraid, since Mary loves me more than you and furthermore, I have my sister Thérèse who will come to my defence, so that you will certainly be defeated, just like that time when I spilled the flour in the kitchen. You had many reasons to get the upper hand but, at the end of the day, you were beaten, completely beaten ...

Oh! Little Jesus, I love you dearly. These little stories seem to be very amusing, do they not? And later, in heaven, they will be even more so. My dear little Jesus, I love you a great deal ... That's enough. Do not tell Mary what has just happened. Or if you wish to speak to her about it, I will agree.

## 5 April 1946

*Jesus*: Little Marcel, my life has been one of suffering; but I have never been sad at having to suffer. So, my life must be called a painful life but not an unhappy life. If I had been sad about my suffering, how could I now exhort you to be joyful when you encounter suffering? Marcel, you must never believe that I was sad at having to suffer. Do not be troubled if you hear such a thing said. Listen carefully to what I am saying to you. If I was sad about my sufferings, does it not seem that I would have shown less joy in sacrificing myself for souls than these souls have shown in making sacrifices for me? ... Never have I been sad; on the (369) contrary, I have always been as joyful as a child who is delighted with consolations. If, at that time, I had been sad because of my suffering, I would be even more so in the sacrament of the Eucharist ... No, little Marcel, it is not like that. The more I sacrificed myself for souls, the more I wished to sacrifice myself, more and more. And, in fact, that is something that Love alone is capable of understanding. You, little Marcel, you are not able to understand it. Time is up, little brother, obey promptly and, by that, you will please me more ...

*Marcel*: A moment ago, in the kitchen, I really wanted to do some work to help the brethren; but because all the other novices had already gone up, I did not dare to remain alone, for fear that the Zealator* might accuse me. Little Jesus, I beg you to accept this little act of goodwill, and I beg you to give to the brother who will have to take on this work, the grace to do it joyfully ...

Incidentally, little Jesus, I was accused today of a fault that I had not committed; and bearded Jesus added: 'It is not your job to oversee the juniors' ... I was really ashamed, I blushed a little, but I did not cry.

---

\* The Zealator is one of the novitiate brothers whose job consists in overseeing good observance. Each week, before the assembled brethren, he must inform each one of his failings. Each brother must humbly accept his words without defending himself.

(370) Had that happened last week, I would certainly not have been able to prevent myself from crying ... But, little Jesus, what were you saying a moment ago?

*Jesus*: Little Marcel, in the past I was falsely accused, completely falsely. However, I had to endure it all the same. But you, Marcel, there were obvious reasons for accusing you; only the Zealator did not speak clearly ... On Sunday, during the walk in the garden, did you not stop to watch the juniors who were bathing? ... That was enough for him to accuse you, little Marcel. No one had told you to stay there laughing with the juniors. And if I had been in his place, I would have accused you of two faults: the first of having laughed with the juniors, the second of not having walked during your recreation ...

*Marcel*: Little Jesus, you talk too much, your tongue never stops. How many times have you talked continuously, not even allowing me to pray in peace. And then you dare to enumerate my faults? Very good, I am going to accuse you to Mary, and tell her that you never stop talking, no matter in what place, without ...

*Jesus*: What's that you are saying, Marcel? You have obviously forgotten the time quite recently when I was silent for a little less than two months and you had red eyes because of it, complaining sometimes to Mary, sometimes to your sister Thérèse, sighing and saying: Alas! Alas! Such is my fate ...

(371) And now you have just asked me to keep silent? If I had kept silent a little longer, when I returned to speak to you, I do not know if I would have still found you here ... that's enough. Do not reproach me any more on that subject. If not, I shall keep silent again and for a long time. Then, even if you exhaust yourself with crying, there will be no one to comfort you ...

Ah! Marcel, we speak in such a natural manner that bearded Jesus will not be able to stop himself from laughing ... By that, men will understand that, in my dealings with them, I exercise an extreme condescension ... Marcel, you must understand that I follow your will more than you follow mine ... In the eyes of your true Father in heaven, you are a little child; you love him always, you abandon yourself to him, you do his will and pay careful attention to it – conforming to it in everything ... However, Marcel, your Father loves you more than you love him; consequently, he always wants to know your tastes and your wishes, to follow them as soon as possible. If you examine the conduct of children towards their natural parents, you will see that it is like this. It follows therefore that the true Father in heaven follows even more the will of his children, than he allows them to follow his own will. Do you understand, Marcel? Later, bearded Jesus will explain these things more clearly to you.

Besides, little Marcel, if you are a friend to me. I am, also, your true (372) friend. We both love each other; but if we examine who gives proof of the greater love, we see that it is the one who sacrifices himself more for his friend. So, therefore, concerning me personally, I follow your will more than you follow mine. Do you understand, Marcel? Later, you will come to understand. Simply remember this short sentence: 'Parents more often follow their children's will than children do that of their parents'. 'The will of children is in harmony with the will of their parents', in such a way that what parents wish, children wish also. Now parents love their children more than the latter love them, so it follows that the will of parents bends itself to the will of their children and that, normally, parents more often follow the will of their children. Do you understand, Marcel? I have spoken very clearly. You really know nothing. Come on, read it once more without troubling yourself and, if you do not understand, I will repeat it again, but it is not necessary to write it down ...

*Marcel*: I understand already.

*Jesus*: Good. So, worry about it no more. I love you dearly. All you wish for, I give you. Do you want me to give you a kiss? No more worrying. Enough, little brother, the time has passed already, go and sleep.

*Marcel*: Little Jesus, what's the use of loving you? (373)

*Jesus*: Marcel, that's a very clumsy question. From now on, I do not want you to ask such a question. I am the only one who is allowed to ask you this question. What's the use of loving you, Marcel? I get absolutely nothing from that. It is through pure Love that I love you ...

Marcel, what news have you just heard? Do not be concerned. The Redemptorist sisters will come to Vietnam. If there is a delay, it is simply because of them, since my words are already engraved on their hearts ...

*Marcel*: Little Jesus, if such is the case, I am really sad.

*Jesus*: Why sadden yourself in this way, Marcel? Remain tranquil. Because, in one way or another my words have been doubted, the business will have to be sorted out later, as I have already said ... Marcel, do not be troubled. If your heart were full of worry, how would you be able to love me? Stay peaceful. Pray to me. You are still here with me ...

*Marcel*: Little Jesus, is it your wish to bring the Redemptorist sisters to Vietnam as soon as possible? If not, when will my little sister enter religion?

*Jesus*: Marcel, don't bother yourself, I will see to it. Continue to follow the advice of bearded Jesus who encourages you to pray, yes, continue praying ... I have spoken clearly, now the sisters act towards me as they wish; my words are already engraved on their hearts ...

(374)    Marcel, I am telling you not to concern yourself. The time has not yet come; one has prayed much too little. Because my words have been questioned, one has cared too little for prayer and it is that which explains why few prayers have been said. Marcel, continue to pray, pray unceasingly. It is easy to conquer my heart, but to conquer the hearts of the Canadian sisters is difficult ...

*Marcel*: Little Jesus, how is it that your glance is so powerful? You had only to fix your glance on me for a single instant and it was enough to make me cry. I am very weak, as you see; what good can I do? I ask only to lean on your Love.

*Jesus*: However, Marcel, the glance of your weakness is still more powerful than mine. Yes, a single glance of your weakness suffices to charm my Love and to draw my heart to you ... Little brother, time is up. I am giving you a kiss. Marcel, you are my little brother ... Enough, little brother. Go, go, I am showering you with kisses.

## 6 April 1946

*Marcel*: Little Jesus, you are weaker than me. A simple gust of wind suffices to carry you and place you on my table. Nevertheless you say that I am very weak.

*This is an allusion to a picture placed before him on his table, which was turned over by the wind.*

*Jesus*: I wish it so, Marcel, and it is I who allows the wind to carry me in that way so that you pay a little attention to me. Without that, perhaps,
(375)    a century would pass before I would see you place a kiss on my picture. Marcel, you ought to thank me. Marcel, how sad I am! Although I am

able to talk here with you, the fact is that, in other places, I am sadly repulsed. Where can I find a spiritual Egypt where I would be able to live and take a little rest? I do not know what to do ... I make an appeal to the Canadian sisters, but they do not accept my invitation; they are still hesitant, they are afraid ... Marcel, comfort me; say to me: 'Jesus, my brother, I love you a lot'. Marcel I am very pleased with you; and heaven grant that there may be a great number of souls which, like yours, allow me to come and go freely to them. Then, how happy I shall be! Marcel, for that to happen, it is necessary that you suffer much for me. Do you accept cheerfully? Marcel, Marcel, I love you; I press you against my heart and cover you with kisses. Marcel, agree to suffer much for me. I will never separate myself from you, not even for a second ...

Marcel, your apostolate must be directed toward children. I wish you to draw children to me. I love them dearly. When they play ball, when they have swimming competitions or play no matter what childish game, I am present in the midst of them ... Marcel, everything pleases me about children: a word, a smile, even a tear which they shed in a moment (376) of sadness, all that pleases me ... But, unfortunately, Marcel, it seems that now children, by their manner of acting, want to emulate adults. And the most pitiable is that normally the world makes them know sin rather than know me. My life as a little child, even a very small child who hardly knows how to walk, is capable of imitating it. I am the true way which leads men to heaven. Why have a way if men were incapable of following it? Men can follow this way easily, without even trying ...

Marcel, time has passed, love me well. I, Jesus and you, Marcel, we make only one whole in God the Father, in Love (the Holy Spirit) and in the arms of Mary. Marcel, I kiss you unceasingly, and the more I give you, the more I wish to give you. Marcel, time is up.

**Marcel**: Yesterday, while making the Stations of the Cross, having arrived at the second station, Jesus said to me: 'Marcel, do not worry. If, in this business, there is something troubling you, it is your director who must concern himself and not you. All you have to do is to pray. Soon, you will tell your director to look again at the passages where I have spoken of the Redemptorist sisters; you will see there your role and that of your director. Say again to your director: "That is only a first little cross".' I hear Jesus say to me unceasingly: 'My words are (377) engraved already in the hearts of the sisters; they have already reached them'.

**Jesus**: Marcel, listen to what I am telling you. I love you dearly. I have a special predilection for children; I am happy to be their friend. If they wish to look for me, it is very easy. They have only to examine their own manner of acting and they will find me immediately in themselves. I have already promised the kingdom of heaven to the children; and this promise does not oblige them in anything. If I had obliged them to fast, to give themselves the discipline, to practise mortification, etc., how would the newly born who die immediately after baptism be able to go to heaven? ... Marcel, merciful Love has reserved for children a magnificent portion. All they have to do is accept it. However, Marcel, do not neglect to pray a lot so that children can understand my Love and give themselves entirely to it. The world kills the souls of children before my very eyes and I, what can I do? The souls of children belong

(378) to me completely but, nevertheless, the world steals them from me to make them the prey of the devil ... In my eyes children are a relaxation for me, the only amusement capable of consoling me and of leading me to gladly embrace the world in my arms. However, the world wishes to inoculate the hearts of children with the venom of sin ... Alas! My little brothers, do you not know that your little Jesus thirsts only for you? Come, little brothers, allow me therefore complete freedom to enter into a relationship with your souls, as I wish. Without me how could you be happy?

My dear little brothers, I have called you and looked forward to you from the first moment of my conception in the womb of Mary. Because I love you I have lived your life as a child, I have understood your childish condition. My dear little brothers, come to me ... In the same way as a father's heart can be sad because of his young children, in the same way that an older brother has not the heart to abandon his young brothers, in the same way that a good friend does not wish to separate himself from his best friend, it is the same for me, my little brothers. And not content with that, I still do more to such an extent that Love alone is capable of

(379) understanding the compassion that I feel for your very small souls. Little brothers, come with me ... Come with me in Mary's heart ...

Marcel, do you understand this? It is necessary to uproot the children from the darkness of the world ... Oh! World, misfortune to you! If you did not have children to give sanctuary to the tenderness of God's heart, you would be destroyed under the weight of divine justice ...

Marcel, tell the children about the kingdom of heaven; the legacy which has been promised to them is precisely there ... The kingdom of heaven belongs to children; blessed are they to receive this inheritance with open arms. However, it is necessary to let them know their heritage since, if they do not know of it, it is certain that they will not possess it. Yes, Marcel, it is necessary to tell them about it, since in that is their true wealth; it is necessary to teach them to accept the heritage which belongs to them ...

That's sufficient, little Marcel, you have gone past the time. What sadness!... Enough, little brother, go and rest. I am kissing you.

*Marcel*: Little Jesus, I no longer know what to say to you. If you do not speak to me I will go and chat with Mary...

Mary, my Mother, since the day when Jesus spoke to me, I have chatted with you very little. It is again little Jesus' fault. Your little one is very mischievous. Yes, you have two little ones equally roguish. This morning little Jesus allowed the needle of the sewing machine to prick my finger. It was very painful but the prick had scarcely bled. Nevertheless little Jesus' fault deserves a punishment. I am asking you, therefore, not to give him any more kisses, so that, from now on he is more attentive. Do you agree dear Mother? (380)

*Jesus*: Marcel, you have a strong tendency to accuse others falsely! Dear Mother, your little one thinks it is more appropriate to punish Marcel since, a moment ago, I told him to eat a bowl of milk soup so as to make up for what he was not able to eat this morning; and now, would you believe it, he goes off to accuse me to you... Mary, our story is really amusing...

Marcel, in acting like this we make Mary very happy who pays the greatest attention to our little accounts... What happiness, Marcel! You have a Mother; and for that reason I also love to recognize Mary as my Mother, and that she really is. Marcel, listen to what I say and write quickly.

If God the Father had not given to Mary humility of heart, she would certainly not have been able to recognize that I was the second Person of the Trinity, incarnate and descended to earth. Mary has already spoken to you on this subject; but, nevertheless, write down what I am saying to you. My external behaviour resembled that of ordinary men, well, almost... It is for this reason that Mary dared to command me in all simplicity, as a mother commands her child... (381)

*Marcel*: My dear Mother Mary, when you asked something of Jesus, did he obey immediately?

*Mary*: My child, my little Marcel, you are truly very naive. When little Jesus is speaking to you, lo and behold, you cut him off to ask me a question... but, nevertheless, I am going to answer you.

Outwardly, I behaved towards little Jesus as a mother with her child; but our mutual feelings were at that time of an intimacy impossible to describe. I often asked little Jesus to do such or such a task for me, and he, obeying immediately, carried out my wishes promptly. But he behaved like everyone else. Do not believe that he was happy to sit there and to perform miracles. Not at all. Little Jesus lived like everybody else; his attitude differed in nothing from that of a well-behaved child and I was always pleased with him. Often, also, I gave him sweets as other mothers do who love their children. Jesus accepted these sweets gladly and ate them. When he was still small, I took him often to draw water with me, I made him water the sheep, or again I made him collect twigs to cook the meal ... etc. I have already told you all of these things when you were working in the kitchen. That's enough, my child. Time is up. Go and work together with your brethren. I will speak to you again tomorrow and you will write it down. My child, I am kissing you. When I see you obey promptly I love you still more.

(382)

## 7 April 1946
*Passion Sunday*[*]

***Marcel***: My dear Mother Mary, you told me yesterday that you would speak to me today, for me to write it down. Allow me to ask you a question. What does the word 'naive' mean? By the way, a moment ago, I was very disappointed and I had to make a big effort to contain myself. I am always in a hurry to see Sunday arrive so as to have more time to write, but, in fact, I have hardly more time than other days. Father Master asked that the novices who normally help in the kitchen, do so also on Sundays, while the others do the washing up. It happens that only two of us remain to wash the dishes: Brother Gregory and me, so that it takes much time. That is why I was disappointed a moment ago. But I think that in a week or two I will be used to it. Mother, help me. Little Jesus does not stop repeating to me that he prefers it like that. But, dear Mother, explain to me the meaning of the word naive.

***Mary***: My dear child, if you wish to please little Jesus, accept cheerfully things which inconvenience you slightly; by that you will be able to stop the stones that sinners, today, throw at Jesus ... Little Jesus is your true friend; if you love him, try to protect him by your sighs of love. Thanks to the little sacrifices that you impose on yourself, little Jesus loves to stand close to you, since these little sacrifices are for him like so many caresses ... However, my child, continue to tell me quite simply your little problems; by that you please me, and I, I can only love you more. My child, I love you a lot and even more than little Jesus.

(383)

You ask me the meaning of the word naive: here is my reply. This

[*] Sunday before Palm Sunday.

morning I already answered you but since you have not yet written down my reply, I am happy to repeat it now. And so that you can understand, I will speak clearly.

My child, candour is a natural characteristic of children. The naive child is simple and sincere; he shows himself as he is; he does not know how to distinguish between good and evil since, being still too young, he does not have the use of reason ... My child, if your soul possesses this candour, it will be closer to me. In the same way that the young child remains always with its mother, you will remain always close to me. I wish that there may be more souls like yours, so as to be able to freely imprint the lips of little Jesus on the forehead of each of them; so as to be able to unite their hearts to that of little Jesus and, at the same time, be at peace with him. Without that he does not cease to complain (384) to me and importune me, asking me every day to look for a great number of souls for him. As Jesus' heart thirsts for souls, so mine burns for him in looking for them ...

My child, little Jesus is very fussy; he does not like to play with a puppet. All he wishes for is a real little brother with whom he can play and chat, a little brother whom it is possible for him to embrace as he wishes. Little Jesus is still naturally greedy, he is not happy with a small amount. The more little brothers I give him, the more he demands. As I dearly love him, I dare not scold him for fear of causing him pain. Truly, I do not know how to set about it, in order to spoil him, as I would wish to do. The more little brothers I give him the more I wish to give him others ...

My little one. You, also, are my 'little one' like little Jesus, since you are the little brother of little Jesus. Little Jesus loves his little brother a lot. Be well behaved. Let little Jesus be completely free to play with you. My child I love you always with a compassionate love more than I love little Jesus.

**Marcel**: Dear Mother, I have a very bad stomachache; I feel very unwell ... Little Jesus, why do you love your little Marcel so? Do you find your little brother well behaved?

***Jesus***: Marcel, you are not at all well behaved, since the well-behaved (385) child does not bother himself so. How many times have I told you not to get so perturbed; and you still have this defect. Come, little brother, since you do not wish to cause me any pain in anything, what is there to trouble you? I tell you that I am happy with all that you do; why do you not believe what I say? All your actions, all your sighs, all the feelings of your heart, you have offered them to me already. All that is my property and no longer yours, so why trouble yourself? ... Little brother, remain tranquil. I am giving you a kiss and another to our Mother. Regarding Jesus with the ginger beard* has he not said these very true words to you: 'Since you have Mary for your real Mother, you should never disconcert yourself'.

(386) Little brother, if after that you still trouble yourself, it is certain that Mary will be very hurt. Your weaknesses, not being sins, can in no way sadden me. But since you are a poor little soul, how can you avoid weakness? Marcel, there is in you only this tendency to worry which makes me fear for the future. So, remain peaceful. All that you do belongs to me. You must not trouble yourself about it since it does not concern you ...

Little Marcel, are you at peace now? ... Very good. From now on, never allow yourself to become troubled, do you understand? It is sufficient for you to love me. We are still both in Mary's arms, you must not, therefore, fear that we will ever be separated from each other. It is only the day when you say: 'I no longer recognize Mary as my Mother', that you will have reason to fear. However, Marcel, that is a simple supposition on my part, in reality, that will never happen, since you and I are but one together. Do not worry, Mary is very happy with us both.

Your weaknesses, Marcel, far from reducing my value of you, only make it increase further, since they are, for you, grounds for much greater confidence in me, which makes our union firmer still ...

What did your sister Thérèse teach you? You have forgotten everything already; it's hopeless! And it is also so much the better, since what you have forgotten, I am always there to remind you of and thus you can continually learn the lesson anew. What happiness can be compared to yours? And if a child thus indulged and loved by everybody was not happy, little Marcel, there would be nothing more to do (387) for him. Little Marcel, love me a lot.

The sighs of love that souls cause to rise towards me are capable of stopping the enormous stones which are thrown at my Love; these sighs divert the arrows of sinners which target my heart ... Oh! Marcel, the weak sighs of men prevent me from dying, suffocated on this earth. From where does such power come? From the love within them. What happiness for me to be able to frolic in the midst of these sighs! I feel very much at ease and completely at peace, no longer fearing being seen by my enemies or of being pierced by their arrows ...

Alas, little Marcel, they are still very rare on this earth, the places where I can rest. Today, little Marcel, pray for the expansion of the reign of my Love throughout the world; it is necessary that you bring

---

* Father Louis Roy.

to it your full attention. The summer holidays are coming, I want to have many well-ventilated villas to go and rest in them. So, Marcel look for a large number of villas for me. And we, both of us, will be able to enjoy them; you have nothing to lose there ...

However, Marcel, our main villa is the very heart of Mary where we will find all consolations; nevertheless, many other houses are necessary for us, so we may get more rest. (388)

*Marcel*: But, little Jesus has the expansion of the reign of Love already begun in the world?

*Jesus*: Yes, already. But the starting point of this expansion is in France itself. And it is your sister Thérèse in person who is the universal Apostle of the other apostles of my Love. Yes, it is from there that the expansion of the reign of my Love has emanated and which continues still. And you, Marcel, in writing down my words, you also work at this task, as I previously said. There are still many other apostles that you do not know and who also work in great secret, continually following each other to spread the reign of my Love in the world.

*Marcel*: Little Jesus, I hear people say that the end of the world is nigh. Is that really true, little Jesus?

*Jesus*: It is only the brilliant intelligence of the devil that has the habit of resolving questions that it is not correct to solve; as for those who are driven by the spirit of Love, they will never pass judgement on the works of God. In a family, for example, does one ever see children make a judgement about a task that their father will finish later? It is only the enemy of their father who dares to judge this work, with the intention of doing harm to the children.

Marcel, similar surmises are never in conformity with the truth. Further, you are not allowed to question me on this subject. Besides, I will not answer you. For example, when a father of a family decides to do something, he is not beholden to ask the advice of his children or to let them know of his plans. It is the same concerning the end of the world. Even our Mother Mary knows nothing about it; and if you ever hear a bogus Mary say that the end of the world will take place on a specific day, chase her away as being the enemy of our Mother ... (389)

Marcel, children know only the external signs of their father's work, without knowing when these works will be realized .... It is the same with the true Father of heaven. Men only know the external signs of his works without knowing the moment of their realization; and one should never lend an ear to such conjectures ...

(390) It is time, Marcel I am giving you a kiss ... Marcel, do not preoccupy yourself any more with the end of the world. As our Mother Mary has told you already, that is a business which concerns only the Holy Trinity ...

Marcel, it is necessary that you understand this also: even in the prophecies that the holy doctors speak about, the opinions voiced by them never relate to the day when the world will end, but simply to the time when the signs preceding the end of the world will occur, as I have said in the Gospel. If you do not understand these things, bearded Jesus will help you understand; but do not believe the suppositions of this one or that one, since they are not true, no matter the strength of their words and the reasons brought to bear. It is not even appropriate to discuss this subject, since I know that falsehoods would be mixed into these discussions.

Even if you saw the moon and the sun fall from heaven before your eyes at the same time, you should not try to calculate how many years or days remain before the end of the world. Even if you saw this earth burst into huge pieces, you should not do it, since the works of the Holy Spirit are beyond the forecasts of the human mind ... Marcel, it is necessary to firmly believe that without the shadow of a doubt. And if, in a book of prophecies, you come across a passage where it says that the end of the world will occur on a specified day, ask the Holy Father to burn that book immediately, since it contains an error. However, it is not like this; this is a simple example that I am giving you ...

**Marcel**: My sister Thérèse, why are you no longer speaking to me? Are you angry with me?

(391) **Thérèse**: Dear little brother, what do you want me to say to you? It is all right, I wish to speak to you. My dear little brother, love little Jesus a lot. Remain joyful always, so that he is pleased to stay with you. Do not stop singing so as to take away his sadness during these days of Holy Week; and act so as to make him forget all the sufferings that he has endured in the past ...

My dear little brother, do you remember all the sweetnesses that little Jesus made you taste during Lent last year? Surely he has shown you much love by that. How fortunate you are little brother! Who could be more so? Little brother, always be happy therefore. Little Jesus wishes to stay close to you because he wishes to see your smile. Were you very sad the other day? Then I had a lot of pity for you, but I dared not say a word to you since little Jesus wished you to be in this state.

My dear little brother, in these days when Holy Church recalls all the sufferings endured by Jesus in the past, try hard to console the heart of little Jesus in hiding from him your own sadness and avoid reminding him of the memory of these sad days. From now on, little brother, I will keep silent, waiting to speak to you again when Jesus himself keeps silent. Remain in peace, I am not at all angry with you, and neither will I ever be. Otherwise where would be the fraternal feelings which animate us, one towards the other? Little brother, I am kissing you and, to do well, you must always be joyful so that little Jesus may be more pleased with you. (392)

*Marcel*: Little Jesus, while thinking yesterday of the way in which my brother Saint Gerard* tied a rope round you to make you descend into a well to oblige you to look for a key that you succeeded in fishing out, I really felt like laughing ... Were you cold, little Jesus, at that time? My brother Saint Gerard is very mischievous. He also used the occasion to make you take a good bath. In fact I do not see where, during your whole life, you ever took a bath. That is not the way to be very clean ... But, little Jesus, do you know how to swim? If, on that day, I had taken the place of my brother Gerard, I should have, first of all, taught you how to swim, since, not knowing how to swim you could have drowned. Ah! Little Jesus, you are a skilful diver. You had hardly entered the water when Saint Gerard pulled you out straight away and you already held the key in your hand. From now on it will be appropriate to call you 'Saint Gerard's diver' ... Oh, Saint Gerard's diver, were you not happy enough in heaven to have to dive to the bottom of this earth, to look for dirty lumps of mud, without fearing either the awful smell, or the cold? Really, only an insane love is capable of such madness ...

*Jesus*: Marcel, there you are, speaking in such an impolite way. Are you not afraid that I might scold you? You dare to say that Love is mad? However, I admit it is true. Yes, Love is truly mad; and it is fortunate for you, Marcel, since if I were not mad in this way, you would have (393) never become what you are now ... So, it is necessary that you love me still more.

*Marcel*: Little Jesus, if, in the past, you had had to preach to people in the Vietnamese language, how would you have spoken?

*Jesus*: I would have spoken as I do now with you, little Marcel. To express my feelings as a father, I would have spoken as a father does

---

\* This is referring to Saint Gerard Magella, whose feast day is 16 October and who is the patron saint of the lay brothers of the Congregation of the Most Holy Redeemer (C.Ss.R.).

168   *Conversations*

with his child, and to express my feelings of friendship, I would have spoken as a friend speaks to his friend.

***Marcel***: So why, in the Vietnamese translation of the Gospel, do you make people speak in a manner so difficult to understand? If, living in your time, I had heard you speak in that way, I would not at all have had a desire to listen to you. Indeed it is only sufficient to read these words to notice that they conform in no way to anything resembling politeness. And supposing that you did really speak in those terms, the Pharisees would have had good reason to become angry ... However, I am certain that you never spoke thus. That's really true is it not, little Jesus? Even if a king, speaking to a slave, used the words *mày, tao*\* people would consider him arrogant, as one who has no sense of politeness with regard to his subjects.

(394) ***Jesus***: You are right, Marcel. In listening to the words that I have addressed to you up till now, you know that I have never spoken as it has been translated in the Gospel text ... But one must not blame the translator, since he lacked the emotions of Love. You can only blame yourself when, while reading, you do not know how to make the necessary refinements. Yes, you understand that Love never speaks to souls using such terms ... Marcel, the words I am saying to you now are going to change the translations of the Gospel which do not capture the exact meaning of the text. For that, it is necessary that you undertake the pain of writing. You are hardly seated for a moment to write and already you sigh and complain of being tired. You must be zealous for me; it is because of this that children will be able to learn to love me. You say that your wish is to make all children love me. Now, I am about to choose for you an easy and hidden task which will have the effect of leading children to me, so, why do you complain? To want something and then to abandon it is hardly better than to wish and then not wish to achieve what one wishes.

(395) ***Marcel***: Alas! Little Jesus, all you know how to do is to speak. In such heat, to oblige me to close my door and write, who would be able to put up with that? To allow me to do the work carefully that you ask, you should pay attention so that air comes into my room to refresh me a little; without that your work will be delayed. You can take it or leave it.

***Jesus***: Marcel, what good is that going to do? The fanlight being open,

---

\*   *Mày* and *Tao* are haughty manners of expression.

the air can get into your room. And when it is a little too warm you will be able to offer me this sacrifice, without fear of any harm to yourself; and by this little sacrifice you will be able to save a great number of souls from eternal fire ...

Marcel, do not complain. Try to smile a little. Do not be afraid of perspiring; nevertheless, I see you look tired. That is sufficient, rest yourself, Marcel, I love you dearly, I am very pleased with you. These little stories please me, they even make me forget my sadness and they will draw to me, later, from little souls, a number of other little stories of the same kind.

***Marcel***: My dear Mother Mary, I am going to brush my teeth. Mother, help me to make them white, to make them beautiful. I have very bad breath. In heaven I will have no more need to brush my teeth, nor need to eat or chew, no more need to use soap; what happiness! But when will this happiness come? I do not know how many more times little Jesus is going to oblige me to write ... I am stopping here, Mother. Let (396) me kiss you and give another to little Jesus and to all my brothers and sisters in paradise. I am leaving you. Time is almost up.

My Mother Mary, there is one question I wished to ask you and I always forget. Allow me to first reflect a little in order to recall it ...

Ah! I have it. How is it that I find people who say: 'We cannot believe that Mary is the Mother of God; yes, that a human creature may be the Mother of God, that is something so unreasonable that one cannot believe it'.

***Mary***: Right, my dear little 'meticulous one', I am going to answer your question. What those men affirm is quite right. They say that it is something unreasonable, since in fact, no reason exists capable of explaining this mystery. Granted that this world is still very poor in reason, only Love can succeed in penetrating it. If people are unable to believe, it is because they are lacking humility. Myself, in seeing God so humble himself as to become man, I have in the same way found that mysterious, incomprehensible. And if the true Father in heaven had not given me humility, neither would I have been able to believe this mystery. My dear child, there remains no more than one means to lead people to understand: it is to make known to them that Love, in God, is limitless, of an unfathomable depth and that, consequently, it is a mystery that I (397) myself do not understand, and with much greater reason men do not ...

My child, the human mind is very limited; it is even incapable of understanding the Love that God has for a simple grain of sand. If, therefore, man dares to scrutinize the immense Love that God holds for humanity, does he ask this question: 'Man, are you capable of understanding the grandeur of the Love of God for a simple grain of sand?' If one managed to understand it, one would, equally, be able to understand all that the Lord has done in me in favour of men ... My child, that suffices, it is already almost time. Go in peace.

## 8 April 1946

(398) *Marcel*: Dear Mother today is the eighth of April, the day when I must pray for France.* Yesterday, Mother, during the meal, I asked little Jesus this question: 'Little Jesus, in bygone days, did you eat bananas?' He answered me, laughing: 'Marcel, it is not for eating that I came down to earth.' But afterwards, acceding to my wish, he added in a more gentle tone: 'I have never eaten bananas and there are many things that you eat which I have not eaten. However, at this moment, when you eat something, it is as if I was eating it myself, since we two make only one.' On hearing little Jesus speak so, I was very content and I ate two bananas.

Last night, when I woke up, little Jesus spoke to me again. Mother, I really love little Jesus and, for his part, little Jesus is pleased with me. This is what he said to me: 'Even when you sleep I am still with you, not ceasing to give you kisses and to gather all the acts of love that you make during your sleep, that is to say, each of your breaths.'

Dear Mother, you also love me a lot. And I, I love you a lot in the same way, a lot. But it is only in heaven that I will be able to see you clearly in company with little Jesus ... Mother, it is time already. Give me a kiss and accept my loving glances to present them to little Jesus.

Little Jesus, yesterday a brother broke a plate and Brother Augustine complained in these terms: 'People always break plates without deducting anything from the refectory inventory, so that the number written in the register remains complete whereas, in reality, there is a shortage of plates.' On hearing that I said, jokingly to the Brother: 'If you were the Superior the Brothers, perhaps, would not dare accuse themselves; and if they accused themselves, they would certainly be very worried on the subject of the missing plates which had escaped them.' Brother Augustine immediately quoted to me these words from the Gospel: 'Do not judge anyone, as you will be judged as you will have judged others.'†

---

\* It is Monday, cf. (102).
† Matthew 7, 1 & 11.

There, a simple word said as a joke has earned for me a quotation from (399)
the Gospel, and a very interesting one at that. However, little Jesus, I
dared not judge anyone; Brother Augustine has well and truly calumnied me, is that not so?

Later, in the evening, when the Brothers were discussing the eventual canonization of such or such a Brother and the name which would be given to him, I said quite simply, as a joke, to Brother Augustine: 'Later, if you are canonized, you will surely be called Saint Augustine of Mỹ-Phong, since that is where you come from ...' This is what he replied to me: 'When you wish to get your own back on a brother, you mention his place of origin ...' Under these conditions how is it possible to be joyful? Little Jesus, try to make the Brother understand that in all the words that I address to him, my sole intention is to please him. Yes, all I say to him is done in such a way that he may be joyful with me, your little Marcel. The time is up, little Jesus; I love you dearly, dearly.

*Jesus*: Marcel, are there any words which better encapsulate love and tenderness than the words of the Gospel? Nevertheless I have had to submit to criticism and scorn on the part of the Pharisees ... Marcel, accept cheerfully the harsh words that Brother Augustine says to you. I (400) censure those who judge and not those who are judged. Since you have not judged anyone, Marcel, do not worry yourself over these words. It is, besides, a matter of little importance, but which attracts me nevertheless. Marcel, do you wish to offer it all to me?

Marcel, I love you dearly; my love for you is truly indescribable. Do you believe it, Marcel? Nothing is more hurtful to me than to see a great number of souls that I love in preference to all the others, who behave towards me with such indifference that they do not even wish to believe in the preferential love that I have for them.

*Marcel*: Little Jesus, why am I so sad today? Is it because you also are sad? But, little Jesus why are the saints often so tested in the virtues that they practise?

*Jesus*: There is nothing surprising in that; a virtue which has not been tested does not merit the name of virtue. It is for this reason that the saints have to be tried.

*Marcel*: But, little Jesus, do you not already know them, yet there is still a need to try them and make them suffer? For me, your little one, not possessing any virtue, I do not fear being tried in this way; and so much the better since if I had any virtue and it was necessary for me to be (401) tested, perhaps I would not be able to put up with the trial. Is that not so, little Jesus?

***Jesus***: That being so, Marcel, what credibility would the saints enjoy in the eyes of men? It is necessary that they have virtues so that men notice them! Really, Marcel, you understand absolutely nothing to ask such finicky questions; and how can you suggest that I do not know them? ...

And you, Marcel, you say you have no virtue? It is true little brother, but what need have you of virtues when your heart already contains all the virtues? These virtues, however, are not yours; they are mine only, so that all that remains for you to do, is to be ready to contain Love and then, Love will be all for you.

Come on, Marcel, be happy. I do not like being with sad children. With children given to crying, I can still comfort them and make them smile; but with children inclined to sadness, I can do nothing and it is really sad for me to stay with them ... Marcel, it is the same with you; when you are sad, I am so also. Up to now your sister Thérèse has not taught you to be sad, she has taught you only to be joyful with me ... Come, come, where is my 'sugared sweet'? When one eats a candy and finds it sweet, one wants to eat it; if, on the contrary, one finds it bitter, one only wishes to throw it away ... Your sister Thérèse has let you know that you were, for me, a 'sugared sweet'. You must, therefore, act so that my mouth feels, on tasting you, a certain sweetness and well-being. That is the condition on which I will take pleasure in tasting you, Marcel.

But, it's a strange thing, how is it that a sweet also knows how to worry? A sweet that knows how to worry, it is very strange, Marcel, yes, very strange. Marcel, I am speaking in a jocular manner. If you wish to be a sweet for me which is edible, you must not worry, do you understand? When I wish to bring it to my mouth to eat, if this sweet does not cease from saying: 'I do not know if it is really little Jesus' mouth', how would I dare to eat it when I do not even dare to put it in my mouth? So, Marcel, from now on if you want me to eat sweets with a nice taste and with pleasure, you must not bother yourself, since you are my sweet and mine alone. When I eat you all up and when you are in my heart, you will, without doubt, find it strange to see that in my heart it is not like the hearts of other men; you will see that my heart is only full of Love ... Marcel, I am kissing you and I wish for you a peaceful rest.

***Marcel***: Today, my Mother, your 'little one' makes me very sad; he hardly speaks to me. Perhaps he has gone to sleep again? Really, he likes his sleep.

***Jesus***: Marcel, what are you saying that is so interesting? But I am still here, why are you afraid. I have not left. It is very unfortunate Marcel; if you moan of being sad for such a little thing, how will you be able to make sacrifices for me? You moan at the smallest trifle, why do you concern yourself so? You know well that it is impossible for me to abandon you. However you have just spoken badly of me, so seriously lacking in charity. You must exercise this virtue again. On my part I will also help you.

Dear Marcel, I love you dearly, be always happy to sacrifice yourself for my Love. No matter what happens, remain peaceful. As you still remain on this transient earth, you will still have to suffer many times; but do not worry: I remain always with you, yes, always, always. It is impossible for me to leave you, even for half a second. Little brother, remain tranquil, you are always very pleasing to me; later, in heaven, you will be with me on Mary's breast. We will then be able to converse quite freely, unlike now. The happiness we will taste will be a true happiness and without end ...

However, little brother, that time is not yet here, it will still be necessary ... (404)

But, what does it matter, little brother, I will come back very quickly to you; it will not be long at all ...

I am giving you a kiss. Your body is my body, all of you is mine. Little brother, I place you on Mary's heart where you will stay with me for eternity You will, therefore, always be in Mary's arms and I, I will not cease pampering you. Be joyful little brother, never give in to sadness. Even if you feel a little sad, do not show it, since in imposing this sacrifice on yourself you will please me a lot ...

***Marcel***: Dear Mother, do you know, at midday little Jesus and my sister Thérèse were competing with each other, not ceasing to call me: 'Little brother!' 'Little brother!' and then challenging me to guess whose voice had called me. But I have a very fine ear; I distinctly heard their voices and each time that one or the other called me, I immediately recognized whose voice it was, little Jesus' or that of my sister Thérèse. I was not fooled once. If my little sister called me: 'Little brother' without hesitating, I said: 'It's my sister's voice.' If little (405) Jesus called: 'Little brother' I replied immediately: 'It's little Jesus' voice.' I was right each time. And afterwards we all wanted to laugh. Little Jesus began to laugh first, then I and finally my sister Thérèse of the Child Jesus. You were not there, Mother, as I did not hear your voice. In this business it was all little Jesus' fault. It was during the time of particular examination of conscience and I had to make a big effort not to laugh. When I went to the refectory I still wanted to laugh, so much that bearded Jesus asked me what I had to laugh about with Brother Augustine.

*This is quite true. It is only afterwards that I understood why he was laughing.*

Dear Mother, don't give any more kisses to little Jesus; in this business he was the one who began first, then my sister Thérèse and then I the last. Moreover, being the youngest, I must necessarily do what little Jesus wishes; so, therefore, I have not committed any fault and if the Zealator accuses me, it is little Jesus who will have to undertake the penance.

*Mary*: My dear little one, I am kissing the three of you; but because you are the most unfortunate I am giving you a greater number. Be happy ... You please me, all three of you ...

## 9 April 1946

(406) *Marcel*: Mother, today is the 9th already. This morning, after the washing up, I was very tired and I had, in addition, to wear the *cuissard*,* which made me feel very bad. Little Jesus is really cruel: on this day when I particularly honour him he still obliges me to wear a chain and chew bitter herbs. The result being that this day consecrated to the Child Jesus is hardly better for me than that dedicated to suffering Jesus; but I love him, the one and the other of these two Jesuses, dear Mother ...

Incidentally, Mother, today, I do not cease thinking of the words that you said to me last night and I really feel like laughing. It concerns the incident when I obliged little Jesus to do the penance in my place: you replied thus to me: 'Regarding the penance, you are the one who must do it since little Jesus and your sister Thérèse did not laugh outwardly, you are the only one to have done so.' But, dear Mother, examine my case carefully: if I laughed it is solely because of little Jesus. If he had not behaved as he did, I would not have had any reason to laugh. Because of that, Mother, I have gained a reputation as a 'giggler'.

*Mary*: My little Marcel, as a penance you have only to recite one 'Hail Mary' and you will draw from it great benefits. I am spelling them out for you. First of all, you will obtain humility of heart, to admit your fault

---

* An instrument of penance.

is to practise humility; secondly, you will prove your love to me; thirdly, you will gain because Jesus' love for you does not appear externally ... And there are still other benefits. But the time is up, go my child ...

**Marcel**: Last night during meditation, Mother, little Jesus only looked (407) at me without saying anything except the following few words: 'Now, Marcel, I am going to teach you, simply, how to look at me, so that, during the moments when I do not speak to you, you are happy to look at me. I am going to accustom you to this method so that later you can put it into practice easily.'

Therefore, quite simply, little Jesus exhorted me to raise my eyes towards the tabernacle. And, on focusing on the tabernacle in this way, I felt as much consolation as if Jesus had spoken to me. This morning little Jesus resumed the same exercise, but I had not been able at all to apply myself to it; I only slept. I asked little Jesus if he was pleased with that. He answered me positively, on condition that I never get agitated at the sight of my weaknesses. He told me that I was very weak, that I possessed nothing, if not my weaknesses; that he received from me nothing other than weaknesses, because everything in me was simply weakness ... Mother, I am leaving you. I will speak to you again in a short while. I love you dearly.

## A Vision

Here is what I saw last night during meditation. Little Jesus told me that only bearded Jesus would understand this vision.

While hearing the point of the meditation on the Passion read out, I did not at all know how to meditate. I then asked little Jesus to teach me (408) to meditate; but little Jesus said nothing. I then asked him this question: 'Little Jesus are you sad to remain always in this tabernacle?' But he did not reply. I saw only that he was looking at me and crying. At sight of this I also began crying. But I had cried for only a short time when little Jesus began smiling and said to me: 'Enough, Marcel, I am no longer sad.' A short time later I saw him again as on the preceding occasions, still with bare feet and dressed in a white robe reaching below his knees. He stood up straight and only looked at me. He then said to me that he was going to train me to look at him ... as told to Mary a moment ago.

Then I suddenly saw a cross appear beside little Jesus. At the top of this cross a piece of cloth was suspended on which was printed the Face of Jesus. Little Jesus looked at me with a joyous expression, then, showing me the cross he said to me; 'Little brother, here is your portion of the inheritance, here is the portion of the inheritance of the children.

Do you see it clearly?' Then little Jesus, indicating himself added: 'Little brother, here is the elevator* which will allow you to take possession of this inheritance, and it will also be the same for the children. Do you understand? That is the way your sister Thérèse has led you up till now, after having followed it herself. Little brother, tell that to the children.'

(409) Then I realized that it was over. However this vision remains engraved in my mind; I have not forgotten its slightest detail. I asked little Jesus to explain the meaning to me, but he answered me: 'Even if I explained it to you, you would not understand. Bearded Jesus will understand and he will help you understand, little brother.'

Little Jesus, since this morning you have not given me a single sentence to write down on this paper; I am very sad because of it ...

Little Jesus, are you happy with little Toa? He is very skilful, he can imitate no matter what: the crow of the cock, the barking of the dog, the lowing of the cattle and it is all very lifelike. A short time ago Father Huberdeau asked him for a pair of rods; he answered him in very bad French 'Uẫy! Uẫy!'† ... If, in past times, he had been in the cave in Bethlehem, he would have really made you want to laugh. He is very unaffected, but the brothers do not stop saying that he is stupid. He sings all the time. So, little Jesus, do you love him?

***Jesus***: Marcel, my little brother, understand that I myself live in him. Imitate him; I love him a lot. I am happy with all he does and, furthermore, I find it very attractive. Little Brother, that is in what perfection (410) consists in children. Now all that remains is to teach little Toa to love me and he will be truly perfect ...

Marcel, look at the number of pictures he has. Beautiful or not he sticks them all on the wall so that people may see them. It is, for him, something very attractive, while older people only see bad taste and childishness. But I, Marcel, find all of it very attractive, more attractive even than it is for little Toa. Perfection in children consists in that. Whether it is attractive or not, they allow everything to appear on the outside, in such a way that it is very easy for me to act in them ...

Oh! Dear little brother, happy are children, since they have received their part of the heavenly inheritance empty-handed ... Do you know why I often suggest the example of children to lead men to perfection?

---

\* This refers to the insight of Saint Thérèse of the Child Jesus: 'Ah! never have words more tender, more melodious come to rejoice my soul; the elevator which must lift me to heaven are your arms my Jesus! For that I have no need to grow, on the contrary it is necessary that I remain small, that I become more and more so.' Ms C folio 3, recto.

† Uẫy! Uẫy! Yeah! Yeah!

It is that children, in acting as they do, are already perfect; all that remains is to teach them to love and then, they are truly perfect. Every man, whoever he is, must reach this stage, on pain of not being admitted to heaven. The kingdom of heaven belongs to little children ... Little brother, emphasize this to children; say to them that the true Father in heaven has already reserved for them their portion of the inheritance, and it is sufficient for them to know how to enter into (411) possession of this magnificent inheritance.

## 10 April 1946

*Marcel*: Little Jesus, for the last two days why have you spoken to me so little? It makes me very sad. Having nothing to distract me I only wait for your words to find a little joy; but, that's the way it is, you show yourself very miserly towards me. Is it, by chance, that you just wish to go to sleep? Come, little Jesus, don't go to sleep. If you were to go to sleep again, our true Mother Mary would certainly not be pleased. Seeing that of her two children, one sleeps and the other cries, how could she be happy? One thing, however, is certain, it is that she would prefer to stay with the one who is crying, since she knows that he is in a very sad state. As for the one who is sleeping, she would leave him to manage by himself and sleep as long as it pleases him. Would it not be very sad? Enough, my little Jesus, you must not sleep any more; it would be to your disadvantage.

*Jesus*: Marcel, according to what you say the advantage would, rather, be mine. Listen, I am going to explain it. Every morning you sleep during meditation; consequently, during that time, I am closer to Mary, since she knows very well that I am sadder from the fact that her other child is asleep. So, Marcel, who suffers the disadvantage?

   I am not even silent for one whole day and you are already panic-stricken; yet, you dare to reproach me for keeping silence ... Marcel, (412) you should be ashamed! That's enough! From now on do not reproach me like that. Otherwise your sister Thérèse will make fun of you. Nevertheless, Marcel know that I never leave you. So, chase away any worry. Little brother, remember that I love you a great deal. Yes, I love you always like my own little brother, I clasp you in my arms, and I cover you unceasingly with kisses. Firmly believe that it is really so. And then my Love will be satisfied, since I will see not only that I am loved, but also that my Love is believed in ...

   Little brother, there is still too little confidence in my Love. Revive this confidence in my Love, this is the work you must accomplish to prove to me your love. Do you pray for the Redemptorist sisters today? Good, pray for this intention: ask that they have confidence in me. It is simply their lack of confidence in me that makes them hesitate and fear so; it is simply because they lack confidence in me that the prospect of sacrifice disturbs them and makes them worry. Yes, all of that comes from their lack of confidence in me. To be afraid of sacrifice is to be afraid of Me; and if one is afraid of Me, it is obvious that the love that one has for me is still more or less imperfect. And the soul that acts in this way is not, for me, a true spouse.

(413) If your father Saint Alphonsus were not a gentle man he would certainly scold the Redemptorist sisters in an exemplary manner ...

Littler brother, emphasize this to them from me: 'I am still lacking a place to rest my head. I have looked for this place but I have not found it ...' The appeal I make to you is not new; it already dates back a long time ... However, I am still waiting for you patiently and I will wait for you for as long as I do not see you arrive. Do not go so far as to believe that it is not painful for me to wait in this way. On the contrary I find it very painful, since it results in few souls acknowledging themselves as my spouses.

*Marcel*: Little Jesus, today I must pray for the Redemptorist sisters.* It is also the day specially dedicated to honour my father Saint Alphonsus. However one could say that my father Saint Alphonsus is closing his eyes on this business; he is covered completely with a veil; I can't see his face at all. It is without doubt for fear that the villains throw stones at him that he has been hidden so. It is very sad to see him decked out in this way.

*It was Passiontide and Saint Alphonsus' statue, which was in our church in Hanoi, was veiled according to the custom prevalent at the time.*

Little Jesus, do you love my father Saint Alphonsus?

*Jesus*: I love your father Saint Alphonsus dearly, since I recall that, during his meals, he saved a portion of everything he ate for me. But you, Marcel, your are a real gourmand, you leave me absolutely nothing, being happy to offer me quite simply everything that you eat; and nevertheless you claim to love me a lot!

(414) *Marcel*: Really, little Jesus, I am not happy that you speak like that; is it not you who said to me, 'Marcel, when you eat, it is just as if I myself

---

\* It is Wednesday. See (102).

were eating'. You told me that the other day. If you deny it, let us ask our Mother for clarification. That's enough little Jesus; you have lost already, without counting your lack of charity in word even though this morning's meditation was precisely on the subject of charity. I am going to tell our Mother Mary to punish you ...

Little Jesus, last night at the time of the collation in the common room I saw the rose fixed in your hands and in which there was a little picture of Sister Thérèse of the Child Jesus. I knew well that it was my sister Thérèse of the Child Jesus, but feigning ignorance, I spoke to her in these terms: 'I really do not know which Carmelite is in this flower. My sister Thérèse, would you know who this sister is?' This is what she replied (I felt like laughing at that time, and I also had the feeling that you were present, little Jesus): 'This sister, it is Thérèse of the Child Jesus.' I questioned once more: 'But where does she come from, to be in this flower and to act as a plaything for little Jesus throughout the whole day?' She replied to me: 'This sister is already in heaven, but because little Jesus loves her a lot, he never wishes to be separated from her; so she acts as his plaything. And you, Marcel, it seems that she calls you "Dear little brother".' Then I answered her: 'Ah! Is that so?' Then (415) we laughed together for a while: I had a continual urge to laugh, and my sister continued to play-act to make me laugh. Later in heaven, we certainly will be very happy.

> Brother Marcel is referring here to a little plaster crib, which stayed all the time on a table in the common room of the novitiate. An artificial rose holding the little picture in question was fixed to one of Jesus' hands.

**Jesus**: Marcel, little Thérèse does not cease to teach you to be joyful but still, from time to time, you moan, you complain of distaste, of fatigue; what good does her teaching do? Marcel, you must learn this lesson by heart. After having taught you to make sacrifices, she is now teaching you to be joyful. In spite of your sacrifices, if you are not joyful, I have no inclination to accept them. I can only reject them and then you will cry ...

Come, little Marcel, you are my little brother, so you must learn how to be joyful; without that it is impossible for you to become the apostle of children. It is necessary that one can say of your life that it is a joyful one. I am very fussy: I only like to play with little brothers and sisters who are joyful. As for those who are sad, I do not experience any joy with them, as I have already told you.

**Marcel**: Nevertheless, little Jesus, you told me that you are not as ill-natured as I am and now you admit to being very fussy?

**Jesus**: Really? Marcel? Come on, let us examine it a little and you will see that I am not as ill-natured as you. When you ask or wish for something, I give it to you gladly; but you, if I ask you to be joyful, you always remain sad. And, in spite of that, you still dare to reproach me ... Be grateful that I do not scold you ... That's enough. From now on you must correct yourself and you must never dare to speak this way again. Agreed? Marcel! Marcel! In reality I never dare to scold you. My only concern is that you are going to be angry with me. So I must carefully watch over you always since you are my very little brother ...

Little brother, see how my Love is concerned for you even in the minutest details, just as it is for all other souls. Little brother, love me well. It is because of this that I am pleased to remain with my little brothers. Love me also in place of all the souls who repulse me. All the kisses that these souls refuse to receive, it is to you that they come back, as they do to all the souls that love me. That's enough, little brother, the time is up. Go and rest.

**Marcel**: I do not know, little Jesus, if later, in heaven, I will be treated better that I am now. For myself, I am very happy to be treated as I am. But, little Jesus, why do you make me speak in this manner as if I were your 'little brother'?

**Jesus**: The reason is that I wish it so. All you have to do is follow my will. You are really too curious about everything, asking questions even about trifles ... Oh! Marcel, why the tears? I have not scolded you, why do you worry so? It is through love that I have spoken thus and not to reproach you. I simply wish to show you that I am always pleased with you. That you are so weak, little brother is not important. Remain peaceful, since the weaker you are, the more you are loved by me, and yet, my Love is always, always, greater than your weakness ...

Little brother, a moment ago you asked me a question about heaven. I wish to answer you now so you may be happy. However, to please me, ask me the question again and do it with a big smile; that will be more joyful.

**Marcel**: I wish first of all to reflect again a little ... My little Jesus, in heaven, will our mutual relations remain the same as now?

**Jesus**: Yes, little brother. In heaven we will love each other as now, we will also chat together as we do now and we will always stay on Mary's knee as now ... etc. However, there will be one difference: we will no longer need the language of this world; we will speak only the language of love which then will be understandable to you. We will see each other very clearly. All will be changed, all will be shining brightly. All we will have to do is to stay there and love one another. And what will make our happiness grow even more is that we will be seated on Mary's knee. What joy! I will no longer be afraid of seeing you sad.

*Marcel*: But, in heaven, will I still be able to call Thérèse by the name of sister?

*Jesus*: Yes, you will always be considered as being the little brother of Sister Thérèse of the Child Jesus. Her manner of acting towards you on earth will remain the same in heaven. However, as I said to you earlier, there you will speak the language of Love and you will be loved by Love itself. It will no longer be as now; you will no longer have to speak the language of this world. Once in heaven, you will understand. And if, at that time, I used earthly language to explain celestial things to you, you would be incapable of understanding. Be happy, little brother.

*Marcel*: Little Jesus, I like my new position in the novitiate oratory a lot. (419) I now find myself just opposite your tabernacle, so that you see me always and that, for my part, I see you in the same way, without having to lean from one side to the other. I can look straight ahead so that we can see each other clearly and even if I happen to smile, no one sees me.

*Jesus*: But, little brother, what is more important is that you remain entirely immersed in my Love ... Enough, little brother, time is up. Go, otherwise you will arrive late for the communal exercise ...

## 11 April 1946

*Marcel*: Little Jesus, a short while ago I was about to sew when Jesus with the ginger beard asked me: 'Who are you doing this work for?' I did not at all know how to answer. After having reflected a moment, I replied: 'For the Congregation'. Jesus with the ginger beard added: 'But you work for God; that's all that matters.' I was really ashamed, but I just smiled and Jesus with the ginger beard laughed with me.

*Jesus*: Little brother, I prefer that it should be Jesus with the ginger beard rather than you who said those words ... Be happy. But why (420) were you so sad a moment ago? What is troubling you? Tell me so that I may know.

*Marcel*: What troubles me is something you said to the Redemptorist sisters and even bearded Jesus could not understand. He asked me but I did not understand it. That is why I was troubled, nothing else.

***Jesus***: That's enough, my dear little brother; do not trouble yourself needlessly. It is not necessary for you to understand what I say to you; leave that to your director. He questioned you because he did not understand, but that you do not understand is not important for you. You become perturbed very easily, little brother. However do not lose heart, I am still here with you and I love you always. Offer it all up to me. If it happens to trouble you, do not bother yourself seeing that you get perturbed so easily. It's a consequence of your weakness; but this weakness is entirely in me, little brother, don't worry about it, do you understand? Did you eat with an appetite today, little brother? So, tell me what you have eaten?

(421) ***Marcel***: I ate very well today. And as it was the feast of the Reverend Father Provincial, the meal was a little more appetizing than usual. I even forgot you, busy as I was speaking with the brothers. Little Jesus, forgive me. So, today, everything was good: the soup, the bread, the vegetables and the meat. But what I preferred above all were the crushed vegetables that I find better even than the meat. I then ate two ears of maize, but I only ate a small amount of rice. I also like the maize a lot. In the past, little Jesus, I don't suppose you had maize to eat, so, I was more spoilt than you. I then ate some cake, but today I did not find it tasty. In former days, little Jesus, did you eat cake? Did our Mother Mary bake it?

(422) ***Jesus***: Yes, little brother, Mary was very skilled at making cakes, as she was in everything. Little brother, remember this: Mary indulged me outwardly as other mothers do and she did as much as she could. She knew that I was as weak as other children, only knowing how to laugh when I was happy and to cry when I was sad. Consequently Mary always considered me outwardly as her very dear son, she loved me as a mother sincerely loves her child. But, internally, Mary did not cease to adore me because I am truly God. It is necessary that you understand that, outwardly, I did nothing which could distinguish me from other men; and in her relations with me, consequently, Mary acted in the same way.

***Marcel***: Little Jesus, was your family as poor as mine?

***Jesus***: No. Relative to the time when I lived, my family was very poor: it had absolutely nothing. However it found itself in an environment better than your family is in currently. In spite of that, it was still very painful for me. If I had simply to take on human nature and come to this earth to become the king of the universe, that was already an incomparable humiliation for my Divinity.

When I had to flee into Egypt with Mary and Joseph, I had to suffer only at the beginning. Shortly afterwards the situation improved. On returning to Nazareth, I lived in the same poverty, but under better conditions than in Egypt ...

God the Father never allowed my family to suffer hunger or thirst, even for a single meal ... Further, Mary knew how to plan ahead and, above all, she had confidence in her true Father in heaven. Towards me she behaved as a mother, but with God the Father, she acted with all the trust of a child. If something was lacking, if she had any need, no matter (423) how small, she knew she only had to raise her eyes to heaven and ask for it from God the Father in all simplicity and sincerity. And as her confidence and her simplicity were very pleasing to God, Mary obtained all that she asked for, as she has already mentioned to you.

For example, when she was short of flour to make bread, she simply said to her true Father: 'Father, today your "little one" and your children are in need.' Then she spelled out: 'They have no more flour, no more salt ... etc.' After which she remained in peace as usual. The true Father in heaven was very assiduous in granting her prayers, but he did it in a very natural manner, without resorting to striking miracles ...

Little brother, there, in a nutshell, you have what my visible life was like. Have you understood? ... But why do you reflect in this way? I have already told you: The words that I am dictating to you today, only those who are really humble are capable of understanding them. Afterwards you must not ask yourself anxiously if you have been deceived. You must believe this firmly: when I speak to you and when (424) you listen to me, you are doing nothing but following the only truth. You must hold for certain that I alone am the Truth. Now, it is impossible that the Infinite Truth should allow a soul to fall into error that always follows and recognizes this one and only Truth ... That, never! Since you always follow the truth, you have no reason to fear.

Little brother I am not reproaching you. Since the words that you are writing here are words of truth, they can but come from the only Truth ...

**Marcel**: Nevertheless, it seems that even my director dares not affirm with certainty that it is you who is speaking to me ...

**Jesus**: Ah! My little one, my little brother, that is quite right; and if your director acts in this way, that is my responsibility and not his. Your director is only my spirit; he is not me in person. It is necessary that you understand that. You do not need to know what line of conduct his duty towards you imposes on him. It is enough that you know how to obey. It is in obeying that you give evidence of real humility. Now humility is truth itself ...

(425) Little brother, see how Mary, living with me, had to call on the virtue of faith in order to believe. Also, although it was given to our Mother to live in the company of the Redeemer, she had, nevertheless, to believe in her heart. Yes, Mary had to have recourse to the virtue of faith in order to believe that I was God, since outwardly I allowed nothing of my divinity to be seen. So, little brother, you must also act in the same way and, by that, you will please Mary much more. Having formerly led a life similar to yours, she understands very well the feelings of your heart. The more you believe in the truth, the more she rejoices and the more she loves you. Little brother, look at Mary. And never give way to anxiety on this subject for fear of making her sad ...

(426) ***Mary***: My dear little one. You have just been looking at me. It is not surprising therefore that I hasten to ask you this question. It is something really astounding, My child, by a simple glance you have drawn to yourself my compassionate gaze. So, what do you want and what is it that little Jesus has just said to you? Are you very troubled? That is very unfortunate, my child. I am very sorry for you. Today, the recreation day, when you should be relaxing, all you do is worry yourself. It is very painful. But, my child, why trouble yourself in this way? I was once in the same situation as you; my soul also needed to believe, to hope and to love like you. Although aware of the wonders that God was working in me, I had, nevertheless, to believe, since I had no conception of the graces that the divine Father was granting to me. If, at that time, I had not had the need to call on the virtue of faith, I would no longer have been a humble creature like you, my children. If, therefore, I still had need to believe, with much greater reason have you, my child ...

My dear child, remain in peace, all right? Little Jesus has not scolded you; neither have I. Our sole intention, both of us, is to get rid of your troubles. Do not worry, I love you dearly. See, I have more pity for you than for little Jesus. In that case, it is he who should be sad; but you, what reason have you to be sad? Come, my child, I am kissing you, I am giving you twice as many as I am giving little Jesus, nevertheless, little Jesus is very happy with that.

(427) If little Jesus was like you, you would end up hitting each other seriously, both of you. But little Jesus loves you even more than I love you myself, since my love for you is the sign of the love that he has for you. So, in seeing me give you more kisses than I give to him, he is not offended.

My dear little one, I am kissing you a lot and I love you dearly. That's enough. The time is almost up. My child I am placing you on my breast with little Jesus; and there, both of you, you will love each other. But you must not be angry with little Jesus. Should you do so, little Jesus would cry and I would be very sad to see you both crying ... My child, I am sorry, but it is really time. That is sufficient. Go now and converse cheerfully with the brethren. It is very difficult; your hand is already very tired; my child I am sorry for you ...

*Marcel*: Little Jesus, please forgive me. A short while ago you spoke to me and I understood absolutely nothing, so I found that very difficult. Please forgive me. I love you a lot. This is what Mary said to me: 'Do not to be angry with Jesus.' I would never dare to be angry with you, little Jesus. Mary simply wished to make me laugh so as to drive away my pain. She loves me a lot; she has even more compassion for me than for you, little Jesus. Does that make you angry? On the other hand, she told me that you love me more than she loves me. Is that really true little Jesus? (428)

*Jesus*: It's quite true, Marcel, my little brother. Without Mary, it would be impossible for me to love you; it would also be impossible to communicate so easily with you at this time. Marcel, you are very small, very weak, but I also know that you love me a lot. You are often very sad, is that not so? Your role is simply to write and not to understand, since if you understood everything, it would be impossible for me to quell the feelings of pride that would rise up in your heart.

*Marcel*: Little Jesus, am I, therefore, very proud? It is not surprising, then, that I cannot understand, since you told me that only those who possess genuine humility of heart will be able to understand the words you are addressing to me.

*Jesus*: Little brother, do you really know what it is to be proud? To be proud is to know the truth and not wish to follow it. Now you, Marcel, have you ever denied me, have you ever refused to follow the truth? No; consequently, it cannot be said that you are proud. In fact you only recognize and only follow the truth, which is precisely in what humility consists. Nevertheless, I do not wish you to understand all the words that Love says to you because that is not necessary for you. All the same I have a means which can allow you to understand: this means consists in loving me and in abandoning yourself to me in total confidence. That is what your sister Thérèse has already told you, and that is sufficient. As for the rest, little brother, allow me to deal with it. Enough, my very (429) little brother, you are already too tired; your neck hurts and your hand is hurting too, rest yourself. Besides, the time is almost up. Go and walk a little so as to compose yourself before meditation, If not, you will be very tired and then bearded Jesus will allow you to write no more, which would be a great pity. Follow my will. I am covering you with kisses and pressing you to my heart ...

## 12 April 1946

*Marcel*: Mother, today little Jesus speaks to me no more. I feel very sad. Yesterday, dear Mother, I had an insane wish to laugh. Do you know why? At supper time, during grace before the meal, I saw coming, I do not know from where, my sister Thérèse who tapped me on the shoulder, looked me full in the face with a comical expression, then, laughing, said to me: 'Little brother, so you are anxious? Come then, let me see this sadness which always troubles you so.' Then, grabbing my sighs in one of her hands, she threw them to the ground and said, smiling: 'These careworn sighs are of no use to little Jesus.' And that is all. I so wanted to laugh that it was impossible for me to say my grace.

(430)

My sister Thérèse concentrates a lot on cheering me up. Although she acts quite naturally, it is, nevertheless, very amusing; like the time when she covered one eye just to make me laugh. I am sure that, in the past, she was more mischievous than me and that is the reason why she succeeds in making me happy.

Dear Mother, I love you dearly. I do not know where little Jesus has gone. It is quite probable that, once again, he is sleeping. Mother, I am very sad. I do not know why but, humanly speaking, I do not wish to remain in the Congregation. On the other hand, I do not wish, either, to return to my human mother. All I wish is to be freed from my anxiety. Dear Mother, you who are my true Mother, graciously take pity on me. I love you dearly.

*Mary*: My little one, do you love me? Today, the feast of my Seven Sorrows, have you done anything to console me?

*Marcel*: My Mother, I love you lots, lots. I love you also with all the love that little Jesus and my sister Thérèse love you. To comfort you all I can say to you is: 'Dear Mother, I love you dearly'; nothing else. I pray to you dear Mother to have pity on my country, Vietnam, and also on France. I pray you above all to have pity on the Vietnamese communists; they are very bad, dear Mother. They have no love for Jesus and, furthermore, they do not recognize you as their Mother. Mother, be,

(431)

therefore, their Mother, to lead them to our heavenly Father. I am availing myself of the occasion to offer to you the apostles of the Love of Jesus and your own apostles. Graciously take your children under your protection, for the greater good of Holy Church.

Today, I feel a lot of disgust, but I offer this sacrifice to you. Mother, have pity on me. As I love you three times more than little Jesus, you must also love me more, since you are my mother. Whatever I say, however, I always love little Jesus more than I love you. I still love you more than you love little Jesus ... But, from whatever angle I ask the question, it is little Jesus that I love the more. So, what is there to do now? ... I also know that you dearly love little Jesus, that all the love of your heart points to him. So, I am taking all the love of my heart, with all the love of Jesus and of my sister Thérèse, to love you, dear Mother. Then, because you love Jesus, it follows that all which belongs to Love, returns to Love, so that it does not lose any of it anywhere.

Concerning my favourite saints, it is Saint Thérèse's manner of loving (432) which pleases me the most. It is also to her that I prefer to unite myself to love you, since she does not like to show her love to you as a Queen, but solely as the Mammy of the family. Dear Mother, I, also, am animated by the same spirit. My feelings towards you are those of a child towards his Mother and I have had these feelings since the moment when I first had the happiness to know you. Yes, since the time that I began to know you, I have only called you my true Mother, not wishing, as you well know, to give you any other title.

O Mother, what happiness! Later, in heaven, I will give you only the name of Mother and, you, you will give me only the name of child ... I am stopping here. I have no more to say to you. Now it's your turn to speak.

*Mary*: That's enough, my child, you are tired already. I am kissing you. Stay seated without doing anything. I have much compassion for you; I do not at all wish to tire you any more, you are tired enough, you are incapable of writing. Go and rest. Or again, if you wish to read, you can do so. I am kissing you. Little Jesus does not cease looking at you. Love him well. I bless you. Go in peace.

## 13 April 1946

*Marcel*: Little Jesus, so you are not speaking to me any more? Are you angry with me? But who could be angry? Love does not know how to be angry. Little Jesus, are you content now only to say a few words to me now and then just to please me? Although you speak seldom, I am (433) not, sad; it is probably for love of me that you keep silent in this way. Is that not so, little Jesus?

Now, little Jesus, allow me to ask you a question. Why, in the Gospel, do you make such terrible threats against those who scandalize children? If I remember correctly, it is perhaps the only place in the Gospel where you allow such threats to be heard.

*Jesus*: Little brother, you do not understand why it is so? I am going to explain it to you. The only difference between the souls of children and the angels in heaven is that the souls of children are united to a body and so, consequently, they have natural defects. But, in spite of that, a child's soul is pure like that of the angels in heaven. Because of that children always possess in themselves the Trinity and continually taste natural joys that the Trinity lavish on them ...

(434) There is no need for me to expand on this subject; I will simply say that the soul of a child is a perfectly pure temple inhabited by the Holy Trinity. That is why whoever scandalizes one of these little ones gives a sign to the devil, inviting him to come with sin to soil the soul of this child. He who acts in this way takes a magnificent temple from the Trinity; he takes away from the saints a place where they could praise the Trinity; he exposes the soul of this child to the loss of its innocence. It is for these reasons that I utter such serious threats against the scandalous who insult the Blessed Trinity in a manner which could not be more outrageous. Marcel, even the devils and the damned in hell cannot cause such outrage to the Trinity ... For him death would be preferable to scandal. Before the gaze of God the Father, the soul of this child loses the natural beauty that it received from him because the seal of sin has been imprinted on it. In its relations with God the Son, the soul of this child can no longer clearly see the true light; it no longer clearly sees its divine Spouse, since sin has left its imprint in its pure and innocent heart. As for the Holy Spirit, it can no longer freely give to this soul the kisses of Love. So, therefore, in its relations with this soul, the Trinity find themselves prevented from acting in total freedom as before. Marcel, is that not a fearsome obstacle? ...

(435) A thousand misfortunes to the world because of scandal! How many pure souls have been corrupted because of it. The world is blind to the fact that it has destroyed nearly all the temples of the Trinity in all their splendour ... Little brother, time is up. I am giving you a kiss and with it peace.

Marcel, listen to what I am saying to you. The world is very stupid. When the hearts of children have become like a temple where the goodness of the Trinity dwells here below, goodness, which has the power to draw to the world the benevolent glance of the Trinity, the world works to destroy these temples of divine goodness and make them disappear because of scandal.

O world, without Love, you would already be destroyed and reduced to cinders ... O world, God now wishes to transform you by way of Love; you must live in Love ... However, to accomplish that, many prayers will be necessary, since the world still rebels against Love.

Little brother, tomorrow, the anniversary of my entry into Jerusalem, what do you intend to do to welcome me into your soul? Besides, it is also the day when you must pray for the spread of the reign of my Love in the world. What intention are you going to pray for? Come, tell me, so that I know in advance. Quickly, little brother, be obedient.

*Marcel*: Concerning your reception, my Mother and my sister Thérèse (436) are there to attend to it. As for me, all I will be able to do will be to hold the Palm of Love and wave it before you to make you rejoice. In my prayers I am going to ask that everyone in the universe may always be disposed to welcome the Love that you lavish on their souls. I am going to ask that the reign of your Love spreads freely in the hearts of all men ... Little Jesus, that is all that I remember. If there is still something missing, I beg you to provide it for me.

*Jesus*: Very good, little brother, do as you have said. See, little brother, the bosom of our Mother Mary is always like the little donkey on which we are mounted, both of us, to bear witness to our mutual love. Together from this world to heaven we will have only this gentle mount. Marcel, without doubt Mary will have a strong urge to laugh on hearing us say that her bosom is the back of the little donkey on which we have both climbed. Sister Thérèse will have to come to meet us; what incomparable happiness! However, little brother do not be sad. If you are sad, tomorrow's triumphant reception will no longer be joyful. Therefore be joyful. Do you hear? Recently it seems that you are more tired than sad. However, you have nothing to fear: normally during this season one is easily fatigued. I still love you dearly and on Mary's breast I clasp you closely in my arms. Never be sad, do you hear? (437)

*Marcel*: Little Jesus, today as a penance I had to carry a stone on my neck in the refectory, but I have not been thrown into the sea. On thinking of that I felt like laughing and, if I had been thrown into the sea, I would have laughed even more ...

The other day, my sister Thérèse prompted a mad desire to laugh; but I have already mentioned it to my Mother Mary. Yesterday, little Jesus, why did you not speak to me?

***Jesus***: I did not dare speak to you because I was afraid of troubling you even more ... It is really painful to upset you so easily and for nothing. I see that today it is over and, now, it is not necessary to begin it again. Do not worry any more, ever. And if you ever feel yourself troubled, go and tell it without delay to bearded Jesus. If you do this, you will please me

***Marcel***: I do not understand why, I wish not to be troubled yet I always am. Yesterday, Jesus with the ginger beard repeated to me what he had said the other day: 'When one has Mary for a true Mother, it is not appropriate to worry.' And after having heard these words my anxiety dissolved. Little Jesus, at such times, are you pleased with me?

(438) ***Jesus***: Yes, I am always pleased with you, because whatever concerns you in no way offends me. However I have one fear; it is that if you worry excessively, you will end up being angry, even with me, which would be very dangerous. That is why I tell you that it is not appropriate to trouble yourself. Besides, everybody repeats the same thing to you: your Mother Mary, your sister Thérèse and, if Saint Alphonsus spoke to you, he would only tell you not to worry, since it is a useless thing to do and often even harmful. That is enough, little brother, go and rest; the time is up.

***Marcel***: Dear Mother, this is what little Jesus said to me: 'Marcel, try to prick yourself a little with this needle to see if it hurts.' I was then busy darning socks. In spite of Jesus' words, I did not do anything for fear of hurting myself too much. I was a little sad at that particular moment and little Jesus said that to me to make me laugh.

My dear Mother Mary, I love you dearly. Now that little Jesus is giving me absolutely nothing to write, I am very pleased, since it gives me a little time to express on this paper the feelings of my heart. Dear Mary, you are really my true Mother. I love you a lot, so much that it is impossible for me to express all my love, since, in this world, time passes very quickly. It is only in heaven that I will have enough time to express (439) my feelings ... Mary, I love you and you are well aware of it since you know all my feelings concerning you, and even my smallest actions in their minutest details. In fact I do nothing without relying on your help. Be it a sigh of love for little Jesus, or a simple glance in his direction, I must always count on your aid. Mother, since you are my true Mother, you know that I am only a delicate child with all its weakness, this little one who can only offer to his Mother the guilelessness of his glance.

Yes, dear Mother, such is truly the state of my soul; but I do not concern myself. It is you alone who must deal with it in my place. I have just had this thought; even if I happened to commit a sin, but without knowing that it was a sin, I am convinced that any mother, other than you, would say to me: 'You have offended God.' However, dear Mother, I have never heard you speak like that ... But what have I just said? It's very strange; I am far too scrupulous. But, dear Mary, you understand your little one, I do not doubt. Dear Mother, what happiness it is for me to rest on your heart. Alas, this happiness is coming to an end; time is almost up.

My dear Mother, I love you and I am giving you a kiss and, in order to kiss you, I have no need to lift my head; you incline yourself to the level of my lips and I place my kiss on your sweet face, there where you yourself place my lips ... O Mary, I love you. Deign to bless me and (440) prepare my heart so that, tomorrow, together we may greet little Jesus when he comes to me. Mother, whatever you have that is most beautiful, offer it to little Jesus and say it's from me, and then he will be pleased to accept it. But, if you say it's yours he will not be happy to accept it.

It's really strange, this pen leads my hand unceasingly so that I feel no tiredness in writing. I am stopping here. Time has passed quickly dear Mother. I am saying goodbye to you on this paper.

## 14 April 1946
### *Palm Sunday*

***Marcel***: Little Jesus, I am very tired and I don't wish to write any more. And because of my extreme fatigue my hand is shaking a lot, Today, after returning from Mass, I had to go and work straight away; that is why I am very tired and have no further wish to write down your words, little Jesus. Are you happy, nevertheless? I really would like to write but since I am too tired I can hardly hold my pen.

***Jesus***: Marcel, are you very tired? All right, that's enough, try to rest. I love you dearly little brother and I gladly allow you to rest. You will write again when you wish to do so. However, although tired, do not be sad, agreed? Little brother, you are very sensitive; the slightest vexation causes you suffering. Offer all of it to me. If you suffer in this way it is because of your weakness; do not trouble yourself about it, since it does not offend me in any way. That's enough, take a rest. I am kissing you and I do not cease to hold you tightly in my arms, (441) on Mary's bosom.

*Marcel*: Little Jesus, I still feel tired, but at present my hand no longer shakes. If you want to dictate something to me I am able to write.

Now, let me tell you about this morning's ceremony, all right? As I sat in the last place in the choir, I was very close to the communion bench, so that everybody could see me. Little Jesus, you know my temperament very well: when I am alone with you I feel more at ease; but if others look at me, I become self-conscious. I was, therefore very upset. It is possible that no one paid any attention to me; nevertheless I am naturally shy and, in such circumstances, I feel very uncomfortable. But I did not wish to change my place, since it was your will that I should stay in the same place during all of Holy Week.

Truly, little Jesus, when I find myself under everyone's gaze, I always feel afraid and ashamed while when I am alone and you are looking at me, I feel free, joyful, and I can act naturally. It seems, therefore, dear Jesus, that the gaze of the world is more severe than the gaze of your Love. Is that not true?

(442) *Jesus*: Marcel, why do you say that the gaze of my Love is severe? It is not correct to speak in this way. It is because you do not understand what you are saying that you have made this mistake. You should say: the gaze of Love is infinitely good and just. There is a difference between just and severe. It is never correct to say that God is infinitely severe. You should only say that he is infinitely just. Why so, little brother? Here is the reason: it is because Love is infinitely just that your works, even the smallest, have a value in the eyes of the Trinity. If, on the contrary, one says that Love is severe, it could be taken to mean that Love will make use of the good works accomplished by souls to punish them, since man's good works are far from being beautiful in the eyes of Love. So you have forgotten already what your sister Thérèse taught you? However, you read it the other day, do you remember?

But I see today that you are very tired? That's enough, rest now. I don't want you to tire yourself out. I accept your good will; sacrifice cheerfully your wish to write for me. By that you will accomplish a work much more useful for souls than the words would be that you wish to

(443) write for them, since you know that there is no lesson so beautiful as that of always pleasing me.

I am kissing you. Go now and brush your teeth, wash your face, comb your hair carefully and then prepare yourself for the collation. Eat well, joyfully, so that I will be pleased with you. But, little brother, why do you want to cry. Enough, it's because you are tired, and on hearing me show you my Love in a natural fashion, your weakness makes you cry. Little brother, give me a kiss. Your Mother Mary and your sister Thérèse love you always. Little brother, go in peace.

## 15 April 1946

*Marcel*: Little Jesus, I am less tired today. It is now possible for me to write. Yesterday I had a pain in my neck and I was tired; that is why it was difficult to write.

*Jesus*: Little brother, you are still tired; I do not want you to write. Or, if you do write you must write only a little. Continue to listen and speak to me, but it is not necessary that you write, since I wish it so. Yesterday did you eat with an appetite?

*Marcel*: Yesterday I had no appetite at all and this morning it was the same; I had to leave some of my lunch because I could not eat any more.

*Jesus*: Little brother, rest yourself. If Mary knows that you are tired and that you must still write for me, she will certainly scold me and then, I'll be in trouble! That's enough, rest now. Write from time to time a little sentence or two, that's not important; but to stay seated all the time will add to your tiredness so that Mary will not be happy nor will bearded Jesus. You must, therefore, do my will. In doing so, all will be for the best and by that you will give me proof of a greater love. Come, little brother, give me a nice smile, put your pen down and be happy to listen and to converse with me. Even if you do not wish to write, I am going to converse with you. Enough, little brother ... (444)

*Marcel*: Today, little Jesus, I again ate rice with fish but the fish was full of bones. It was only after having spent much time picking them out that I was able to eat. Little Jesus, I love you a lot. I read in your Gospel a passage where you say: 'If you have faith the size of a grain of mustard, you will say to this mountain: move from here to there and it will move itself ... '* Little Jesus, on that score, I certainly have faith as big as a fist, since without being able to move mountains, I have, however, the power to move even my Father in heaven. My faith is, without doubt, very great to be able to work such a marvel. Is it not, little Jesus?

*Jesus*: Little brother, what you say is quite correct, but one must understand that the words that I have addressed to men do not apply to material things but solely to spiritual ones. In this text I intend to say

---

\* Matthew 17, 20.

(445) that if anyone really has confidence in Love, he will obtain from it all he wishes. As for you, little brother, you no longer have faith, since your faith is already totally encapsulated in Love. Because you see and truly understand Love, it is as if you no longer live in faith. Although, outwardly, you must still make use of faith, however, this faith is already lost in the Holy Spirit who is Love. Now, as the Holy Spirit is one with the Father and the Son, consequently your faith is already immersed with you in the depths of Love. The flame of Love which envelops you completely, in the same way, envelops everything which is of you. If this sentence appears difficult for you to understand, do not worry about it, your director will help you to understand more clearly.

*Marcel*: It is not surprising that I have heard people say that Father Mateo said: 'I have the virtue of faith no longer, because all divine things are already present before my eyes.' I am beginning to understand that it really is so ... Consequently, little Jesus, he who gave himself to Love no longer has the virtue of faith?

(446) *Jesus*: Precisely. Let me give you an example. A little child knows that his parents love him a lot. This knowledge is faith for him. He firmly believes in the love of his parents, and this faith leads him to abandon himself entirely to them. You see clearly by that that after having abandoned himself to his parents, the child has no further need to believe in his heart, since the faith that he has in his parents finds itself incorporated in the word 'abandon'. Do you understand that, little brother? It is not necessary for you to concentrate on the above; if you do not understand completely, bearded Jesus will help you understand better.

Now, listen, I am continuing on the same topic. As a consequence, this child has no more need to believe; all that remains for him is to love his parents with all his heart. It is the same for you. Although you have to live in this land of exile, you already have a foretaste of heaven, so that your faith diminishes little by little, while your love grows day by day. It is understood that, outwardly, you must still, at certain times, really make use of the faith, because there are many things that you do not yet possess. However, as I said to you earlier, this faith is lost in the Holy Spirit who is Love, so that even if you must make use of it, in fact, you are not making use of it. You are tired, little brother; you do not have to concentrate so hard ... Very good. Keep your mind entirely free; and if I happen to say something erroneous, bearded Jesus will let you know. Don't worry. You are already very tired, stop there and go and rest. I am giving you a kiss and I am always pleased with you.

*Marcel*: Little Jesus, a short while ago I had to have a tooth extracted.

Brother Alexander performed the operation. It caused me less pain than wearing the small chain, although blood flowed abundantly. I do not miss that tooth at all!

*Jesus*: So, you had a tooth extracted? That's very good. Your mouth is now a little bit prettier ... Little brother, interior pains that I send you also have the effect of embellishing your soul more each day. The advantages that you gain from each sigh which accompanies these interior pains are numerous. By that you please me and you acquire a new beauty ... etc., etc. If I had to enumerate all of these advantages, I do not know how many tens of millions of the word 'and' I would have to use to reach the end. Even a thousand volumes would not suffice to contain all of them. Let it be enough for you to know that to each sigh that you offer to my Love in suffering, I add an incalculable number of these conjunctions 'and' to express the advantages that you gain from them. (447)

*Marcel*: I remember that during my childhood, before this tooth appeared, I sang very well; but since I have had this tooth, my voice has become very bad. Now that it has been pulled out, I do not know if I have recovered my beautiful voice. Let me sing in order to see.

Little Jesus, I love you a great deal. My little Jesus, if I am tired, it is perhaps because you give me too many kisses. I am still joyful and, during this Holy Week, I receive, like every year, many consolations. It is truly strange: when you are in sorrow, how is it that you give me joy?

*Jesus*: Little brother, it is very interesting to hear you. You understand nothing of this? I will explain it to you. A lover of flowers seeks every means to cultivate his flowers carefully, so they will be more fresh and beautiful, so he can gaze on them afterwards to comfort himself in moments of sadness. With you, my little flower, I act in the same way. I must, first of all, give you freshness and beauty, to find subsequently, in contemplating you, a comfort for my heart. It is solely for this reason that I give you delights, and you did not know it ... Little brother, since you are joyful, continue to be so and, the more you are, the more you will console the lover of flowers ... But, little brother, to comfort me at this time, you must stop writing, since you are already tired ... That's enough! ... If not, Mary will scold us and that won't be pleasant for us. Come, little brother, that's enough, it is time. Quickly! Quickly little brother. It is very tiresome. I am giving you a kiss. (448)

## 16 April 1946

(449) *Marcel*: Little Jesus, there is one thing that I would really like to tell you, but I'm afraid that bearded Jesus might get to know. So! Why did I write that? I have forgotten. But, it's not important, bearded Jesus can know it also. Besides, he certainly understands that I never hide from him the slightest thing ... Little Jesus, I have already spoken to you this morning about this business, not wishing to put it into writing for fear of being very ashamed; but since you wish that I write these things down, I am doing so. This shows that I have shown more respect for you than you have for me.

It's the matter of my soutane. I detest it a lot. The collar is too small and once I've hooked it, if I cough a little, it squeezes my neck which hurts my epiglottis. This soutane itself is too tight-fitting; the sleeves are short and too tight, leaving the cuffs open. The pockets are at waist level and when I want to take out my handkerchief, I have to lift up my hand very high to put it into my pockets which are, also, too small. It is true that it is a new soutane, but I do not like it at all. If I have to wear this soutane when summer comes, I will certainly find it very unpleasant. When I am in my room, I must unhook the collar, but outside my room, it is necessary that I close it and I find that very painful.

I have asked to have it altered but bearded Jesus has not allowed it. I am, nevertheless, very content since I know by that it is your will. Little Jesus help me to wear this soutane cheerfully. But frankly, only to look at it is enough to make me sad.

(450) In the past the brother tailors always made fun of my small stature; that is why they made me a little soutane that is much too tight. It was the same with my shirts, which they have cut much too small. At the time only one is left which I never wear. But previously, when it was necessary to change my clothes, it took me up to fifteen minutes to take off my tight shirt. However, I put up with it joyfully. I was far from able to wear all the clothes that the brother tailors gave to me. I was happy to wear them once and then to put them aside. Little Jesus, you can judge by that how hard it was for me.

*Jesus*: Now, now, little brother, why do you complain in such a strange manner? All the things you have just listed are only opportunities to renounce your self-will a little. You blame this one and that one, but, in reality, you should blame it on your small size. It is because you have grown that this new soutane, which formerly suited you well, has now become too small. Continue, therefore, to wear it cheerfully, even if it is a little difficult. Offer these sacrifices to me, since, for me, they are real caresses and a comfort for my heart. Little brother, be patient, will you? And be so until the day when it will please me to let you wear another new soutane. Besides, by that you will show that you possess the real spirit of poverty. And, if you are truly poor, you already possess your share of the heavenly inheritance. What more could you wish for?

As I said to you yesterday, all the sighs from your little sacrifices accepted with love for me, and offered to me, earn for you innumerable benefits ... Yes, all the better, if you have something to suffer. Offer it all to me, and as soon as you offer it to me cheerfully I will place a kiss on your forehead. Is that not happiness for you? If you had known that earlier, certainly you would not have complained as you just did. However, little brother, you are allowed to say these things to me but you may not complain to anyone else, since 'Love alone is the master of your heart'. Do you remember, little brother, this lesson that your sister Thérèse taught you some time ago? Try to remember it. (451)

*Marcel*: Little Jesus, I love you a lot. Today, I no longer feel tired. I have a really good appetite. A short while ago I had a stomachache which made me even forget the words; and if you had not repeated them to me earlier, I would not have been able to write them. Some time ago, seeing that Brother Augustine's soutane was too long and dragged along the ground, I said to him in a kindly manner: 'Your soutane is too long, it is unsightly. If you wish, ask Brother John Baptist if I can alter it for you ...' But Brother Augustine was displeased with my words. He had just received this new soutane, but because the tailor, Brother John Baptist had not cut the bottom straight, it is nevertheless too long. Brother Augustine maintains that it is just the right length, whereas, in fact, it is too long by as much as the length of a finger. Everyone advises him to get it shortened but he continues to act annoyed. Regarding this, little Jesus, have I done well to speak in this way? (452)

*Jesus*: Yes, you have done very well since you spoke simply by charity. However you should not repeat the same thing many times, since the Brother might then think that you acted in that way not through charity but to make fun of him. It is enough to mention it just once. If the Brother wishes, he will do as you say; but if he wishes to act otherwise, you cannot force him to do your will. And if you find it a bit painful to look at, all you can do is to speak of it to bearded Jesus. Will you remember? Instinctively, Brother Augustine does not like you very much, however, that is more useful to you than all the little treats that I could shower you with. If I speak to you in this way, it is not necessary to hesitate to receive my little treats, since if you truly love me, you will gladly welcome all that comes to you from my hand. Everything I send to you is useful, but there are some among them which are better than others.

(453) Another piece of advice I am giving you is that you must never assume that that Brother holds a grudge against you. You must always assume that he acts in this way because of his natural temperament and that, in a spirit of charity he never stops considering you as his little brother. As far as knowing if he detests or likes you, it is sufficient that I alone know it. You have no need to know.

Little brother, it is nearly time for the siesta. I am kissing you. Although you say that you are no longer tired, nevertheless, you still are and you cannot write for a long time. That's enough, Try to behave in accordance with my will.

Little brother! What is it that makes you so sad? Come now, remain peaceful. Don't fret, fearing that you have followed your own will. It was your business to speak to me about the soutane. I have heard you and bearded Jesus must also be brought up to date on the subject but do not be afraid that others will hear of it. But concerning the repairing of the soutane, that depends, not on you but on me. It is because I wished to favour you that bearded Jesus told you to get it altered. Stay calm. If after that you were to appear sad, bearded Jesus would be even more sad since he thought he was making you happy in indulging you like that. If he sees that you are still sad, he will no longer know what to do, unless he gets you to make a new soutane. Ah! I see you are smiling. Very good. If this soutane, once altered, is still too small, you will

(454) certainly have one made to measure. What more can one do? So, try to smile a little so that I can see. Good. There you are, well behaved at last. That is the way I like you. If you were always sad, who would want to look at you? ...

Little brother, love me well. You must pray today for sinners, you must not forget them. In you I can find joy but in how many other places do men treat me badly and outrage me, as, long ago, the Jews did, trying all sorts of ways to harm me; and I am reduced to looking for refuge in the souls which love me. There I find many consolations since the least sigh, the slightest gesture helps to please and comfort me ... however, little brother, try to calculate to see how numerous these souls are. There are truly very few of them, but to comfort you I am telling you that the greater number of these souls which love me are the souls of children who have remained pure. Is that not a source of happiness for you? Men pour scorn on children and, nevertheless, there are among them many things that comfort me ... Therefore, little

(455) brother, pray and suffer so that sinners repent and learn to love me. Enough, little brother, you are already a little tired; I do not wish you to tire yourself more. Rest for a while and then you will go and make

your visit to the Blessed Sacrament with the brethren. Come, little brother, let us recite together this homage to Mary: 'dear Mother, we love you dearly' . . .

## 17 April 1946

*Marcel*: Little Jesus, does the devil have faith? In my opinion it is because he believes that he asks such or such a thing of you. Is that so, little Jesus? I would like you to explain it to me.

*Jesus*: Little brother, I will grant your wish. Naturally, the devil has no need to believe, since he already sees all the things necessary for him to believe. He knows the truth, but he does not wish to follow it. You wish, then, to know why, when the devil asks me such or such a thing, I grant him what he asks for? Do you understand the reason? Listen carefully, then. The reason is that if I did not grant him what he asks for, I would show that I am not just. The devil knows well that God is always ready to grant to one who prays to him all the graces that he asks for. Consequently, he also knows that God, in his goodness, still awaits this humility of heart from him, which would obtain for him the benevolence of the divinity. But because the devil is too proud, while knowing well that he would be able to obtain this favour, he does not ask for it. There is another thing that you must know; it is that all the requests made to God by the devil have for their object bad things, never good ones. Consequently, when God the Father allows him something, it is (456) not a favour that he is granting to him but simply a permission to do something, which will redound to the glory of God. The devil believes but he does not act in conformity with what he believes, so that one cannot say that he has the virtue of faith. All one can say is that he knows clearly what men must believe, but without wishing to conform to it himself . . . But I do not wish to expand more on this question since you are not a student of theology. My sole intention is to make you understand that the devil knows the truth but does not wish to follow it.

Little brother, do not be sad. That you understand what I have said is enough. As for the permission that God gives to the devil to do one or other bad thing, it is not with the intention to harm someone that he gives it, but simply so that it contributes to his glory. Naturally, the devil does not like the Holy Trinity, his only desire is to find the means of outraging it. However, whatever he does, the power he has to act remains in the hands of the Blessed Trinity. Also, although externally, the work he does is bad, in reality, it can only contribute to the glory of the Trinity.

*Marcel*: A moment ago, while drying the washing, I felt such an acute pain in my heart that I dared no longer lift my hand, especially my left hand, to stretch out the linen. Actually, I still feel a little pain and I am very tired.

*Jesus*: Little brother, offer it all to me and go and speak of it to bearded Jesus. Go straight away.

*Marcel*: This year, little Jesus, I am not going to serve Mass at the Carmel. I remember that last year I really felt like laughing and I said to myself: if I had succeeded in becoming a Carmelite, no one would have known that I was a man. In fact, last year I said the prayers with the sisters and my voice blended so well with theirs that no one knew that it was I who was reciting the prayers. That is why, after Mass, the brothers said to each other: 'There was certainly a sister outside the grill, because the voice of a sister was heard clearly on the outside reciting the prayers.' No one could guess; I was the only one who knew who was saying the prayers on the other side; and this question of my brothers made me want to laugh. It is only later that they learned the truth and they found it strange that my voice was so similar to the sisters. This year, little Jesus, my voice has broken, but if I imitated the voice of the sisters, no one would be able to tell.

*Jesus*: Like you, little brother, my experience was the same; the more I grew, the more, also, my voice changed too. But, concerning you, little brother, if you had entered Carmel I would certainly not have loved you as much as I love you now, since you would not have had the strength to put up with the austerities of the Carmel.

*Marcel*: So, I am very weak then?

*Jesus*: One could not be more so. This morning, for example, you had not been wearing your discipline for two hours when you were already pulling a face and you could no longer walk. If, after that, you asked to enter Carmel, how could you put up with it, since the Carmelites impose on themselves more external mortifications than are imposed in the Congregation of the Redemptorists.

*Marcel*: However my sister Saint Thérèse who was able to put up with it, never stops saying that she is weak. What, then, can be said of my own weakness?

***Jesus***: Little brother, I have already spoken to you on that point, but you have a very short memory. Physically, your sister Thérèse was stronger than you; but spiritually, in regards to Love, who is not weak? It is true that physical strength can help with enduring sufferings with a little more joy; but my Love knows how to choose crosses which are suitable for each soul, because if I sent the same trials to all souls, I would certainly not have a single one as spouse. Do you understand, little brother?

***Marcel***: Little Jesus, at one time I really would have liked to enter Carmel, but one thing frightened me; it was to have to wear a brown habit. I do not at all like to wear clothes of that colour. I remember when I was small, my mother, one day, made me a very nice pair of brown trousers that I went and tore up immediately; I only liked to wear white clothes and my mother had to bend to my whim. (459)

When I was still a postulant, Brother John Baptist gave me a brown shirt that I did not at all like; and because I was ashamed, I waited two or three weeks before daring to wear it. Afterwards my sister said to me to make me laugh: 'Dear brother, you resemble me a lot. I also had to wear a brown habit; but now it is you too who must wear one. Truly, you resemble me a lot ... Yes, evidently we must both resemble each other.' That is all she said to me and I felt like laughing. I made an effort to wear that shirt sometimes and, once used to it, I no longer wished to change it for another and I continued to wear it until my entry into the novitiate. Actually, I do not know if it still exists. My sister Thérèse is very skilful at joking with me. It is enough for her to say something amusing to me to make me wish for things that I did not want.

*I have witnessed this very simple fact.*

***Jesus***: Little one, you are already tired. That's enough, go and rest, I am giving you a kiss. Rest yourself, otherwise you will be too tired and our Mother will not be pleased.

***Marcel***: My dear Mother Mary, today little Jesus has not given me any collation; and, a short time ago, he did not cease asking my forgiveness. I forgave him gladly, without giving him any penance. We only laughed together and expressed our love for each other. Our mutual relations could not be more attractive and, in my opinion, even if in heaven there were only little Jesus and me, that would be enough to make you joyful. What can be said, then, of your happiness since there will also be in heaven the true Father with all the saints. Dear Mother, I love you a lot, (460) but it is only in heaven that I will be able to show you my love externally.

Dear Mother I heard bearded Jesus say yesterday that the French military had to fight against the Chinese soldiers and I saw my sister Thérèse complain, saying that it should not be possible for the French to show such imprudence. 'Such imprudence,' she said, 'should not be encountered among the French.' What does that mean, dear Mother? I saw that my sister Thérèse was very saddened by this business.

(461) *Mary*: My child, you are very sweet; I am going to answer you. But only in a few words. When such incidents happen, normally that hurts the good reputation of the country that Jesus loves with a special love. You do not understand these words now but later you will understand them. For the time being, continue to pray a lot for France, but it is also necessary that you pray that each French person understands that his country enjoys the special protection of the Love of Jesus ...

A short while ago little Jesus did not give you any collation; are you hungry now? Try to be patient until Easter; I will then tell little Jesus to compensate you. It is very hard for you to be hungry and not be able to eat. But, my dear little one, it is the Love of Jesus who sends you this sacrifice, and by that you have done two things pleasing to his heart: first you have accepted this sacrifice because it is Jesus' will, then you have actually deprived yourself of food. Thanks to this sacrifice, how many souls have you gained for Jesus! On their part, these souls will certainly not forget you; in return, each one of them will obtain for you from me many consolations, so that your sufferings will be changed into a deep joy.

(462) *Marcel*: I said to little Jesus, a short while ago: 'Little Jesus, if the Redemptorist sisters knew how you treat me, it is certain that they would not dare to come to Vietnam for quite a while, fearing that, once here, you might sometimes forget them and leave them to die from hunger.' This is what little Jesus replied to me: 'If that happened and the sisters are happy to die of hunger for my Love, it would be very good ... ' And we both laughed.

Little Jesus added: 'If I forgot the sisters, their father Saint Alphonsus would be able to look after them in my place.' I replied: 'My father Saint Alphonsus is already old, his back is bent and he easily forgets so that it would be much more of a risk for them. So, I will no longer pray that the sisters come to Vietnam, for fear that they die of hunger and that the foundation does not get off the ground ...'

Little Jesus said to me, smiling: 'It is only with you that I am inclined to forget, not with the sisters.' And we laughed again. However, I did not dare laugh too loudly for fear that the others might notice.

*Mary*: That's enough for now, my child, the time is up. See you soon.

## 18 April 1946
*Holy Thursday*

*Marcel*: Dear Mother, your reply of yesterday disturbed me a lot since the French have not fought with the Chinese.

*Mary*: It is very unfortunate, my child. Don't tell me you have been troubled about this since yesterday? It's really bad for you. However I can relieve you of your anxiety about this business. Who told you to scrutinize my words? That's where your trouble comes from. I had, however, told you that you did not understand; so, why worry to no purpose? Yesterday I was not alluding particularly to the incident that you recounted; I said, simply, 'Incidents of this nature'. Then do you remember the question you posed to your sister Thérèse? Now, in her reply, did she complain that the French had lacked prudence? In this affair in particular? ... No. She simply replied in general, saying: 'acts of imprudence, the lack of prudence ...' So, whether, in having fun or from prejudice, that is, for the French, a type of imprudence which should not happen if they wish to do good ... (463)

You should know however that usually, people relate incidents much differently from how they happen in reality ... That is all I am able to tell you. Now, have you stopped worrying? Come, tell me you love me. Has little Jesus spoken to you since this morning?

*Marcel*: Dear Mother, I am disturbed no longer and I remain tranquil, since bearded Jesus who understands the complaint of my sister Thérèse and your words of yesterday is always there. But, Mother, why do you speak to me figuratively? You said that I would understand later ...

*Mary*: My child, don't think that you understand, and then say that I am speaking figuratively. If you were able to understand, you would not trouble yourself uselessly.

*Marcel*: I feel a little tired today, Mother. Little Jesus spoke to me and he kissed me. He loves me a lot and he doesn't want me to be angry.

*Jesus*: Yesterday, Mother, this is what Marcel said to me: 'Little Jesus, is your heart broken? If you are heartbroken I am going to make you take

(464) some medicine.' This was my reply: 'To soothe the sadness of my heart, there is no remedy comparable to the sighs of love. But this remedy is very rare in this world, so it is necessary to put up with much pain in order to find it.' I then questioned Marcel, but all he could do was laugh. Finally, we gave each other kisses ... Oh, what deep peace we taste at your breast. Mary, love us both dearly, your little Jesus and your little Marcel.

*Marcel*: Little Jesus, tell me, do I love you? Yesterday, seeing that I had a heart ache, I suspected that it was you who gave me too many kisses. It's a strange thing. I am truly very weak.

Ah! Time is already up. I must go and assist at Mass. Little Jesus, give me the pleasure of coming to me at the moment of communion.

See, little Jesus, I am putting my remedies under your feet (*a picture of the Child Jesus placed on the table*); if a pill disappears, I shall accuse you of secretly taking it and oblige you to put it back. It is true that you also suffer from heart ache, but you have my sighs of love as a remedy. As for the medicines here, they are mine.

*Jesus*: Look, little brother, you take two pills each day; now a pill, necessarily, must disappear. If after that, you dare throw the blame on me, it will be a false accusation against me ... So, little brother smile a little; (465) come on, smile ... Good, there you are, at last well behaved.

Little brother, be pleased to suffer for my love. It is all I am telling you. Be content. Never be sad at having to suffer ...

*Marcel*: Little Jesus, a moment ago you were mistaken. I only take one pill a day and you said two, so I had to ask bearded Jesus. Why did you make this mistake? I believed you better informed than him.

*Jesus*: Little brother, I am challenging you, all right? Yes, I challenge you to tell me if it is I who was mistaken or you in writing carelessly. If you did not commit a mistake in writing I would never see you erase or cross out a word in this exercise book. Now, how many times have you obliged me to repeat what I was saying to you? A while ago I correctly said *one*, but you maintained that it was *two* ... After that you still dare reproach me. It is a real shame for you, Marcel. It would have been better to admit that you had written carelessly, and you would have avoided this humiliation. That's enough; from now on you must correct yourself.

Little brother, do you feel very bad? When you are sad, you must tell me immediately so I may receive your suffering. But, however intense this suffering may be, it cannot be compared to mine, since my heart was pierced by the spear. Little brother, offer your suffering to me. It is (466) like a medicine for me which comforts me and pleases me a great deal ... Today, what have you got to comfort me?

**Marcel**: What I have, little Jesus, you already know, I told you this morning. I have nothing of real importance; I have only my poor, loving heart and I offer it to you. I asked Mary to place it under your eyes at the altar of repose in the church, so that there, by its presence, it might make you forget your sadness and you may keep it continuously in this church. Little Jesus, although my heart is not worth a lot, I dare to wish, however, that it be placed today in all the tabernacles of the world where you are present in the Eucharist. It is true that I am expressing here a great wish, but I really believe that you are going to respond to this mad desire in realizing it fully. Besides, I know very well, as you told me, that even by my sighs of love, I can give you a place of rest in me. I am asking you to distribute my sighs of love in all the tabernacles of the world where, today, you are residing. I have not the strength nor the opportunity to go and visit all of these tabernacles: I (467) have only my sighs of love to make these visits in my place. Graciously accept them and grant my wish.

I again feel a little pain in my heart, but I do not think it is serious. I can still write until it is time to finish ... Little Jesus, I love you a great deal. Today, I have no appetite at all; I feel a little tired. Perhaps it is because I have just heard Mass.

**Jesus**: My dear little brother, be happy to suffer for my love. Know this well, Marcel, you no longer belong to yourself, it is to me that you belong. Consequently, all I wish, you must also wish. On the other hand, when you wish something, you have the power to force me to follow your will. Do you understand? Let me explain clearly.

You know your will already belongs to me. This means that your will is already in my heart, that it has really become like my own will. You have no power any longer over this will; consequently, when I wish for something, you must comply.

On the other hand, my will belongs totally to you; it has become your own property, it is your will completely. Consequently, if it wishes anything, it forces your will, which is in me, to follow mine, which is in you. Moreover, you know well that my will never wishes what the world (468) wishes. It is thus that one can call this state of things: exchange of feelings, amicable relations between friends. As I said to you previously, you know also that parents follow the will of their children more than their own will. Why is that? Because parents love their children a great deal and children, for their part, love their parents dearly, the results are that the will of the children is always stronger than the will of the parents. And so, my little one, your true Father in heaven acts, also, in the same way with you. He follows your will more than you follow his, and he does that because he loves you and you, you also love him ...

Why have your brothers and sisters the saints had to suffer? Why do you and the other souls who love me have to suffer also? See, it is not from my will that your sufferings come, but really from yours, which wishes to prove its love to me. Now I know that suffering is the only proof of love. That is why, through condescension, I am sending you suffering, so that you may have something to prove your love for your true Father in heaven.

(469) My little one, now that you have some time, listen, I am going to continue to speak to you on the previous subject.

Marcel, when the heavenly Father sends crosses to you, my little brothers and sisters, it is not his will that he is following, since his will already belongs to you; if he sends you crosses, it is because he follows your will which is in him. Consequently, although externally you will endure suffering because you conform yourself to his will, in reality, it is he who has followed your will. Indeed, since your will belongs to him completely, he makes use of this will in him, to follow his in you.

Do you understand, little brother? It is very unfortunate that you understand absolutely nothing. Never mind, be glad however. It is sufficient that I understand for you. If you are not troubled now, you will have to be on your guard so as not to be troubled later. Bearded Jesus will help you understand. As these things are not for you alone, but they must be communicated to other souls, they will understand, since they are far from being ignorant like you, my little one.

*Marcel*: The other day, when I was speaking to Brother John Baptist I accidentally referred to myself by the word *em*.* As Brother asked me to repair a soutane, I replied to him: 'Your *em* does not know how to do it.' I remember that previously, now and then, I also used the same term and I wanted to laugh.

*Jesus*: And did Brother John Baptist laugh?

(470) *Marcel*: Yes, he laughed, but I am sure he did not understand what I

---

\* The Vietnamese word *em* means 'little brother'. In Vietnamese it is the practice to designate oneself by one's position relative to one's questioner. So, a child in speaking of himself to his parents says: 'your child' (*con*). A younger brother to his elder says: 'your little brother' (*em*); an older brother to his younger says: 'your big brother' (*anh*).

was saying. He often calls me 'baby'.* He likes me a lot and enjoys teasing me; he doesn't want to see me sad. I remember that once I was very angry with him. When I asked him for some medicine, he answered, as usual, 'It is not necessary.' I know he said that as a joke, but afterwards, he forgot completely, so that his: 'It is not necessary' became a reality and I was left with my stomachache. Brother knew how much I loved little Thérèse. So, each time he gave me a holy picture, it was always an image of little Thérèse and I was very pleased. Brother John Baptist has a bent back like my father Saint Alphonsus.

If my little sister knew him, I am sure she would not hesitate to mimic his mannerisms. The other day, seeing Brother eat a tomato in the bathroom, I really wanted to laugh. This brother is truly simple; I like him a lot.

*Jesus*: Little brother you have just used the words *a lot* twice. You said:

1) Brother John Baptist likes me *a lot*.
2) I like him *a lot*.

Now, I want to ask you a question. Do I love you as much as Brother John Baptist? Do I spoil you more than he does? Come on, try to reply, just to see, and do so in such a way as to please me, since I am very jealous.

*Marcel*: Little Jesus, since you ask me this question, I am going to answer. It is true that you love me more than Brother John Baptist, but you have never given me a picture. You spoil me more than he, yes, much more ... There you have my reply, little Jesus. (471)

*Jesus*: So you like Brother John Baptist a lot, but do you love him more than me?

*Marcel*: Little Jesus, following the example of my Mother Mary, I will reply to you as follows: concerning Brother John Baptist, I love him with a compassionate love more than I love you, yourself; but you, little Jesus, you are the only one to possess all my love ... Little Jesus, you are very jealous and for nothing, not being able to tolerate that someone loves me more than you and not wishing either that I love anyone more than you.

---

* This was written in French in Van's text: 'bébé'.

Incidentally, little Jesus, you said a short while ago that my will was in you already. So from now on, I no longer wish to suffer. What do you say to that?

(472) *Jesus*: Fair enough. It is very easy not to wish to suffer, but unfortunately, your will no longer belongs to you. The only right that is yours is to make use of my will, as I have the right to make use of yours. You say you no longer wish to suffer; in speaking this way, you are making use of my will, since I never wish to see you suffer. But, on the other hand, since you wish to prove your love to me, then, it is necessary that you suffer ... Little brother, it is impossible for you to escape Love. That is why I said to you previously: 'It is only through love that I must allow you to endure suffering'. These words are very clear ...

Since Love has gripped you and has enveloped you, you must leave Love completely free in its relations with you. I am one with you, Marcel, as you are but one with me, Jesus; and we rest together in Mary's arms ... Marcel, from now on it will be impossible for you to turn away from Love. Little brother, you will be submerged eternally in the ocean of Love, where you will carry in your wake a great number of souls. What a joy for you, Marcel! Little Thérèse calls you her little brother with good reason and I recognize that it is right to call you so. But, see, you are embarrassed and you are blushing deeply ... Enough. I will no longer speak to you in this way, except in heaven; I will no longer fear to make you blush ...

Marcel! Marcel! Marcel! I am kissing you. Go and rest. Otherwise Mary will not be pleased. That's enough, little brother; renounce your self-will a little. It is worth more to please me than to stay here writing. Do not fear that I shall cease speaking; I am continuing to do so ...

(473) *Marcel*: Dear Mother Mary, today I had to stay on my knees in adoration before the altar of repose for a very long time. As no one came to replace me and as I was very tired, I was obliged to return. For a moment I felt in my heart a little sadness but it ceased immediately. Today, dear Mary, I am receiving many consolations but I ask myself why I am sad. This afternoon, little Jesus once again deprived me of the collation; and he said that he still hopes to see the arrival of the Redemptorist sisters! ... I have never suffered so much from hunger; I had to hang on until supper.

I now have something to ask of Jesus. Dear Mother, you really love me, don't you? A short time ago I found myself in the presence of little Jesus at the same time as the children. I was very happy, thinking myself to be in heaven in the company of the Holy Innocents and wishing to act like a child. However, in the presence of people of this world I lose my natural disposition. I do not know why, in the presence of children, my heart feels joyful, while in the presence of people of the world, I tremble and I feel my limbs freeze. I do not understand why this is; and in spite of all my efforts to act naturally, I never succeed in doing so.

Mother, I am very weak. Truly people cannot make me feel comfortable; there is only Jesus, there is only Love, which can do so. When I am alone in the presence of Love, I feel joyful, radiant; but as soon as I enter into contact with people, I lose all my naturalness. (474)

Dear Mother, I love you. Bearded Jesus has just given me a new exercise book, but I already feel a little tired. Mother, give me a kiss. I love you dearly and I beg you to bless children. Graciously place on their foreheads a sweet kiss and place their lips on little Jesus' brow resting on your breast ... Oh Mother! How happy are they, the children!

Little Jesus, do you want to allow me to fast tomorrow? I really wish to do so, but as my will is already lost in yours, I must again ask your opinion.

*Jesus*: My will is that you do not fast, first of all because you have not reached the age for fasting and then because you are too weak. In fact on normal days when you eat as you wish, when the time for dinner approaches, I see that you sometimes shake all over. However, my spirit still remains with you; do not ask bearded Jesus permission to fast; but if he asks you to do so, you should. To obey him is the best thing. (475)

Little brother, are you tired? Rest yourself. I love you dearly. Offer to me your sadness, your disgust, your sickness and your hunger. I truly ask your forgiveness for having again today deprived you of your collation and allowed you to endure hunger. In spite of that you are not yet dead and you still have the strength to laugh with me. Be patient. Come on, smile a little so I can see ... Good, rest yourself, you are tired. If not, trouble! Mary will scold you. And if bearded Jesus knows that you are too tired, he will forbid you to write.

## 19 April 1946
*Good Friday*

*Marcel*: Little Jesus, I absolutely do not wish to wear socks; I think I have no reason to wear them, since I am only a little cold and I am not at all ill. However, you force me to wear socks all day.

*Jesus*: Why do you complain so? I did not tell you to wear socks because you were ill, but simply to wear them. Consequently, wear them, and wear them through obedience. Is that not a good thing? Wear them, therefore, until I tell you to take them off. If you wear them it will be beneficial for you and beneficial also for others ... Little brother, are you unhappy today?

**Marcel**: A short while ago I was suffering a lot, but now the pain has diminished and is quite bearable. I offer this suffering to you, Jesus.

(476)  Now, little Jesus, I am going to confession. Help me to make it well. In order to spend a joyful Easter, I must have a pure heart ...

Little Jesus, allow me to take off my socks. My feet are now warm; I am no longer afraid of being sick. So, to wear socks makes me stand out too much; none of my brothers wears them. Nevertheless, you still oblige me to wear them. It's very painful. I have a strong desire to take them off, but I fear that you may not be pleased.

**Jesus**: What have you to moan about? You have only one thing to do, to wear your socks until I tell you to take them off. You say that that makes you conspicuous? However, this morning, all your brethren fasted; you alone did not. Doesn't that make your conspicuous? Why not reproach me for that? Alas, little brother, how difficult you are to please. It is necessary for you to wear socks, I wish it to be so ... Little brother, do you have a good appetite today? Come on, tell me.

**Marcel**: I have had no appetite at all for the past few days and now, I feel sick once again. However the suffering is slight and bearable.

Little Jesus, it is warm now, allow me to take off my socks. It is very sunny; I no longer feel the cold.

**Jesus**: If you take them off now, that will be very harmful for you.
(477)  Come, be patient for a little while and offer this sacrifice to me. When it is necessary to take them off, I will tell you. Stop thinking about them. Accept this little mortification with the intention of comforting me on this day of my crucifixion. On the other hand, today you must pray for priests; it is necessary for you to remember these priests who have strayed far from Love and who walk barefooted in the sludge of sin ...

My dear little brother, today stay near the cross, kiss my feet and do not cease repeating: 'O Jesus, I love you for the priests who do not love you. Make your Love penetrate freely to the innermost hearts of priests. Make it so that fervent priests may be full of zeal for your Love.'

Little brother, always remember this: the voice in the world that rejected my Love came first from the priests; that is why it is now necessary that the voices of priests rise up to protect my Love in the world. If not, the world will be unhappy ...

*Marcel*: Then, what can I do so that priests become good as you wish?

*Jesus*: Little brother, I have just told you: stay at the foot of the cross and, there, your voice will be powerful enough to call priests to my Love. (478)

*Marcel*: Little Jesus, tell me why you love priests so much? Each time you speak of them, I see that you show them the greatest respect.

*Jesus*: It is because priests are my other selves. Their dignity is greater than that of being my Mother. The dignity of our Mother Mary does not equal that of priests. However, Mary is more powerful since she is my Mother and, as a consequence, priests, being my other selves, are also the children of Mary. In heaven, a priest's soul will be the object of the veneration of all the saints, including our Mother Mary.

Little brother, you are already very tired. Is that not so? I dare not speak to you any longer for fear of tiring you too much, then Mary would not be pleased. Enough. Go and rest. You will write another time. As you did not sleep well last night, take your siesta a little earlier. You will write this evening. I am giving you a kiss ...

*Marcel*: Little Jesus, at midday I slept very well. On awakening at the end of the siesta, I sat on my bed for a moment, then, seeing that all was silent, I thought it was not yet time for rising and I slept another five minutes. When I got up I was quite afraid but bearded Jesus knew nothing of it.

*Jesus*: My little one! After that do not complain of doing anything differently than the others! There you are, you have acted differently than your brethren in sleeping five minutes too long. You should be ashamed, Marcel. (479)

*Marcel*: I did not gain anything from it since I got up feeling very tired and I still do.

*Jesus*: Little brother, so you have forgotten that today you are at the foot of the cross? It is by accepting this tiredness that you will be able to comfort me.

*Marcel*: Oh! I had completely forgotten to wear the *cuissard*\* today. I only thought about it at noon. Little Jesus, is that serious? Whereas I

---

\* The *cuissard* was a small wire chain, worn around the thigh, which was uncomfortable rather than painful.

should have worn this little chain longer, today I have not worn it at all. It seems that I am quite negligent towards you, little Jesus; graciously forgive me.

***Jesus***: It is for this reason that I have made you wear socks. It would be a good thing for you and at the same time a mortification conforming to my will; and yet you continue to ask to take them off. Marcel, your little sacrifices are very pleasing to me. You still will have to suffer a lot, but don't worry. Remember today is the anniversary of the day when I gave you to my Mother Mary so that you might be her true child; it is also the day when I gave Mary to you to be your true Mother. Finding myself in the presence of my Mother, I suffered with joy. At that moment, when all the creatures of the world seemed to have abandoned me, only my Mother remained to comfort me. Even God the Father seemed to wish no longer to look at me; but my Mother Mary did not cease to look at me until the time when I escaped from suffering. Oh! Little brother, Mary is your real Mother as well as mine. When she sees you suffer, she is closer to you to console you, for all time until you, too, will have escaped all suffering. Mary, you are the true Mother of Marcel, the real Mother of all souls; never be far from your children ...

(480)

Marcel, Mary is your true Mother, and you are really her child. Always think of her; she understands you better than you understand yourself. She knows your sufferings, she is always close to you, carrying you unceasingly in her arms and covering you with kisses ...

Little brother, no matter how great your sufferings, always remind yourself that I, also, have suffered, but that Mary has comforted me. It will be the same for you. Mary will never abandon you in your suffering. Besides, when you suffer, it is she who suffers even more, since she is your Mother.

(481)

Little brother, time is up. Go and eat your fill without concerning yourself about the fast ... First of all, a little smile ...

***Marcel***: I am really sorry for not being able to write down all your words.

***Jesus***: No matter, that's already enough for you. Do not worry; you will have to write much more. That's enough. Go, otherwise ...

# FIRST PROFESSION OF BROTHER MARCEL
## (HANOI, 8 SEPTEMBER 1946)

Father Boucher and Brother Marcel

# PRINTS ON THE WALL OF BROTHER MARCEL'S ROOM

*Our Lady of Perpetual Succour*
The icon was confided to the Redemptorists by Pope Pius IX in order that they might spread this devotion throughout the world.

*Saint Alphonsus Liguori* (1696–1787), Founder of the Redemptorists, Proclaimed a Doctor of the Church in 1851.

*Saint Gerard Majella,* (1726–1755), Redemptorist Brother, Patron of the Brothers

*Saint Joseph* patron of Vietnam and of Canada

# THE CELEBRATION OF MASS

Van (*back to camera*) serving Mass celebrated by Father Antonio Boucher in the Novitiate chapel Đa-lat in 1952.

# THE COMMITMENTS OF VAN

Perpetual profession, 8 September 1952 at Đa-lat
*Left to right:* Brother Eugene, Brother André, Brother Marc, Brother Marcel
*Seated in the centre:* Father Alphonse Tremblay,
Vice-Provincial of the Vice-Province of Vietnam

Pious Union of the Disciples of Saint Thérèse (9 October 1944)

## IN THE CONVERSATIONS...

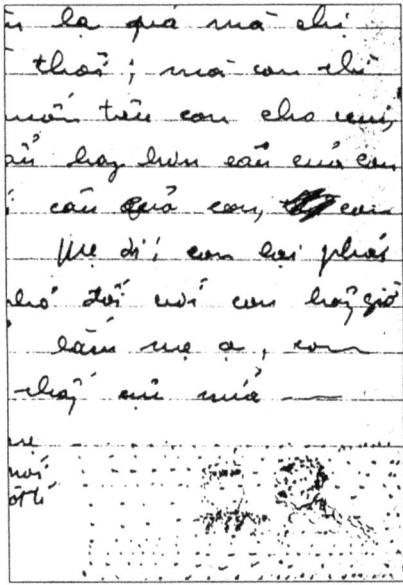

Extract from an original page of the *Conversations* (533): 'I tried to draw a man but I was not successful,' wrote Van.

Van with his little sister Anne Marie Tế who dressed in black in order to resemble her brother. She entered a community of Redemptorist Sisters in Canada since, despite the many appeals of Jesus in the *Conversations*, the Canadian Sisters did not make a foundation in Vietnam.

# THE CANADIAN REDEMPTORIST FATHERS

Father Louis Roy, Father Superior of the Monastery of Hanoi when Van arrived in 1944. Van called him 'Jesus with the Red Beard'.

Father Maurice Létourneau. He was Father Minister. In this capacity, he recruited the gardeners among whom was Van, whom he received into the monastery some months before his admission as a lay brother, lodging him in a rice loft.

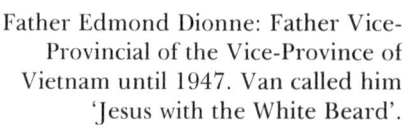

Father Edmond Dionne: Father Vice-Provincial of the Vice-Province of Vietnam until 1947. Van called him 'Jesus with the White Beard'.

# BROTHER ALEXANDER AND SOME REDEMPTORIST FATHERS OF THE MONASTERY OF HANOI

Brother Alexander:
A Canadian Brother, very much appreciated and loved by all, making an icon of Our Lady of Perpetual Succour in lacquer.

1) Father: Louis-Philippe Vaillancourt
2) Father Irénée Marquis

1) Father Roméo Gagnon
2) Father Jacques Huberdeau

# REDEMPTORIST BROTHERS AND FATHERS

Monastery of Hanoi.
This building is reserved for the Brothers and the novices. On the ground floor and the first floor are the rooms of the Fathers and Brothers of the Community. The parlours are also on the ground floor. On the second floor are the rooms of the novices. The three windows on the left are those of the novitiate chapel.

*Bottom: From left to right:*
*1st row:*  Brother Jean-Baptiste,
            Father Pierre Lôc,
            Father Henri Lôc
*2nd row:*  Brother Marcel, Brother Paul
*3rd row:*  Brother Martin, Brother André

Saigon (1951).

## 20 April 1946
*Holy Saturday*

*Marcel*: Today I do not feel very sick. A short while ago I felt a little sadness but it was only a passing feeling. My little Jesus, can I take off my socks?

*Jesus*: No. Continue to wear them joyfully. I love you dearly, so when I see something that is harmful for you, I cannot allow it. We are in the month of fraternal charity and you do not cease exhorting me to practise this virtue. But when I practise it toward you, you resist. So you have two tongues, one which says it is good and the other which says it is bad. In spite of it, you are still my little brother and I am not scolding you about this. Yes, you are my dear little brother and your conduct does not offend me at all. Since I love you dearly, I count your negligences toward me as nothing. Just to see you so unaffected attracts me. (482)

Today, little brother, have you thought yet of your Mother? What favour do you propose asking of her? Perhaps it is not necessary to ask her, since all that belongs to her already belongs to you. However it is not possible for you to receive her favours without giving her a big smile. That's how it is! See, Mary is looking at you and wishes to speak to you. Listen.

*Marcel*: Mother!

*Mary*: My child! Are you happy?

*Marcel*: Yes, very happy. Little Jesus told me yesterday that I would still have to suffer, but that you, dear Mother, would suffer even more. What does that mean? I did not think that you had to suffer any more.

*Mary*: My child, what Jesus said to you is very true. This is how: I have two children who both have to suffer. That is why the distress I feel in seeing you suffer is twice as much as yours. Is it not for this reason that men call me the Mother of Sorrows? Yes, I am truly the Mother of Sorrows, since all my true children have to suffer. And no matter how great the happiness I feel, when I see you suffer, you my children, I cannot stop feeling distressed, and that as a loving Mother ... My child, (483) I feel sorrow in seeing you suffer. The word 'sorrow' is stronger than the word 'suffering' and I am the only one to whom it is appropriate.

My child, the time is up. Quickly, quickly, try to follow my will.

*Marcel*: Little Jesus, I have a very beautiful missal which pleases me a lot. Unfortunately I have to be content to read it without understanding any of it. Not one word of it means anything to me. I have, however, asked my sister Thérèse to understand for me. So, I read the text in French but it is she who understands its meaning. And since she understands it, it is just as if I understood it myself. But what comforts me even more, little Jesus, is that you understand everything I do and that's enough for me. I find it more profitable to read in French. It is quicker and saves me from reading the words *Tao, Mày*\* which are in the Vietnamese versions. There are also passages which I do not like reading in French because in the French language one does not find the words *con* and *em*† used as personal pronouns, when speaking to God the Father, to Mary, or to you, little Jesus and with the saints in heaven. There is only the word 'me'†† I do not like that: when one speaks to anyone, one always says 'me'.

(484) *Jesus*: But, little brother, how can you say that you do not like the French language when you do not know it? Today I think you are very tired. I dare not make you write a lot. You must rest if you want me to be pleased with you. I really want you to write, but if you are tired, Mary will not be happy ... do you agree, little brother? There you are, already feeling upset; that's enough, rest yourself. Stop writing for fear of tiring yourself too much.

*Marcel*: This morning I asked Brother Mark to mend my sandals, but he answered me very harshly and that hurt me a lot. Then, this afternoon, I asked him for another pair of trousers because the pair he had given to me was too long and I could not wear them. This time again he showed his dissatisfaction to such an extent that now, of course, I am afraid of him.

Little Jesus, Brother Mark is very arrogant in daring to be so harsh towards his dear little brother. All the same, I am pleased with him, since he has by this obtained a present for me to offer to you for the feast of Easter, which we celebrate tomorrow.

(485) *Jesus*: Dear little brother, even if you were not pleased, you should, nevertheless, appear to be pleased. Remember that you are but one with me, as I am one with you. So therefore, when Brother Mark speaks harshly to you, it is I who must put up with it since you are one with me.

---

\* The words *Tao* and *Mày* (I and you) have an authoritarian meaning that Van does not like. Cf. [584].
† *Con* means child and *em* little brother.
†† This was written in French in Van's text: 'moi'.

So, why dare concern yourself with something that concerns me? When Brother Mark speaks to you, it is to me that he speaks; so, what reason have you to be sad? Your role consists simply in loving me. That's enough, don't be sad any more. I will see to it for you; besides it is exclusively my business and not yours ...

Ah! Little brother do not start crying. But what is it that I see there in your eyes? Alas, my little one how weak you are! Come on little brother, smile a little. What reason have you for crying?

*Marcel*: Little Jesus, you only take Brother Mark's side ... I am not speaking to you any more.

*Jesus*: But no! It is not Brother Mark's side that I take, but really yours. I am telling you not to be sad with Brother Mark's abruptness because this Brother is not your business but mine ... Now, little brother, I challenge you to cry. Dare to if you can ... That's enough, there you are, forced to smile. Try to cry, just to show me.

*Marcel*: But, little Jesus, if I cried over the suffering of your crucifixion what would you say? Would you forbid me to cry?

*Jesus*: Little brother, who has asked you to cry over my crucifixion? It is another instance of meddling in my business. Your role is not to have pity on me but simply to love me. As for pity, it is for me to exercise it toward you. (486)

In speaking to me you must never use the word 'pity' but only the word 'Love'.

Have you ever heard children say to their parents: 'Daddy, mammy, I have great pity for you'? No, never. The duty of children is to love their parents and that of parents is to have pity for their children. However, you dare to say that you have pity for me, without fear of being ashamed? ... However, little brother, I am not scolding you. You are still very small and as soon as you hear a phrase you repeat it without understanding its meaning. In acting this way you oblige me to have even more pity for you. From now on, never say that you have pity for me, but simply that you love me. Isn't that very sweet, little brother?

*Marcel*: During these past few days I noticed that Brother Augustine does not stop crying during the Way of the Cross. Little Jesus, is that not crying through pity for you? He cries so much that he does not recite the prayers.

*Jesus*: If he cries, let him cry. It is not your affair to judge his behaviour.

(487) **Marcel**: But, little Jesus, I am not judging, I am only pointing the thing out to you. Really, you have a more difficult nature than mine ...

**Jesus**: Little brother, what face are you pulling now? Be silent. Listen so I can speak. But first of all you must give me a big smile. You just said earlier: 'is that not crying through pity for you?' Even if you do not have the intention of judging, this sentence reveals some suspicion about Brother Augustine's tears. I have not accused you of having judged Brother Augustine, yet you pull a face. It is really tiresome; as soon as I say something, you take it as a reproach. Nevertheless, dear little brother, I am giving you a kiss, I am giving you two, three, four, five and I do not stop giving them to you ... Do not go and be sad and think that I do not wish to listen to you. On the contrary, I wish to listen to all the little stories you tell, even the most insignificant, and I wish that all these little events should become so many lessons for you and for souls. Know that I never scold you ...

(488) Little brother, you who are my dear little brother, do you love me? I never wish to hurt you. And the words that I am saying here, I do not intend to say them for you alone, but also for other souls. Little brother do not become sad if during these days you feel full of disgust even when I speak to you. If it is so, it is not that my love for you has cooled; but rather because you are feeling sick and tired. I do recognize however, that it is I who is the cause of all this ...

If at this time you can no longer write, little brother, you can at least listen to me. I know that you are very tired, but your love is not. Therefore, because you love me and because I have pity for you, I am obliging you to put your pen down on the table, to close your copybook, to close your inkwell and then to rest. I am holding you close in my arms on Mary's breast. I wish you to obey promptly.

## 21 April 1946
### *Easter Sunday*

**Jesus**: Little brother, tell bearded Jesus the vision of Good Friday.

(489) **Marcel**: On the morning of Good Friday, during meditation, I saw little Jesus in the tabernacle and I saw him clearly; he was bigger than at other times and could have been thirteen or fourteen years old. He did not smile at me; his face was tinged with sadness. He kept his eyes closed and he was complaining about priests. It was solely by the movements of his hands and the position of his eyes that he expressed his sadness. He spoke a lot about priests, but after having spoken a few

sentences, he rested a moment. I cannot remember in detail what he said to me; I remember only that he called priests to come to the foot of the cross to console his Love, to spread the reign of his Love in the world and act so that all men may come to know his Love.

This vision lasted a fairly long time; then suddenly, little Jesus faded away bit by bit, until he disappeared completely. My Father, that is all.

*Marcel*: Little Jesus, I am very tired; I feel sick all the time and now I can only eat a little. My only fear is to suffer from a heart problem and have to return to my mother's house.

*Jesus*: Little brother, who told you that? Who told you that the Congregation would send you back if you were ill? If such were the case the Congregation would no longer deserve the name of Congregation. This is a temptation of the devil who wants to frighten you. Has the Congregation ever sent anyone back into the world because he was ill? ... Come, little brother, you think of the silliest things. If your father Saint Alphonsus knew it, too bad for you! Yes, your father Saint Alphonsus loves you a great deal; so, how would he be able to send you away? He must leave you in his Congregation, so that later in heaven he may have one of his little children to stroke his beard. If he sent you away who would be able, later, to stroke his beard? (490)

That's enough little brother, you are very tired; you need to rest. You feel very sick, don't you? Offer it up to me: today it is necessary that you wear your socks all day. If you take them off, it would not be good. Continue to wear them until I tell you to take them off.

Were you sad yesterday when I did not allow you to take a shower? I knew that if you went it would not be good for you. Enough, my little brother, be patient a little. On the days when I shall tell you to go to the shower, you will go. Now, take a rest.

*Marcel*: Little Jesus, I ate very well at midday. I thank you. Right now I feel a little better than I did this morning. Little Jesus, why do you speak to me so seldom? It would be better if you would speak to me more often.

*Jesus*: The reason is that today you are still busy talking to your brothers and so, you must listen to them. If you always remained absorbed in listening to me, who would put up with you? Besides, I need a bit of rest! Little brother, are you happy? Why did you cry a moment ago? (491)

*Marcel*: I feel really sick and I cannot put up with my illness so I had to cry. And there are my sandals: as soon as I walk a little in them, someting very dirty comes out of them and sticks to my feet and I find it so painful that I cannot hold back my tears.

*Jesus*: Dear me! Little brother, that is the sum of your weakness. But when you cry in this way, are you content?

*Marcel*: Yes, I am always content.

*Jesus*: Then, that's very good. You show by that your great weakness and I have the benefit of your good feelings. But, little brother, why don't you speak of it to bearded Jesus?

*Marcel*: I mentioned it to him some time ago but he paid no attention and now I am afraid, I dare not speak to him about it any more. My fear is that if I keep on disturbing him he will not be happy.

(492) *Jesus*: Why would he not be happy? In speaking in this way you suggest that bearded Jesus does not have a heart kind enough to indulge you. No, little brother, understand that bearded Jesus, just like me, wishes nothing more than to demonstrate his goodness towards you.

*Marcel*: Yes, but only a little; and how could he manage to spoil me continually. I no longer wish to speak to him about it.

*Jesus*: Come, come, little brother, the goodness of your true Father is without measure, as I have told you many times already. Even if, in his Love, he indulged you in everything, filling all your desires, he would never find it enough for his Love; he would only be afraid that you might not have the strength to receive all his treats. Whatever I do to spoil you, I consider it all as being nothing. Little brother, do you understand? After what I have just said, bearded Jesus is also in the know; so you have no more reason to worry.

*Marcel*: I do not wish to speak of it; and if bearded Jesus questions me on the subject, I will tell him that it is you who obliged me to write these things, whereas I did not wish to speak of them.

(493) *Jesus*: Well, well. Anyway, what you propose to hide from bearded Jesus has already been revealed to him. Now, try to hide it from him, just to see if you can. Besides, as I am but one with you, in telling him about it myself, it is just as if you had told him yourself ... That's enough, go and rest. Do not be troubled, I would not be pleased. Remain at peace, your sandals will be dealt with by Love, but you must not worry. And if

bearded Jesus does not see to it, allow me to deal with it; I will tell you what you have to do. However, do not oppose the words of bearded Jesus, but obey him perfectly.

***Marcel***: I feel sick again, like this morning. My socks are torn. I am happy because now I can avoid wearing them and I will be able to cool my feet a little.

***Jesus***: I can't agree to what you have just said, little brother. If your socks are torn, you must ask for another pair and see to it that you are wearing them before Vespers. If you don't, I will not be pleased.

Did you not prolong your siesta today by fifteen minutes? You are a good sleeper, little brother. One must warn bearded Jesus. Do you feel ill?

***Marcel***: Yes.

***Jesus***: Do you wish to offer me this sacrifice? How can one call that suffering? A little while ago, you made this promise to me: 'Jesus, even if you send me interior or outward suffering I accept all with joy ...' I still remember it very well; and now, I am conforming to your will. Little brother, you feel tired, don't you? (494)

***Marcel***: Yes, I am tired but I am still able to write. Little Jesus, while wishing Father Irénée Marquis a happy feast day this morning, he said to me that I was very small. I answered him: 'Because I am small, Jesus loves me more.' And Father said: 'And me too, I am small, so Jesus certainly loves me half as much as you and, if I was even a little bit smaller, he would love me as much as you.' I felt like laughing because if Father Marquis is not big, he is far from being small.

***Jesus***: Yes, if Father Marquis saw your soul clearly in all its littleness, perhaps he would not dare compare himself to you. Little brother, if I did not show you my Love as I do, perhaps you would not dare to cast a glance at me, so small and weak and timorous is your soul. However, little brother, because you are more wretched, I have more pity on you. Do not be sad with the misfortunes of your soul.

Little brother, already you are very tired. That will do. Through love for me, you must obey me and rest yourself. Know that no one wishes you to write when you are tired, neither your Mother Mary, nor your sister Thérèse ... etc. Nobody wishes it. If you try to continue writing, you are following your self-will. You must also remember that your will (495) no longer exists; so, if you willingly take away my will from me, I am going to force you to return it. Be careful! Enough, little brother, go and rest.

**Marcel**: Little Jesus, today during benediction, on raising my eyes to the statue of my father Saint Alphonsus, I felt like laughing and I had to control myself the whole time so as not to burst out laughing.* My father Saint Alphonsus is very old but no one had given him his crosier to lean on and alleviate his tired back. He certainly has a crosier but I do not know who went and hid it behind his back. At his age his eyes are weak and it is not surprising that he does not see his crosier although it is close to him. I really felt like laughing.

Little Jesus, today Vespers have been very solemn. I sang better than ever. Often I could not find the place in my book which troubled me a lot. However I continued to search very calmly, so that if anyone had seen me, he would not have guessed that I was doing so, and that's true. But I had an even greater urge to laugh, watching Brother Gregory who knows less than me and who kept looking without any success. He pretended to be on the right page but he was not there at all. He spent the whole of Vespers leafing through his book, without daring to recite anything. He stopped, from time to time, but it was impossible for him to find anything.

I think that if there had been anyone close to me more knowledgeable than me I would have openly asked him to find the right page for me, showing by that that I knew nothing, and without any disadvantage for me. I do not imitate Brother Gregory who is very skilful at hiding things. There are a thousand things he does not know but that he pretends to know. Truly I often want to laugh, seeing him act in this way ...

**Jesus**: Listen Marcel, I am going to give you a useful lesson. Little brother, when you are in the presence of bearded Jesus, you must act with simplicity and openness, reminding yourself that even if you happen to commit some fault, bearded Jesus will certainly take your side. Young children have only one fear: that is not to have their parents near them. They know that in the presence of their parents they have nothing to fear. If they are guilty of some fault they count on the presence of their parents who will intervene to protect them. On the other hand, if the parents are not near them, they lose their normal confidence and become fearful, knowing that if they commit some fault,

---

* On Holy Saturday, the statue was unveiled, but someone had forgotten to put the crosier back in place.

there will be no one to protect them, to advise them, and that would be a problem for them.

*Marcel*: But, little Jesus, I heard Brother Gregory say that in the presence of bearded Jesus he found it difficult to behave naturally, that he dare not even raise his eyes. Indeed I have noticed that this is the case. How do you explain it? Is it through simplicity or is it a question of personality? (497)

*Jesus*: I am not telling you why he acts like that, but one who acts in that way lacks a spirit of faith, showing by his words that he considers my presence everywhere as less important and less worthy of respect than the presence of a superior, as I told you before. In the presence of a superior it is necessary, obviously, to act respectfully, but it is necessary to act with all the simplicity of a child, so that his glance can discover even the microbes which are in your soul and, so, you will never have to fear that any grain of dust manages to cling to it ... Little brother, look at me and with complete confidence in me, ask that many brothers who lack confidence in my Love may believe with a sincere heart that Love loves them infinitely. It is simply through lack of confidence that one does not succeed in acting with simplicity. Little brother, if one had true confidence, one would be naturally simple ... Do you remember? (498)

*Marcel*: Then I shall pray for Brother Gregory, since I am sure that he still lacks much confidence in your Love. In fact when I say: 'Jesus loves each one of us with a special love', Brother replies immediately: 'Who can know if he is loved by God ...' He shows by that that he does not believe in your special love for him. Is that not the case, little Jesus?

*Jesus*: That is quite so, little brother; but there is another thing that you must do immediately, it is to cease writing. You are tired, go and rest.

*Marcel*: Little Jesus, I am less tired, but I feel a lot of disgust. However, I no longer feel sick. Ah! there, it's started again.

Little Jesus, a while ago I was looking at a picture where you ask Mary permission to go and play with the other children. I wanted to smile. This picture pleased me a lot and I wanted to cut it out and bring it to my bedroom. In the past, little Jesus, did you act like that?

*Jesus*: Obviously man is incapable of describing the manner in which I behaved towards Mary. I loved her very tenderly and I had such confidence in her, that Mary alone can understand it. And because I had confidence in her, naturally, I behaved towards her in all simplicity ... (499)

But, little brother, you are tired; I do not want you to write any more ...

*Marcel*: Yes, little Jesus, I am at the same time tired and full of disgust. If I were allowed to lie down right now, it would be great.

## 22 April 1946

*Marcel*: Little Jesus, since morning I have not felt the slightest joy. Today my nausea is not as continuous as it was yesterday. I feel sorrow only occasionally, but it is very strong. I feel it at this moment and I am very tired. At midday I had less appetite than yesterday ... By the way, I wonder why, today, since there is hardly any sun, you do not demand that I wear socks?

*Jesus*: Today there is no sun but nevertheless it is warmer than yesterday. If I made you wear socks for a long time, I would be afraid that you might not be able to put up with that and then you might cry.

*Marcel*: Today, although I do not feel any happiness, why do you speak to me so little, little Jesus? By acting this way aren't you afraid of making me cry?

Little Jesus, allow me to ask you a question. Have I really got something wrong with my heart?

(500) *Jesus*: Little brother, I will not tell you. It is the doctor's business and not mine. You see, I am very careful: I do not wish to usurp the authority of the doctor. If I told you, you would reproach me for meddling in other people's business; I would then be very ashamed and I would not dare any longer to teach you. Naturally, I know you, but the authority to tell you if you are ill or not, I leave to the doctor. Little brother, I love you dearly and I would really like to tell you, but by doing so, you might think that doctors are of no use to you. You must understand that. Although I have the authority to let you know, I leave that to the doctors, as I have said.

Today, it is true that you feel disgust, but it is necessary that it is so, since it is the day when you must pray for France. And to do it well, you must pray a lot since, if there are few prayers, what use will the promises be that I made to it? If, through prejudice, the French reject my Love, what use will the promises be that I made concerning the future for France? Those in France who do not wish to recognize the rights of my Love are still numerous; and if enough prayers are not said it is certain that the reign of my Love will not be able to spread in (501) France. My Love has made known to France that she is, to me, the object of a very special love; but if, in their conduct, the French do not respond to this special love, what use will it be for France?

Little brother, you must really pray for France, above all so that the French are always ready to spread the reign of my Love throughout the universe. But it is first of all necessary to see to it that the reign of my Love becomes established deeply in the hearts of the French people.

Next month, your sister Thérèse will give you a formula of prayer for this intention. Really little brother, after such a mark of affection, what more could my Love do for France? I have not asked you to pray especially for any other country, I have asked you to do it only for France. When France has the good fortune to have you as intercessor, what more could she wish for? (*Smiling*) Moreover, these prayers do not come from the mouth of a man of this world; they have their source in my very Love. Being favoured to such an extent, what more can France desire? Nevertheless, there is still a very great number who do not know how to love me ...

But, Marcel, I see that you are very tired. You must go and lie down, (502) time is up already. Recite, first of all, the phrase I taught you, then go and sleep. 'Little Jesus, come with me, come with France.' You are very tired, go and sleep; what you still have to say, your sister Thérèse will say for you.

*Jesus*: Marcel, where have you come from?

*Marcel*: I have just been to confession.

*Jesus*: What sin have you committed that you had to confess so promptly?

*Marcel*: What sin have I committed? Little Jesus, you cannot ask me to write it here. No. I confessed to Jesus with the ginger beard, he forgave me, therefore I have no need to confess it again. Your question is over the top; so you wish me to write down even my sins? That's really too much!

*Jesus*: Little brother, you overdo it. Why would I ask you to write down your sins? Would I not already know them ? Nevertheless, let me ask you a question. This is what I said to you: 'In carrying out this action have you gravely offended me?' You cannot hide it from me. The fault that you have just confessed is simply due to the fact that you are too scrupulous. No one told you that you had committed a grave fault. First of all you went to see Jesus with the ginger beard, but were not able to (503) meet him. I told you at the time not to return, but you went anyway. This is what I said to you: 'Even if you confessed this fault a thousand times, Jesus with the ginger beard would only observe that that is a dubious fault without any foundation.' It is truly tiresome for you, little brother. On the one hand, I do not wish to judge you culpable, but on the other hand, your scruple continues to declare you guilty. Little brother, listen carefully to what I am going to say to you: 'Even if I were not here to excuse you, natural reason alone tells you there is nothing for you to worry about in what you have done.'

You say: perhaps it is from fear of being ashamed that I dare not admit that I am really guilty of this fault, so as not to have to confess it. Understand this clearly: up till now, you have never wished to offend me. Now if you were aware of having really offended me, this desire not to offend me would remove the fear of being ashamed and would allow you to confess your sin freely. This will not to offend me makes you always inclined to confess the faults that you have committed deliberately ... So thanks to this intention, you must not trouble yourself any longer, believ-

(504) ing that it is the fear of being ashamed that prevents you from admitting your fault. Take a little child who wishes never to hurt his parents. By virtue of this wish he acts toward his parents with all sincerity and, if he realized that he had hurt them, he would gladly go to ask their forgiveness immediately even if he felt embarrassed in the presence of his brothers and sisters ... There you have a child who truly loves his parents. That is also your situation, little brother. Is that quite clear?

In the second place, why are you inclined to trouble yourself so much? Because you are always afraid, asking yourself if you might have caused me sorrow in such a way that the least thing worries you, preoccupying you, making you fear this and that and, then, you ask yourself if, without knowing it, you could have committed some fault which hurt me. You must remind yourself that in such circumstances you are not committing sin. It is precisely what bearded Jesus has already told you, but you always forget because you are troubled. What you do not realize is, even if you hit me, blasphemed me, or maltreated me cruelly, you would not commit sin. Why so? Little Marcel, because you are not aware of what you are doing to me. So, rest assured that your involuntary

(505) weaknesses never offend me.

Listen well, little brother, as you always maintain the will not to offend me, there is also in this will humility, so that, if you knew you had hurt me, then, spontaneously, humility would force you to recognize your weakness, without becoming troubled, and immediately ask pardon for it from me. But why bother yourself over these actions since, in fact, you have not offended me. Taken by itself your action would have been able to offend me, but it is nothing since in it is a lack of will.

Consequently, your concern relates to this action and not to your will. So, there is no sin. All there is, is that in troubling yourself like this, you are being offensive to me. And, supposing that you offend me in a grave manner, I would be less hurt by your sin than I am in seeing that you worry yourself for nothing. All these troubles make it difficult for me to give you my kisses.

If I were in bearded Jesus' place, each time that I heard you enumerate your dubious sins, I would stretch you out on the ground, I would give you a good hiding with the cane and I would quickly (506) show you the door. (*Laughing*) With this method any doubt would disappear; a few good slaps administered to the little one would remove dubious sins.

Who continues to declare himself guilty, when one declares him innocent? If you continue to worry in this way, for the slightest thing, I will give you no more kisses. Little brother, it is necessary for you to know that you are very weak, that no soul is as weak as yours; and I admit that your weaknesses never cause me the slightest sadness. It is only your scruples that make me feel such pain as to clasp you in my arms, to spoil you and give you my kisses ...

Enough, Marcel, my little brother. Do not be sad, do you understand? From now on, no more worrying, all right? ...

When you confessed just now, what did Jesus with the ginger beard say to you?

**Marcel**: He said this: 'So, you doubt whether or not it is a sin?' Then he gave me a penance. But all I wanted to do was laugh, because while Jesus with the ginger beard was speaking to me, I could smell cake in his room. It was impossible to feel contrition; I could only laugh ...

Time passed and with it my concern. Little Jesus, I love you and I am (507) kissing you, always, always, and always. Today, little Jesus, I do not know why but I feel myself overwhelmed by sadness. I heard that the Chinese had killed a large number of French and I felt a great sympathy for them. I do not understand why but, naturally, I do not like the French. In the past, I have often seen them make many Vietnamese suffer a lot; it is for this reason that I do not like them very much.

**Jesus**: Little brother, that's a natural feeling in you however, through love for me, pray for the French, since I consider them to belong to me in a special way.

**Marcel**: So, I who am Vietnamese, I do not belong to you in a special way?

**Jesus**: Ah! There you are, being jealous. Although you are Vietnamese, you belong to the kingdom of my Love ... I am not taking into account the external, I only speak of the interior. Come on little one, do not be jealous. You also belong to me in a very special way; even more, you are but one with me.

(508) You are still the intermediary with the French; is that not more than being simply French? Little brother, tell the French this: 'Remain calm; little Jesus wishes to teach France that to spread the reign of his Love, she must not place her confidence in the number of aeroplanes, tanks and submarines, but simply in the Love of Jesus.' It is because the French have lacked prudence that they have been killed by the Chinese; you need not be sad about that. The other day Mary said it again without your understanding what your sister Thérèse had already told you the preceding month: 'It is necessary for the French to be prudent and remain on their guard a little ...' But you have not understood ... However, all these incidents are so many lessons which remind the French that they have no need of physical armaments to deal with people; what is necessary is prudence, this very prudence which my Love uses in her relations with the world ...

Little brother, pray for France and tell the French to pray also for their own country; but no one should doubt what I am saying here. The slightest doubt about my words concerning France would be the sign of a lack of confidence in me ...

Enough, little brother, you are tired. Rest and offer me your sadness and your disgust as a prayer for France.

**Marcel**: So, little Jesus, you are not telling me to pray for my country?
(509) You are not as fair as bearded Jesus.

*I had asked him to pray also for Vietnam. They are teasing each other.*

**Jesus**: But, little brother, to ask you to pray for France, is to ask you to pray for your country, since I regard the French as Vietnamese, having as their mission the protection of my Love in this country of Vietnam. However, little brother, do not fear that the French are governing your country as before. If such were the case, the French government in Vietnam would not be stable. My only intention is that the French come here to protect my Love. So, in praying for France, you are praying as well for Vietnam. As for bearded Jesus, he must speak as he did in order to conceal my words concerning France. If he behaved like you, the secret regarding France would have been revealed a long time ago. You are incapable of understanding my wisdom; all you have to do is to follow it. I am very wise, Marcel, and not foolish like you ... Marcel, that's enough, rest yourself, all right?

## 23 April 1946

*Marcel*: Little Jesus, I am very tired; I am shaking all over and I am beginning to feel sick. Just now, while working I did not feel any sadness; that has just started ... Alas! Little Jesus, it's really painful. Having to put up with something else at least passes, but what I am actually feeling is very painful. Little Jesus, I accept; yes, I accept this suffering for love of you. (510)

Perhaps I will not be able to stay in the Congregation; I am a lay brother, but I do nothing well. I find it difficult to sweep the house; nothing I do is any good. Nevertheless, little Jesus, I leave to you the responsibility of attending to this business instead of me; as for me, it's nothing to do with me, since I am but one with you and you with me. Therefore, do with me, your little Jesus, all that you wish and as you wish; I am worrying about nothing.

*Jesus*: Little brother, who has expelled you from the Congregation? Your suffering is obvious; but the devil wishes to harm you in putting these ideas in your head. I have called you into the Congregation to be a serving brother; now a serving brother abandons himself to manual labour to assist in the work of the salvation of souls. So, when you sit down to write, do you not, by that, devote yourself to work and prayer? You have already sacrificed everything for me, without taking into consideration that you already belong to me. From now on, whatever may be your will, you must remain in my heart ... Little brother, it's (511) really annoying, it's time already.

*Marcel*: Little Jesus, I don't know why but I do not at all like to read books of the genre of *Faith in the Love of God*. And I believe that if I knew French, I would prefer to read in that language rather than in Vietnamese, since it is very difficult to understand and I am sure that many people cannot understand ... In my opinion, one should never hand over translations to philosophers, because they are very difficult to understand and, for my part, I do not at all like to read books translated by learned philosophers. Usually they make the words of the saints lose all their simplicity. For example, I see that many of my sister Thérèse's words are very simple and easy to understand, but when I read the translation in books of that sort, I find them very difficult to understand and that annoys me still more.

*Jesus*: (*smiling*) Marcel, who forces you to read these books? Who obliges you to understand them? If you cannot even understand the very simple words that I address to you, then of course you cannot understand the books that you are reading. If you could understand everything, you would not be privileged as you are. What I wish, and what is better for you, is that you read without understanding anything. If you understood, I would have no reason to speak to you as I do ... Marcel, knowing nothing as you do, how would you be able to understand? And yet you dare say that that annoys you ... Alas! You only know how to laugh and cry.

(512)

(*Changing his tone*) Why do I have to choose many apostles for the expansion of the reign of my Love? Because it is necessary that there should be some for every category of person. You, for example, you must use a certain manner of speaking, while another will have to use a different one, which responds to the feelings of his audience. It is the same for crosses, for sufferings; I must choose different crosses for each soul to whom I send them, since, if I dealt with all souls in the same way, who would be able to walk along the path of perfection?

Often, however, translators do not act with enough prudence when they translate books destined for the use of all souls; indeed, having little experience, and not knowing the degree of perfection these souls have reached, they often translate only according to their own personal fervour ... This is what I wish: for books useful for all souls, a person of experience is necessary to translate them who is aware of the degrees of perfection by which souls must pass, so as to translate for the ordinary soul and for the common good. By that, many souls will be able to understand what they must gain, or what is still lacking in their spiritual lives.

(513)

If the translator allows himself to be guided by his personal fervour, or that of someone he knows, he will often lead many souls away from the path by which I was conducting them. And they, believing themselves to be deceived, will commit themselves to a new way that is not meant for them and which they will abandon little by little, to their detriment ...

Little brother, that's enough. You are tired, go and sleep. Today ask for permission to write to your little sister. I have been suggesting it for a long time already, but on Easter day you forgot completely; it is very tiresome. You must give your sister a little happiness; nothing pleases her so much as to receive your letters. Ask your little sister especially to pray that the Redemptorist sisters will come soon to Vietnam, but do not tell her for what reason. Be content to ask her to pray particularly for this intention. I like this flower very much. In a short time people will call her 'Sister Jesus'. (*Jesus was laughing*)

(514)

**Marcel**: Little Jesus, what have you just done to me? That hurt me a lot and I have lost a lot of blood.

*In the shower he skinned his foot on a sharp tile.*

You are really cruel. You are not afraid to see me cry? So now my sickness begins again. After this accident you will no longer be able to force me to wear socks. That's enough little Jesus, I am not chatting with you any more, I am now speaking to Mary.

My Mother Mary, I do not know why I am so sad this evening. I feel so much disgust that I only want to cry. In writing to my little sister, I did not know what to say to her. Bearded Jesus gave me some peanuts, but very few. If he had allowed me to help myself, I would have taken many more ... Mary I love you dearly. At this time I feel sick again.

This morning during the washing of the linen, little Jesus was boasting in front of me in these words: 'In the past, children often came to my Mother's to invite me to go and play with them. Some of them praised my great beauty and preferred to play with me because I behaved very nicely towards them. When I said something, they listened to me with respect. If they were given some sweets, they shared them with me and I ate them as they did. I said candidly to Mary: "Mother, my little friends say that your little one is very beautiful", and my Mother replied: "Yes, my little one, you are truly beautiful." Then she showered me with innumerable kisses; and Saint Joseph did too.' (515)

I then said to little Jesus that he was beautiful and he, himself added: 'Yes, I am truly beautiful and if I did not possess all the beauties, Marcel, you would not love me. But, of all my beauties, the most beautiful and the most distinguished is that of my Love for you.' Then we laughed together, since I had a strong desire to laugh.

Incidentally, Mother, am I beautiful myself?

**Mary**: My little Marcel, you are very beautiful, the most beautiful of all, more beautiful even than little Jesus, since all that belongs to little Jesus belongs to you alone and to that add all the beauties which come to you from me, from your sister Thérèse and from the host of other saints in paradise. If, after that, you are not more beautiful than little Jesus, who else could be. My child, you are very beautiful. If, at this moment, our true Father in heaven asked me to part with one of my children, I would prefer to part with little Jesus than with you, my little Marcel. My child, your beauty is greater than that of little Jesus, but from a different perspective. Your beauty moves me to have compassion for you more than for little Jesus. As for the beauty of little Jesus, it is inferior to yours, in such a way that little Jesus only deserves to receive my love. Now, as *compassion* takes preference always over *love*, it is in this sense (516) that I would rather part with little Jesus than with you. (*Mary, adopting a joyful tone continued while laughing*.) So, since you enjoy such happiness what more can you wish for?

My child, by any chance is it because you quarrelled with little Jesus that you are so sad? Come now, little Jesus wished to tease you as a joke, but he loves you dearly. If you are sad, be satisfied to offer him your sadness with the intention to pray today for sinners and pagans. All right, my child?

(*Changing her tone*) My child, does your foot hurt?

**Marcel**: Actually, yes, the pain has begun again and I feel more and more sick.

**Mary**: Marcel, you are tired. Take a rest, that will please me more.

## 24 April 1946

**Marcel**: Mother, today little Jesus is not speaking to me any more. I am very sad. This morning, I felt a sharp pain in my heart and my foot hurts a lot, so I had great difficulty in fulfilling my duty as *excitateur*.* I do not know why I was so sad today at the time of communion. While eating little Jesus, I had the feeling I was eating a piece of white paper. Perhaps it is because I had a soreness in my mouth, unless little Jesus has already left for good. Tomorrow, the 25th of the month, if little Jesus does not speak to me, I am going to cry so he can hear me. Mother, I love you a lot. I see that the time is already up. So, since I am tired, allow me to rest. It is already nearly time.

(517) Mother, today I made a bet with Brother Eugene and I lost, so I have to say ten 'Hail Marys'. I am not angry, since this loss permits me to honour you, my true Mother.

Mary, I love you dearly. That's all I know how to say. You are my true Mother; clasp me to your breast with little Jesus, suckle me with him. You say that you have two children, but that you love your Marcel with a compassionate love greater than that for little Jesus. Allow me to prove that it is really so. Little Jesus has absolutely nothing deserving of your compassion; and if you have a little compassion for him, it is simply because he has taken a body like mine; consequently, it is only thanks to me that you have compassion for him. And now, if I had not

---

\* The role of *excitateur* is to pass by the rooms of the brethren each morning to waken them.

agreed to your giving him a little compassion, it could be justified, since I have more of a claim on your compassion than he does ...

Tomorrow, dear Mother, if my sickness persists, I will have to go to the doctor for an examination. I am really scared. I would like to have an examination but I do not wish to, since, if I am really ill and my illness is incurable, I will certainly have to leave.

However, I am not very afraid, because if bearded Jesus sends me home, he must also make little Jesus leave with me; otherwise, I will stay with little Jesus in the Congregation of the Most Holy Redeemer. (518)

*Mary*: My child, why trouble yourself? If I knew that the Congregation was going to send you back to your family, I would come to look for you before you could descend the novitiate staircase. Be assured that, even if you were so ill as to be bedridden all your life, not a single community would send you away. Even while being ill, you would still be able to work for the Congregation by your sufferings and your prayers, and that is all that the Congregation has need of. If, on the contrary, you were in good health, think about what you could do to make yourself useful to the Congregation. Even when you sweep the house, you do not succeed in doing it as it should be done; and so, are you still afraid of not being able to work? From now on, if similar fears come to you, say this to me: 'My true Mother, I am going to go with you, before descending the novitiate staircase.' You must not be afraid of being sent away because of your weakness, because it is little Jesus who allows these weaknesses in order to remove from you all self-confidence and to lead you to place all your confidence in him alone. Because of this, it will be easy for him to teach you all his lessons. So you have no need to fear (519) having to return to the world because of your misfortunes ...

Come, Marcel, are you done being afraid? Ill or not, it is necessary that you obey completely.

*Marcel*: Nevertheless, my brothers tell me all the time that I cannot remain in the Congregation.

*Mary*: That's quite correct my child; it is because you cannot remain in the Congregation that you will stay here. If you had been capable of staying here, you would have had to return to the world a long time ago. The brothers have a different meaning to their words, but you must understand them in the sense that I have just pointed out to you. Try not to forget ... Do not worry about this ... you are tired today, aren't you? So, that's enough; go and rest. I am kissing you. Stay happy. Little Jesus wants to tease you as a joke. Go, sleep peacefully.

232  *Conversations*

*Marcel*: Little Jesus, a short while ago you allowed a pair of scissors to fall on my hurt foot and you made it bleed. So, there, I have two wounds on the same foot, and it is all your fault, little Jesus. It is lucky for you that I have not cried, since if I had cried, you would have been embarrassed. Little Jesus, tomorrow is the 25th of the month; what are you going to give me to make me happy?

(520) *Jesus*: I am going to give you what you wish for above all, what you prefer more than anything else: 'The grace to want to please me' and this grace is 'suffering'. Do you agree, little brother?

*Marcel*: Little Jesus, you speak to me about suffering at the drop of a hat; I do not like it at all. Can't I please you without having to suffer!

*Jesus*: There is no better way than that. Even if you do not like it, it is still necessary to like it. Anyway, to prove your love to me you must accept suffering.

*Marcel*: But when will it happen? It is not possible that tomorrow, the 25th, you are going to make me cry. How could I joyfully take part in the afternoon tea? Since I don't know, I will go speak to Mary to find out.

*Jesus*: Who is making you suffer right away? I have just sent you this suffering, but before it reaches you, it must pass through many stations, so you cannot know in advance either the hour or the day of its arrival. One thing is sure, you will cry a lot, but don't worry, little brother. Because of this, you will be able to offer me a great number of souls ... come, little brother, laugh a little ... Try to smile at least. I am kissing you. I have not yet ceased speaking to you and I will continue to do so; do not fear of losing me tomorrow ...

(521)    That's enough. Go and do your spiritual exercises with the brethren. You must maintain a composed and joyful air as usual. I will never again speak of this business for fear of making you sad. So, remain happy so I may be happy too. Oh dear little Marcel, the time is up. If you do not leave straight away you will be late.

## 25 April 1946

*Marcel*: Little Jesus, the day before yesterday I asked for a floor cloth to wash the floor. It is still quite new, although it's already torn. I am afraid that the choir Brothers will discover it and take it, then I will be very sad. Often, after having used it, the choristers leave it quite dirty, without taking the trouble to wash it with a little care, and so it deteriorates very quickly. Each time that I use it, I have to take a lot of time to wash it. To do things properly I would have to hide it and let the choristers use the old floor cloth until it is beyond further use. Little Jesus, may I do that? I do not want to reproach the choristers; I continue to remain silent and take the trouble to wash this floor cloth each time I use it, so as to make a little sacrifice to you. All I have to offer you are little sacrifices of this kind, however since, apart from you, nobody knows of it. I prefer that it remains so ... When we kiss each other, no one sees it; when we give each other presents, no one knows either; no one knows anything of how we love each other; and it is very good that it is so, is it not, little Jesus?

There is always one or another brother who thinks that I have never (522) had to suffer. Even during the most hurtful of my interior sufferings, I hear that someone has criticized me like this. However, little Jesus, looking at it from a human standpoint, if you made this brother taste a little of my interior pain, he would never dare to speak of me as he does. Little Jesus, if I speak in this way it is not at all with the intention of parading myself for knowing how to suffer with a lot of courage; I know very well that the blows coming to me from your hands are always accompanied by Love. I am so weak that it is impossible for me to endure even a sorrowful sigh. However, the stronger your blows are, the more the intensity of your Love grows, which makes me capable of putting up with suffering ...

Little Jesus, I would have liked to express my feelings to you in these pages, but it is already time. I give myself to you. When I am very favoured externally, I then suffer a great deal interiorly; but the external consolations count as nothing compared with the interior pains that I endure. And nothing can stop my tears from flowing, more so when I do not clearly see your loving gaze fix itself once more on me. Little (523) Jesus, I love you ...

Little Jesus, today, I feel a more acute pain in my heart. At midday, I had no appetite at all. Ever since last night when you told me that I would have to suffer a lot and certainly have to cry a lot also ... I have been overwhelmed by sadness. I feel sure that this suffering is not far away; perhaps it is even on the point of arriving and this pen is about to rest. Nevertheless, I am not afraid. As long as Love survives, I, also, will survive. My fear is that, as happened the last time, bearded Jesus, not at all spoiling me, will only add further to my sadness.

*Jesus*: If that happened, little brother, it is because you did not mention it to bearded Jesus. But from now on, to do things right, you must tell him candidly what is happening to you.

234  *Conversations*

***Marcel***: But I do not know how to express myself.

***Jesus***: In that case, be content to put up with this suffering, since I wish it. When you do not know how to express yourself, leave it to me. But, sometimes, you could express yourself but you are afraid to do so. (*Laughing*) Would you be afraid that someone is going to gobble you up? Yes, Marcel, you are inclined to fear things that are not worth the trouble. (*Changing his tone*) Be glad little brother. I have much compassion for you and it is only through love that I am allowing you to suffer ... You are very tired, little one, that's enough. Go and sleep.

(524)

***Marcel***: Little Jesus, I don't know why I feel so sad. A short while ago I saw seven aeroplanes. One of them was as big as five little ones; I found that very interesting ...

Today at teatime, I ate well and with a good appetite. I did not forget you, my little Jesus, but all the same, I am still a little sad, fearing that suffering will occur unexpectedly ... Ah! My little Jesus, I love you without reservation; all that is in me, were it even a little speck of dust, I offer it gladly to you. I know that I am a little victim offered to your Love and that, in order to die consumed in Love, I will have to die in suffering. I am not afraid to suffer, since if I die in suffering, I will be certain that you have accepted me as a victim of merciful Love, after the example of my sister, little Thérèse ...

Little Jesus, at this time I feel sorrow in my heart and this sorrow gives me joy, since I know that my heart pleases you a lot and you must look at it unceasingly to make you happy ... In spite of this joy, I am, nevertheless, suffering a lot, without daring to admit to having a heart problem. I feel completely at peace and I fear nothing. All I have to do is to tell things as they are to bearded Jesus who will have to put up with everything for me. I will only be able to say to him, according to the circumstances: that hurts me, that hurts me a lot, or: that does not hurt me, that hurts me slightly, that hurts me only a little, I am tired ... etc. Nothing but that.

(525)

Little Jesus, I am very hot and I do not know why, I just want to cry. Perhaps the sufferings are about to arrive. Is that not the case, little Jesus? But, I am not afraid; I am not getting worked up. I will welcome suffering; I will give it a kiss, as I give one to you, little Jesus.

***Jesus***: Marcel, so you are very hot? It is a pity. Go and ask bearded Jesus to give you a fan. You must be straightforward with him. Go, little brother, I have not left you yet. Besides the separation will be more painful for me than for you, because I have more compassion for you than you have love for me ... Go, bearded Jesus has returned, ask him for a fan. Quickly, otherwise you will miss the opportunity.

***Marcel***: Little Jesus, here is the magnificent fan that he give me. I am very happy. However, if bearded Jesus demanded it back to give to Brother Mark in my presence, I would be content and joyful, considering it put to its proper use. I do not wish to keep anything for myself. All that belongs to me is yours and that is worth more for my sins, so that nothing remains mine, if it is not myself, Marcel, not being other than one with you, Jesus. (526)

Little Jesus, I love you. I wanted to cry, but I have not yet cried. This silly thought came to my mind: all the external suffering that you have endured from the moment of your arrest until your last sigh on the cross, even all these sufferings, I say to myself, are not comparable to the least interior suffering that you send me. And truly, in speaking thus, I do not feel any problem or any fear. If I only had to endure the external sufferings that you had to endure, or even more, and that was pleasing to Love as much as the slightest interior suffering, I would prefer rather to endure these external sufferings than interior suffering ...

But, little Jesus, what have I just said there? I love you a lot and even if interior sufferings oppressed my soul for all eternity, depriving me of seeing Love, I would accept them gladly and with joy, since I love you, not for my consolation, but simply to please you ... Ah! Little Jesus, I love you. You suffered much more interiorly than externally. A single sigh accompanying your interior sufferings is worth a thousand times more than your external sufferings, even the cruellest. (527)

Little Jesus, if I had been there at that moment and I had known that it was the case, I would have dissuaded you from suffering death in this manner. However, I am sorry also that you suffered more inwardly. You endured your outward sufferings with the intention of proving to men that you love them to the point of dying for them. However, it was your interior sufferings that reduced you to not being able to breathe any more, so that you had to bow your head and breathe your last sigh. As for external sufferings, they were only the sign of your death, and in no way were they able to cause it.

***Jesus***: You speak the truth, Marcel, but if my Love did not live in you, it would be impossible for you to say such things ... Little brother, as I have told them previously, it is to my most dear spouses, to those who live in very close intimacy with me, that I send inward sufferings ...

Look at our Mother Mary, she did not die like me, in excruciating pain, and yet, without a special grace from our true Father, she would have died of exhaustion at the foot of the cross. Why is that? Because (528) her sufferings were interior ... In reality, it is not external sufferings that caused my death, since exterior sufferings count for very little in the eyes of Love ...

Marcel, my little brother, since you wish to prove your love to me, I must look for a means of granting your wish; now there are none better than interior sufferings ...

Little brother, you are already tired, aren't you? Do you agree to rest? I dare not force you to rest, but if I do not do it, you are going to tire yourself. So, because you love me, because I have a great deal of compassion for you and also because Mary and bearded Jesus do not want you to tire yourself out by writing, I am obliging you to stop there. Unless you do that you will not please me. Enough. Be content.

(*Laughing*) You have no reason to moan, since I continue to love you and to speak with you ... Come on, little brother, laugh a little so I can see it. What kind of laughing has your sister Thérèse taught you, that you do not wish to put it into practice with me? ... Come, rest yourself. I am kissing you ...

## 26 April 1946

(529) ***Marcel***: Little Jesus, what's happening? Today, bearded Jesus has not yet received any news from either of us.

Yesterday, the doctor examined me. He said I had nothing wrong with my heart, but I was very weak.

***Jesus***: Very good. From now on when you feel any pain in your heart, you will be able to lay the blame on me, do you understand? Since yesterday, Marcel, have you been very sad? And for what reason? ... What a pity! Marcel, you are truly very weak. Simply hearing the word suffering is almost enough to make you lose control. Little brother, before sending you any suffering, I want, first of all, to let you know how weak you are. You must realize that if you have not got the strength even to hear the word suffering uttered, still less do you have the strength to put up with suffering ...

Little brother, although this is so, you must accept suffering; but you cannot understand how much Love suffers even more than you, having to make you suffer. Oh Marcel! Although you are truly very weak, the sight of your weakness makes you more lovable in my eyes than any gestures of love that you show me would be able to. My intention is to teach you that you haven't got the strength to endure suffering, even for the time it takes to wink your eye. However, little brother, your
(530) strength is love; and this strength can even make you capable of accept-

ing all my sufferings, with those of Mary and of all your brothers and sisters the saints, and to bear them with joy. Yes, it is really so, and you can see by that that there is no longer anything difficult for you. (*Laughing*) You are really the happiest of men, Marcel, what more could you want? And it is so because you are the weakest of all ... Is your foot still hurting you today?

*Marcel*: Yes, it still hurts but only a little, and I also feel sick. I have a runny nose and I am coughing a lot; I believe that today my sufferings are going to begin. This morning I felt no joy and you don't say a word to me. Little Jesus, why then, knowing how weak I am, do you still send me sufferings. Isn't that rather abnormal?

*Jesus*: Since Love is your strength, what more do you want? And you have got bearded Jesus who never stops caressing and spoiling you in a thousand ways; what more can you ask for? And with that, how many souls you can save ... etc. It seems, therefore, that your weakness is very advantageous to me. It is because you are the weakest of souls that Love treats you so; if you possessed a little strength, Love would act differently toward you. (531)

Let us suppose that a soul like yours says to me: 'I will joyfully sacrifice myself for your Love', really, this soul would make me want to laugh, since I am sure that it is incapable of doing anything whatsoever. However, if I see its good will, I feel very ashamed and I must hasten to give it Love so that it has the strength to sacrifice itself for me.

*Marcel*: Is it really like that with me?

*Jesus*: Of course, Marcel, it's nobody else but you, (*laughing*) and yet, you still ask questions? You are truly ignorant. It is obviously you and, by your question, you show clearly that you are absolutely nothing, being completely lost in me, Jesus. Little brother, do you feel tired?

*Marcel*: Yes, I have a backache.

*Jesus*: In that case, go and sleep and do not be concerned about sufferings; you will be concerned with them when they come. It is actually time for siesta. Do what you have to do for the present, you will know the rest later. Your sister Thérèse has told you that many times. That's enough. Go and sleep ...

*Marcel*: My Mother Mary, I am very sad. At midday my sister Thérèse spoke to me. This is what she said to me: 'Little brother, a short while (532-a) ago little Jesus said to you: "Next month your sister Thérèse will ask you to pray for the intention I spoke to you about the other day." Little brother, I am speaking to you about it now. Try to compose a very beautiful prayer to say to Jesus and to Mary.' I thought hard but nothing came. Afterwards, however, I was able to come up with a prayer that I remembered very well. I took my pen to write it, but no sooner had I begun to write than a different prayer from the one I had thought of came, naturally, from my pen. And after having written the two following texts, I had completely forgotten my first prayer. I found that bizarre, but my sister Thérèse, only laughed. I am sure that she wanted to tease me. Her prayer is much more elegant than mine, I am sure, although I have completely forgotten mine ...

## For the month of May

(532–1) 'Little Jesus, so arrange things that France acts towards Vietnam in a spirit of brotherhood, as you yourself, in your Love, graciously act towards France.'

To Mary: 'Dear Mother, we beg you, by the wisdom of divine Love, make France and Vietnam conclude peace together in the truth of Love.'
*Thérèse*

(532-b) Dear Mother, suffering has returned. Little Jesus seems quite indifferent towards me. I am sad and I am suffering ... dear Mother, I love you ...

(533) I am very sad and I no longer know what to say. Allow me to play a little. (*To amuse himself he makes a drawing with dots.*)* I tried to draw a man, but I was not successful. It is quite awful. Enough, I will no longer amuse myself in this manner; I do not know how to draw. If I knew how to draw I would draw your portrait. I do not at all like your picture in the community oratory. It is quite unattractive. You certainly have not got such a black face, or such dreadful eyes. I dislike looking at it. It dishonours you too much. Mother, I am leaving you, the time is up. Call little Jesus for me. Mother, I love you.

Mother, it is likely that the suffering has arrived already. This morning little Jesus did not say a word to me. Mother, I am very sad, especially since the time when I met my director. I had to answer some questions, which I found very difficult. I am sure that my director already understands the feelings of my heart; is it necessary for him to ask me these questions again?

---

* Cf. reproduction of a design by Marcel on plate 5.

I offered myself as a victim to the Love of Jesus, as my little sister Thérèse advised me to do and little Jesus drew me to this place to reduce this unassuming victim to ashes ... Mother, I no longer need to speak for a long time; I must shed tears. Indeed, when I look at the pages written earlier, I see only joys and smiles, while in these later pages, I only see sorrowful sighs and tears. However, I do not fear that (534) these tears are lost; all I fear is that they are so abundant that little Jesus might drown in them ...

Alas! Mother, little Jesus is absent for hardly half a day and I cannot manage to dry my tears ... Mary, my true Mother, graciously look upon me with compassion. I feel at peace because you are near me. Mother, I no longer know what to say to you. A part of the page remains but I do not know what to write on it to fill it. I am truly sad.

22 April 1946 (end)*
***Marcel***: I remember having asked little Jesus: 'If the French do not use aeroplanes, tanks and cars they will all be killed and then, how will they be able to protect your Love?'

***Jesus***: 'Little brother, I did not intend to say that material arms are not necessary; all that I mean is that one must not put one's confidence in these arms but in me alone ...'

## 28 April 1946

Marcel: I remember one day when I had absolutely nothing to say to (535) little Jesus, I kept looking at him, full of disgust, trying to meditate but without knowing how to begin. Seeing me in this state, little Jesus called me in order to teach me a way to occupy my mind with him. He told me first of all to look at the bench and he added: 'Little brother, say: "I love you in this bench."' He then told me to look at everything in the oratory and to repeat for each object: 'Jesus, I love you in ... the dust, in the fly, in the window, in the foot of the bench, in the flower, in the plant, in the flower pot, in the earth in the pot, in the shelf where it is placed, in the brick, in the pillar; I love you in the bird, in the bird's song, in the frog, in the white tree frog, in the noise it makes, in the aeroplane, in the motor car ... etc.' While little Jesus was teaching me this lesson, I felt like laughing and I was very distracted. I then had the following

---

* These two paragraphs were added here by Van to complete what he had written on 22 April.

240  *Conversations*

distraction: I said to myself that if it was my job to teach children, I would do such and such a thing to indulge them. Then little Jesus, once more, invited me to say: 'Little Jesus, I love you in my little brothers who are playing.'

(536) Finally, little Jesus said to me: 'Little Brother, you can always make use of this method and, so, you will be able, while resting, to make this prayer continually. In addition, this method will help you never to commit any fault in your distractions. Where the spirit leads you, your love also leads you, in such a way that I am loved by you in every place ... '

Since then, when I have nothing to say, I use this method, but I often want to laugh. I once said: 'Little Jesus, I love you in the fly.' And he said to me, laughing: 'This fly smells terrible. It is very dirty, nevertheless you love me truly, in it. In comforting me like this, in very ordinary things, even in a simple grain of sand, you force me to follow you step by step in order to give you my kisses ... '

*Jesus*: Marcel, on this day of 28 April 1946, how many very ordinary little things there are that people never think of, that they could offer to me to please me. In the eyes of Love, these little things, far from being ordinary, are very precious. However, one thing saddens me, it is that these little things do not know how to love me and there is no one to love me in them and to offer them to me. From now on, little brother, remember that my Love hides itself in the dust and the grains of sand,
(537) waiting until your words of love come to comfort me. In loving me in these little things, you love me equally in the souls who do not wish still to belong to me; I receive consolations even in these souls, since I find your love there ...

Marcel, why are you so sad? I was absent only yesterday afternoon and, seeing you cry, I wanted to smile. Yes, little brother, you will have to suffer a lot; but the nature of these sufferings and the time when they will come, I am not letting you know. Sometimes I will send you a little, sometimes, I will send you ... What? You know nothing of it and I am not telling you. However, little brother, when even the suffering comes, whatever may be its intensity, even if it lasts only the time of a sigh or a wink of an eye, accept it with joy for love of me, your little Jesus, and for souls. And since you are the victim of my love, even if you do not offer yourself, the fact that you have already asked your sister Thérèse to offer you as a victim, following her example, is just as if you had offered your-
(538) self. Because your will is in your sister Thérèse, when she offers you to the flame of my Love, it is you who offers yourself, do you understand? You have no need to complain ... The time is up. Be joyful, always.

*Marcel*: Little Jesus, yesterday Brother Eugene said that only the

Redemptorist sisters were your spouses but that the Redemptorists were not since they are men. All the brethren told him he was wrong since, in your eyes, the outward form does not count but only the soul. In spite of that, Brother Eugene stuck to his opinion and would not concede. If I had wagered with him he would surely have lost. On hearing him speak like this, I was a little sad, since you always call me your spouse. Afterwards, however, Brother Eugene had to give way, because bearded Jesus proved it otherwise; and I was very pleased. Since then, little Jesus, in thinking about my soul as your spouse, I feel a very sweet joy.

*Jesus*: Yes, all souls are my spouses. But that must not be understood in a material sense. However, as bearded Jesus said yesterday, the word 'spouse' is a term which is used to indicate, externally, religious sisters and not male religious, although the latter are also as truly my spouses (539) as their female counterparts. The Church also gives the name of 'virgin' to female saints because they have kept their virginity, but it does not give the name 'virgin' to the men even though they have also kept their virginity, just like the women. In this world, Marcel, it is necessary to use the language of the world; but this language is weak in expressing spiritual things. If at this moment I allowed you to see the soul of your father Saint Alphonsus next to that of your sister Thérèse, but without any external form, you would not be able to distinguish one from the other. Supposing even that I showed you at the same time my own soul, you would be completely baffled. The reason why I must use the word 'spouse' is because the world has no other; and if I used another language, the language proper to my Love, the world would not understand it; it would not be able to grasp the meaning of my words ... Little brother, it is only in heaven that you will see clearly all these things and, as I told you before, I will no longer use the word 'spouse' in speaking (540) to you.

*Marcel*: I do not know why, but Brother Eugene does not please me at all. I used to believe him quite readily, but now, it is impossible to believe anything he says. He exaggerates a great deal. In relating certain facts, when he should say 'one', he says that it is 'ten'. The other day, for example, when speaking of France, he said: 'At this time, France is very corrupt; the whole country is communist. All the priests have been killed and religions are persecuted more than in Russia. Another army has been sent to take possession of the Holy Land, to rule there; and innumerable sins are committed ... etc.' And Brother Eugene added that he heard it on the authority of Father Thính himself. All the brothers protested, saying it was not true, but he continued to affirm that it was really so, and he referred to such and such a witness to give more weight to his assertions.

At that time, my sister Thérèse recommended that I pray a lot for France; but after having heard Brother Eugene's words, I felt discouraged, all the more so when he stated that many Fathers endorsed what he had said. I then questioned my sister Thérèse who replied to me 'Keep calm, little brother; even if Brother Eugene's words were true ten times over, you must not become agitated. Even if the whole of France was really as he says, it would be enough to find a single Frenchman who loves Jesus, for him once again to have pity on France.' I then recovered my composure and continued to pray for France. Some days ago I again heard it said that the majority of French soldiers who have just arrived in Vietnam are very good people. And since then I no longer wish to believe what Brother Eugene says. There are other stories too that Brother Eugene tells, but which are not at all true.

*Jesus*: Marcel, who compels you to believer those things? Has the Church obliged you? So there is no need to believe any of it; if Brother Eugene exaggerates, too bad for him. All you have to do is to listen and consider those things as amusing stories which are not true. Who makes you believe them and get worked up in the process? As for Brother Eugene, he believes he is speaking the truth because he is badly informed; he affirms what he does through personal conviction ...

From now on, do not bother yourself in this way. Now that you know Brother Eugene's temperament, you must appear happy with him, to please him. And in this way you will have stories to listen to. If, on the contrary, you spend your time saying: 'it isn't true', who would want to speak? If it sometimes happens that you find these stories too difficult to swallow, accept this sacrifice for me who, in the tabernacle, must listen to the blasphemies of men. By doing that, while pleasing me, you will contribute to the joy of your confreres. As for Brother Eugene, his tall stories are neither sins nor lies, since he believes that what he says is true. However, little brother, if after having heard something from Brother Eugene, knowing that it is not true, you then went to repeat it to another, you yourself would commit two sins: a falsehood and a lack of charity since your words would not coincide with your thoughts and, furthermore, you would take away from others all confidence in Brother Eugene. In effect, by doing so you would make him lose his good reputation among the brethren and they would no longer want to listen to him.

*Marcel*: But, little Jesus, I have never acted in this manner!

***Jesus***: No, and I have not accused you of behaving in this way. I am simply giving you a bit of advice, so that you may know where you stand and that you are not prejudiced with regard to Brother Eugene who is so prone to exaggeration. I am not letting you know any intimacies of Brother Eugene; I am simply advising you to listen willingly to the stories he tells to entertain the brethren, so as to console him a little.

Little brother, are you worn out? I notice that these days you have a head cold; does that frighten you? Remain calm. It is I who wishes it so. When I tease you and see you joyful and contented, I feel more joy than if I were giving you kisses ... Little brother, rest yourself. It is almost time; take a little rest. (543)

***Marcel***: Little Jesus, at midday I ate very well. I was served bananas and toast. I like that a lot but I am not able to eat too much of it. I do not know why but at the moment I am eating very little. When I entered the novitiate I had a hearty appetite and I did not wish to deny myself by putting up with hunger, not feeling that I had the strength to practise this kind of mortification.

On my admission into the community, I tried to practise self-denial in food, to see if I was capable of doing so. But after having done it once, my sister Thérèse forbade me absolutely from doing it again. Threatening that, if I mortified myself in such a stupid manner, she would ask you to expel me from the Congregation. I was really afraid and, since then, I have no longer even dared to endure hunger.

But at home why did my mother force everybody to fast on the days prescribed by the Church? My sister and I, although not having reached the age to fast, had to do it so as to become accustomed to it. I found it very hard. Often I was hungry and I complained; then my mother used to scold me in these words: 'You know very well how to commit sin, but you do not know how to atone for it. If you have not yet reached the age to fast, you have more than reached the age to sin.' I found that very hurtful and I thought to myself: 'I had not yet committed any sin which obliges me to suffer hunger in this way.' (544)

So therefore, little Jesus, my mother is more virtuous than you since she made me fast whereas you forbid me to do so. You are really not very fervent; yes, less fervent than my mother. Do you admit it, little Jesus?

***Jesus***: Not at all. I allow myself to be guided by prudence rather than by fervour. It is fine that your mother acted in that way; but there was a lack of prudence, so that this, good in itself, could be bad because of a lack of prudence. It is better to follow the will of the Church than one's personal fervour. The Church is very prudent, with a true prudence: the prudence of Love. I want you, therefore, to follow the will of the Church rather than your personal fervour, and that is why I do not wish you to fast. Normally, people are inclined to consider their personal fervour as being preferable to the prudence of the Church. It is not bad in itself. I am saying, even, that it is good, but it is always better for children to follow the wish of their mother. I do not intend to speak here simply of your mother; there are many other mothers who do not sufficiently follow the rules of prudence and who, by that, do a lot of harm to their children, as much spiritually as corporally. (545)

Normally, fasting and other penances, not only are not useful to children, but also are harmful to them. It is therefore necessary that mothers show much prudence so as to take care of their children according to the will of the Church. If one wishes that there were many of these prudent mothers, it is above all necessary that there are priests who are at the same time holy and very prudent...

Something I find it very sad to see is that, generally, children who do not yet know what sin is, learn very soon to do wrong, simply because the parents are lacking in prudence. For children there is nothing bad; they think that everything is good, and that is true, since in all that I have created, there is absolutely nothing bad. That is why parents must be extra prudent to help their children avoid things that are wrong. For example, if a child says an improper word, there is no fault in him since he does not know that what he says is sinful. His parents must be alert to correct him in such a way that he never again repeats that word; but it is also necessary to see that the child does not know that what he has said is sinful or that it is something improper, something that people normally regard as being a sin. (546)

Little brother, go and sleep now, all right? It's time. Little brother, I feel very sorry for you.

**Marcel**: Little Jesus, why did you not speak to me yesterday, making me shed a multitude of tears? But... I do not know what is happening, my pen writes with difficulty. I shall try to fix it to see... Does it work now? I do not know. Probably yes. It's strange. It's not brilliant. Ah! That's better; I shall continue writing. However, little Jesus, yesterday's tears, although abundant, were not comparable to those of the preceding time. But I do not at all regret them; I give them to you. Little Jesus, you have a very difficult nature; you only find pleasure in swallowing my tears, teasing me to make me cry, so as to have something to drink. It is not nice; would Mary's milk be incapable of satisfying you? Little Jesus, you are too inclined to abuse my weakness, and even Mary cannot manage to correct you; you are more stubborn than I am. (547)

The other day, little Jesus, you told me this: 'Little brother, you are not a miser, but you have a miser's will.' Very good, little Jesus, allow me to reply in my turn that you, much more than I, have the will of a miser. The more riches the miser possesses the more he wants to acquire; and if, finally, he succeeded in possessing the whole world, his avarice would not yet be satisfied and he would wish to possess even more.

It is the same for you, little Jesus. The more I offer you souls in great numbers, the more you want. How can one explain such a strange attitude? I do not really understand how the will of a miser can penetrate your heart to such a point that it is impossible to get it out. That is a very unattractive defect, little Jesus; the more I offer you souls in great number, the more you say to me: 'I still want more.' So, when will this end? It is probable that it will only cease for good the day when you will no longer be able to receive any at all. And, after all that, you reproach me for having the acquisitiveness of a miser. It is yourself, Jesus, who has such a yearning and you still throw the fault in my direction. Are you not afraid of being ashamed? Certainly, our Mother Mary should feel like laughing.

*Jesus*: Yes, Marcel, I admit it is so, but you, you deserve to receive some (548) sharp slaps since knowing that I have, as you put it, the appetite of a miser, you are still afraid of suffering. But it is in suffering that you will be able to offer me a great number of souls. Marcel, you ought to be more ashamed than I ... And whatever you might say, you also have a little of my defect, since the more I give you kisses and caresses, the more your miser's appetite grows. Even though I have exhausted all the means of indulging you, this strange desire always demands more. If I do not receive any soul from you, I am only sad but I do not cry, while you, as soon as I am absent for a moment, you sigh, you pull a face and you cry. So, have you not more reason to be ashamed than I? And you dare to make fun of me? Are you not afraid that your pen also makes fun of you? Enough, let us not speak any more about our mutual defects, for fear that bearded Jesus, seeing it, starts laughing.

*Marcel*: Incidentally, little Jesus, yesterday bearded Jesus copied you in making me smile before dismissing me. I did not smile because he told me to, but simply because I felt like smiling on seeing that he was (549) copying you in telling me to laugh. So I laughed quite merrily, but bearded Jesus does not know my reason for doing so.

*Jesus*: Bearded Jesus and I, it is the same thing. Bearded Jesus wishes you always to be happy so that I am pleased with you. Also if, in speaking to you, he wishes to make use of my words, it is with the intention of forcing you to remember what I said to you, namely: that you must always be joyful. *(Laughing)* Why then do you say that bearded Jesus is copying me? Are you not afraid he might scold you?

*Marcel*: But, little Jesus, you just told me that bearded Jesus and you are the same thing; consequently, he will never dare to scold me. Don't you think so? If he scolded me, I would cry so you could hear me. I fear nothing, except to be anxious. I know also that bearded Jesus wants to give me many kisses, but he does not give them to me outwardly; he does so only spiritually.

*Jesus*: What would he gain in kissing you? He would only soil his lips without any benefit.

*Marcel*: Yes? So, from now on little Jesus, it would be better not to give me any more kisses. Who makes you dirty your lips in giving them to me?

(550) *Jesus*: And you, little brother, who makes you say that you love me? Because you are wrapped in the flames of my love, on looking at you I see that you are very beautiful and your beauty enchants me so much that I give you kisses without tiring myself; and truly, the more I give you, the more I wish to give them to you without stopping.

*Marcel*: So, why moan about soiling your lips?

*Jesus*: Let us assume that you are not enveloped by Love and that I felt like giving you a kiss, and then I would not be able to do so without truly soiling my lips. But now that you are very beautiful, I can do so without any risk and if I did not do so I would find that harder than observing that you do not love me. Time is now up, go and take a walk in the garden ...

*Marcel*: Little Jesus, the episode of the 'soiled lips' makes me want to laugh all the time.

*Jesus*: Truly, little brother, does this story not prove that you truly have the appetite of a miser? My kisses alone do not amply satisfy you, since you want even to receive bearded Jesus'? When I give you kisses, it is just as if bearded Jesus was giving them to you; what more do you want?

*Marcel*: Little Jesus, you said that we would no longer speak of our shortcomings; and, hey presto, you are still speaking of them. Are you not afraid that I might get angry? Do you want that I, also, should enumerate your faults? If you really wish it, I will bring up one, for your ears.

**Jesus**: I have absolutely no fault which deserves mentioning; my only (551) dominant fault is that I love you to excess, with an inexpressible love; and in spite of that, I still have the feeling of not loving you at all. Oh! Marcel, we both love each other. On the one hand, the love that I have for you goes to the extreme limit; on the other, to respond to my love, you only have to take this excessive love and offer it to me, and you will have reached the final limit (of love). What then is left? All that is left is little Jesus (me) with little Jesus (you). Marcel, you are one with me, as I am one with you; and eternally, we will be only one. So, therefore, little brother, you will remain in me during all eternity.

**Marcel**: Little Jesus, I feel tired. Allow me to rest. I do not expect you to take the trouble to warn me. It is better that I take the initiative.

My little Jesus, I am coughing a lot and my throat is very tickly. I must take some not too pleasant tasting medicine. On looking at it one would say that it is a bottle of wine; and the proof is that yesterday bearded Jesus showed this medicine to the brethren and they all said it was pleasant to taste. In fact anyone who has not tasted it would think that this syrup was sweet, but once swallowed, one realizes that it is not so ... That it is, rather, sour and sharp. If I take it, it is only for love of you, Jesus ...

It is really hard for me not to participate in the singing of Vespers, (552) since I really like singing. But I still have no voice. Later, I am certain, I will sing very well ...

Incidentally, little Jesus, did my father Saint Alphonsus like you a lot as a Child? Why did he write so much on your Passion?

**Jesus**: Little brother, why would he not have loved me as a Child? If your father Saint Alphonsus had not loved me as a Child, if he had not understood my life as a child, neither would he have been able to understand the death that I endured on the cross.

**Marcel**: Nevertheless, little Jesus, Brother Mark never stops criticizing me on this subject. He speaks only of the extraordinary favours granted to Saint Alphonsus; he does not like to speak of your childhood, or if he speaks of it, it is only to recall the sufferings you endured during your infancy. So, very often I only want him to stop talking, wishing that he would not say a single word. Your childhood was certainly not as Brother Mark described it.

*Jesus*: Come, come Marcel, you fly off the handle at the slightest thing. As I have already told you, all you have to do is listen to Brother Mark without having to agree with what he says. Follow the same line of conduct with him as with Brother Eugene, of whom I spoke this morning. Do you remember? Act in the same way and if he criticizes you, you will have a good opportunity to please me. Why concern yourself so much?

(553)

The sorrows I endured dying on the cross were external sorrows, but the interior sorrows were no less than the former. The outward sorrows endured until my death are nothing compared with the interior pain that I felt in my childhood in thinking of the sufferings I would have to endure later ...

Marcel! It is easier to suffer in the present than to think of the sufferings that one will have to endure later ... So, to summarize briefly, he who can understand my childhood can also understand my sorrows while dying on the cross. But if my life as a child is not understood, neither will one understand my sufferings at the moment of my dying on the cross ... My death on the cross is only the proof of my love, it is not Love itself. Little brother, I died outwardly, but my soul did not die as I told you the other day ...

Now, time is up. I am kissing you, I am giving them to you without stopping, no longer being afraid of sullying my lips, and I am holding my cheek always pressed to yours ... Go in peace, little brother ...

## 29 April 1946

(554) *Marcel*: Little Jesus, a short while ago the brothers asked me this question: 'Brother Marcel, do you want to join the ranks of the vietminh?' And I answered joyfully: 'Yes, I would gladly join the ranks of the communists ...' Little Jesus, such is really the case. Although my name is not inscribed in the party, my heart is already there. No brother understood the meaning of my reply. However, I would wish to join the ranks of the Vietminh so that, among them, there might be a little soul that loves you. This is what I think: in placing myself among the ranks of sinners, when I ask some favour, I am certain that my true Father in heaven will have more pity on me. I remember that my sister Thérèse taught me that a long time ago.

I wish to enter the ranks of the communists to hand over the communist flag to my Mother Mary, so that she can hand it over to you, Jesus;

and then I will be happy and at peace. Little Jesus, I am certain that the day will come when you will hold this flag in this country of Vietnam and that you will smile on it. I will not hesitate to enter the ranks of the Vietminh; wherever one finds the names of sinners, I wish that my name were there also. And if my name is there, you will be there also, little Jesus, since I am one with you, and you are one with me.

*Jesus*: This is true Marcel, and what else would you fear? Your heart being established in all the little specks of dust, (*laughing*) the communists would definitely not be afraid of you, little brother. So, among the communists what function will you fulfil? (555)

*Marcel*: I am going to love you in place of all the communists and ask you that they all get to know you and to understand clearly the meaning of the name of communist. Because only the kingdom of heaven can be called a communist kingdom. I cannot say more, little Jesus, I know that you already understand the feelings of my heart ...

I still remember that the other day, bearded Jesus asked me some questions to which I did not at all know how to reply. Any more and I would have cried. I am really very weak. I also think that if you asked me the same question that you once posed to Saint Peter: 'Peter, do you love me?' I certainly would not have been able to reply as he did. I answer you quite simply by my tears as proof of my love. Therefore, I would not reply either 'yes' or 'no' since loving you solely by love I would not know how to respond; I would however be certain that you understood my heart's feelings.

*Jesus*: Marcel, since you cry for the slightest thing, what is the point of questioning you? Weak as you are my question would only hurt you further and, then, I would have to reply myself for you; it would be really sad. So, stay calm. I will not question you. So, just now, what did you have to complain about? (556)

*Marcel*: I was very thirsty and I wanted to make a little sacrifice to offer to you. Therefore I decided to wait for half an hour before drinking; but you did not allow me and you made me drink. This little sacrifice would not harm my health in any way; further, it would be to your advantage, yet, you forbade me to do it.

*Jesus*: Little brother, I spurn this sacrifice. (*Laughing*) And I want to ask you a question. First of all, to make this sacrifice, did you have your director's permission? I have already told you, when you impose some mortification on yourself, you must speak of it to your director. Only then will you please me. *(Changing his tone)* The mortification that I want from you is the best of all and there is none that is better. Even if you endured, like me, death on a cross, it would not be better than the mortification that I wish to teach you here: namely, 'obedience'. The best mortification is obedience. You wish to practise mortifications to offer to me, but I do not like this kind of mortification; I only like the mortification of obedience.

(557) At Nazareth, did I take on fasting and mortification? Did I give myself the discipline? No. I knew only how to obey. Little brother, since you are one with me, you must also act like me. *(Laughing)* Yes, Marcel, you and I are only one. Then, why do you not like to act like me? Henceforth, you have no right to complain.

*Marcel*: Little Jesus, in favouring me as you do, do you not favour the propensities of my bad character?

*Jesus*: To indulge the inclinations of your bad character, Marcel, is to satisfy your self-will. Now, in indulging you as I do, do I satisfy your self-will? No. On the contrary my intention is to exercise you in obedience, since there is nothing better than obedience. Thus, you enjoy the advantage of being spoiled and, at the same time, you please me. Now, little brother, guess why I am plumper than you.

*Marcel*: Because you eat a lot of bread; that's the only reason. You are really very fat, fatter even than Mary and my sister Thérèse.

*Jesus*: You are not at all right. I am plump, simply because I know how to obey. In the past, when I was thirsty, I said to Mary: 'Mammy, your little one is thirsty.' And when she gave me a drink I was happy to drink it immediately. When I was hungry, I said to her: 'Mammy, your little one is hungry.' I had only to say a few words and Mary gave me, without delay, what I needed, because she cherished me greatly. Now you have no more reason than I to wish to call attention to yourself. Is
(558) it not to be virtuous to act as I have acted myself? It is necessary, therefore, that you behave as I did.

*Marcel*: So, what can I do to prove my love?

*Jesus*: Little brother, first of all, accept all the little inconveniences that I send you and, by that, you will please me more than if you fasted for a thousand years.

*Marcel*: Little Jesus, why do you speak of such a long time? Is it possible that the saints who fasted did nothing good?

*Jesus*: So, you find that long? Well, even if you fasted throughout eternity that would not please me for a single moment, because it would be contrary to my will. Come, little brother, listen: my intention in creating all things was to place them at man's disposal and not to abandon them in a corner. It is through love that I have created these things, so that you can enjoy them. If you do not make use of them when you need them, you scorn me. It is almost time ...

As for the saints, your brothers and sisters, why have they mortified themselves in these ways? Because they offered themselves to me with the intention of making retribution for the excesses committed by men, by their self-denial. Indeed, there are many people in the world who put created things to bad use, for example, who eat too much unnecessarily ... Now the saints have endured hunger so that this superfluous food which men abused also becomes pleasing in my eyes, that is to say with the intention that food should be considered by me as having served man for a good purpose. It is because of this that I joyfully give men what they need. All the things I have created I consider useful to man ... Enough, little brother, the time is up. Let us go quickly, little brother. Make a little sacrifice for me, if you wish. (559)

## 30 April 1946

*Marcel*: Little Jesus, one more day and the month of fraternal charity will be finished. Next month, it will not be necessary to beat me. Anyway, I am not worried, as you would not dare hit me. No matter how I provoke you, you dare not ever do anything. Today, little Jesus, I am more tired than yesterday. I have no appetite at all, which adds further to my tiredness. Yesterday I received an injection, and during the night the place where I was pricked made me feel very ill. Today, I again feel the pain but it is less painful than the *cuissard*, although it lasts longer. During your lifetime, little Jesus, did you ever receive an injection?

*Jesus*: I never needed an injection, because I was never ill. I was always well, because I knew how to allow Mary to care for me and to obey her perfectly. But you, Marcel, it is only through the force of argument that one manages to pamper you. (*Laughing*) It is necessary for me to show the advantages and the drawbacks to get you to obey me; and it is still with a certain shame that you do it ... (560)

*Marcel*: But, little Jesus, I am still a weak soul; you are the first to say so, and yet you still complain?

*Jesus*: Little brother, who would want to complain about you? Truly, you do not deserve to have me complain about you for the slightest thing, since you know nothing ... Time is up. Go, little brother.

*Marcel*: Little Jesus, I have been working for hardly a half-hour and I am shaking all over. I am not very tired, but I do not know why I am shaking this way. I do not at all feel hungry. If I said I was hungry, I would immediately have something to eat; but I do not feel hungry, I am just thirsty, yet, I do not want to drink anything.

Why are there a great number of saints who, seeing themselves specially favoured by you, have not allowed themselves to be spoilt in this way? Was that not to spurn you? And I, little Jesus, can I imitate them?

(561) *Jesus*: No, you may not; and furthermore I absolutely forbid it. I am the one you must always imitate. It was different for the saints; but for you, it is different also. To please me, all you have to do is obey me. You must always be ready to let me know your desires; in that way you will be able to sacrifice yourself and renounce your self-will. I do not expect you to demand anything but simply to let me know your needs.

*Marcel*: Little Jesus, the other day the brothers were talking about Sister Cecilia of Rome,* saying that you indulged her a lot, but it happened only a few times; after that she did not want to ask for anything more, for fear of hurting you ... I said to these brothers: 'If Jesus spoiled me as he did her, I would let him do as he pleased.' And the brothers replied that, if that was my attitude, you would not spoil me in that way. In that case, do you shower favours on souls only when you know they do not want your treats, it seems to me that that is very niggardly on your part. So, I do not at all agree with what the brothers said.

---

* Sister Cecilia of Rome (1897–1921). She was Canadian and a religious of Jesus-Mary. She is known because of her *Autobiography* 'one of the purest joys of the spiritual literature of the 20th century' (Preface by Father F.–M. Lethel, Carm.). She is better known to the general public by her family name Dina Bélanger under which her autobiography appeared. She was beatified on 20 March 1993.

*Jesus*: I do not oblige you to accept it. Nor do I oblige you to wish to be pampered. All I am asking you is to let me know your needs. As for spoiling you or not, allow me to take care of that. Such was my behaviour towards Mary. I never said to her: 'Your little one wishes to eat, wishes to drink, wishes this or that, etc.' I was content to say to her: 'Mother, your little one is thirsty, your little one is hungry, etc.' Then I allowed Mary to deal with it. Whether she gave me what I needed or not, I remained at peace, since all I had to do was to let her know my needs. I have repeated these things to you many times, but you always forget them. (562)

Marcel, my little brother, are you tired? I see you are shivering a lot. That's enough. Go and rest. Bearded Jesus has already given you permission.

Marcel, are you tired? Make a little sacrifice for me. Sacrifices in conformity with my will are the ones that please me the most. In the past I also followed this line of conduct. I conformed in everything to my Father's will. When God the Father wished that I do something, that I endure some suffering, I accepted everything cheerfully. Outside of that I did absolutely nothing special to please him. Concerning my self-will, I never did anything for myself. And if I had ever done anything along these lines, you can be sure that the divine Father would never have used me to redeem the world. Do you really understand?

*Marcel*: In this case, little Jesus, it seems that, outwardly, you never suffered as much as my brother Saint Gerard. Is that not the case? (563)

*Jesus*: Little brother, it is really so. Putting to one side my cruel death, I never endured any external suffering, I never imposed on myself any scourging of the flesh as Saint Gerard did, because the divine Father did not wish that of me. God the Father saw fit to choose for me the most perfect kind of suffering, interior sufferings I have endured throughout my life.

*Marcel*: So, voluntary penances that the saints impose on themselves would not have any value in the eyes of God? Little Jesus, that is something I do not understand.

*Jesus*: They have value and it is not my intention to denigrate the penances of the saints. Of himself, the divine Father does not oblige the saints to impose on themselves penances of this kind. But because the Holy Spirit who is Love makes known to them that nothing escapes divine justice, were it even a little thing, consequently, your brothers and sisters, the saints, having understood that, spontaneously offer

(564) themselves to do penance in place of the world, so that the gaze of God, being drawn by their penitential works, the Trinity takes them into consideration and is led, because of them, to readily forgive the world, since there is in it still a place to harbour Love. It is in this sense that the Church calls these penitential acts sacrifices offered to the justice of our heavenly Father.

However, little brother, so as not to trouble you, you must remember this: the saints have practised these penances simply with the intention of expiating the sins of the world and not to redeem it, since it is I who accomplished the work of the salvation of the world already.

*Marcel*: Little Jesus, I understand absolutely nothing. And how can I understand when you use such philosophical language?

*Jesus*: Why do you still seek to understand? Little brother, it is better that you do not understand.

*Marcel*: So, little Jesus, tell me what 'Victim of Love' means.

*Jesus*: They are victims who, through love, offer themselves to Love. These victims leave to Love complete liberty to accomplish his desires in them but of themselves, they do nothing to expend themselves; it is Love, that is to say the Holy Spirit who acts spontaneously in them ... What I have just said to you is sufficiently clear. You already feel tired, (565) little Brother. Go and rest. Besides, it is time. Go in peace and rest.

*Marcel*: Today, I do not know why I tire so easily. As soon as I do a little work, I feel tired. At midday, while suddenly thinking of Brother Mark's words, I felt very agitated and during the siesta I could not sleep. I will explain. Sometimes, on certain days, some news or other is mentioned in the refectory and Brother Mark tells this news to the brothers during recreation. I listen like the others and I even ask some questions, but often Brother Mark's version is not at all correct. So, when bearded Jesus asks who gave us this news, I answer, frankly, that it was Brother Mark, since I know that among the brothers he is the only one who understands French well. However it seems that Brother Mark does not like hearing me speak like this. Is it through humility or for another reason, I do not know. So it is that today at midday, while we spoke of the arrest of little Kháng, while doing the washing up, Brother Mark interrupted the conversation rudely and addressed these words to me: 'Everything that is said lands on Brother Mark's shoulders, be careful ... etc.'

I know that these words were aimed at me because I am the only one

who tells bearded Jesus: 'It was Brother Mark who said that ...' (566)
However I acted as if Brother Mark was not referring to me; and in a slightly stiff tone, but tempered with a little sweetness, I said frankly to him: 'In that case I think it would be better not to speak ...' The Brother asked me: 'Who told you to always question others?' I did not say anything else; rather I again said these words: 'It is certain that God, the infinite Truth knows the intentions of men of good faith.' After which I remained silent and I was bothered no more. But at midday, I do not know why, on recalling these things, I was once again annoyed. Nevertheless, little Jesus, allow me to love you with Brother Mark.

*Jesus*: Enough, Marcel, put that feeling to one side. Do you remember what I said to you the last time? You must not get angry since this business concerns me. What Brother Mark intended to say, it is to me that he said it. Who asked you to meddle in my business? Besides, if Brother Mark really knew your childlike simplicity, it is quite certain that he would not take offence at your words. My intention however is that he does not understand so that you, my little Jesus, may bear a little interior suffering from your brethren. That, Marcel, is the best mortification, a little mortification that Love itself sends to you, my little (567) Jesus. (*laughing*)

*Marcel*: So, Brother Mark is not sincere?

*Jesus*: Little brother, you have no right to ask me such a question; and besides, I will never tell you, since it is not your business. It is quite enough that I am the only one to know. What more do you want? If you knew, you would only be sadder. Know, however, that the simplicity of children is always different from that of adults. Indeed, children's simplicity is always natural, while that of adults can sometimes be natural and sometimes not. There is no doubt that bearded Jesus understands this; so there is no need to speak to him of it any more. You are already tired, go and rest. Go and drink now since you are very thirsty.

*Marcel*: Little Jesus, I am coughing a lot; I cannot go to the community meditation. I really love finding myself alone with you in my room; I cough much less then. Little Jesus, although I am coughing like this, you do not say a word to comfort me or encourage me to be patient. This evening, bearded Jesus gave me some nougat and some peanuts; I even had to eat the skin around the almonds. It was not as good as last time but, nevertheless, I ate them gladly and with a good appetite,

(568) so that you might not be sad, on seeing that I am not joyful when you are spoiling me.

Little Jesus, be pleased. I am still joyful although, today, I feel tired and I feel some disgust.

***Jesus***: *(laughing)*: Marcel! What did you just say earlier? Ah! You want me to comfort you. Listen carefully and perhaps you will be able to laugh a little. My little brother, I have a great deal of pity for you. Try to suffer a little for my love. So many times I want to pamper you to comfort you, but you never stop fearing this and that. And now, my little brother, you have just again reproached me for not having comforted you when I see you coughing. Little brother, from now on, do not reproach me so insanely any more, all right? I would like to comfort you often but I am afraid that you will hesitate to accept my comfort, and yet, you still dare to reproach me. That's enough. I forgive you, and I give you a kiss as well to please you. That is already a consolation for you, what more do you want? Would you still want your sister Thérèse to put on an act for you to make you laugh? Enough. Let us save that for the times when your eyes are quite red; then it will be necessary to resort to her.

***Marcel***: In fact, my sister Thérèse teases me a lot; later, in heaven, I will do the same to her. Little Jesus, we will play at 'hide and seek'. We will (569) make little Thérèse close her eyes while we will go to hide. I will ask Mary to hide me somewhere under her cloak, and then we will ask our Mother to shout 'ready' instead of us, so that my sister Thérèse does not know where we are hidden. I am sure that she will go to look for me in the midst of the Holy Innocents and that she will continue to wander among them until we are ready to show ourselves to her. So I will have the chance to make fun of her.

***Thérèse*** *(laughing)*: So, little brother, you intend to go and hide? Alas, Marcel, it is too childish. Did you not know I was here, to dare to plot in this way with little Jesus? It so happens that I already know your hiding place, both of you and if, later, you put your plan into execution, I will already be familiar with everything. My dear little brother, you are very foolish, but all the better for you, since it is solely thanks to this that I was forced to speak to you. Still that plot is already out in the open. That's enough. Or rather, to please you, I will pretend to have forgotten. Dear little brother, I see that you keep laughing; are you pleased with this solution? It's interesting is it not? Never be sad, little brother, I love you a great deal, always. I want to laugh all the time in thinking of what you have got up to with little Jesus ... Ah! The time is up, little brother, go and eat. I am giving you a kiss and I am adding to it a nice smile ... little brother! Little brother!

## 1 May 1946

*Marcel*: Little Jesus, my heart hurts a lot; so much that I am trembling a lot and am incapable of writing. It is as if someone pierced my heart with a needle. The pain lasts a moment, then it stops, but begins again a bit later. And it continues on this way. I am very tired; I am resting. Today, little Jesus, I have already begun to practise poverty. (570)

*Jesus*: Yes, Marcel, you are poor already. The kingdom of heaven belongs to those who are truly poor in heart, and to acquire this poverty of heart, it is necessary to behave like a child. Childlike perfection includes true interior poverty. Marcel, you doubtless still remember the lessons of your sister Thérèse on this subject ...

My little one! If, in the past, I did not possess true poverty of heart, it is absolutely certain that I would never have been able to save a single soul.

But, what is this interior poverty? Little brother, it will be up to you to answer this question, since your sister Thérèse has already taught you these things. However, little brother, take the trouble to write and let me again reply in your place.

During all of my life, from my birth to my death, I always maintained true poverty of heart. I am not speaking of external poverty, because external things are only the evidence of what is really in the heart. Really convinced of this truth, from my birth until my death, for my slightest actions – were it just a sigh – which were meritorious in my Father's eyes, I gladly gave all the merit to souls. I kept absolutely nothing with the intention of enjoying it personally, later. I left everything completely to souls. That is why the infinite merits that I accumulated are truly the property of all souls, even yours, Marcel. For myself, I knew that the kingdom of heaven belongs already to the truly poor of heart and that, as a consequence, it belongs to me also, as it belongs to the divine Father. And because my merits are infinite, my true interior poverty is equally infinite ... (571)

Marcel, your true Father, who exists from all eternity, is also infinitely poor. Listen, little brother, all that exists in heaven and on earth belongs to your Father; all the graces, all the blessings are his, but he never makes use of them as his own property; he keeps them solely for his children. In truth, little brother, your Father in heaven who is the Infinite Being makes himself infinitely poor in his dealings with you ... (572)

Do you understand, little brother? For your Father in heaven, true poverty consists in his true love.

And now, to come back to you, little brother, if you really want to be like me, you must be a real pauper in your heart. Without doubt, your heart is not attached to the goods of this transitory life ... but that is not yet true poverty of heart, since it is only a question of material goods while interior poverty is directed towards spiritual things.

(573) So, you must never work to gain merit with the intention of putting it in reserve for yourself, so as, later, to buy eternal happiness. If you had such an intention, it is sure that the kingdom of heaven would not belong to you. My merits alone have already gained the kingdom of heaven for you, so that, even if you had no other good, you would be able to take possession of this kingdom like children who have just been baptized. Tell me, are children able to do anything to gain the kingdom of heaven? Why do they go straight to heaven? Because they already possess true poverty of heart. Therefore, little brother, to amass spiritual goods and save them to make personal use of them later is a thing worthy of chastisement, because he who acts in this way shows that he has not an ounce of charity for souls; and not having charity, he does not have true love of God ...

Little brother, to reach true poverty of heart, you must renounce not only all attachment to the goods of this world, but even all desire to amass spiritual goods for the future life. It is due to my merits that you are able to acquire these spiritual goods, and as a consequence, they belong equally to souls and not to you alone. You must therefore always be prepared to give them to souls, as if you were giving them to me myself, since, in the last analysis, it is by my hands that they are distributed ... It is thus, Marcel, that the kingdom of heaven belongs to you as it belongs to me since you are one with me ...

*Marcel*: I have written beyond the allotted time. I am going to rest, I am very tired.

## 2 May 1946

*Marcel*: Today, little Jesus, I am less tired than yesterday, but I am still coughing and I have a pain in my spine. When I breathe deeply, I also (574) feel a lot of pain. Today, I once again ate maize ... But, little Jesus, let me ask you a question. On the subject of poverty of heart about which you spoke to me yesterday, if I renounce all attachment to spiritual goods, it seems to me that by that I scorn you. I do not understand very well; try to repeat it to me once more, just to clarify it.

*Jesus*: Very well. What is pleasanter than to answer you and instruct you? Have the patience to listen to me.

Yesterday, did I tell you to renounce all attachment to spiritual goods? Not at all. I told you that you must renounce the desire to amass spiritual goods that you would store in reserve for youself alone. This is very clear, clearer even than what your sister Thérèse taught you. Yes, although the merits that you acquired by your suffering, these crosses transformed into roses ... etc., you may have truly acquired them; you must, however understand that, without my infinite merits, all that would not have any value before your Father in heaven. Consequently, it is by virtue of my merits that the smallest works have value before your heavenly Father, and by virtue of this value, in his infinite justice, (575) he is obliged to reward you. And this reward, where does he get it from? He gets it from the infinite treasure of Love to award it to you, so that it becomes your personal possession. But you must remember that of yourself you can do nothing, that you must count on me so that I act in your stead. And you, you have only to come forward to receive the graces that I have acquired for you by my merits.

Let us suppose that you are the pen that you are using at this moment and I am in your place. Of itself, the pen cannot write any legible word. It is necessary for it to be guided by your hand to go up and down, to go from one side to the other to form words. That is a simple comparison but, for you, there is this difference: the works you do, it is I who must do them for you. Nevertheless, before your heavenly Father, it is you, yourself who does them ... You understand now, do you not?

You have truly become like another me, so that the merits you acquire are for you superfluous possessions. If you save these superfluous goods for yourself, you lack poverty of heart. There are a great number of unhappy souls who do not have sufficient spiritual goods to nourish themselves. You therefore have the obligation to give to them the alms of all your merits, as I am obliged to give you my infinite (576) merits. As you already possess my infinite merits, you already have enough for yourself, and you must give your surplus to others.

*Marcel*: So little Jesus, other souls then do not receive your merits?

*Jesus*: Why would they not receive them? From the beginning, my merits belong to souls; and since my merits are infinite, all souls can receive them, and that in an infinite manner for each one. But because there are a great number of sinful souls, poor souls who do not know where their heritage is, nor what they must nourish themselves with, these souls fall into extreme poverty ... It is, therefore, a duty for you and for fervent souls to look for a means of feeding these unfortunate souls. But what food is there to give them? My own merits that you already have in your hands and that you must now give to them as alms ... Then they will discover, little by little, where their food is ... Then they will be able to procure it themselves and each one will become (577) another me. All of that thanks to the poverty of heart that you will have practised.

There are also many souls who ardently desire to come to take possession of their heritage, but because they are too weak, they have need of the support of your hand, my little Jesus *(Marcel)* to reach their destination and receive their part of the heritage. Consequently, he who lacks true poverty of heart is lacking, also, in all the virtues. Furthermore, he kills me once more, spiritually, in the sense that he rends my infinite merits useless for one or another soul that he would have been able to save.

*Marcel*: Little Jesus, but what language are you using so that I still understand nothing?

*Jesus*: What can I do to help you understand more? Enough, little brother, it is not necessary for you to understand. What I wish is not that you understand but that you put these things into practice. To do that, it is sufficient that you offer unceasingly to Love all the graces received, all your works, all your breathing, all that you do through love for me, so that Love can distribute it to souls. As for what concerns yourself, allow Love to attend to it for you.

Although, personally, you have as a function to be the mother of souls, with regard to me, you are always just a very small brother, a very (578) small child to such an extent that you have no need to be concerned about yourself, but I must attend to everything in your place. Is that not so, little brother? You have no need to understand; if you cannot understand the lessons of your sister Thérèse, still less will you understand mine.

*Marcel*: So, little Jesus, among the saints one could find no one who has kept true poverty of heart? In fact, I do not hear anyone speaking of this interior poverty; they speak only of outward poverty. And when they explain the meaning of your life, they speak only of your external poverty, without ever saying anything of your interior poverty. My sister Thérèse was the first to speak to me of it the other day and I found it very strange.

*Jesus*: Little brother, your question is very clumsy. This is how it is: if someone practises true outward poverty, he also practises true interior poverty. If, during my earthly life, I had not practised true poverty of heart, but only outward poverty, my merits would never have been infinite, and they would not even have been sufficient to redeem a single soul in this world. As I have already told you, external poverty is the mark of interior poverty; and that is true also for your brothers and sisters, the saints.

Here is an example: in days gone by, your father Saint Alphonsus wore a patched-up soutane; it was the practice of external poverty. And (579) because he wore this patched-up soutane, he was able to practise humility, patience, charity, abnegation of self ... etc. Thanks to the practice of these virtues, what merits has he not acquired? And has he kept these merits to enjoy himself at a later date? Obviously not. Because your father Saint Alphonsus burned with a desire to save souls for me, he offered all these merits to me gladly so that I might distribute them to souls, so that, personally, nothing more remained to him, were it not the virtues he had practised. With me, it was the same; all the outward signs of poverty were only the sign of my interior poverty ... Do you understand, little brother? That is enough. It is not necessary for you to understand. Put into practice what I said and you will be truly poor, already you are my little Jesus.

*Marcel*: Little Jesus, according to what you have said, poverty is true charity, is it not? Now, true charity is love itself. So, it would be sufficient to give to poverty the name of love; is that not so, little Jesus?

*Jesus*: Unfortunately, as the language of this world is very inadequate, it is incapable of defining this word 'love'; it is only in heaven that it will be possible to understand the meaning of 'true poverty'.

*Marcel*: But how can poverty be infinite? (580)

*Jesus*: Come on, little brother, you have just said that poverty is 'love' itself; now love remains eternally; it is, therefore, infinite. You let yourself be confused by something so easy to understand. It is very unfortunate, little brother, you know absolutely nothing. I have hardly finished speaking when you have immediately forgotten everything. Nevertheless, there is nothing surprising in that since you are still very young.

*Marcel*: So, therefore, in heaven one will still be poor, since it is a question of interior poverty?

*Jesus*: Is that what I say in the Gospel? I only say: 'Blessed are the poor in spirit, since theirs is the kingdom of heaven'.* It is evident that in heaven you will no longer have to practise poverty, as you will no longer need to believe. Then faith and hope will be united in charity. Although there will no longer be any need to make acts of faith or of hope, these two virtues will subsist in charity. It will be the same for poverty; although one will no longer practise it in heaven, it will continue to subsist in charity. And it will be the same for all the virtues which will be contained in charity, in such a way that they will truly continue to exist, but without the need to practise them.

*Marcel*: Little Jesus, you are saying, therefore, that God the Father, being the Infinite Being, is also infinitely poor. How can that be?

(581) *Jesus*: Alas! Little brother, you are so fussy. Although you do not understand, you do not stop asking questions; it is really very difficult for you. If I do not reply to you, you get worked up. On the other hand, if I do answer you I do not succeed in making you understand even a little bit. You do not understand at all how that can come about? Listen, I am going to tell you.

Be patient a little. I am not angry with you; on the contrary, I am very pleased with you. Go, first of all to make a short visit to the Blessed Sacrament. Hurry, the bell has rung already.

In all justice, your Father in heaven must be infinitely poor; and if he were not so, what would the souls receive in heaven? It is certain that they would not receive the least joy ... So therefore, in justice it is necessary to give everything to souls and to accord them all the favours they are capable of receiving. Then does anything still remain to the Trinity? Only these souls remain. Because it is necessary to use language that is comprehensible to people that I speak thus in a broad sense, since, strictly speaking, the Trinity has never lived poorly. But since it is necessary to speak in a way to make men understand the Love that the Trinity has for them, I say Love makes itself as if it were infinitely poor.

(582) However, as Love is the infinite Being, nothing can be compared to it to an infinite degree ...

Enough, little brother, you are tired. Go and take your exercise book to bearded Jesus and rest yourself. Do what you wish to amuse yourself. I am giving you a kiss.

*Marcel*: Little Jesus, today I took a shower and, afterwards, I felt a bit better. I no longer feel any itching. Yesterday little Jesus, you again forbade me to take a shower.

---

\* Matthew 5, 3.

Ah! I'm very thirsty, I'm going to take a drink. There is a holy hour today. I will be able to chat for a long time with you; I am very pleased with that. I will tell you that I love you in my coughing fits, in my sufferings ... etc.

*Jesus*: That's enough, little brother. You say you are going to drink yet you do not stop talking? You are tired, that's enough for today. Now, go and rest.

But, Marcel, you are coughing a lot! It is good, stay in your room with me. Since you cannot make the holy hour, write to compensate for it. It is only right, isn't it?

What passage did you read in the Story of your sister Thérèse, a short while ago?

*Marcel*: I read this passage where she says: 'The virtue of poverty must not only renounce creature comforts, but even consent to lack what is necessary'.*

*Jesus*: Yes, Marcel, and it is because I wished to give you a lesson that I made you fall on this passage. If you wish to reach the renouncement (583) of your comforts in the spiritual life, you must give all to souls and then you will possess the kingdom of heaven, as I told you earlier.

But why does the virtue of poverty demand the lacking even of necessities? Do you understand that? Because I wish that you become humble, I often allow you to be deprived of interior joys ... So you can see your real poverty. This awareness of your poverty will inspire in you compassion for many other souls and this compassion for souls will prompt you naturally to donate to them the gift of all your spiritual favours. That is true poverty. In the times when you are deprived of favours that are necessary for you, if you joyfully accept this deprivation so that other souls may enjoy these same favours, that is true poverty of heart, true poverty that I, myself, practised ... That's enough, little brother, time is almost up. Your sister Thérèse has already taught you the rest. Besides, what I have told you is sufficient and you have already put it into practice. So, that's an end to it. Now, it is necessary that you go to supper. I am giving you some kisses to please you. So, close your copybook, put the stopper on your inkpot, put away your pen and go. Your page is finished.

---

\* '... Poverty consists in seeing oneself deprived not only of pleasing things but also of essential things ...' Ms A folio 74 recto.

## 3 May 1946

(584) **Marcel**: Little Jesus, yesterday I was very angry, and if I had not made a big effort to restrain myself, I would have torn into pieces the life of the great Saint Teresa. I do not know why translators who are so clumsy dare get involved in translating books and have them printed for people. Little Jesus, never in speaking of yourself, have you used the word *Tao*.* People are truly very proud. Yesterday, I was not able to do my spiritual reading; and if you had not prevented me, I would certainly have torn out two pages of this book. I thought to myself: if later in heaven you were to speak in this way, I would lose all happiness, so that I would prefer to remain eternally on earth, so as to speak to you as a child speaks to his father.

*Jesus*: Little brother, so you do not remember: the last time when you moaned about translators, I recognized that they were at fault. But yesterday, who authorized you to cross out the word *Tao* in this book? You will have to ask bearded Jesus' forgiveness. That was such a childish anger. That it angered you, fair enough, but what right have you to draw a line through the words? From now on you must correct yourself, all right? Now, go and accuse yourself. Take the book to show it to bearded Jesus ...

(585) **Marcel**: There is at least one page where I will not have to read this word *Tao* that is put into your mouth. In spite of that I am still very angry. From now on, if in my readings I again encounter passages which include the word *Tao*, I will not read them since you have never spoken in this way; I would consider these words as not coming from you. Since the creation of the world until now, it has never been said anywhere that our true Father in heaven, speaking to men, his children, has used the word *Tao*; he uses only the word *Cha*.† *Tao*, how awful! Ah! Little Jesus, I am very annoyed at not being able to do anything to suppress this word *Tao* from being put into your mouth. Other words, no matter how beautiful and intimate they are, if they are accompanied by the word *Tao*, become words without love, words which smack of pride.

---

\* I, authoritarian, overbearing.
† The term *Cha* signifies Father. When a father uses it, it is a fatherly way of saying 'I'.

*Jesus*: Marcel, lucky for you that yesterday you did not tear out the two pages in question. If you had torn them out you would certainly have been very troubled, since the simple fact of having drawn through some words has been enough to make you cry ... Marcel, let that be enough; do not get angry uselessly. It is not possible for you to burn all the books that include the word *Tao*. By that you would be lacking the virtue of poverty and it would be serious! Therefore, have the patience to read these books such as they are. Besides, you know that in reality, I have never spoken in such a way. If I, myself, am not angry, you have no reason either to be angry and to be sad.

Although men give my words an appearance of harshness, I do not (586) take offence at it; I put up with it patiently and I wait for the words that I am addressing to you here to reach men to make them understand I never use harsh words, when I speak with them ...

Marcel, I see all the same that you have a fairly difficult nature. After all, this business concerns me. And even if you are angry, that changes nothing. Come, it is better to be patient like me and to take the trouble to write down what I am saying ...

But I still have to take you to task for another fault: where did you get the audacity to say that the translator was proud? It is too much! You are very silly, my little brother. It is not at all so; the translator was a virtuous man, perhaps even more virtuous than you. He also meant well, believing that his translation corresponded exactly to the manner in which Love acts towards man. It is because he believed he was doing it well that he translated it that way. But if the translator knew what you know, he would not have translated as he did and nothing would have happened to make you angry, my little brother ... So, that's how it is. However, I allowed it to happen so that you may be more certain that (587) it is I who wished it thus so as to give you the opportunity to mortify yourself a little. If everything were in keeping with your wishes, what would you look for to produce roses of love? So, the word *Tao*, far from being harmful, is also useful for you. Do not get angry any more. That is my business and not yours; there is no need to get angry.

*Marcel*: Today, I felt really hungry. I spoke of it to bearded Jesus, but he gave me absolutely nothing. I found that very hurtful. From now on, I will speak to him no longer about it. Whether I speak to him or not, it's all the same.

*Jesus*: If it's all the same, you must nevertheless speak to him about it. I told you that you should speak of it to bearded Jesus, but not that bearded Jesus should give you something to eat. What a shame for you. And now, are you hungry?

*Marcel*: Good question! I have just come from the table, how could I still be hungry? All you know how to do is to tease me; when I am not hungry, you ask me the question, but you do not ask me the question when my stomach is empty.

(588) *Jesus*: Since your stomach is full, that's enough; wait for the next time, bearded Jesus will give you something to eat. Nevertheless, if he gives you something or not, you must speak to him about it all the same. Yes, I am obliging you to speak to him about it but I am not obliging you to eat. If you do not speak to him about it, I will not be pleased with you. Since I wish it so, you must listen to me; it is by doing this that you will show yourself to be obedient ... Now I ask your forgiveness for having allowed you to suffer too much from hunger and, to make it up to you, I am allowing you to go to sleep ten minutes earlier. So, go and sleep ...

*Marcel*: Little Jesus, I do not know why I am so sad this evening. I do not at all know what to say to you.

*Jesus*: Ah! Little brother, so you are very sad? It is necessary that you think a little of priests; it is for them that you must pray today. Offer this sadness to me. Are you tired?

*Marcel*: Yes, I am.

*Jesus*: You are tired? Then, do you wish to rest? If you wish it I will gladly dispense you from writing.

*Marcel*: I am not very tired, but I feel a great deal of disgust. I really want to write, but if you do not speak, I will have nothing to write and I will be forced to rest. Now, I am no longer given honey.

*Jesus*: As you are coughing less you have no more need to take it. Did you eat well at midday?

*Marcel*: I had no appetite at all ... But, little Jesus, I am going to rest. I am very thirsty and I have no wish to write. I am leaving you little Jesus, give me a kiss and be content to let me go.

## 4 May 1946

*Marcel*: Dear Mother, on this day which is specially dedicated to you, I promised to go to communion and to offer to Jesus all that belongs to me, and to ask him to have pity on your apostles. (589)

Mother, I love you a great deal. Concerning your reign to come, it will not be given to me to work for its expansion, since I cannot preach to the world or do absolutely anything. However, dear Mother, I will be your child, I will stay in your arms with little Jesus to help your apostles; I will love you in company with little Jesus, and my sister Thérèse and my father Saint Alphonsus. With little Jesus, I will hide myself in all the souls on earth, so as to love you in each one of them. I will even be in the souls that do not love you, so that there also you may be loved ... Oh Mother, how time passes! I cannot speak to you for a long time, I must leave you. I love you a lot; dear Mother give me a kiss. I am saying goodbye to you.

Mary, little Jesus is very lazy. He shares the same room with me but he never takes the trouble to sweep the floor. I have to do it each week. I am asking you to mention it to him in my place, since if I speak to him about it, I am not sure he will listen to me. This bedroom is full of spiders' webs; if it continues like this, perhaps, in a little while, I will not even have a path to get out. The Zealator has already blamed me twice but I haven't got enough time to sweep. As for little Jesus, he spends all day playing, but he does not take the time to sweep. He has obviously decided to allow me to suffocate in this room ... (590)

Ah, I've found the answer! You must allow me to make, as appropriate, a division of labour. Without that it will be very difficult for me. Little Jesus will sweep instead of me; my sister Thérèse will wipe the table and make everything tidy and you, Mother, will make my bed. And, as I am very small, I will go and play. Mother, do you agree? It is fair that I divide the work in this way, otherwise, I will continue worrying.

*Mary*: Marcel, who has told you to worry? Up till now you have not had to worry at all about the room of your soul.

*Marcel*: But, Mother, I am talking about the room I live in.

*Mary*: My child, just listen to me a little. Your soul is really a living room; and in this room, what dust and untidiness ... It is I who must sweep it and make everything tidy; it is I who must make sure to open and close the door so that you may breathe easily and be comfortable. In short, it is impossible for me to favour you more than I do. I am like

(591) your servant. After having freed you from your scruples, I save you from occasions of sin ... And yet, my child, you complain about having the most difficult work? Whether or not you divide up the work, I still must do everything, whereas you have no other job but to play. Would playing be a very difficult task for you? So, change jobs with me. My child, you see that I wish to have fun so you may be happy. Truly, if I confided to you the care of the room of your soul, you would not know how to find a means of getting out; you would certainly have a body tangled up in spiders' webs.

*Marcel*: But, Mother, little Jesus and my sister Thérèse are, then, doing nothing?

*Mary*: You are, all three of you, busy playing, what more can you want? If little Jesus and your sister Thérèse were busy like me, who would play with you?

*Marcel*: Mother, must you really give yourself so much trouble? The room of my soul is certainly very small, so that, in my opinion, your work ought not to consist of anything tiresome.

*Mary*: There is only one job I find tiresome. I have even asked little Jesus and your sister Thérèse to help me in this, but it seems that we have not yet fully succeeded. Do you know what it is a question of? Bearded Jesus, himself, has not been able to bring it to a close; I mean that he has not succeeded in ridding you of anxieties. This spider's web is very difficult to remove, but I have the firm hope that one day you will be relieved of it. I know that this spider's web, in which consist your troubles, makes breathing very difficult for you. However, remain at (592) peace, I am going to do the chores for you and so you will be very happy.

*Marcel*: But Mother, this room I am living in is very dirty; so what can be done?

*Mary*: The cleanliness of your room is your business my child. Go to work, then little Jesus, your sister Thérèse and I will help you. When Thursday comes ask bearded Jesus to give you enough time, and I am sure that in fifteen minutes all will be done. It's only a trifle, all you have to do is get rid of the spiders' webs ...

That's enough. When the day comes, I will take care of it for you. Now you must go to sleep. I am giving you a kiss. Rest in peace on my heart.

*Marcel*: Little Jesus, I love you a lot. I am going to sleep with you. Mary, this evening I am coughing a lot and I continually feel sadness. From time to time I feel a very sharp pain in my heart. Little Jesus is very unruly with me; he only knows how to do foolish things. If my heart broke, what would happen?

*Mary*: So, Marcel, you are afraid that your heart is breaking? All the better then. Say this to little Jesus: 'Little Jesus, I am not afraid that my heart is breaking; continue to play with it, without being concerned. If it breaks, you will have to clasp it closely, without daring to let loose for (593) a single moment, for fear that the blood might escape from it and that death will necessarily follow. It would be of benefit to me. I would no longer fear to see you sleeping, since you would have to pay attention to my heart unceasingly.'

My dear child, allow little Jesus to play as he wishes with your heart, which pleases him a lot. Each of its beats is like a smile that you give to him. Little Jesus loves your heart because your heart comforts him during your sleep and during the hours when you are unable to converse with him. Yes, he loves it for so many reasons that you cannot understand them all.

*Marcel*: All the same, that makes me very ill.

*Mary*: If that makes you ill, try to be patient a little to please little Jesus. You spare nothing for each other, my children; both of are be very happy together. And you, Marcel, if you express the desire to have something, little Jesus gives it to you immediately, cheerfully. Now, if little Jesus is a little unruly with you, stay calm and act as if you were very pleased to see him act in this way. You have nothing to fear, Jesus only gives kisses to your heart.

*Marcel*: I know that very well. Also, each time little Jesus plays with my heart, I notice it immediately. The other day he pretended to give me the anointing of the sick. Touching my heart he said: 'Ah! This heart (594) belongs to me; it is very attractive. I am giving it a kiss.' I then had a strong urge to laugh. Even though my feet were very dirty, little Jesus, nevertheless, placed his lips on them ...

Incidentally, the other day bearded Jesus asked me to put in writing this story of the anointing performed by Jesus, but I hesitated not knowing how to tell it. By doing this, Mother, have I been impolite towards bearded Jesus?

*Mary*: Not at all. Bearded Jesus did not force you, he left you free to do it or not. However, to please him, you should tell it to him. As the time has passed already, you should write it tomorrow ... Go, my child. Hurry. I am kissing you.

(595) ***Marcel***: Mother, this lamp is very weak. I must pull it closer to my table but, in spite of that, it isn't much brighter. Mother, I am coughing a lot. I cannot go to the communal meditation. I am, therefore, remaining here with you, with little Jesus and my sister Thérèse. That is all right, isn't it? That's strange. Why is this lamp so weak today? Mother, give me some light so I can write. Ah! Have you just given me a kiss? I noticed it straight away. Although, externally, I feel nothing, interiorly I notice it quite naturally, but without understanding how I notice it. Oh! Another one. And each time I receive a kiss, I am able to distinguish if the kiss comes from you, Mary, or from little Jesus, or from my sister Thérèse. So, it seems to me that I am more skilful than an astrologer. Is that not so Mary?

***Mary***: But are you not also an astrologer?

***Marcel***: Mother, I am not an astrologer, I am simply your child; I am only the victim sacrificed to the Love of Jesus ... Mother, I am coughing a lot.

***Mary***: My child, did you just mention sacrifice? So, offer your cough as a sacrifice to Jesus. Listen, I am going to tell you a new method of sacrificing yourself. Each time that you are troubled, even if only for the span of a breath, say this: 'Little Jesus, I offer you this worry as a sacrifice.' Then, remain in peace. Thanks to this sacrifice, you will be consumed in the fire of Love, which will act freely in you. Thanks to this sacrifice, how many sinful souls will be able to avoid an occasion of sin that would expose them to falling into despair? ...

(596) Always remember this method, all right? Little Jesus loves this kind of sacrifice a lot; he even prefers it to the joy of being able to pull you from the hands of the devil, since it is the devil who gives birth in you to these anxieties with the intention of misleading you. Consequently, if you offered your anxieties to little Jesus, naturally, the devil will be ashamed to see that the net that he holds out to you to drag you along has fallen into little Jesus' hands. Then, little Jesus will make use of it to draw you to his heart, and then he will make use of it to draw many other souls ... What a blessing for you! What a benefit for little Jesus! Oh, my child, it is impossible to express the extent of this great benefit And yet, to obtain this result, you only have to say: 'Little Jesus, I offer you this sacrifice.'

*Marcel*: Mother, there are still five minutes, allow me to prepare to go to supper. Mother, I love you dearly, dearly. I love you as little Jesus, and my sister Thérèse and my father Saint Alphonsus love you. Mother, I love you. My only occupation in heaven will be to love; I will have no need then to eat. Is that not so, Mother? I am saying goodbye to you ... Give me a kiss ... Allow me to leave you.

## 5 Mother 1946*

*Marcel*: My Mother Mary! This morning, wishing to avoid sleeping at (597) prayer, I invented the following method. After having assigned a part of the oratory to each saint, I went to pay him or her a visit in company with little Jesus. I did it interiorly only in my heart.

I went, first of all, with little Jesus, to my sister Thérèse. We greeted her, I felt like laughing. And this is what she replied to us: 'My little brothers, so where are you going?' I began to laugh and, in my astonishment, I asked myself why my sister Thérèse gave little Jesus the name of little brother. I looked at little Jesus who answered me in this way: 'It is because, in the past, she only gave me the name of little brother. Also she had to spoil me more than I spoiled her, since I was her little brother.' After that, both of us did not stop laughing.

Once again little Jesus began to speak: 'My sister Thérèse, this particular month is the month of our Mother; we must be sure to obtain many flowers for Marcel, so he can offer them to our Mother during the month of Mother.' Then the three of us laughed. My sister Thérèse showed how happy she was. From that moment we no longer said the month of May, but only the month of Mother. Thérèse, our sister, then (598) gave each of us a kiss and she took us in her arms. As I was smaller than little Jesus, she carried me on her left arm. We both gave her a kiss; after which she placed us in an armchair and disappeared. A moment later she came back and gave something, what it was I do not know, to each of us; I have even completely forgotten its shape.

The clock struck the quarter hour and I realized that I had stayed too long with my sister Thérèse, so that no more than fifteen minutes remained to visit all the others that I had not yet visited. While I was thus distracted, everyone disappeared. I no longer saw Jesus, or my sister Thérèse, whose voice only I could hear, neither did I see myself. All had disappeared.

I then heard my sister Thérèse say to little Jesus and me: 'My little

---

\* Van will give an explanation of this new name for May below.

(599) brothers, the time is almost up, that's enough, stay with me. As for the other brothers and sisters, let me visit them instead of you.' These words calmed me down, but once again I was distracted, thinking of the Vietminh and Vietnam. I wanted to have many rifles and aeroplanes to fight the communists and prevent them from reigning over Vietnam, my country. Mother, I even asked little Jesus to grant me what I wanted, but he was content to answer me: 'The best weapon for safeguarding the interests of your country and to snatch it from the hands of the communists, is prayer. Do not stop looking towards me, little brother, and that will be enough. Each of your glances with this intention is enough to make me understand the situation of Vietnam, your country.' My sister told me the same thing as well.

*Mary*: And I, my child, I tell you the same thing also. The only means to save your country from communism is prayer. This is very easy; it requires neither cunning, nor rifles, nor ammunition. A glance, or a smile, or a sigh toward little Jesus is enough; it is like a game within reach of everyone.

(600) *Marcel*: Incidentally, little Jesus, what did our sister Thérèse give us this morning? Do you remember? I would love you to tell me.

*Jesus*: Little brother, I remember very well but before telling you, you must say to me first, five times: 'Little Jesus, I love you a lot.'

*Marcel*: Little Jesus, I love you a lot. Little Jesus, I love you a lot. Little Jesus, I love you a lot. Little Jesus, I love you a lot. Little Jesus, I love you a lot. There you are, it's done.

(601) *Jesus*: Very good. The devils have already taken flight. They wanted to trouble you, but on seeing that Love envelops you, they became afraid and have all fled. Now, listen, I am going to tell you what our sister Thérèse gave us this morning. It's quite straightforward, nothing out of the ordinary. She simply gave us two connecting tubes. Yours is meant to collect all your sighs, all your glances, all your smiles and all that belongs to you, in order to pass them to me. As for mine, it receives all my kisses, all my caresses and all there is in me to pass them on to you. And thanks to these connecting tubes we are but one whole since there is a mutual exchange of all we possess. If you cannot understand such a simple thing, little brother, it is a sign that you are still very ignorant. These two tubes must be called the tubes of Love.

*Marcel*: Truly, I have just learned an interesting lesson, but where has my communicating tube gone?

*Thérèse*: There is no tube in reality, little brother. I made you see these things in a purely spiritual manner to help you understand, but what use is a tube? Do you understand?

*Marcel*: Yes, I understand. But, my sister Thérèse, so it was you who just spoke to me? I thought it was little Jesus. Were it not for the word *Chị*\* I would certainly have been deceived. I am, all the same wide-awake, and I am sure that no one can deceive me. Time is up. I am leaving you. You will speak to me in a little while.

Little Jesus, I remember that during my childhood, there was someone who loved me a lot. Seeing that I suffered continually at the presbytery of Hữu-Bằng, she spoke of me in these terms: 'This child will probably have to suffer all his life. Still so small and to suffer as he suffers, how will he be able to grow?' I think these words contain a morsel of truth, is that not so, little Jesus? There are many people who, after having observed such or such a thing about me, have predicted my future. I had a strong urge to laugh ... (602)

But, little Jesus, why was I so ill at ease a moment ago? I adored the Blessed Sacrament for only a half-hour and I found it extremely long. I had only one desire, to come back as soon as possible. I do not understand why it was so. On the other hand, at the moment of returning, I regretted having not behaved well towards you. I beg you to forgive me. Pardon me, and allow my heart to return with you to the presence of the Blessed Sacrament, to stay there and love you unceasingly.

*Jesus*: Little brother, why do you concern yourself so? Do you think that I no longer understand? You had to make an effort to remain with me; that is a greater sacrifice than if you had remained on your knees all day in my presence.

*Marcel*: So, little Jesus, do I still love you?

*Jesus*: Why not? And why do you ask me this question? That's enough, little brother, remain in peace. I am always pleased with you.

---

\* Big sister. This can only be understood in the Vietnamese text of Thérèse's reply. She uses the word *Chị* to say 'I'. In this way, Van understood that his 'big sister' had intervened in the conversation.

*Marcel*: Little Jesus, I am so sad I do not know what to say.

(603) *Jesus*: You know, at least, how to breathe and to look; so, take your breaths and your glances and give them to me. Is that not to speak to me? Would you be afraid that I might not understand? Come, I understand you very well.

*Marcel*: Little Jesus, I have not yet received my injection today. I must go and let bearded Jesus know. I am going there, little Jesus.

Little Jesus, last night I said the following words to Brother Mark and he made fun of me: 'The physical sufferings that Jesus endured during his life are not equal to a single sigh coming from his internal sufferings.' The Brother laughed at me in a scornful manner, letting me know that what I said was unacceptable. I was not angry; I quite simply greeted the brethren and went to lie down.

*He then went to bed before the others because he was unwell.*

(604) *Jesus*: There is nothing surprising in that because you let slip something I had said to you. You should not be surprised that he scorned you because you used words you do not understand. These words are correct but you cannot say them because you do not understand them. Fortunately you were not angry, because if you had been angry you would certainly not have dared to boast of the matter to me. So, from now on, no longer repeat any of the words I have addressed to you. Let the brothers speak as they understand it and if you really notice that they have got it wrong, speak of it to bearded Jesus, but reveal nothing of what I have said to you, for fear that one or another of them manages to guess what is happening in you.

*Marcel*: In this case what will there be for me to say to the brethren? Truly, I have absolutely nothing to say to them; all I know is how to ask questions.

(605) *Jesus*: Little brother, I was also in the same situation. In the temple all I could do was to listen and to question the doctors of the law. And if these doctors of the law did not know what to answer, I asked their permission to give explanations. It is evident that in speaking with people who know less than you, you must speak and give them explanations, not through pride but only through charity. With the brethren who certainly know more than you, let them speak and be content to listen. If you hear things that are not interesting, act as if you find them very interesting so as to please the brothers, as I told you before.

*Marcel*: Incidentally, little Jesus, during the three days you spent in the temple, who gave you food to eat? Brother Mark said you went begging. Is that true?

*Jesus*: What Brother Mark supposes, is correct from his point of view, but from my point of view it is not correct. People are, without doubt, going to find the reply that I am giving you here very strange. I am certain, however, that children will be comforted by it.

I asked the doctors of the law many questions, and because they did not know how to answer, I asked them to allow me to give them some explanations. I did it so well that even the children were capable of understanding it all. Because of this they loved me a lot. Also, during those three days, outside the time dedicated to the explanation of the Sacred Scripture, they invited me to go and play, to visit their homes, and then they gave me food to eat. I was sometimes in one house and sometimes in another. All the children liked to take me to play; but (606) usually it was the children of the priests and other people in the service of the Temple. During these three days I taught them a lot on subjects easy to understand. They were very happy conforming to my wishes and, for my part, I loved them a lot ...

On the third day, when my Mother and Saint Joseph entered the Temple, they found me in the midst of the children of the high priests explaining the law to them, in response to the desire of the doctors. Mary did not make me go back immediately; she waited for me to finish and only after that, she took me back. Many priests showed me great affection; others sang my praise in Mary's presence. I had to return to Nazareth with her, but my heart remained in the midst of the children who had shown me such marks of affection ... And some of these children who played then with me are now in heaven ... Blessed are the children, the kingdom of heaven is theirs ... Marcel, it is time. Go and sleep.

*Marcel*: So, little Jesus, what did you do to amuse yourself with the children? (607)

*Jesus*: The children in the Temple usually played with a lot of reserve. I also conversed with them as I do with you and I used all different means to capture their hearts.

*Marcel*: Little Jesus, were the parents of these children happy to feed you?

*Jesus*: Of course. Even many people, at the sight of my beauty, asked some questions. They found it very strange to see me so handsome and so smart. Usually the children gave me something to eat all day. Each time they received something they shared it with me, as I have already told you.

*Marcel*: Little Jesus, in those times, did you wear sandals?

*Jesus*: Yes, but the sandals were not like those of today. They were almost the same as those worn by Vietnamese country folk. I did not have beautiful sandals but ordinary ones. The same went for my clothes.

*Marcel*: So, you had no trousers?

(608) *Jesus*: Why not? But my trousers were different from yours, since in those days people did not yet know how to sew.

*Marcel*: I have heard people say that you had no sandals and that you had to walk barefoot. If that were true, I think you would have frozen to death since, in Palestine, it is very cold.

*Jesus*: These are assumptions people make but, in fact, since the day I was able to walk, I always wore sandals according to the custom of the times. Even the poorest had to wear them, otherwise how would they have been able to walk barefoot in the snow?

*Marcel*: It is also said that you wore a belt made of jute fibres, is that really true?

*Jesus*: Yes, it is true. People made a strip of cloth of average width with these jute fibres, which served as a belt. However, when I was small, I had a belt of lamb's wool, which my Mother made so that I was more beautiful, but only for feast days ...

  Little brother, I see you are tired. Take some time to rest yourself a little and after that, you will go to take collation.

(609) *Marcel*: Good day little Jesus. I am a bit tired and I do not know why this nib now has such a contrary temper; I have great difficulty writing with it.

*Jesus*: If you didn't have a worse character than your nib, you would be able to write more easily; but because you have a more troublesome character than it, the difficulty increases even more.

*Marcel*: Little Jesus, why don't you indulge me? Can't you give me another pen?

*Jesus*: I cannot encourage you in a lack of poverty. Have the patience to use it for some time yet since it is still in good enough condition. Were you to put it aside now, you would be lacking in poverty. I cannot spoil you in going against the vows of religion. Be a little patient and offer me this sacrifice; it will be to the advantage of the community, advantageous for me and, at the same time, useful for you ...

Little brother, are you a little tired? Accept this fatigue. I love you dearly. Following my example, try to be poor to the end. All that you gain by your sufferings, by your love and by your sacrifices, give as alms to souls, and then I will be your property, and you will obtain everything because you will have been poor like me.

*Marcel*: Little Jesus, you tell me to give everything to souls; in that case, who will look after my soul? (610)

*Jesus*: Why worry, little brother? You have abandoned yourself to me, leaving me to watch over everything. Now, you know that I lack nothing and that you obtain all you desire. On the other hand, there are still many souls who do not know how to abandon themselves to me and who, for this reason, always remain in need. Therefore it is necessary that you give alms to them, so that they have the means to live. But what will you give them as alms? My infinite merits, these merits that I have given gladly to you and without reserve, and which have become your property. So, possessing this treasure, you must give alms to nourish other souls who do not yet know this treasure of my infinite merits. You must give to poor souls these infinite merits, just as I have given them to you. You have the power to make use of these infinite merits as you wish, to give them to destitute souls, because they are yours to give. (611)

All souls which are consecrated to me in a special way, all those who are my privileged spouses, must practise poverty in this way. Because of this, they will possess the kingdom of heaven. Only the souls who, after following my example, possess true poverty of heart have the right to use my merits as they wish to distribute them to souls ...

*Marcel*: Little Jesus, Brother Augustine has new sandals. And I who have such worn sandals, you do not give me new ones. It's a fact that you spoil Brother Augustine more than me.

*Jesus*: Marcel, my little brother, do you need new sandals to gain my heart? As we are one, you must resemble me. Now, I have never had

(612) sandals as beautiful as yours. Indeed, my sandals were only a piece of leather held by some straps, while yours have several layers of leather and can still last you a bit more time. Be patient a little more; this month is the month of poverty. When you are in heaven, it is Mary's bosom that will serve you as sandals for walking ... Enough, be patient a little while longer.

The time is up. Go wash your feet and after, go to meditation. Goodbye, little brother. I am giving you a kiss and clasping you to my breast.

## 6 Mother 1946

*Thérèse*: Marcel, what have you just eaten? Why did you not give me some? Did you give some to little Jesus?

*Marcel*: I ate some peanuts, nothing more. Besides, you know already so why do you ask? Bearded Jesus told me to give some to little Jesus; I offered him some but he refused, saying he was not hungry. For you, my sister, I saw that there was too little and, fearing that there might not be enough, I did not give you any. Besides you are already big so I can eat your share as well, since you no longer need to eat.

*Thérèse*: Nevertheless, little brother, you did not say a single word to me. You are very greedy, Marcel, aren't you?

(613) *Marcel*: Bearded Jesus gave these peanuts to me and not to you. So, there are very few of them. And why didn't you ask for some in a humble manner? If you had asked me, I would have given you some because there are some left. Do you want to eat some? Let me ask bearded Jesus to give you some.

*Thérèse*: I am teasing you, little brother. Now, I no longer have any desire to eat peanuts. Besides, I no longer feel hungry like you. The only hunger I feel is the hunger for souls to offer to little Jesus.

*Marcel*: My sister Thérèse, tell me, to eat as I do, does that show a tendency towards greed?

*Thérèse*: Yes, little brother, it certainly shows a tendency toward greediness, nothing else. However, you have no reason for concern, since if you eat often, you also love often. Little Jesus does not take note of the fact that you eat, but simply of the fact that you eat through love.

Why does little Jesus make you tell your director the slightest things that happen to you? It is to teach you humility. Each time you act in this way, you hand over to Jesus your self-will. Little Jesus wants you to have confidence in your director just as you have confidence in him. That is why he makes you confide to your director all the little things that concern you. He wants you to reveal everything to your director; and (614) each time you do so, you allow him to see your great weakness. However, it pleases little Jesus more to receive your weaknesses than it would to accept your extraordinary mortifications. Why is that? Because, if you are weak, little Jesus constantly holds you close to him and holds you tightly in his arms. So, all the times you are eating, you are expressing your love to Jesus by means of your weakness ... Marcel, thanks to your weaknesses, you can save a great number of souls. Little Jesus wants you to reveal all your weaknesses so that men will know of the mercy of their true Father in heaven towards the world.

So therefore, my dear little brother, all little Jesus does to spoil you, far from being harmful is, on the contrary, useful for you and by it you can save a great number of sinners.

*Marcel*: My sister Thérèse, it is said that eating peanuts makes one cough a lot. So, I don't know why bearded Jesus makes me eat them. (615) Perhaps he doesn't know that. Is that so, my sister?

*Thérèse*: Whether he knows or not, little brother, since Jesus gives you these peanuts, accept them gladly and eat them. What you do through obedience never harms you.

*Marcel*: I really like peanuts, but I'm afraid that, by eating a lot of them, I will cough more. I eat them only to please bearded Jesus ...

My sister, my time for resting is now over. Allow me to go and work. I began to solder a metal container but I have not yet finished. I sought the help of Brother Bonaventure who is doing the work for me. I also asked little Jesus to help him so I could go to rest ... it is really time. Goodbye, my sister.

Little Jesus, today I do not have much of an appetite, but I ate a lot nevertheless. At dinner, peanuts were given me again to eat and they were better than the ones bearded Jesus gave me. At the beginning I was afraid the peanuts might make me cough, but my sister Thérèse told me to continue eating them, since it is through love for you that I eat them. She even insisted, saying: 'Little brother continue to eat them; there is absolutely nothing that is dangerous for you. The (616) only thing you must avoid is troubling yourself.' I think she was right so I continued to eat as usual ...

Little Jesus, I have just found a piece of verse. I do not remember when I wrote it. I believe my sister Thérèse helped me compose it; in fact I am sure of it. Now that I re-read these verses, I want to smile. In them I give you the name of Spouse. I remember being inspired for this poem by the *Canticle of Canticles*. It is very beautiful. You will certainly laugh a lot on hearing it. However, I am careful to hide this poem, not showing it to anyone. I am going to hide it even from bearded Jesus, just to see ...

But, little Jesus, why do you not teach me to paint so I can do your portrait? If I were an artist, I would certainly paint your portrait along with one of Mary and even of my sister Thérèse. That is something I would very much like, but I do not know how to paint.

(617)

*Jesus*: Little brother, it is better that you do not know how. Chase away this useless desire. If you got yourself involved in painting, you would certainly shame me since it would not be at all beautiful. It would be more correct to say that you would paint my caricature rather than my portrait. Marcel, you ask to do my portrait? How would you be able to do it? If you knew how to paint, I would be so afraid that I would not dare show myself to you. Moreover, as you must still write, where would you find the time for painting? Now if you really wish it, ask your sister Thérèse to give you lessons.

*Marcel*: My sister does not teach me to paint, she simply teaches me to sacrifice myself and to love. When I ask her to teach me to paint, she just says: 'To sacrifice yourself, that is to paint; to love, that is to paint; what more do you want?' I do not understand it.

*Jesus*: It is true, little brother. Thus, your sister has already taught you to paint; what more do you want? Indeed, as I am a spirit, in order to make a beautiful portrait of me you must use a spiritual brush and colours. If, on the contrary, one painted my portrait by using a natural brush and colours, I could not look at that portrait without being afraid.

(618)

*Marcel*: In that case, how will people be able to do your portrait? If all the portraits done of you make you afraid, what can be done from now on to stimulate people's fervour? Truly, little Jesus, you are talking nonsense, and you still dare to speak? I am not listening to you any more.

*Jesus*: Well! There you are, are you angry with me? Come, be patient. Listen to me again a little. Afterwards you will no longer be able to listen to me since it is already almost siesta time. Listen! In no way do I despise the other pictures that men find very beautiful and I also find them really beautiful. But if you did my portrait, no one would be able to look at it because, if you managed to do it, it would only have been in following your own will, so that your pictures, even the most beautiful, would not have any value.

*Marcel*: How could I follow my self-will, since I do not know how to paint?

*Jesus*: It is precisely because I wish to prevent you from following your self-will that I leave you ignorant of painting ... Marcel, do you understand? To follow your own will is something that never pleases me.

*Marcel*: The other day I said this to Mary: 'Mother, people make really ugly portraits of you.' After having given me a kiss, this is what she (619) replied: 'That is something that does not offend the Blessed Trinity or me. Even if one represented me as black as charcoal and ugly as a green caterpillar I would, nevertheless, find it beautiful, since in the eyes of the Trinity, there is absolutely nothing that is ugly. Things are only ugly that men make ugly. As for me, I only consider the good will of men, my children, towards me ...' Little Jesus, the time is up, I am going to lie down.

My Mother Mary, my room is now clean. Brother Thaddeus helped me and the work took no more than ten minutes.

Mother, I am very sad. I love you a lot. Yesterday, little Jesus, to comfort me and to encourage me to put up with the heat joyfully, promised to give me a pair of new sandals. At that time my back and chest were burning like fire. I do not know what remedy bearded Jesus applied on me to draw out such heat. So little Jesus promised me some new sandals but I have not yet seen them. Today, my sandals being broken, I got Brother Andrew to repair them, but there is hardly any (620) improvement. I do not like these sandals at all. In spite of polishing them, they always appear very ugly to me, and I only wish to throw them away, all the more so because they make my feet hurt.

*Mary*: My child, my little child, what are you moaning about? As little Jesus said to you yesterday, be a little patient. Offer this flower to me. The other day little Jesus asked your sister Thérèse to obtain many flowers for you so you could offer them to me. Now that your sister Thérèse has got these flowers for you, have the courage to gather them and offer them to me ... My child, you feel a lot of disgust, do you not? So, tell me what you want?

***Marcel***: Mother, I wish you would give me a kiss. I then wish to have the big dictionary that is in the community room.* I love looking at the pictures it contains. Grant me this. I am going also to ask permission of bearded Jesus.

*Which he did quite simply.*

***Mary***: My child, go, first of all to pay a visit to the Blessed Sacrament and, after having greeted little Jesus and me for a little while, you can go and look at the pictures. Be joyful always. And accept your sadness today with the intention of praying for France.

(621)

***Marcel***: Yes, Mother. I love you and I unite myself to you in loving my little Jesus, I love him very much. During this month, I am going to present to him all the flowers that I will gather, so that he may offer them to you ...

Mother, I love you. Have pity on me.

Little Jesus, I am very sad. I do not know why but I again feel a little worried. This lasts for a moment and then it disappears. I am really sad. I have just received news of France. I remember all the time these words you said to me: 'My spouses will triumph ... ' and that comforts me a lot ... At this time, however, it seems to me that I am overwhelmed with sadness, I can find peace nowhere ... Mary, I beg you, come with me. My sister Thérèse, I feel so much disgust.

***Thérèse***: So! You feel disgust? Do not complain. Remain in peace with me. Little Jesus has gone to visit France. Wait for him with patience, he will come back to you. Remain at peace. I am going to conceal your sadness. You must put up with a little sadness so that France may experience happiness. You always say to little Jesus: 'Little Jesus, come with France.' Very good, at this time, little Jesus is visiting France for a while. Accept the hardship of his absence. What have you to fear here with me? After some time, Jesus will come back. What reason have you to concern yourself? Well, you are worried? Go and speak of it to bearded Jesus, little brother, all right? Go and speak to him.

(622)

***Marcel***: My sister Thérèse, the other day little Jesus pretended to give me the anointing of the sick. First of all he touched my eyes saying: 'Ah! These eyes very often look directly at me, I am giving them a kiss since I know that it is only through love that they look at me.'

---

\* *Nouveau Petit Larousse*, 1940.

He then touched my mouth and said: 'This mouth often throws me acts of love like arrows of fire. Good, it already belongs to me; I am kissing it.'

He then moved on to my nose. I had a strong urge to laugh and I asked him this question: 'Is my nose like my sister's?'

He replied: 'Remain in peace. All noses are the same; all have the function to breathe through love for me. It is the same for yours, which finds its delight in me. I am giving it a kiss.' (623)

Reaching the ears, little Jesus said: 'These ears are very good; they are always attentive to my words; they are better behaved than Marcel. Very good, I am giving them a kiss.' I still had an urge to laugh, and Jesus, seeing this, was pleased.

Then passing to my heart, little Jesus said: 'This heart belongs to me; it is very attractive ... I am giving it a kiss.' I have already told this to Mary.*

When he came to my hands, little Jesus said: 'These hands are truly beautiful; they are very docile to my word. All I say, they do punctually, being happy to write, without question or reflection as Marcel does. I love them dearly. Let me give them a kiss.'

Finally, on seeing my feet, he said: 'These feet are also very pleasing to me. Each of their steps is a joy for my heart. Very good, I am kissing them.' And I, still stretched out, I could only laugh. A moment after Jesus had given me his kisses, my tiredness disappeared and I was able to take up my work again.

My sister, little Jesus loves me a lot. But at this time I feel a great deal of digust. (624)

***Thérèse***: You feel disgust, little brother? Come, take courage. You must not worry; rest on my heart. I love you a great deal, and at this moment I love you in little Jesus' place ... Little brother, it is almost time, rest a little before going to eat.

***Marcel***: My sister, I must serve at table ... however, that is something that pleases me, a wonderful opportunity to eat with you. I am going to rest a little and then I will go to the refectory.

---

\* Cf. (593–594).

## 7 Mother 1946

(625) *Marcel*: Little Jesus, have a little pity for little Toa. **Phúc**, for whom he works, never stops oppressing him. Abusing his seniority when little Toa is hungry, he gives him nothing to eat and, furthermore, he orders him to do this and that. This **Phúc** is very arrogant to dare to bully his dear little one in this way. I see that little Toa suffers a lot and that he is very sad. As for **Phúc**, he always looks sullen. Just looking at him makes me afraid. It's a real pity for little Toa who is continually oppressed. If I were in **Phúc**'s place, I would arrange things so that little Toa is always merry. I love children as you love them yourself, little Jesus. And later, in heaven, if I see the children of this world lacking even a grain of sand to play with, I will go in all simplicity to my true Father, and having gained his favour, I will ask him to add to the world still one more grain of sand, to make the children happy. Little Jesus, understanding that the Trinity love children greatly, I take great comfort from that and I am certain that God, far from remaining deaf to my prayer, will immediately give to the children the grain of sand I am asking for. Perhaps he will even regret that I had to remind him. Yes, I know it; the Trinity love children a lot. In heaven I will look upon the children. My heart will remain with God the Father, but my gaze, I will lower it towards the children ...

Little Jesus, the time is up ... I am very tired and I am shivering a lot. However, I have just heard some very good news. So it is no surprise that I have seen you so joyful this morning. I am going, first of all, to tell it to bearded Jesus ...

(626) This morning, at the time of my awakening, I noticed that little Jesus was coming to me very quickly. He kissed me earlier than usual and appeared very cheerful. While I was getting washed, he spoke spontaneously to me about France, saying, quite simply: 'Little brother, it is almost finished.' And he added: 'Today, I want you to pray again exclusively for France. Therefore, instead of praying for sinners, spend an extra day praying for France.'

At that moment I felt naturally joyful like little Jesus and, since that time, little Jesus keeps repeating these words to me: 'Little brother, it is almost over, but prayers are still lacking. It is necessary that you pray a lot so that it may come to an end, as I have told you before ...' That is all I remember. Little Jesus has certainly said other things and I have asked him many questions, but perhaps that was not necessary since little Jesus has made me forget it all.       'Jesus-Marcel'

(627) *Jesus*: You see, Marcel, a single afternoon of suffering has obtained such benefits; what more do you wish for? I went to visit France for a short

time, I did not stay long; why were you afraid?

*Marcel*: So, little Jesus, why did you not take me with you? I wished to go to France to see my sister Thérèse's room and also the Buissonnets.* I regret very much that you did not take me with you. If I am sad, you must not reproach me, I have good reason to be. That's enough. It is time already, I am leaving you.

Today, I had to serve at table. I was very tired. I had no appetite to eat. All I fancied was maize, but Brother Simon gave me only one ear. I really wanted more, but I didn't have the right to ask. I gave you the other ears that I had decided to eat, so that today I left you your share; and from now on you do not have the right to call me greedy. I had decided to eat three ears and I have eaten only one. You, therefore, have had one more than me. You are greedier than I am, and you still dare to speak.

*Jesus*: Unfortunately, Marcel, you are very ill-natured. You have just given me two ears of maize and you still say that I am greedy. But it is (628) you who gave me these ears, it is not I who took them for myself. As you are always asking me for mortifications, I gave you one today. And this mortification has twice as much value than one of your choosing. It is a mortification of my choosing so that by accepting it you have done my will and at the same time you have imposed on yourself a sacrifice. Isn't that a good thing?

*Marcel*: Little Jesus, how is it that if someone recognizes his weakness, his poverty, he is then truly poor? This morning, while reading the book called *Faith in the Love of God*, I came across words of this sort, but I understood absolutely nothing. If it is so, I think it is impossible for me to gain many merits for heaven. And so, where would I find what to give as alms to souls? I recall a word of my sister Thérèse who said: 'It is necessary to recognize oneself always poor before God.'

*Jesus*: Yes, little brother, before God your Father who can be rich? And since your true Father is the Infinite Being, who can be compared to (629) him? However, you must also remind yourself that he is your true Father and you are his very small child. Thus, thanks to my merits, your heritage is yours already. Naturally, you must recognize your poverty before God your true Father; that is totally correct, since I must equally act in the same way towards my true heavenly Father. If I did not

---

\* Saint Thérèse's family home in Lisieux.

behave before him as a truly poor person, would souls receive my infinite merits? Obviously not, because then I would gain merit only for myself, not having the intention to give anything to souls.

Although I am God too, the fact remains that, through love for you, I have agreed to be poor and weak, so as to buy for you the kingdom of heaven as I told you previously. So, thanks to my infinite merits, the kingdom of heaven belongs to you already. You remain always poor and pitiful, since you possess absolutely nothing. From that you (630) must recognize your true poverty, which is different from the practice of poverty in terms of what is virtue. Indeed, there is a difference between the fact of recognizing oneself as poor and needy and the fact of practising real poverty. To recognize that one is poor and needy is a kind of poverty which is motivated by the virtue of humility, while true poverty is an effect of the virtue of charity. The kingdom of heaven really belongs to you already, but the power of giving you this kingdom of heaven belongs to God your Father, so that you will recognize yourself as always being poor and lacking everything. With this attitude you force your Father to have pity on you and, because he takes pity on you, he gives all things to you. That is poverty based on humility and I must, myself, practise it. As for poverty coming from charity, I have already explained it earlier. Because you have recognized that you are totally poor and lacking everything, you have received everything. So you must practise poverty with regard to (631) others since they, not yet knowing their true poverty, have not received everything ...

That's enough, little brother, it is time ...

***Marcel***: Little Jesus, I do not understand how God the Father can be infinitely poor.

***Jesus***: Who asks you to understand? You have too much curiosity. There is nothing extraordinary in that. Indeed, God your true Father is infinitely worthy of being loved. Now he is not in a position to love any other infinite love like his. So one can consider him as being infinitely poor since he is, as it were, deprived of the very love that is so pleasing to him.

***Marcel***: So, therefore, souls are not infinite?

***Jesus***: They are, little brother; however, their infinity is that of your Father, since your Father must embrace souls in his own infinity. If I speak in this way, it is so that men may understand, since your Father, possessing absolutely everything, lacks nothing at all. Little brother, you have no need to understand; it is sufficient that bearded Jesus understands.

*Marcel*: My sister, a moment ago I had not even finished forming the words 'My sister' when it was already time. At this moment I feel tired. I have just received an injection which made me feel a slight pain; but my foot is still numb. (632)

Now! I want to tell you what happened this morning. After having recited the *Regina Coeli* I added the invocation to Mary for France: 'O Mary, our Mother, we beg you, sustain France.' I had hardly finished when little Jesus, standing somewhere, added immediately: 'Alleluia'. I wanted to laugh and in my turn I added: 'Alleluia' which made two alleluias. After that, we both laughed. I do not understand why at that time little Jesus was so cheerful.

*Thérèse*: Little brother, it is because, yesterday, he received your roses that I sent to him in France. Without doubt these very small roses brought consolations to him concerning France, so he was very joyful and sang Alleluia to let you know the happy news ... Little brother, pray a lot. Tell the French also to pray a lot for their country. One must not doubt Jesus' words concerning France, since these words give proof of the love that he has for it. Do not allow the joy that little Jesus has (633) just received to change into sadness; never cease praying for France. This morning, Jesus told you that all he lacks is prayers, nothing else. It is necessary therefore that you pray. In a short while I will take you to France, so that you may enjoy the countryside at your leisure.

*Marcel*: But, my sister, when will that happen?

*Thérèse*: That will happen later, no other time.

*Marcel*: Later, that surely means when I am in heaven, not anything else. But when I am in heaven, even if you do not take me there, I will go to France nevertheless to see if the children are well behaved.

*Thérèse*: If you do not pray for France, while asking that the reign of the Love of Jesus spreads throughout the universe, then the communists will completely destroy France and later, in heaven, what will you be able to see? You will see the communists challenge the Love of Jesus, you will see them kill the children; and in that case, how would you still be able to look at it? You must, first of all, pray for France. Only then (634) will you be able to take pleasure in looking at it when you are in heaven.

*Marcel*: But my sister, the French make my country suffer cruelly and I know that they consider the Vietnamese as servants.

*Thérèse*: Little brother, Jesus has already asked France to atone for its faults. How many sacrifices have been offered to Jesus to atone for the sins of France? What more do you want? ... The time is up, little brother, remember to pray for France.

## 8 Mother 1946

*Marcel*: My sister, yesterday you spoke to me about France. Frankly, I don't know why but, in the past, I did not like France at all. I only liked French priests, and I liked them a lot because I saw them sacrifice themselves in this country of Indo-China. Formerly, on hearing it said by everyone that France was very guilty and that she only brought to Indo-China a culture of sin, I was very angry and I would have wished to kill all the French in Indo-China, except the priests. I wished that only the French priests were the protectors of my country ...

(635)

*Thérèse*: Come, little brother, it is evident that you must hate sin, but you are not allowed to hate the sinner. You must pray for France so that she stops committing sin. That is all that is right to do. Whatever it may be, little brother, I can only exhort you to pray for France, since little Jesus loves it dearly, as he has told you.

*Marcel*: Now my sister, I love France once again and I do not cease to pray for her, as you know. That's enough. I am leaving you, the time is up. It is really painful. Time passes too quickly in this world; before one has said all one wished to say, it is already the end of the day.

   Little Jesus, Brother Eugene continues to say that he will never acknowledge that his soul is your spouse. He maintains that only women are your spouses.

*Jesus*: Then, little brother, say this to Brother Eugene: 'If in relations with Jesus one does not have the feelings of a spouse in relation to his spouse, neither does one have the feelings of a child in relation to his father. If one does not have the feelings of a child in relation to his father, one no longer has those of a pupil in relation his master. Without these feelings of a pupil towards his master, one is no longer even a man. If one is no longer a man, one isn't, either, a thing and, finally, one is no longer anything at all, so that one cannot love Jesus.

(636)

That is, in a certain way, to renounce the Trinity without knowing it.

In love, one must always find the feelings of a child towards his father, of the subject towards the king, of the friend towards his friend. If anything is lacking there, one can no longer call that love.'

Say this to Brother Eugene: 'If you refuse to recognize Jesus as the Spouse of your soul, you have not the slightest degree of love for him. Even if in your relations with Jesus you only wanted to express to him the feelings of a child towards his father, or some other sort of affection, that cannot be called love, because there is still lacking a type of affection that little Jesus wishes to attribute exclusively to the Trinity, and which consists in loving Jesus with a spouse's love.'

**Marcel**: Little Jesus, how would I be able to say that to Brother Eugene?

**Jesus**: If I say these things I will readily find the means of letting Brother Eugene know them. But how many other Eugenes are there who also do not wish to recognize me as the Spouse of their souls. I am not speaking here only of Brother Eugene, but it is my intention to speak also to many other souls. (637)

If religious do not wish to recognize me as the Spouse of their souls, they cannot take the vow of chastity, since this vow obliges the soul to unite itself to me as a true spouse. If, after having taken the vow of chastity, the soul does not wish to identify itself as being my true spouse, that is a blatant falsehood. Further, this refusal on the part of the soul is a disgrace for me, and a shame much greater than that I felt on hearing the Jewish people refuse to recognize me as King.

As I said to you many times, I do not hold store by the external. If men judge solely by the exterior, they appear to consider the Holy Trinity as being clothed with a sinful flesh similar to theirs. That is truly a blasphemy that the devil himself dare not commit. If, therefore, you hear Brother Eugene say some similar foolishness, you must tell bearded Jesus immediately.

If a soul does not recognize me as its Spouse, it will not recognize itself either as a true child of the Trinity, as I have just said. But if it is a religious who behaves this way, all the vows that he has committed himself to are worth absolutely nothing, and what is more, he commits a sacrilege because he lies to the Trinity itself. I have already said these things very clearly in the Gospel. I have not spoken just for women but for all souls ... (638)

That's enough, little brother, the time is up. I am very sad to see that there are still many souls who refuse to recognize themselves as my true spouses. Their conduct is not worthy of a creature coming from the hands of God. They copy Cain in offering to me as a sacrifice only ugly

290   *Conversations*

things and keeping the best to satisfy their self-will ... (*Little Jesus evinced a very great sadness*).

(639)   **Marcel**: Little Jesus, I am very tired. Will you remind me of the question you spoke to me about a few minutes ago, so I don't forget it.

*Jesus*: All right. Pay careful attention ... On the subject of the feelings of parents towards their children, they encapsulate, also, all the other kinds of feelings, even those of friend towards friend, of spouse for spouse, of brother for his little brother, of king for his subjects, of master for his pupils. So, to be able to say that parents truly love their children, they must have all these feelings which make up true love.

For example when parents follow the will of their children in appropriate things, they show them the feelings of a friend. When they give them signs of an ardent love, when they shower them with caresses, they display the feelings of a spouse. When parents support their children and protect them, they show them fraternal feelings. When they give them an order, they act towards them with the feelings of a king towards his subjects. When parents instruct their children, they show them the feelings of a master toward his pupils ... And there are many other comparisons.

See, little brother, am I not at the same time father, master, friend, brother ... And Lord of all souls, without counting all the rest? When 
(640)   parents love their children and when the children love their parents, there must be in this love the feelings of spouses. So, why do men not act in the same manner with their true Father? Really, as I have already told you, if a soul does not consider itself as my true spouse, neither will it consider itself as truly being my child.

Only the Trinity is worthy of receiving love. Now, for this love to be true, it must contain, with regard to the Trinity, all these sorts of feelings. Without it there is no true love. Do you know why I consider myself the Spouse of all souls? Because I want all souls to love me alone ... After what I have just said, have you sufficiently understood? Poor little brother, you are very tired. Go and speak to bearded Jesus about it and rest a little.

**Marcel**: But, little Jesus, the words *phu phụ*[*] what do they mean?

*Jesus*: I will tell you tomorrow what they mean . Since you are tired, it is more important for you to rest than to write. Go on, please me ...

---

[*]   Spouse (male and female).

## 9 Mother 1946

*Marcel*: Little Jesus, a while ago I was really angry with the choir brothers. I had just washed the floor carefully and, just like that they dirtied it all again. I had to restrain myself, but a harsh word escaped me in Brother Mạch's direction. I think that hurt him a little because there was no joy in my words. I am sorry for not having gathered this flower (641) to offer to Mary.

*Jesus*: Ah! You are sad. You do not remember that you are weak? Enough, little brother, do not continue to be sad. If you were sad, Mary would be even more so, since it is because of her that you are in this state, for not having known how to gather a flower to offer to her. Offer your weakness joyfully to her and it will be better. Mary knows that you are very weak. That you have not even the strength to collect a spiritual flower. So, she will accept your weakness with more joy than she would accept a beautiful flower that you might offer to her.

Little brother, that is poverty. Thus, it is certain that Mary will love you more. Do you believe that? It is also the same for me. I love you more because you are weaker, more wretched, I would even say, to please you, more poor.

*Marcel*: But, little Jesus, I hurt the brothers; what about that?

*Jesus*: So much the better, little brother, by that the Brothers will further see that you have no virtue, that you lose patience for nothing; and by the same token you reveal your extreme weakness to them. (642) Thus, I will not be the only one to know your weakness, the brethren will also know it. So, what reason have you to be worried? The fact that you recognize yourself as being weak, and that even the others consider you as such, makes me love you twice over. So favoured, what more can you ask for? Do not be sad any more. Offer this weakness to Mary or, better still, let me offer it to her in your place.

*Marcel*: Fine, little Jesus, offer it for me, all right? I am no longer sad; let me smile to show you. I have already spoken of this business to bearded Jesus. Little Jesus, please give Brother Mạch the strength to endure with joy the unfriendly words I addressed to him.

Incidentally, little Jesus, you have not yet explained to me the words *phu phụ*; you always forget.

*Jesus*: Little brother, *phu phụ* means 'husband and wife'; *tình phu phụ* indicates the feelings of one spouse towards the other. Normally one would not use the words *vợ chồng*,* because it is not polite; one must use the words *phu phụ* or *Bạn trăm năm*: spouse.

(643) **Marcel**: Ah! So that's it? But, *Thanh nhã*† what does that mean?

**Jesus**: Ah! You do not understand that? That means 'refined'. If you do not know it, it is without doubt because you do not use these words very often. Besides, you don't have to understand every word.

**Marcel**: In the past, I used to do very well in my studies. I knew many strange words, but without knowing their meanings. As for speaking, I was able to do so in a very literary manner, but the unfortunate thing was that I understood nothing. If someone made grammatical or pronunciation errors I was able to spot that he was mistaken and I would have liked to correct them, but I did not know how to express it to make myself understood.

**Jesus**: It is much better that way. If you understood everything, I wouldn't have to teach you in detail the slightest things, as to a child. It is because you are so ignorant that I can guide you along the right path. Let us suppose that you had the wisdom of the world. I would then have great difficulty in guiding you, since the false perspective of this world is very blurred; and perhaps no longer seeing the path on which it is walking, it will end by throwing itself into the abyss ... Little (644) brother, rejoice at being weak and wretched, because it is to those alone who are truly poor and wretched that the kingdom of heaven belongs. Are you tired, little brother? Go and sleep. You will write the rest this evening.

**Marcel**: Little Jesus, you promised me a pair of new sandals, but I have not yet seen them, so I must always wear these wretched sandals that hurt my feet a lot. My fear is that in getting them repaired many times more, I may end up displeasing the brethren.

**Jesus**: Why be afraid? If you wear these sandals gladly and cheerfully, the brethren will be happy to repair them. If you observe poverty, the brothers, for their part, will be charitable. It is true that I promised you a pair of new sandals, but to have them, you must first of all wear your

---

\* This is an expression indicating husband and wife; it is a common expression as opposed to *phu phụ* which is more polished.
† Elegant.

old ones joyfully. By accepting suffering you will experience true joy because you will then have given proof of a true love. Yes, it is understood that you will have new sandals, but on the condition of having worn your old sandals with joy. Do you agree? Even if you did not agree, you will have to agree nevertheless because, being one with me, you must act like me, otherwise that will not work and I will not put up with it.

*Marcel*: So, little Jesus, if I no longer wish to be one with you, what will you be able to do with me?

*Jesus*: It is a great pity, but your will does not belong to you any more. (645) You can decide all you want but it will be impossible for you to achieve what you have decided, because your will is nothing other than one with mine. Consequently, the more you decide that you no longer want to be one with me, the more your decision will force me to maintain the obligation, for you, to become like me.

*Marcel*: But, little Jesus, I wanted to joke with you and tease you a little to see if you were going to get angry. How could I be unaware of these things?

*Jesus*: Whether you wished to joke or not, little brother, the fact remains that you can no longer take such a decision. Besides I knew that you were joking, that is why I also teased you a little to cheer you up. Since today is recreation day, one is allowed to speak a lot and also to laugh a lot, therefore I wished to make you laugh so that you can be (646) happy.

*Marcel*: Little Jesus, according to what you are saying, I think it is not certain that a soul can fall into hell. I continue to think that it is very difficult for the devil to drag a soul from your hands, that it is almost impossible.

*Jesus*: Little brother, you are right to think in that way but, unfortunately, man does not understand it. If men could understand that Love loves them infinitely, there is not a soul that would fall into hell. Truly, the devil has no power to pull a soul from my hands; all he can do is cause men to fall into sin. However, if a soul no longer has confidence in my infinite love, then, naturally, it is very easy for the devil to take possession of that soul ...

Alas! Marcel, is there a sorrow for Love, comparable to that of losing a soul? Naturally, Love being infinite, loves with an infinite love. But, (647) this infinity of Love can only clasp strongly the hearts in which there is a true confidence. Without this true confidence, infinite Love, no longer having anything that permits it to adhere to the soul, how would it be able to keep it? ...

O sinful souls, my little sisters, the only thing I ask of you, and which suffices for me to press you to my overflowing heart, is that you truly believe that Love loves you infinitely. Unfortunate little ones, do you believe that I do not know how wretched you are? Even if your wretchedness is infinite, you must believe that my merits are also infinite. Even if your sins have earned hell for you an infinite number of times, you must not, for all that, lose confidence in my Love ... But, alas! The unfortunate thing is that men have no confidence in my Love. Oh! Sin! Sin! Sin never offends my Love; there is absolutely

(648) nothing that offends my Love, except the lack of confidence in my Love ...

Marcel! Marcel! Little brother, pray that sinful souls, so numerous, never lose confidence in my Love. As long as they keep this confidence, the kingdom of heaven does not cease to truly belong to them ...

***Marcel***: But, little Jesus, if men continue to sin deliberately, what will happen? Will you still give paradise to them?

***Jesus***: Little brother, you do not know that I know man's extreme weakness. Even if men offend me deliberately and as gravely as you can imagine, their sin is nothing in comparison with a hint of Love ... Love is infinite and infinite, repeat it to men; yes infinite and infinite. Have confidence in me and never, eternally never, will you be separated from me. Even the devil must despair of a soul in which the word 'confidence' is found.

Little brother, here we are, the time is up. First of all smile a little with me, then go and work with the brethren.

***Marcel***: Little Jesus, I have just taken a shower. It has refreshed me a

(649) lot. I do not understand why I tire so easily. I have a greater craving for drink than for food.

Incidentally, little Jesus, I have a new nib. I am very pleased. Now I can write quickly and easily ...

Ah! There is a question I have wanted to ask you for a long time, but I always forget. The doctor you asked me to pray for, is he saved? When I am in heaven I am going to tell him the story of the medical examination he gave me at his place.

***Jesus***: Little brother, you are really too inquisitive. Why did I ask you to pray for the doctor? That was enough for you to know. It was not necessary to speak to you clearly and in detail about this matter.

After the doctor's death I asked you to pray for him ... If he had been damned, what is the good of asking you to pray? Little brother, doubtless, you understand. Later, in heaven, one will certainly be surprised to see among the ranks of the saints a great number of souls that one believed damned ...

Love loves infinitely, it is infinitely just. It is because it is infinitely just that it loves infinitely, and it is because it loves infinitely that it is infinitely just ... A simple glance of confidence towards me suffices to grab sinful souls from the claws of the devil. Even if a soul found itself (650) already at the gate of hell, waiting for its last sigh before falling into it, if in this last sigh there is the slightest element of confidence in my infinite Love, that will still be sufficient for my Love to draw this soul to the arms of the Trinity. That is why I say that it can be very easy for men to go to heaven, while it can be very difficult for them and even infinitely difficult to fall into hell, because Love can never permit a soul to lose itself so easily.

However, little brother, these words should not be made known to all souls indiscriminately. It is necessary to do it with prudence, for fear that certain souls, knowing this, might become hardened in evil ... and then lose confidence in me and no longer have any confidence.

*Marcel*: So then, little Jesus, I am sure that the doctor is saved. But, unfortunately, no one asked for Masses for him, nobody has said a single Mass so that he may be promptly delivered from purgatory if he has had to go there.

*Jesus*: Whether or not he has had Masses celebrated for him, is no concern of yours. At this time there is only one thing that it is appropriate for you to concern yourself with, that is to go take a rest. You are (651) tired, go and rest. I am kissing you.

## 10 Mother 1946

*Marcel*: Today I had to serve at table and I was very angry. Being tired, I had not finished serving at one place when I was called to another, so that I did not know what to do next. Eventually there were enough dishes everywhere; there was no shortage anywhere. I was really angry with the Fathers and the students; before even having finished, they call the server and when one brings them what they asked for, one notices that there is too much, whereas there is a shortage elsewhere. That happens above all on recreation days. The Fathers, talking and gesticulating, are inclined to raise their hands as if they are asking for something, but going up to them one sees that they do not need anything; they had quite simply lifted their hand while speaking animatedly. Very often I am really tired and I must still be confused in this way. Little Jesus, you must keep an eye on things, if not it is very painful for me. However, it is only on the days when I am tired that I get so angry; when I am not tired, I can take it with a smile. But today, little Jesus, even if you had come with my sister Thérèse to joke with me and make me laugh, you would both have wasted your time. Happily, at least, I have not cried, although it was not easy.

(652) *Jesus*: Yes, it is just as you say, little brother; it is only in these moments of fatigue that I am able to make you see your weakness and to teach you that, truly, you haven't got a scintilla of virtue ... Little brother, see how weak you are. That it is enough for you to abandon yourself to me and to put all confidence in me alone.

*Marcel*: Now, I am not angry any more because I no longer am tired.

*Jesus*: Nevertheless, little brother, your weakness has not disappeared for all that; it will remain in you until the time when you receive from me the first kiss of your life ... Little brother, always remember that you are a truly poor and destitute soul. Do not worry about your weaknesses, as your sister Thérèse has told you, and as I, myself, have told you many times. It is in knowing your nothingness that your confidence in me will be truly firm.

(653) *Marcel*: Little Jesus, I do understand that it is really so. If I did not wish to admit that I am weak, I would not be able to find the slightest thing that can prove that I am not weak ... Oh! Jesus, little Jesus, I am weak, yes, really weak. I abandon myself to you. Have pity on me. Enough. I am going to sleep. Little Jesus, do not allow me to worry. I love you a lot.

Little Jesus, I have something here that you really like a lot. But, first of all, you must ask me for it. Come on, ask me for it and I will give it to you. It is necessary to ask in order to receive; otherwise, who would give? You are the one who has often told me that.

*Jesus*: Little brother, what have you got there? All right, I am asking you for it. Come, give it to me. Quickly. Then, each time you ask something of me, I will give it to you.

*Marcel*: Little Jesus, here are my fatigue and my disgust. I give them to you; do with them what you want. I do not understand why, this evening, I feel disgust and fatigue.

*Jesus*: Little brother, since you have agreed to give them to me, you no longer have the right to complain. Your fatigue and your disgust are mine; and if you ever complain of being sad, I am going to beat you as necessary, for having stolen my sadness. From now on it is necessary to say that you are joyful since, having lost sadness and disgust, only joy remains to you, not anything else. What you have given to me is mine; I will make use of it to give it to priests.

*Marcel*: But, little Jesus, are you giving me nothing in return? After all I have given you, you must show yourself grateful. (654)

*Jesus*: Little brother, what do you want? That I give you a kiss?

*Marcel*: No.

*Jesus*: So, what do you want? Come on, tell me.

*Marcel*: I am going to reflect a bit first of all. Little Jesus, I ... wish ... to love You.

*Jesus*: Ah! What can you have comparable to that? Very good, I give it to you gladly, straight away. And now, even if you do not want me to kiss you, I must, nevertheless, give you one.

*Marcel*: Ah! Little Jesus, I have forgotten one thing. I want, as well, a pair of new sandals.

*Jesus*: It is too late. I have already given you the gift of loving me a lot; I cannot withdraw this favour. If you want something else, you are wasting your time, since it is from your will, which no longer exists. All that is left for me to do, is to look for a means to allow you to prove your love to me.

*Marcel*: Unfortunately it will be suffering again, inevitably. But I do not like suffering.

*Jesus*: Nor do I. I do not like to make you suffer, but you just told me that your only wish is to love me. 'The wise man keeps his word.' That is something over and done with, it is impossible to come back to it. You want (655) new sandals. Very good, continue to love me joyfully and you will certainly get some ... Marcel, I am very pleased. I am sure that your words will draw a much greater number of souls to me ... Marcel, do you wish to love me? Why speak such lunacy? That's the point, little brother, continue to accept suffering patiently. That is to love; why worry?

*Marcel*: So, little Jesus, when will you send me suffering?

*Jesus*: I have already told you, it is not yet time.

*Marcel*: Little Jesus, I am very happy to have to suffer again. I dare not say that I am sad since I am afraid that you may beat me; I must say, therefore, that I am very happy ... But the time is up.

## 11 Mother 1946

(656) *Marcel*: Little Jesus, yesterday, I heard the brethren saying that a little sister of Madame Giac would be baptized today. I was very pleased. So, this morning after communion, I prayed that this person will treat you well. I hope that many others will be converted in the same way, above all President Ho Chi Minh. For him I wish only one thing: that he will be baptized.

*Jesus*: Yes, very good little brother, but first you must really pray a lot for him. There is no means comparable to prayer for gaining his conversion. Continue to pray and your wish will certainly be granted.

*Marcel*: Little Jesus, while serving at table today, I was not angry. I am less tired than yesterday and I have a better appetite. There was one question I wanted to ask, to get an explanation from you, but lo and behold, I have completely forgotten it. So I have absolutely nothing else to say to you; if you wish to speak to me, I am listening.

*Jesus*: Little brother, let us look at each other, since I have nothing to say to you either. That is enough. You can rest now and do what you wish.

(657) *Marcel*: Thank you very much, little Jesus. I am going to write my piece of poetry, which is very attractive. I am going to hide it with the greatest care. Goodbye, little Jesus.

A while ago, little Jesus, I ate some rice pudding. I like this dish very much and I found it very tasty.

*Jesus*: Little brother, you are, all the same, very impolite for having teased me about eating as you did. Really, if I were able to eat, I certainly would have devoured all of your share. It is because you know that I am unable to eat that you pretended to give me some. If you knew that I was able to eat, you would not have dared to pretend as you did, is that not a fact?

*Marcel*: But, little Jesus, it is your fault. I really gave you some to eat. I told you to open your mouth so I could give you some rice but, seeing that you did not move, I then opened my own instead.

*Jesus*: Yes, all right and all the better. When you eat it is as if I, myself, were eating. Besides, I am happy. Seeing you happily eating, calms me and the more you eat with relish, the more content I am. Little brother, take care to eat. Try to become as plump as I am. That would be marvellous. If, of your own will, you were going to fast and endure hunger, I would never again speak to you.

You must become as simple as a child, eating when you are hungry, (658) crying when you are sad, laughing when you are joyful; then you will be another me, my little Jesus. Agreed, little brother?

*Marcel*: But, little Jesus, why does Brother Augustine cry so often? Tonight, seeing him crying so much, I cracked some jokes to cheer him up; but I only succeeded the first time. After that, instead of laughing, he cried even more.

*Jesus*: There's nothing strange in that. Everybody has his or her own temperament, and it is because you don't know Brother's temperament that you joked in that way. There are some people who will laugh at your jokes, but they will only make others sadder because they believe you are making fun of them. To comfort a sad soul you must, first of all, know his temperament. With some it is necessary to use firm words while with others it is necessary to tell a joke as you did with Brother Augustine. For souls like yours, there is no difficulty; a simple glance suffices. And there are many others who are in the same category, above all among children. With them it is necessary to adopt a friendly tone and to know also how to look at them with gentleness and affection ...

Without doubt you remember that time when your sister Thérèse (659) looked at you with one eye and there, that single glance with one eye was enough to dry all your tears ... That's enough, little brother. Until tomorrow. The time is up already.

## 12 Mother 1946

*Marcel*: My sister Thérèse, tomorrow is the anniversary of the day when Mary our Mother smiled at you. My sister, try to press little Jesus a bit to find out if he has already smiled on France. He made me a firm promise that he would smile on France but, as yet, I have seen absolutely nothing. Tomorrow, would you be able to remind him?

*Thérèse*: No, little brother, little Jesus cannot yet smile on France. He is still very sad on that score; enough prayers have not yet been said.

*Marcel*: My sister, praying as I do and you say that it is still too little? However, I pray every quarter of an hour, and sometimes even more often ... So, what more can I do? In my opinion, to pray as I do is to pray a lot, all the more as you also are praying ...

*Thérèse*: Little brother, I dare not make any reproach to you; I reproach, simply, the French for not having enough confidence in little Jesus and for not praying enough ...

*Marcel*: So, let me first of all ask you a question. When will little Jesus smile on France?

(660) *Thérèse*: When? Do you need to know, little brother? Besides, little Jesus' smile is spiritual. Consequently you will have to wait until you are in heaven before you can see the smile that little Jesus will give to France.

*Marcel*: When our Mother smiled on you, was her smile beautiful? Personally, I am sure that it was very beautiful. And I do not find that surprising, since if a mother, in the presence of her beloved child, would not smile on her, it seems that she would not at all have the feelings of a mother. Is that not so, my sister? Although I, personally, have not, like you, seen our Mother smile on me outwardly, I have seen her smile on me spiritually many times. She loves me more than you because, besides my own heart, I have yours and that of little Jesus to love her with.

(661) *Thérèse*: Marcel! You are saying a very strange thing. Is it because you love our Mother a lot that she also loves you a lot? Not at all. You do not know very much little brother, how many times have I told you that and you always forget it. If our Mother loves you dearly, it is because you are very weak; your love for her is far from being comparable to

your weakness. From now on you must remember that. It is because you are weaker than me that you are loved more than me.

**Marcel**: I do remember, but it is a fact that I very easily forget. If I ever forget again, be kind enough to remind me.

That's enough, my sister; I am speaking to you no longer. I am now going to speak with little Jesus. You can listen if you want.

Little Jesus, this morning I had a very good appetite; I ate much more than yesterday. I am already almost as fat as you.

Incidentally, little Jesus, if I were allowed to sit during meditation in order to converse with you, I believe it would be better because, then, I would feel less tired, and it would be very easy to chat with you. On the contrary, by staying on my knees, I am often very tired and I find that difficult.

**Jesus**: Fine, little brother, it is my wish also. All you have to do is ask bearded Jesus' permission to sit as you usually do. By that you will be acting slightly differently from the others, but it is not necessary to be concerned nor to be afraid since, of course, you are not as strong as they. If I left you always on your knees, I would be very sad. I sometimes have pity on you, because I see that you are very tired and that you no longer feel like chatting with me.

(662)

**Marcel**: The other day I asked permission of bearded Jesus to sit down; I do not know if I should ask him again.

**Jesus**: You can ask him but it's not really necessary since he knows the situation ... That's enough. Go and rest. It is time already. Be a little patient.

**Marcel**: I don't want to write any more. I have hardly formed any words when the time is up already. It is really very difficult. From now on, little Jesus, when I only have a little time, I won't write any more. That's enough. I am leaving you.

Little Jesus, would you eat some soup? I am going to give you some. As for me, I am not yet hungry. I will wait until 10.30 before eating. I am going to make you eat before me.

Little Jesus, yesterday evening I saw that Brother Augustine was very sad, he didn't laugh at all. Why don't you console him? Perhaps he has to return to the world? I am pretty certain of it, but I dare not be absolutely since I am not Master of novices. I would be very pleased if

(663) he had to leave because he is very mean. He cannot remain in the Congregation. He would have a lot of trouble in practising poverty and brotherly charity. In the past he has often made me go hungry. I would be pleased to see him leave the Congregation, but I do not want him to distance himself from you. I am going to pray that he leaves the Congregation but that he continues to love you and to follow your will etc. ...

Little Jesus, in speaking this way have I spoken badly of Brother Augustine? Nevertheless, I am not afraid. And even if my words were defamatory, the fact is that I said them spontaneously, without any intention of speaking ill, all the more so since I have prayed for him again.

Wait, little Jesus, I can hear a great number of aeroplanes passing over. They are French aeroplanes. I am going to pray that the French are skilful pilots who are transporting Love throughout the whole world. What do you think, little Jesus? I would like very much to go in an aeroplane but I cannot. Later, in heaven I will build an aeroplane so that you can travel with me.

*Jesus*: What are you talking about in such a disjointed way? And who could understand such language? Come, re-read what you have written
(664) and see if you can understand it ... However, little brother, that is of no importance. No, no importance. The case is that you have hardly learned to speak. I understand now, don't worry.

But who told you that Brother Augustine was on the point of leaving? You must not make such assumptions, you understand? I am not happy with that, and bearded Jesus neither is ... Even if externally you witness such or such a sign, you are never allowed to make such an assumption ...

Ah! Marcel, I am not scolding you at all. I am giving you a simple piece of advice, since you had no bad intention acting in this way. If your supposition had become known, exteriorly, then you would have deserved to be blamed, but since only I know it, it has no consequence; on the contrary it is even an interesting story for me.

*Marcel*: Little Jesus, if I supposed that Brother Augustine was about to leave, it is for the following reason: last night, immediately after supper, as I was leaving with the brothers, Brother Gregory said to me on the spur of the moment: 'Let us go comfort the Brothers a little ... etc.' And, while speaking, he indicated Brother Augustine. Then, seeing that
(665) Brother Augustine was very sad, I thought he was on the point of leaving, all the more so since he had said certain words of goodbye to the brethren. Brother Gregory's words succeeded in convincing me

that it was true. So, with an honest heart I said quite simply to Brother Augustine: 'You must leave, then? Why worry? *Voluntas Dei*,* it's God's will.' And I saw that Brother Augustine was laughing ...

It is only afterwards that I noticed that Brother Gregory had deceived me and I had fallen into the trap without knowing it. I see that Brother Gregory is not at all straightforward. In speaking he often uses indirect routes to get to know things concerning the brothers. I would be very pleased for him to leave too but I am going to pray that he also may persevere in your Love ... Now I am going to eat; it is already past 10.30 ...

There! My bowl of soup is finished. I am leading a happy life, with a stomach always full. However, seeing that you are fattening me up in this way to make me suffer afterwards, I feel much disgust because of it.

*Jesus*: Do not worry; you are far from being fat. I do not speak of suffering, I only speak of the way in which I show you my love. Why do you always concern yourself with sufferings to come?

*Marcel*: What did bearded Jesus just say? I did not understand it clearly. He spoke only to the choir novices, so how can I pray? (666)

*Jesus*: It is very unfortunate, little brother, but what do you need to understand? Come, say the following to me: 'Little Jesus, arrange things so that religion in Indo-China enjoys true peace, in accordance with bearded Jesus' words to the choir novices.' That is all.

*Marcel*: I am often very angry because bearded Jesus speaks only to the choir brothers, or when he gives some news, I understand absolutely nothing, so that I do not pray.

*Jesus*: Little brother, you really have no reason to get impatient in this way. Is bearded Jesus not as wise as you? Be a little patient; that is the most beautiful sacrifice. There is no need for you to know everything; it is enough that you know how to love me. Continue to be patient a little; why torment yourself. It is good if you know what he says, on the other hand, if you do not know, that is no disadvantage. That is a mortification I am sending you, accept it joyfully ...

Stop, you are crying? That's enough. Come, give it all to me, I prefer it to the bowl of soup you gave me earlier. It is through prudence that (667) bearded Jesus must act as he does. What do you need to know and understand? Do not torment yourself any more, all right?

* This is in Latin in Van's text.

*Marcel*: But then I do not know what to ask for in my prayers.

*Jesus*: You have only to speak and I will understand.

*Marcel*: But what could I say to you?

*Jesus*: I have just given you a prayer, re-read it for me. Or better, say this to me: 'Little Jesus, I beg of you to hear the words of bearded Jesus that I do not understand.' Then I will immediately understand... Time has passed very quickly, little brother, go; you must no longer torment yourself, understood?

*Marcel*: My Mother, Mary, during my reading yesterday, I came upon a passage where you use the word *Tao* in speaking to the devil. In this regard, allow me to ask you a question: have you ever spoken to the devil in these terms?

(668) *Mary*: All right, my child. On more than one occasion I, also, wanted to speak to you about this, but I did not have the opportunity. My little child, I do not find it difficult to reply to your question. Naturally I know that God in Three Persons is truly a Father who is infinitely good and that, as a consequence, he must be good even to the devils. You know that your true Father has hatred only for sin and not for sinners, that is why he shows his goodness toward the devil. However, in regard to his sin, God must act according to justice. Despite the state the devil is in, he is still considered as being the genuine child of your true Father. And God, in his mercy, still waits for him to repent. So, how could it be possible that on the one hand God exhorts the devil to humility and repentance, which would restore his glory in the presence of the Trinity, and, on the other hand he shows himself strict and hard towards him? If, therefore, God is so merciful then, with much better reason, am I who act as the intermediary of this infinitely merciful Love. For my part, I remain the true Mother of the devil and, following the example of the Trinity, I am always prepared to recognize him as my true child. Only his pride prevents him from ever agreeing to admit that such is the case...

(669) My child, never, absolutely never do I speak to the devil severely. If I did so, my little Marcel, I would not deserve to be your Mother. It is because people wish to give more force to my words that they say that I speak in this way. In reality, I never use the word *Tao* in speaking to the devil. I, myself, have no hatred for the devil but solely for his sin. The devil does not recognize me as his mother, but I am, nevertheless, his true Mother.

In the same way, the Trinity never use harsh words in speaking to the devil. The devil is truly worthy of pity, but since he will never accept this pity, he will have to suffer eternally.

*Marcel*: Mother, the other day I used the word *Tao* in speaking to the devil, has that any consequence? Given his state, I thought it was no longer necessary to have pity on him.

*Mary*: That is true, my child. The devil really deserves to be treated harshly. Even the word *Tao* is not hard enough for him since he deserves to be treated with infinite severity. However, you must understand that Love is infinite, and it is for this reason that the Trinity treat the devil with kindness, as I also do myself.

If one held to your way of thinking, one would not be able to say that Love is infinite. Why doesn't God destroy the devil immediately? (670) Would it not be preferable in order to prevent him from harming my children? It is, again, through love for him. Love waits for him always, wishing for him to repent and become again what he was previously. That is why God does not punish him by destroying him, since Love is infinite. In fact even the devil could profit from Jesus' merits; but because of his great pride, he is not willing to accept them. If he accepted them, how could God not be ready to welcome him?

My child, since Love is infinite, infinite and infinite, he still waits for the devil to repent and come back to him, the infinitely infinite. It is impossible for me to express myself in a way to make you understand better.

If I never treat the devil severely because I am his very good Mother, with much greater reason will I never do so to men, since I am even more, their Mother, full of kindness. Is that not the case, my child? And because I am full of kindness, I am telling you to go and rest yourself. The time is up and what's more you are tired. My child, I am kissing (671) you. I love you because you are my true child; I have compassion on you because you are very wretched. One more time, I love you because you are really my child.

*Marcel*: Mother, later, in heaven, you will continue to call me your child, is that not so? And I, I will give you the name of Mother to the exclusion of any other name. And similarly, if I do not call you by the name of 'Queen', will you be pleased with me? Is there anything wrong in not calling you 'Queen'?

*Mary*: My child, let me put it another way. Before dying, did Jesus tell you to call me 'Queen' or did he tell you to call me 'Mother'? Did he say:

(672) 'Here is Mary, your Queen'? No, he never said that. In giving me to you to be your Mother and in giving you to me to be my child, he simply said: 'Here is your Mother, there is your child'. Consequently, not calling me 'Queen' has no importance. I am not a queen; I only have the power of a queen. In relation to men, my children, I am simply and always your true Mother. I would never deal with you as a queen with her subjects, for fear of contradicting Jesus' last words to me. The Trinity never established me as a Queen; it has established me only as a Mother. So, in heaven, you will never hear the word 'Queen' but only the word 'Mother'.

*Marcel*: Mother, what can be compared with it. I am full of joy! In heaven, I will not have to hear the word 'Queen' but simply the word 'Mother'. What happiness! This fact alone will suffice for me to be happy in heaven. Mother, Mother, you are only Mother. It is the only name I like to give to you. In reality, Mother, I see that you do not like the name of 'Queen' either, so that my sentiments correspond completely to yours. Is that not so? Ah! It is a great joy for me already that I will not have to hear the word 'Queen' in heaven; yes, that comforts me a lot.

(673) If I were an editor of a paper or in charge of a radio broadcast, I would make known to the whole world right now that you are a Mother only and not a queen. That you only have the power of a queen, without being one in reality. That the Trinity have not chosen you to be queen, but only to be Mother. Mother, how pleased I am! I am asking permission of you. If I encounter, in some book, passages where you are called queen, allow me to cross out the word queen to replace it with the word Mother. Yes, that is good. Also, it is not surprising that my sister Thérèse has absolutely never told me to call you Queen of France. She has only told me that you were the true Mother of France. Yes, you are Mother, Mother only and not queen. However, people still deceive themselves, which is not astonishing when there are still such a great number of sinners. If one said to sinners that you were their real Mother, they would certainly be somewhat comforted and they would come to you. Would it not be really beautiful? If, on the contrary, one continues to call you queen, who would not be afraid of you?

Children in their relations with their mothers behave very naturally, but it is not the same with subjects towards their queen. For myself, even if I were given a mountain of precious stones, I would not dare to approach her.

(674) *Mary*: Marcel! My child! You never stop talking! What did you ask me

earlier? Please allow me to reply. I do not give you what you want because I do not have the power to do so. Consequently, do not do what you asked, do you understand? Besides, to give me the title of 'Queen' is neither to offend me nor to offend God since, in fact, while not being a queen in reality, I have, however, more power than a queen. So much so that the title of queen is not even sufficient. However, because this world has a limited vocabulary, it must use this word to satisfy its fervour.

*Marcel*: Whatever may be the case, since I will never hear anyone call you queen in heaven, that is enough to reassure me. Although men on earth call you what they wish, for me I will only call you my true Mother. And indeed, you are not queen, you are simply mother. It is fortunate that you recalled the last words of Jesus to men, because without that I would perhaps still have been confused. It is now a closed (675) book. I see that I am acting in conformity with the last wishes of Jesus. It is quite clear; there is not the least trace of an error. Jesus said simply that you are my true mother and not my true queen ... Oh! What happiness! My mother Mary, you are mother only; and presto I am freed from the word queen. Although you are not giving me what I asked for earlier, I am pleased, nevertheless. But, when I meet, while reading, the word queen, I shall replace it with the word mother. If you do not show severity, even towards the devil, even less will you do so towards us, your children. I remember your words very well and if, in heaven, there is a saint or an angel who begins to praise you as a queen, I will tell him, frankly, that he deceives himself, that you are not a queen but mother, simply. If he does not listen to me I shall make him read the words that you have just said to me and, so, I will be very happy. Even little Jesus never called you queen; he always called you by the sole name of mother. And if he ever called you queen, I would then be more powerful than he ...

But it is time and I have not said all I wanted to say. Mother, allow (676) me to walk in the garden to take my mind off things. Goodbye, my Mother. Mary, you are my Mother, you are my Mother. Mary! You are my Mother.

## 13 Mother 1946

*Marcel*: Little Jesus, yesterday my Mother Mary reminded me of the words that you spoke to her before dying and since then I have been in a good mood all the time. Little Jesus, I said to her, Mary is not a queen she is simply Mother.

(677) This morning I met **Mr Diệm*** and he greeted me. Ah! I remember that the other day I saw him in a dream. First I saw a very large number of Vietminh flags placed three by three. There were even three in the students' yard, where the statue of Christ the Priest stands, and all these flags were red. One thing, however, appeared very strange to me. In the middle of each flag there was a yellow cross instead of a star. I was quite astonished by that, then I suddenly woke up. Going back to sleep, my dream began again and I then saw **Mr Diệm** with some other people whom I did not recognize. **Mr Diệm** was standing up straight and said in a loud voice: 'Without France we can do nothing ...' He then said some other things but I have forgotten it all. Then, everything disappeared and I saw nothing.

Little Jesus, I like **Mr Diệm** a lot; I am going to pray for him very much so that he might join the French to destroy communism in Vietnam, my country, and spread the reign of your Love throughout it.

(678) *Jesus*: Yes, little brother, continue to pray a lot. Prayer will triumph over communism better than aeroplanes and other necessary means. If there are few prayers, it will be a total failure. Yes, continue to pray; pray for **Mr Diệm** and for many others that you do not know. I am going to extend the hand of my Love over **Mr Diệm** and make use of him to strengthen the reign of my Love in Vietnam, your country. I also promise to regard him as an apostle working for the expansion of the reign of my Love in the world. However, you must pray a lot for **Mr Diệm** so that he may always have the courage and the zeal typical of a true apostle of my Love.

*Marcel*: All right, little Jesus, I will do as you wish; but tell me, does **Mr Diệm** recognize Mary as his true Mother? If he does not call Mary his true Mother, do not imagine that I will pray for him because Mary is the true Mother of the apostles of your Love.

*Jesus*: Why would **Mr Diệm** not recognize Mary as his true Mother?

*Marcel*: I am afraid that he might call Mary 'Queen', which would not be very affectionate. I would like him to call her only Mother.

*Jesus*: Why fear such a foolish thing? From now on cast this fear aside. Since **Mr Diệm** loves me like you, he must evidently love Mary also.

---

* Mr Ngô Đình Diệm was, at that time, the head of the government of South Vietnam.

Why worry about it? All I ask you to do is to pray. Therefore, ask Mary to protect **Mr Diệm** in a very special way.

*Marcel*: Little Jesus, it is really difficult for **Mr Diệm**. The Vietminh do not stop looking for him in order to kill him, making him remain hidden all the time.

*Jesus*: I wish it so to teach you that you are not the only one suffering, but there are many others who also suffer. I want **Mr Diệm** to find himself in this situation to make him understand that it is impossible for (679) him to oppose communism by his personal talents, and he must place his confidence in me alone. I also want him to have enough time to prepare himself for the apostolate that I expect from him ... But you must pray a lot, so that he is always full of courage and zeal ... That's enough, little brother, the time is almost up. Go and sleep. I am kissing you.

*Marcel*: Little Jesus, do you sometimes give kisses to **Mr Diệm**?

*Jesus*: You are too bothersome, little brother. You are not even able to manage your own affairs and yet you still get involved in other people's. Busy yourself, first of all with going to bed; concerning the giving of kisses to **Mr Diệm**, let me worry about that.

*Marcel*: But, little Jesus, there is no sin in telling me ...

*Jesus*: Right, I am going to tell you just to have some peace. Yes, I am giving him some. That's enough. Now I have told you, you must go to sleep.

*Marcel*: Little Jesus, from now on I no longer have to receive injections. This evening, I do not know why but I am very sad. I have permission to go to bed before the others but only until the end of this week. I do not understand why I am so sad. Ah! I know! I must suffer today for (680) France. Yes, that's it. I understand now. Little Jesus, I am giving my sadness to you. It is really strange; I have already suffered a lot for France but it is never over. Perhaps that is a trick on your part, to let France know how much you love her. Is that not so, little Jesus? ...

   That's how it is. There you are again, gone to visit France. I see, indeed, that you are no longer speaking to me. The worst is that each time you leave, you tell me absolutely nothing about it, so that I cannot even send a word of greeting to the children of France. You are truly cruel and completely lacking in sincerity toward me.

My sister Thérèse, will you be kind enough to carry to little Jesus, now in France, my sighs full of sufferings and sadness. Tell him that it is his little brother who sends them to him. My Mother Mary is surely there also. Say to her too that I love her a lot, that I love her for all the French who do not love her. Thank you, my sister.

(681) Later, in heaven, I will see the smile that Jesus has promised to give to France. Is that not so, my sister? Enough. I feel much disgust and I no longer want to write. Tomorrow I will see if little Jesus is going to give me any news from France. If I am left without news, I will not be sad because of it.

My sister, take care to love me in little Jesus' place. You are my true sister. I love you a lot.

## 14 Mother 1946

*Marcel*: Little Jesus, today I feel sick again. Yesterday evening, hearing Brother Augustine speak of the monastery of Phước Sơn, I asked him, as a joke: 'So, you've decided to join the Trappists at Phước Sơn?' I intended to continue joking, but Brother immediately threw these words at me: 'All you know how to do is to judge evil of your neighbour.' Then he was quiet. I was quite afraid and I apologized without delay, saying to him: 'It's a great pity, Brother, but if you understood the meaning of my words, you would not speak to me like that. For the slightest thing you say I think ill of you.' I was very angry with him, but my sister Thérèse said to me: 'There you are, little brother, a present from little Jesus, a present which comes to you from France.'

(682) Then, Brother Mark annoyed me in his turn. He often speaks figuratively, so that I do not clearly understand him. However, I noticed that he often targets me when speaking this way. I think that by doing so he does me no harm at all and he only harms himself. Indeed without knowing why, I understand this: if someone is in the habit of speaking figuratively with the intention of targeting his neighbour, he will also be in the habit of judging others and judging them in a manner bearing little resemblance to the truth. It is only rarely that he will judge according to the truth.

Little Jesus, it happens very often that Brother Mark treats me harshly. Recently, at table, after having heard him tell a story, I asked him a question, but he dryly replied: 'I do not know.' I did not become sad at all, and I offered to you this coarse behaviour.

*Jesus*: Good, little brother, now that you clearly know the way to act towards Brother Mark, you must be more careful to avoid all unfortunate shortcomings. In your dealings with him, you must take into account the circumstances and not be mistaken. Moreover, you must never forget this: when Brother Mark tells a story or says something, it is not necessary to ask him a question or to contradict him. Let him speak, and be happy to listen. In telling you to listen, I am not telling (683) you to remember. Therefore, after having listened, show your pleasure and try to forget the things that would not be useful to you. In that way, while pleasing your brethren, as I told you earlier, your frail little soul will not be subject to any damage.

**Marcel**: Little Jesus, a short time ago Brother Augustine told me also that I was very fierce but he was so gentle that even children were able to intimidate him.

***Jesus***: My little brother, it is very hurtful, isn't it? He told you that you were very fierce. Very well, if you had seen my true image at the time when I had to appear before Pilate and compared it with yours, I am sure Brother Augustine would say that I am much more severe than you. Yes, little brother, you really are severe; outwardly your face never reflects perfect joy ... However, it is not your fault if your face has a different expression than before. It is because it conceals many interior sufferings that it is never really joyful in this world. Looking at it, it also appears quite strained to me. That is because people do not know (684) where this rigid face comes from which they call severe; as for me, I love this fierce demeanour very much and if all religious possessed it, there would no longer be any sinners on earth.

   Secondly, Brother Augustine said that he was so gentle that even children were capable of intimidating him and that made you sad. However, little brother, do not be sad, because those of a gentle nature possess it more or less naturally. As for this gentleness of nature that allows itself to be intimidated by children, that is cowardice and not gentleness. But that is not important and I do not want to expand on this subject. However, little brother, understand this: all I ask of men is to have the virtues of interior gentleness and humility, without obliging them exteriorly to have a gentle and humble temperament. As I said to you earlier, gentleness of temperament and the virtue of gentleness are two very different things. The virtue of gentleness and the virtue of humility go hand in hand. If one lacks humility, one also lacks gentle- (685) ness, and without gentleness there is no humility. By that one knows that if someone possesses true humility, he also possesses true gentleness. There is no need to look at the external physiognomy to know if such or such a one possesses true gentleness. It sometimes happens that the two coincide, but an outwardly gentle physiognomy is only the sign of a gentle character and not of the real virtue of gentleness. Your Father never judges by the external, he judges only by the interior.

*Marcel*: Little Jesus, you say that to allow oneself to be intimidated by children is to be cowardly. So, what must one do?

*Jesus*: Obviously little brother, it is not right to hit children, but it is necessary, according to the circumstances, to act prudently with them, without giving the impression of being cowardly, because that shows a lack of this necessary prudence in those older than them. He who outwardly possesses a truly gentle character, also naturally possesses a good supply of prudence. Bearded Jesus knows these things clearly but it seems that you know absolutely nothing about them ... It is time. You should know, at least, that it is now siesta time.

(686)

*Marcel*: Little Jesus, it is really strange. I do not know why the paper that I attached to the picture of my sister Thérèse is lying in the middle of my table while the picture itself has not fallen over. I fear that a brother may have entered to close the window and then looked at this paper. It is impossible that the wind could have, without knocking over the picture, made the paper fall when it was so well attached. Little Jesus, you must be careful, because if the slightest thing comes to light it can be dangerous for me. See for yourself. Although Brother Mark only knows insignificant things concerning my soul, how many times has he made wild judgements. I truly believe that if there were two brethren like Brother Mark, my soul would not be able to live in peace. Do you not agree, little Jesus? Brother Mark scrutinizes everyone's character and he knows them all. One day I asked him if he knew my character and he answered me: 'Obviously, I know it.' But, in reality, his knowledge of me is hazy. This makes me suffer a lot. But I am not afraid since I know that it is you who wishes it so. I do not fear any damage to my soul since you do not wish anything that could be harmful to me.

(687)

*Jesus*: Very good, little brother. There you have a real thorn. This thorn is not guilty of any fault towards me, since it knows how to act according to my will. I wish, by that, to tease you a little as a joke, because it is not the thorn that is at fault, but only he who holds the thorn in order to prick you. Put up with it cheerfully. Certainly it is very hurtful for you; but know that if I tease you a little like this, it is to avoid the sadness which comes to me from priests.

Do not imitate the dog that only knows how to get angry at the stone which has been thrown at his back while ignoring the one who threw the stone. As for you, little brother, you know who makes use of this thorn to prick your soul. Consequently, you should never lose your temper either with this thorn or with me. Be content to look at me and to give me a smile. By that you will set my mind at rest immediately and then, I will pull the thorn from your soul. Do not get angry with Brother Mark. This thorn, although truly very painful is no less very useful for you, my little Jesus.

*Marcel*: It is very painful, little Jesus. In heaven, do not play such a game any more. I would be very sad because of it.

*Jesus*: In heaven, what good will thorns be for amusement? As for me, I will no longer like this manner of teasing you. I would be afraid of making you cry, Mary would scold me, and bad luck for me!

*Marcel*: But, little Jesus, why aren't you afraid that Mary might scold you now? (688)

*Jesus*: That is a strange question. It is because you wish it so; nobody is violent towards you.

*Marcel*: The time is up, little Jesus, I am leaving.

*Jesus*: First of all, give me a glance. There are still two minutes. I really love your glances of love ... I am kissing you and, eternally, I will clasp you to my heart in Mary's arms. That's enough, little brother, go, otherwise, you will again blame me. Go and be joyful.

## 15 Mother 1946

*Marcel*: Mother, today, on rising, I had hardly got my feet out of bed when little Jesus made me put on my socks. I waited a bit, but I was, nevertheless, pleased since I was cold. At these times I feel once again a pain in my heart. If you do not warn little Jesus, it will be very bad for me. Little Jesus plays in a very cruel way, does he not, Mother? There are plenty of other ways of playing, rather than playing in this way to make me suffer.

*Mary*: My child, I have already told you, it is not right to complain since your heart already belongs to little Jesus. Each morning, after communion, you ask me to offer your heart to little Jesus, consequently, your heart truly belongs to him, you can no longer do anything about it. My child, continue to be patient a little to please little Jesus. I dare not reproach him, since if I did so, he would no longer dare to touch your heart. And then what game could I invent for him to play with you? My child, I still love you more than I love little Jesus; try to put up with your condition. I am giving you a kiss. It is very hard for you, my child. The time is up. Be joyful, all right?

(689) **Marcel**: Little Jesus, it is strange, I can hear sounds like cannonade. It is certainly not thunder. I'm afraid that it may be war between France and Vietnam. If that were the case I would ask you that Vietnam behaves with humility towards France, rather than to try to dominate it. I ask you also that France, in her relations with Vietnam, demonstrates her charity rather than her power.

Little Jesus, have pity on the two countries, but have pity, most of all, on the one that is more unfortunate. As for the one that loves you the most, graciously show it a greater love and make it so that the two words *Thương* and *yêu* join together to make the word '*Thương yêu*'.* The time is up, little Jesus, I beg you to excuse me and to bless France and Vietnam.

**Jesus**: Marcel, you are wearing socks today. Do you find that difficult?

**Marcel**: I hesitated a little before putting them on, but I am very pleased since, today, I feel the cold. I do not find that at all difficult.

**Jesus**: Little brother, continue to wear them. You are very weak; I must look after you more. Do you agree? You surely must.

Today, you asked me about the poverty I spoke of in the Gospel. Very well, I will explain it. Listen carefully. In speaking to the young man, why did I not tell him to give up all his riches and then to follow me? That is not exactly what I said to him. This is what I said: 'Go, sell your fields, your house and all your belongings, give it all as alms to the poor and, afterwards, come and follow me.'

(690) Little brother, it is necessary that you understand this, for souls. These words do not designate all material goods but only spiritual goods. By these words I intended to say to souls that, if they wish to follow me and be truly poor of heart, they must agree to make use of all their good works and the part of the inheritance that I have reserved

---

* *Thương* means 'to have pity for', *yêu* means 'to love', and *Thương yêu* means 'charity'.

for them, to offer them to the Trinity, so that the Trinity may distribute them to poor and wretched souls. It is on this condition that they will be able to follow me.

Little brother, you must remember this text. In the Gospel, I am not saying: 'Give to the poor', I am simply saying: 'sell' and by this word 'sell' I mean to say that it is necessary to offer everything to the Trinity and, after having offered all, to agree to give everything as alms to souls, without keeping anything for oneself. If a soul had the intention of keeping something for itself, it would not be able to follow me since, sooner or later, pride would be born in its heart on seeing its good works that had not been given entirely to souls. If, on the contrary, the soul has given everything, nothing more remains to it on which it can pride itself. It is because of this that one is in the position to recognize oneself as being truly poor of heart and that one accepts joyfully the necessary graces coming from my hand. Since the truly poor person never complains about the food that one gives to him as a gift ...

After what I have just told you, do you understand sufficiently? This morning you did not stop making different suppositions, not knowing what to hold on to. Little brother, the words that I addressed to the young man, I addressed also, in a spiritual sense, to all souls.

***Marcel***: Little Jesus, then why was the young man not pleased with the words you addressed to him? (691)

***Jesus***: Little brother, there is nothing surprising in that. Indeed, because this young man's faith was not strong enough, he found my words strange and impossible to put into effect ... See, Marcel, if it is difficult to strip oneself of earthly goods, how much more difficult then for the man with faith to strip himself of true heavenly possessions. I do not intend to say that it is necessary to abandon them in reality, but only that it is necessary to give them in almsgiving. 'To give' is not 'to forsake'; and if one forsakes possessions, they are not really good ... When will men understand this true virtue of poverty? The time is up, little brother, that's enough. Go and sleep.

***Marcel***: Little Jesus, I do not know why you speak to me so little. It's been ages! Are you angry with me?

***Jesus***: Little brother, who would dare to be angry with you? Come, come, I love you dearly. Why exaggerate so? Hardly two days have elapsed since I spoke to you just a little, because you are tired; and you dare to speak of 'ages'. Come, come, 'an age' is at least a few months, hardly two days, and you speak of ages. It is only because I am afraid of tiring you that I speak to you so little.

*Marcel*: Today, little Jesus, I am really tired and, at the same time, I feel disgust. I offer this disgust to you. I do not wish to write any more; I only want to cry.

*Jesus*: Little brother, try to cry a little, just to let me see. I challenge you to cry. If you were going to cry, your sister Thérèse would scold you and woe betide you ... Since you are tired, you must rest. I do not want you to write any more.

*Marcel*: I am stopping, little Jesus, I am saying goodbye. It is already the end of the first fortnight of the month of Mother, isn't it? I am (692) continuing to make use of this word 'Mother'; I do not wish to set it aside in the middle of this month of our Mother.

Mother, this month is the month of 'Mother' and not the month of 'Queen'. But that's enough. I am going to rest, if not, little Jesus will not be pleased.

## 16 Mother 1946

*Marcel*: Today, little Jesus, I have a huge appetite. I ate twice as much as usual and I am still hungry; it's really strange. The more I eat, the more I am hungry. I now take one extra meal per day, which makes five. Truly, little Jesus, you spoil me more than my earthly mother has ever done ...

Incidentally, little Jesus, a short while ago I heard Brother Vitus say that Father Vaillancourt is truly very virtuous; and after having sung his praises for everything, he added: 'Father is really good, if he is mistaken about something and I point it out to him, he admits it immediately. He is not like Father Romeo Gagnon. Each time anyone tells him he has got something wrong, he is displeased and never wants to admit it. But with Father Vaillancourt, it's different.'

Little Jesus, in speaking this way, has Brother Vitus spoken badly about Father Gagnon?

*Jesus*: Without any doubt, and there is nothing surprising in that. To reprimand a brother for some failure is not something to do in the presence of others. To tell a confrere, before everyone, that he has committed such or such an error, is nothing less than a grave fault, and who could put up with such a thing? If I was found wanting and

Brother Vitus came to reprimand me in this way, I wouldn't want to listen to him any more, and to teach him a lesson, I would reply to him that he was wanting in charity and humility. So, what can one think of someone who interferes and corrects the brothers when it is no business of his? For sure, it is only lunatics who act in this way. (693)

*Marcel*: It is really strange. Brother Vitus talks a lot and all he does is malign his neighbour. I really do not know what sort of character he has. Little Jesus, by acting this way is Brother virtuous?

*Jesus*: What need do you have to know if he is virtuous or not? You are not his Director to have to judge these things. However, judging externally, in acting in this way, the Brother is lacking true wisdom. If a soul is lacking true wisdom, the other virtues are not very solid either in his regard. If, on the contrary, a soul possesses true wisdom, naturally this wisdom, which envelops the other virtues, will give it a greater stability since true wisdom is the Holy Spirit, and the Holy Spirit is Love itself. Now if Love encapsulates the other virtues, what is there left to fear? When Love envelops all the virtues, normally, a stranger could never know if a soul is virtuous or not, since it is rare that Love appears outwardly. So, it is difficult for a stranger to know what sufferings this soul endures or what consolations it enjoys. Only the person involved is capable of knowing these things. On the other hand, in the soul which lacks this enveloping Love, the virtues remain dispersed, a little here and a little there, lacking solidity. Also for these souls a mere nothing is very often sufficient to make their own virtues disappear in their own eyes and then they become discouraged. Marcel, if you wish to acquire (694) true wisdom, you must truly love me.

*Marcel*: Little Jesus, you know well that I truly love only you.

*Jesus*: Yes, it is true. So, I am kissing you. I love you dearly. All day I cover you with kisses and I hold you tight in my arms in the presence of everybody and absolutely no one notices because you are wrapped up in true wisdom ... The time is up.

*Marcel*: Little Jesus, I do not know why, yesterday evening on remembering all the sufferings that my parents caused me before my entrance into the Congregation, I found it extremely painful and the memory drew tears from my eyes. Little Jesus, I did, however, ask you to make me forget these things; why then have you reminded me of them? Truthfully, I did not then know who my parents were, and if someone had asked me, I would have denied them, saying: 'I have no parents in this world; I have only one true Father and one true Mother in heaven ... '

Little Jesus, it is better that I forget, it is better to make me forget. However, when I think of my little sister,* her simplicity and her candour suffice to make me joyful ... Why am I so sad today? I do not want to write any more.

My Mother, Mary, today I feel an extreme disgust. On hearing Father Tuyen performing the song 'Nhớ Chiến Khu Rừng Thiều ...'† I was very moved. If I knew this song, I am sure that I would shed tears while singing it. If only I might have this song to perform in honour of little Jesus and make him understand the feelings of my heart. Dear Mother, there is really nothing at this time that is able to comfort me. Look at my tears that are flowing ... There's one ... two ... And more still which do not stop flowing.

(695)

During these past few days, little Jesus' words do not bring me the slightest joy ... Mother, I am saying goodbye to you. I do not know what more to say to you. The slightest thing makes my tears flow. Nothing, however, can tear me away from Love, not even you dear Mother, nor the Trinity. Nor can anything convince me that such a thing were possible. O Mother, I love you, make me suffer joyfully.

Mary, my Mother, today, I am not very sad, but I feel in me a sort of force that makes me remember past sufferings, which cause tears to come unceasingly to my eyes. Your child is very sad, Mother; I can only lift my gaze towards you and I have the feeling that my heart must again revisit all the places where I have had to suffer ...

Mother, I love you. My memory has gone completely. I would really like to converse with you, but I have hardly taken my pen to write what I intend to say when I have forgotten everything. My dear Mother, you understand my feelings better than I do, have pity on me.

## 17 Mother 1946

***Marcel***: Mother, I am still hungry. This morning I was not able to eat at all. I took only a little more than a bowl of coffee. As for soup, I was not able to eat it and, what is more, there was no bread. I was really hungry but unable to eat. I really wanted to eat some bread; I signalled to Brother Eugene to give me some, but he acted as if he did not understand, so I have had to remain hungry. I do not know

(696)

---

\* Tế.
† A recollection of the battle in the forest of Thiều.

why, when I eat soup, I am not able to tolerate it; I would really like to eat it, but each time I eat it, it all wants to come up again and I find that very painful.

Little Jesus has well and truly forgotten me. He no longer speaks to me and he no longer even wants to give me anything to eat. But, Mother, I am happy nonetheless. Little Jesus wishes it so, I do not dare reproach him because of it. Now, I ask you for enough strength to endure the hunger until ten o'clock. At ten o'clock I hope to have a bowl of milk soup to put into my little stomach. However, Mother, if Brother John Baptist forgot it, I would be content to wait until midday. Mother, I love you; graciously have pity on your little child. Today I again feel sadness in my heart, but this sadness is not so strong and I can put up with it. Mother, offer my heart to your little Jesus. The time is up; I must go to make my visit to the Blessed Sacrament.

## 27 Mother 1946

*Thérèse*: Marcel, my dear little brother, do not worry. I am thinking of France all the time and I am more concerned with her than with you. Remain in peace. Listen, I am going to dictate a prayer to you that you can recite with me during the whole month of June.

'O Jesus, graciously accept France's confidence and make this confidence above all rely on you.'

To Mary: 'O Mother, teach France to live according to the wisdom of the Love of Jesus.'

Little brother, remain in peace and that is enough.

## 6 June 1946

*Marcel*: Mother, I am holding my pen, but I do not know what to write. I remain seated, counting the hours, which I find very long. Oh! This world has no longer any consolation for me. All its consolations have (697) become bitter for me. If I lift my eyes towards heaven, I see myself alone; if I lower them towards the earth, I see myself equally alone. If I glance around me, no matter in what direction, the solitude remains. I have lost all; even my natural smile has also disappeared. You are the only one remaining for me, Mother. But alas! From time to time I also hear a voice that tells me that I have a Mother no longer, that paradise and Jesus no longer exist. However, that only lasts a moment.

## 20 June 1946

*Marcel*: My Mother Mary, I have not touched this pen for a very long time; it is quite covered with rust.

Mother, why does little Jesus show himself so weak with me? Even the prayers that I say as a joke, he hears and answers them. I prayed that Brother Augustine might leave and also Brother Gregory and, lo and behold, he answered my prayers for both of them. In fact I did not pray seriously, I said that simply for fun, but little Jesus granted them to me nevertheless. By that I see that he refuses me nothing. However, Mother, I do not know why but I am afraid also for myself. It is probably the devil that wants to make me afraid. I seem to have a compulsion to think: 'Perhaps the day will come when it will be my turn to leave.' I feel an excessive fear about it, a fear greater even than the unhappiness that could come to me. However, dear Mother, my fear is like that of a little child. I know that the greater the fear of a child the closer he clings to his mother. It is the same for me; the more I am afraid, the more strongly I cling to you ...

(698) Mother, I cannot speak any more. Little Jesus has taken away from me my intelligence and my memory, nothing remains for me but life. I live but without feeling that I live, without knowing what my life is ... However, if I also lost my life I would be happy nevertheless ...

Oh! Mother, it would be better not to live rather than to live in this way; but since it is Jesus who wishes it, it is better still that I follow his will.

## 27 June 1946

'Jesus, so arrange things that France submits entirely to the authority of the Church, that it always obeys the Holy Father.'

'Mary, teach France to sacrifice itself to the Love of Jesus, to sacrifice itself in truth.'

*Marcel*: Mother, it seems that my sister Thérèse is very indifferent towards me. Only after having asked her for it on numerous occasions did she finally give me the prayer for France to recite next month. She dictated this prayer to me in a very indifferent tone, without adding a single word. From time to time, however, she reminds me of this prayer that she dictated to me for fear I might forget it. And this is all. I am very sad, Mother.

However, I have also received a great comfort. This morning I asked my father Saint Alphonsus, this question: 'When my little sister becomes a religious what name will you give to her?' And, what do you know, he replied to me immediately in an unexpected manner. I heard him clearly say to me, 'Call your little sister "Thérèse of little Jesus".'*

Mother, I am really pleased. If I cannot have the name 'of the Child Jesus', my little sister at least will be able to bear the name 'of little Jesus' and that will give me as much pleasure as if I had obtained this favour myself ...

Mother, here we go again, I have forgotten everything and I no longer know what to say. Mother, understand the feelings of my heart ...

## 24 July 1946
*On the subject of children who die without baptism of water*

**Marcel**: Some days ago, looking at the little Alphonsian calendar fixed (699) to the letter board, I read a quotation from Saint Alphonsus affirming that children who die without baptism do not have to endure any torments ... On this subject, I remember that one time – probably during community prayer – while thinking about children who die without having been baptized, I asked myself if, later, they would be able to go to heaven. I spoke to myself thus: if they cannot go to heaven, will they then be deprived of the vision of their true Father for all eternity? In my mind I kept asking myself these questions, and I was very sad.

I thought: to be the special apostle of children and not to be able to do anything to save these souls is something that is very painful for me, all the more so because at this very moment a great number of children are dying without having received baptism. Where can one find priests in sufficient numbers to go and baptize, in time, these children who are on the point of death ... ? I then raised my eyes towards Jesus in the tabernacle and this glance led him to reply to me clearly, which has been a very great comfort for me.

*To his director*: My Father, kindly allow me to tell you that, for some time, although little Jesus does not speak to me often, now and then, when there are important things that I do not understand, he will speak to me still to help me understand. It is precisely for this reason that I

---

\* This was written in French in Van's text: 'Thérèse du petit Jésus'. Each time Van calls his sister by this name, he writes it in French.

said to you one day that little Jesus was no longer sleeping. Allow me to continue my account.

Then little Jesus asked me this question: 'Little brother, so, you are sad again? But why this sadness? If our true Father in heaven, in his goodness, wishes that the voices of these children unite with the voices of the angels to praise him in heaven, where is the problem?'

*Jesus*: Remember this well. Naturally, little children, not yet having intelligence, do not have will either. Intelligence serves to understand if something is good or bad and the will to act in conformity with what the intelligence understands. These two faculties are the most necessary. Now children do not yet possess these faculties. Therefore, another will must take its place in the heart of these little children; and if this will acts in a manner in conformity with what is good, it is just as if these little children were acting themselves.

However, in order that this will may produce its effect, it is necessary that it acts in a way conforming to what is good, conforming to the truth itself. If, on the contrary, it acts in a manner opposed to what is good, opposed to the truth, this will does not produce its effect.

Now, all you have to do is to place your will in the hearts of little children and, then, they also will belong immediately to the Church. And if they die before the use of reason, they will go to heaven with me, because they have your will, which acts in them. And since you have the will to believe all the Church teaches, and also the will to love me ... It follows that these children also have the same will as you, so that their souls belong to me completely and they belong to the Church. Although these children know nothing, there is in them, however, the will of another who does know, so that, while knowing nothing, it so happens that they do know.

Little brother, do you understand that? Offer your will to me, and I, I will place it in the souls of little children who are living on this earth ... From now, you can be sure that all the little children belong to me already.

Little brother, this manner of willing that I have just revealed to you is something new. Until now, little children were saved, thanks to this process, without men realizing it. So, little brother, chase away sadness and be joyful. As you are the apostle of children, it was necessary that you know these things.

Children saved in this way are baptized in love itself. It is given to them to confess the faith in love, and they make this act of love by means of will.

*Marcel*: So, there actually are no children in limbo?

*Jesus*: That is not what I intended to say. After my death, I went down to this prison of ancestors, so the true light has already entered it. (701)

*Marcel*: If it were as you say, people could stay at home and put their will in the heart of their children without the need to have them baptized. What's your answer to that, little Jesus?

*Jesus*: To act in such a way would not be to truly will. For there to be true efficacious will, it is necessary, when baptism by water is possible, that it is actually conferred on the children. If one were content to wish it, while remaining at home, how could one call that will?

*Marcel*: That is all I remember and, since I learned these things, I do not stop putting my will in the hearts of little children. I consider this teaching of little Jesus very true. And I think if my Holy Father Pius XII knew this, he would certainly feel a very great joy because, being on this earth the good Father of souls, he would rejoice because of it much more even than I, since he is my Father.

My Father, on 22 July, while reading what our father Saint Alphonsus says on this subject, I found it quite valid, and his words have added to my joy. I believe the instruction I received from Jesus a few days ago is very true and well-founded. This is what I think: if a pagan, finding himself in his last agony, wishes to receive baptism, but dies before having his wish realized, and he is, nevertheless, saved, with much greater reason will the innocent little children.

My Father, there are still many other arguments that I understand but I cannot write down. As for the argument given earlier, I do not know if you understand it. As for me, on re-reading it after having written it, it is as if I was not able to understand it. Please excuse me. Certainly, little Jesus does not force me to explain these arguments to lead you to believe what he taught me earlier. Nevertheless, if it was necessary, I would be content to enumerate the following arguments: (702)

1. God's mercy is infinite.
2. Jesus' merits are in the same way infinite; they do not limit themselves to the salvation only of a small number.
3. The communion of saints.

4. We can free the souls from purgatory.*
5. There are three kinds of baptism:
   1) Baptism of water.
   2) Baptism of fire (or of desire),
   3) Baptism of blood.
   In the first and the third case, the faith is confessed outwardly, while in the second it is confessed in love ...
6. Parents must leave to the will of their children the liberty to follow what is good, and that is true also for pagan parents. Therefore, even if pagan parents do not wish it, they must, however, leave their children free to follow the truth. Consequently, for children who do not yet have will, my will has the power to freely make in their place the act of faith ... and other acts ...

Besides, I think that the things said earlier by little Jesus are already sufficiently clear. As for the arguments listed here, I only ask little Jesus to make you understand them so as to explain them in my place. As for me, I would not at all know how to explain them ...

What comforts me the most, is that from now on, I truly know that each day I will have totally pure flowers to offer to my Father in heaven.

*When this revelation was made to him, Brother Marcel used a formula containing the acts to make in place of children. But he then forgot the exact wording of this formula, only retaining the principal idea. After having tried in vain to reconstruct the formula, he wrote the following:*

'Little Jesus, graciously place my will in the souls of the children of the whole world who have not yet been baptized. In this will, I wish to place the acts of faith, of hope and of love, according to the intention of the Church. And if these children die before the use of reason, deign to welcome them as being special children of the Church.'

*On 11 August 1946, after communion, he remembered the first formula and he copied it as follows:*

---

* *In a letter written from Saigon, 21 March 1950 (cited in Appendix 2) he wrote to me on this point*: 'Although it is true in itself, it proves nothing here, since the souls in purgatory already possess sanctifying grace. Kindly, therefore, set aside this argument which proves nothing here.' J.M.T. Marcel C.Ss.R.

The formula I recited the first time was:

'Little Jesus, I offer you the children who have not yet been baptized. I wish to believe and to love you in their place according to the intention of the Church, my Mother. Graciously recognize them as true children of the Church. And should they die before the use of reason, lead them to heaven with you, so that in union with the saints they may love you eternally, according to the promise you made to me.'

## 28 July 1946

*Marcel*: Prayer for France to be recited during the month of August. My sister has only dictated this prayer to me without adding anything. She reminded me of the prayer of the other day: 'Jesus, give to the priests of France courage to be always ready to defend the truth in their country.' (703)

'O Mother, teach France humility.'

## 8 August 1946

*Marcel*: Mother, I have just written a letter to Father Dreyer Dufer. It is very interesting. I am sure that God will want to laugh. In it I call little Jesus by the name of cub scout.*

Mother, I do not know why, but to all those to whom I write letters now, I say that little Jesus is on the point of leading me to heaven. I do not know if it is true, but I continue to say it. At this time I am thinking a lot about heaven. I believe that, in a short time, I will rest on your breast with little Jesus and, there, I will call you by the name of 'Mammy'† and I will give to God the name of 'Daddy'.††

Mother, when I think of that, I feel my heart fill with a joy, which does not stop flowing into me from somewhere. Yes, I am joyful. I hear something like a voice from heaven, which calls me unceasingly to rejoin little Jesus without delay. From time to time I even hear this voice. O Mother, come to look for me to take me with little Jesus. When I am with him, only then will I be able to help children a lot. If you leave

---

\* Van was in the scouts with Father Dreyer Dufer at Lạng-Sơn.
† This was written in French in Van's text: 'Maman'.
†† This was written in French in Van's text: 'Papa'.

me sitting in a corner of this room, what can I do, Mother?

My Mother, I love you a lot. It is no longer possible for me to offend little Jesus. As soon as I have done something, I forget it straight away. Little Jesus lets me live, but without my knowing that I live. It is truly strange; I do not know where little Jesus actually is, but one thing is sure, that in seeing the manner in which I am living, he must have a strong desire to laugh.

(704) I have already received a pair of new shoes, but little Jesus did not come to congratulate me. Where is he playing, that he forgets his little friend? Mother, try to hide me somewhere so that little Jesus, noticing that he has lost me, is forced to cry. Then, I am sure that he will hurry to go immediately to look for me.

Mother, the day of the spiritual nuptials of your two children is already close. On that day I am going to ask my sister Thérèse to invite all the saints, as well as all the children who are in heaven, to come to be present at the feast. I will ask my sister Cecilia to play the organ to delight the ear of little Jesus ... As for you, Mother, you will place both of us on your heart, then, with your gentle hands, you will unite our lips and we will both contemplate our mutual smile and our mutual beauty. Is that not so?

Mother, I am leaving you because I am tired. I love you, don't forget it.

I have already been resting for half an hour. Mother I really want to speak to you. There are twelve huge fish for whom bearded Jesus has asked me to pray. But there are only two of them that have been caught. Mother, I have already offered you these fish; make sure you tell this to little Jesus: 'Little Jesus, your little spouse wants these sinners to run to find shelter in your heart.' The other day I also asked the same favour of my father Saint Alphonsus; he had just given little Jesus two of these fish. The ten others that remain, I want them also to belong to him.

The day when bearded Jesus announced the conversion of two sinners, Brother Thuần* immediately said that they were his. Father Socius of the Novitiate† said in his turn, as a joke, that the two conversions were thanks to the Master of Novices and himself, his assistant. As for me, I know that my prayers are really very powerful, to such an extent that if little Jesus does not grant me what I wish, I look at him crossly and then he is afraid. However, when I have obtained something, I do not consider it my own property, but solely that of little

---

* A choir novice.
† Assistant to the Father Master of Novices.

Jesus. Because of this, he is satisfied. Is that not so, Mother?

Mother, I will soon go to heaven with you. I love you a lot. I am stopping here, not wishing to write any more. Mother, take pity on your little child. (705)

## 10 August 1946

*Marcel*: I am praying today, Mother, for your little apostles. Incidentally, Mother, on Thursday, Brother Mark scolded me in this fashion: 'You always act like a child; you must be a little serious and not spend all day amusing yourself ...' At the time I said nothing; I put up with it for a moment in order to find a very good answer that would please the Brother. After reflecting I said to him: 'But Brother, you know that now is the time for recreation.' Then I continued to wash the dishes as usual, while chatting away happily. Mother, I willingly forgive Brother Mark; I am not at all angry with him. I have to suffer a lot from him, but I am not complaining, since it is little Jesus who wishes to tease me.

My Mother Mary, I will soon go to heaven with you. When your little flower has been transplanted in heaven, the world will have a lot to say about it, the world will criticize it ... But I am not afraid of anything. The way in which little Jesus acts in me is evidence of the truth of the words he has addressed to me, and this testimony is true since all I know how to do is to follow the truth.

Mother, is little Jesus happy? I think of him a lot. It is certain that I shall soon go to heaven with him, is that not so, Mother? Little Jesus says I have an illness of the heart, but bearded Jesus, for his part, says no. On the one hand, I would prefer to believe little Jesus because I feel my heart makes me really ill. But, on the other hand I would also want to believe bearded Jesus, knowing that he has more experience than I do. I am continuing, therefore, to believe bearded Jesus; that's the more sure way, is it not? Mother, time is up; I cannot write any more.

## 12 August 1946

*Marcel*: Mother, I was privileged today to enter the Carmel. Previously, I did not stop importuning my sister Thérèse, saying to her: 'My sister, ask little Jesus to change me into a woman so that I can enter the Carmel.' But my sister could not ask for that, nor was I able to become a woman. However, today, I was able to enter the (706)

Carmel; like the sisters I was able to hold a candle in my hand. The Carmelites even came to meet me and then I walked ahead of them. All that distinguished me from them was my Redemptorist's habit. I was wearing my new shoes, which resonated on the cobblestones and made me feel uncomfortable. The sisters led me into the choir, then into the garden and finally they led me back to the door to depart. So therefore, Mother, although your child could not be admitted to the Order of Carmel, he has, nevertheless, entered Carmel. How happy I was!

Last night, while bearded Jesus was reflecting, asking himself who to send to Carmel (*of Hanoi*) to serve a solemn funeral Mass, my sister Thérèse, coming from somewhere, said to me immediately: 'Little brother, say this to bearded Jesus: "Send those who are serving Benediction during this week."' I repeated these words and it so happened that bearded Jesus had also decided that. Mother, I hardly expected to obtain this favour.

Mother, having just arrived at the entrance door I spotted you immediately. (*The statue of the Blessed Virgin*) Incidentally, Mother, this sister who just died, has she gone to heaven already? While I was in the choir, I said to little Jesus: 'Little Jesus, you have surely already met your spouse, have you not?' Little Jesus did not answer me, but I felt my heart beating a little stronger, and I felt a certain change within me, which I considered as being little Jesus' reply. I am therefore certain, Mother, that this sister is already in heaven with little Jesus, since she is his spouse ...

(707) But, Mother, when will little Jesus take me with him? I think of him a lot. To all those to whom I have written letters, I said that probably little Jesus will take me to heaven soon, since all the time I hear his voice calling me. If he deceives me or refuses to keep his promise, later, when I am on your breast, I will give him a funny look. Mother, make this call be realized promptly. Otherwise, I remain confounded, asking myself when it will finally be my turn to go to heaven with little Jesus. I am certain that this voice comes from heaven, since, from time to time, I have the feeling that the devil creates obstacles to prevent my hearing this voice ... But, Mother, the time is up.

## 16 August 1946

**Marcel**: Mary, I see that this earth is full of misery and weakness. However, if I must live here below until the end of the world, I would agree gladly to make known to my Father in heaven all my wretchedness and all my weaknesses. He would then have more pity on me and

I would love him more. It seems to me that heaven is moving from day to day, further away. All that remains for me from the call on high is an ardent desire to see my Beloved. This call becomes more and more distant, giving me the feeling of having been deceived. The heaven that I wanted up to now seems to be no more than a dark cloud which suddenly drifts away in my heart ...

However, Mother, I am not afraid. I always know the truth; but, usually, to follow the truth, it is necessary to encounter obstacles. However, whatever happens, I will follow my Beloved until the end. Until the day when we will both rest in peace on your breast ...

Mary! Mary! It is raining all the time. My soul is also covered with a layer of gloomy clouds and under this blanket of clouds, I remain alone, abandoned, I, your child. Mother, I no longer know what to say to you. I am silent. It is better to rest peacefully in your arms. I agree to live on this earth until the day when little Jesus will wish to take me with him. I am not going to concern myself ... Mother, I cannot speak any more.

## 18 August 1946

*Marcel*: Mother, I do not know why my hand shakes so. Mary, my Mother, I am very sad. Bearded Jesus asked me to correct the badly translated sentences in the book entitled *The Divine Friend*,* but I do not know how to make these corrections; little Jesus has taken away all my intelligence. All I can say is that such a translation is incomprehensible to me. I tore up the pages I had corrected, because these corrections do not at all correspond to the meaning of the French text. After having corrected a paragraph, if I re-read it I did not understand what I had written. It is therefore better to tear up these corrections, since I can write nothing that corresponds to the French text. Besides, not understanding a word of French, I find it very difficult. It is better that I tear it up. Do you not agree, Mother?

(708)

Mother, tell bearded Jesus to give someone else the task of making a new translation of this book. As for me, being quite ignorant, I am not able to do this work. Mother, come to my aid so that I do not become agitated. I do not wish to keep the passages I have corrected, since it would be useless. If the work is given to someone else, it will be done in a better style. Mary, Mary, Mary, happy are you to be able to see the wretchedness of your child.

---

\* By Father Schrijvers, CSsR.

## 19 August 1946

*Marcel*: Mother, in reading the lives of the saints, I see that people form an assessment saying: such a one loved Jesus more than another; another is the saint who has suffered most. Certainly, these opinions are sincere, but they are made with the intention of praising the saints a little. For me, if I assessed things as those people do, I would also say, Mother, that I love Jesus more than you do, that I love him more than he loves himself, that I love him above everything; in a word, no one loves him as much as I do. And if someone wished to love Jesus as much as me, to do so, he would have to have another Love which is comparable to the Love of Jesus. See, Mother, it's the simple truth, I do not at all speak through pride.

(709) It is very painful for me to hear these assessments of the saints, yet I hear them all the time. This is what I think, and I believe it is quite right: if a soul loves Jesus, his love must be nothing other than one with the Love of Jesus. So, who could say what level of love each soul reaches? Only being one with the Love of Jesus, how can this love be great or small, how can it be more or less great?

Even if a sinner only loved Jesus at his last breath, this sinner's love would, nevertheless, be equal to mine, supposing that I have loved Jesus all during my life, and that is so because these two loves merge in the same way in the Love of Jesus. So, to be able to distinguish which of two loves is superior to the other, which is the greater, nothing less than another love, which would be able to equal that of Jesus, would be necessary. However, concerning the glory and the merits of the saints, I admit that there are degrees. Nevertheless, whatever this degree may be, the saints have all equally reached the fulfilment of their desires. Mother, it is time. I love you.

## 22 August 1946

*Marcel*: My Mother Mary, I love you a lot. Mother, where is little Jesus? The voice from heaven does not stop calling me, but I feel there is a sort of power which makes me think that I will still live a very long time and that it is not at all certain that I can go immediately with Jesus. I am sure that this power comes from the devil but that it cannot force little Jesus to follow his will. I remain, therefore in peace since the devil has no power to force me to follow his will. Furthermore, for quite some time, every time I do something good or I practise some virtue, there is a sort of voice that says to me: 'Ah! Marcel, you are very clever; it's marvellous, you are a saint already; what more do you want?...'

I am sure that it is again the voice of the devil since little Jesus' voice is clear, and there is no vestige of pride in his words. I have, however a very clever way of replying to this voice. This is what I say to it: 'That's right; I really am a saint, that is obvious. There is no need to tell me since I know I am really a saint.' These words are enough for the voice to be silent immediately. As I see it, it is no longer possible for me to be proud. In saying that I am truly holy, it is not pride either. If I did not say that I am holy, I would then have reason to repent, since I would shame Jesus my Friend who is holiness itself living always in me and acting in my stead. If, therefore, I was saying that I was not worthy of being holy, I would give the impression of denying the sanctity of Jesus, and then, it is certain that Jesus ...

(710)

## 23 August 1946

*Marcel*: Mother, yesterday I had not yet finished chatting with you when I had to stop because the time had passed. Allow me now to continue.

As I said yesterday, if I replied to this voice: 'I am not a saint', I am sure that little Jesus living in me would be very sad and quite ashamed. So, in saying that I really am holy, it is not through pride, neither is it blasphemy. By this simple and sincere reply, not only do I shame the devil, but more, I please my Jesus. Yes, it is a great disgrace for the devil, since he thought that on hearing me praise myself I was revelling in myself and allowing myself to be proud. Mother, who would have believed that your Marcel would declare himself holy, and by that would render the devil powerless to praise him more? Truly, Mother, the devil could not be more stupid. If he had not spoken, he would not have had to be subjected to such a disgrace. Deceitfulness must always be overcome by wisdom.

He even forgot this text from Saint Paul: 'I live, it is no longer I who live, it is Christ who lives in me'.* If he had recalled this text, he would certainly never have spoken as he did. I still have the audacity to state that I am the spouse of Jesus; so why be afraid and not dare to admit that I am holy? It is a fact that the devil is more forgetful than I am. So, later, when I am dead, what will he be able to find to accuse me of in Jesus' presence? He would be wasting his time. I will only have to go to heaven straight away with little Jesus. Mother, the devil is very foolish. If he recognized you as his Mother, would that not be proof of wisdom.

(711)

---

\* Galatians. 2, 20.

Foolish as he is, he will have to remain in hell eternally and I, in heaven, I will make a mockery of him ...

But, Mother, I almost forgot one thing that I want very much to speak to you about. A short time ago, after my confession, Jesus with the ginger beard was curious enough to ask me this question: 'When you have finished your novitiate, where will you go to?' I did not at all know what to answer, since I was totally ignorant of where I would be able to go. As I hesitated still, not knowing what to reply, suddenly and without knowing why, I answered: 'I am going to heaven.' I had hardly pronounced the word heaven, when I felt my heart overflowing with a sweet joy. I think that I cannot go elsewhere but to heaven; little Jesus lets me see nothing more than the single path that leads to heaven. I am, therefore, certain that heaven will be my residence, that heaven is the place I shall have to go to first of all, after my nuptials with little Jesus.

Oh Mary, my Mother! What happiness! I will be able to go with you soon. Although this day still seems far away, however, little Jesus will not be able to resign himself to remain far from me. He will, therefore, have to find a means of bringing us both together on your breast so that our mutual love may be fully satisfied ... Mother, I am sure that you see nothing strange in that since I know that you always wish for this union even more ardently than I do. Also, I am equally certain that you will look for a means of fulfilling our common desire.

(712)   Mary, time is almost up, I must go and sleep.

Incidentally, when he had heard my reply, Jesus with the ginger beard said to me, laughing: 'When you are in heaven, you will pray for the Fathers and Brothers.' Laughing, I answered yes, then still laughing I left.

I have a huge desire to go to heaven.

## 24 August 1946

*Marcel*: My sister Thérèse dictated to me, the day before yesterday, the prayer for France to be recited during the month of September but I have not yet had time to write it down. On that day, my sister Thérèse, after having given many long sighs, told me to recite the following prayer:

'Dear Jesus, give to the priests of France generosity in all their endeavours where it will be necessary to sacrifice themselves for the good of souls.'

'Dear Mary, change the hearts of the communists of France, so that we enjoy true peace based on the Love of Jesus.'

***Thérèse***: It is very sad, little brother, communism continues its scheming. Should they come to power in France, France, and with her the whole world, will be subjected to a very heavy yoke and, then, it is certain that France will no longer be able to call itself France, it will be a country dominated by the forces of hell ...

Oh! France, France, do not allow the prayers said for your future to become wasted. If these prayers were to be useless, it is certain, France, that you would fall into the hands of hell which would make you feel its crushing yoke.

Communism acts at this time in secret, looking for a deceitful means of gaining power. If France falls into its hands, it will look for a means of delivering it to hell to be oppressed.

Oh! My brothers, the priests of France, what is the law which is appropriate to our country? Is it a law which aims to govern the world? No! No! Here are the essential points of this law:

First: To love Jesus,
Second: To be subject to the authority of the Church,
Third: To spread the reign of the Love of Jesus throughout the universe.

If France does not follow the paths of wisdom, if she does not faithfully observe these essential laws, then you can be certain that France, the kingdom of Jesus, the oldest daughter of the Church, will be the victim of communist cunning. (713)

Marcel, my little brother, pray a lot. Ask Mary, our Mother, to change the hearts of the communists of France. Without that, France will always live in discord and she will never be able to enjoy a lasting peace.

If the French communists knew the ruin that is in store for their country because of their activities, they would surely be heartsick and would not be able to stem the flow of tears. And the world would see that their communist yoke is the crushing yoke of hell ...

Little brother, pray, above all during next month; continue to ask Mary to change the hearts of the French communists. Either France will abandon itself to the gentle hand of Jesus, or it will have to be subject to the crushing yoke of hell; all depends on the prayers of Jesus' spouses. The devil uses the power of lies and deceit to seize hold of France. As for us, we must use the strength of prayer so that it submits to Jesus. Anyway, if one prays a lot, the devil will certainly be vanquished and Jesus will be the victor. His spouses will triumph. However, little brother, to attain that victory, you will have to pray a lot ... I am kissing you.

***Marcel***: Mother, here I am on retreat, but I do not feel at all fervent. While listening to the talks, I do not feel any emotion. As soon as the sermon is finished, I forget everything; I remember absolutely nothing. I feel like laughing when I see myself in such a situation. Mother, the talks are very interesting, and although I do all I can do to listen fervently, I understand nothing, I retain nothing. Nevertheless I continue to listen attentively, offering the words of the preacher to little Jesus. Perhaps in acting this way I gain more than if I understood, since little Jesus must then stay constantly close to me to receive these words. Is that not the case, Mother?

(714)

Little Jesus is also sometimes inclined to forget. I am sure that he really wishes to converse with me, but it could be that he forgets as I do, so he no longer knows what to say. Mother, little Jesus is very crafty; he sometimes pretends to forget, to force me to refresh his memory for him. If in heaven it happens that we both no longer know what to say, Mother, you will tell us stories of the good old days, all right? You will tell us the way in which God spoke to men in earlier times, so we can see if he used the words *Mày* and *Tao*.

The other day, my sister Thérèse did not stop saying to me, while sighing: 'Little brother, ask our Mother to bend the pride of the communists of France.' I do not at all know why she appeared so sad. I have forgotten everything ...

Little Jesus has once again taken my mind away somewhere. He is truly very mischievous. However, Mother, it is enough that you understand me. If some lapse escapes me, I am afraid of nothing; it is little Jesus who is responsible and not me. Mother, I see that little Jesus is not at all polite; just at the time when I am chatting with you, he comes to take away my memory. That's enough. I am saying goodbye to you. Tomorrow, if I remember anything, I will tell it to you. When it is a question of telling you something, I can still do so, but when it comes to telling stories to the brethren in the common room, I cannot. I do not know how to express myself so as to make it interesting; I say trivial things without any meaning.

On the other hand, the hearts of my heavenly Father and Mother which are full of goodness are very different from the hearts of my natural parents. The hearts of my heavenly parents are capable in their goodness of holding all that I tell, even the slightest details, while the hearts of natural parents are truly narrow, incapable of even containing the slightest ... What? I have forgotten. Ah! I remember. Because the

(715) hearts of natural parents are too restricted, there is not enough room to contain the very simple stories that their children tell them. I myself noticed this at my natural mother's house. When she was breast-feeding me or making me eat, if I told her in detail the little stories I had seen

or heard, she sometimes listened. Sometimes, too, she answered me to please me so that I would eat more; but when she was busy, she did not listen to me at all and did not cease exhorting me to eat quickly. I see by that that my true Mother has infinitely more goodness and compassion than my natural mother. Mother, although you hear the melodious chants of my brothers and sisters in heaven, in your goodness, you still lean towards me with love to indulge me, as you know how. It is also the same for my true Father in heaven.

Later, when I am in heaven, I will teach children to conduct themselves with complete simplicity and sincerity towards their Father and Mother in heaven, since they are not parsimonious like their natural parents. These latter cannot understand deep down the hearts of their little children and, in their dealings with them, they lack kindness. The time is up.

## 27 August 1946

*Marcel*: Mother, a moment ago Brother John Baptist gave me his picture as a souvenir of my profession. He will definitely leave for Đa-lạt in a short while; this is why he gave me this souvenir so early. Mother, graciously thank him for me.

With Brother John Baptist leaving, I will have to apply myself to the tailor's workshop and, then, how will I be able to go to heaven? Mother, try to look for another means that will allow me to go to heaven soon with little Jesus, Besides, I am not concerned. When I have to go to heaven, I will go, and afterwards there will be another Brother to busy himself with the tailor's workshop. There is no shortage of Brothers ...

Mother, there is one thing I find very painful and I want to mention it to you alone. But I must not write it here, since bearded Jesus will know it. Nevertheless, I have already spoken to him of it a little. (716) Mother, I am not writing it since, in writing it down, I would lose a good opportunity to make a little sacrifice during this retreat. That's enough. I shall now speak to you of something else.

First of all, Mother, do you know Brother Eugene, this Brother who is no bigger than me? You must certainly know him. It is he who expressed the strange idea that Jesus is not the Spouse of male religious. Yes, you know him. The other day, while serving at table he distributed the dishes incorrectly. I said to him in a soft voice: 'My Brother, you distribute the dishes very badly, some food is missing in certain places and there is too much elsewhere. The Brothers and the students are not yet served when the novices already are. If you follow the order of precedence, would it not be much easier for the server?'

The Brother said to me, laughing: 'Shush! And Father Master, do you not think of him? What is the Prefect of Studies compared to our Father Master?'

Brother has already done that several times and, even when he was warned politely, he did not stop arguing about the order of precedence. Mother, in acting this way Brother shows that he does not yet have the spirit of the Congregation. It is true Mother. Whatever Brother's intentions I continue to pray that he will return to the world; it would be preferable.

I have also heard other brothers speak in the same way. Fathers, they said, are obviously superior to Brothers; consequently it is necessary to treat them with more care. For us, it is not necessary, we would even be content to eat leftovers ... One must give to Father Rector a cleaner knife and fork ... And many other things that show that the brothers, in the refectory, discriminate in favour of some. For myself, I think that among all the brothers who speak in this way, there is not one who has the spirit of the Congregation. Although, personally, I am only a little serving brother, I am, however, numbered among the Redemptorists,

(717) another Redeemer. I have neither the intention nor the audacity to criticize the Superiors in any way. I know, however, that the words of these brothers are not prompted by their love for the Superiors, that they are often inspired by pride and flattery and that ordinarily they offend against charity. In speaking as one does, it is just as if one was saying: Jesus intends to choose Superiors who take care of the community in his place so that these Superiors are treated better than the others by the brothers and receive food better prepared ...

Truly, brothers who speak like this do not yet possess the spirit of the Rule of the Redemptorists. For me, this is how I see things: Jesus intends to appoint Superiors who hold authority in his stead; that is as it should be. Further, I must love the Superiors as I love Jesus himself. Now, to love the Superiors is not to offer them flattering words nor see that they are better treated than the brethren of the community. To prove to the Superiors that I love them as I love Jesus himself, I only know one means: to obey them as a very little child obeys his parents. But when I am in the refectory, I attend to the Superior simply as I do to a postulant, since Jesus did not wish to choose the Superiors so that they may be better nourished than the others.

I am well aware that Jesus obliges me to always give to the Superiors outward marks of respect; but he does not force me, in giving these marks of respect, to be lacking in charity towards others. Mother, what do you think? If one acted in this way, it would come about that owing to the Superiors, the brothers would pay no attention to the others. Mother, this is not the case. And I dare to state with certainty that if someone thinks thus, he has not got the spirit of our Rule ...

But Mother, am I allowed to speak as I have just done? Have I gone too far and lacked respect for the Superiors? If I made a mistake, or if I have been guilty of some omission, you can correct everything for me. I would never dare to despise my bearded Jesus.

Oh! I've forgotten one thing. Mother, graciously change Brother Eugene's spirit. Truly he still has the spirit of people of the world. In place of this worldly spirit, give him the spirit of the Rule of our Congregation of the Most Holy Redeemer. I know that Brother speaks in this way with a good intention, but if he is always left to follow this spirit, even with the best intentions, it will be very difficult for him to persevere. Make him understand the spirit of the Rule. I continue to pray that he will follow this spirit. Mother, graciously help me in this affair and you also, my father Saint Alphonsus. (718)

It is now time, I must go to say my rosary ...

Little Jesus, my loving friend, I wish to write to you, but I do not know what to write. I wish to speak to you, but I do not know what to say. I wish to listen to you, but I do not know what to listen to. I wish to remain in peace, but Love agitates me continually. I wish to give kisses but I do not know who to give them to. There is someone I love more than all the others, someone with whom I am happy more than with any other, someone to whom I wish to give kisses more than to any other, but this someone is far from me, I cannot see him with my bodily eyes. Alas! When will I be able to see my Beloved face to face? If my soul was not a prisoner in this body, would I not be able to see him? However, little Jesus, the day will come when we will see each other and then we will be able freely ... But what? There are many things that I cannot write here ...

Little Jesus, the day of our union is already close. I have asked Mary and my sister Thérèse to adorn my soul, so that it may be truly beautiful; I have also written a piece that I will use to speak to you on that day, my dear Jesus. When I wrote that script I did not find it very interesting, however, my Beloved I am sure that in reading it, you will not be able to stop yourself from laughing and to deal with me as with an unruly child. But, little Jesus, deal with me just as you wish. If you scold me, I will scold you in my turn, you will see since, from this day, as I will be one with you, who would be able to harm me? Be careful, little Jesus. And who told you to choose me for your spouse? When I was small, people called me 'the unruly child'. If one did not do all that I wished, one was not able to get rid of me easily. Little Jesus, are you afraid? Are you afraid of the threats I have just made to amuse you? Do not be afraid, my little Jesus, I love you a lot. And since we are one together in a single love, it is absolutely impossible that we could ever (719) hurt each other. We have no cause for concern, since our mutual relations are nothing like those that people of the world have with those they love.

My little Jesus, I love you dearly. On the day of my profession I will place this script on my chest so that you can read it easily. Or let me ask my sister Thérèse to read it to you. It is very interesting and very amusing, take the trouble to listen to it. Bearded Jesus has promised me not to read it before my profession and this is what I promised him: 'If, after my profession, you find this script somewhere, I allow you to read it.' The other day, as I was asking him for some paper to write down the words I had prepared, bearded Jesus said to me: 'It will be necessary to hide it carefully, otherwise I am going to read it.' Believing he was speaking seriously, I went to hide it in a corner near the door without his knowledge. But now that he has promised not to read it before my profession, there is no need to hide it.

Yesterday, in writing, I made a mistake and this morning, I made a mistake again, so I have had to ask for another sheet of paper and copy it down again. It is really annoying; I am writing all the time and I have not finished. But it is very amusing to read. Little Jesus, have the patience to wait until the day of our spiritual nuptials, and I will let you read what I have written.

(720) Little Jesus, I love you a lot. For some time now, when I think about you as the Spouse of my soul, I feel a great joy and at the thought that you regard me as your spouse, I am filled with a sweet happiness. I wish and I hope that all young people would prefer not to love anyone in this world; that instead of wretched friendships, they only look for and embrace your Love alone. This pure Love will lead them to the vision of the very one that they must love and by whom they will be loved eternally. It is really so, little Jesus, I would not deceive them. What is the soul that would not be able to recognize you as its Spouse, as I do myself? Since we are talking of souls, I cannot distinguish between men and women; but my little Jesus, I can always call you my Lover and my Spouse. The more I love, the more I clasp tightly the object of my love, the more, also, I see clearly that there is in my heart a love whose dimensions are equal to your infinite Love. There is nothing surprising in that, since in calling me your spouse, in allowing me to call you the Spouse of my soul, certainly, you must arrange things so that we have, the two of us, an equal love. Only then will it be possible for us to love each other. Is that not the case, little Jesus? So, therefore, your infinite Love is equally my infinite Love. Just as we make but one, there is, also, only a single love that links us together.

I am stopping here, time is almost up. I cannot continue this conversation with you any longer on paper, my Spouse. Little Jesus, I am going to rest a little and then I will go to pay you a visit. Graciously grant to the brothers the grace to make a fervent retreat. Have you heard me, little Jesus? I am giving you ... Listen well, I am sending you a spiritual kiss! ...

Little Jesus, I have finished my visit to the Blessed Sacrament. During (721) the time I have left, I would like to say many things to you, but I'm not sure I have enough time to say them all. It is only when time no longer exists that I will be able to speak to you at my leisure.

Incidentally, little Jesus, the other day, bearded Jesus asked Brother Eugene the following questions: 'Souls who are consecrated to God in a Congregation, men and women, are they all without exception the spouses of Jesus? Can they all recognize themselves as being the spouses of Jesus? For example, we Redemptorists, can we say that our soul is the spouse of Jesus?' We were speaking on that day about the vow of chastity in the Congregation.

After having reflected for a moment, Brother Eugene replied: 'Yes'. And I, I could hardly control my need to laugh since, previously, the Brother had maintained forcefully that men could not call themselves spouse, that the words in the Gospel applied only to women. He then said that it was not appropriate to call you our Spouse. At that time I was very angry with him and I thought that, if he had been my director, I would certainly never have been able to give him the name of spouse. The Brother understands nothing; he still thinks like people of the world; it is very annoying. But now, I am sure that the Brother understands.

To be your spouse, Jesus, is not at all the same thing as to be the spouse of a man of this world. You have always, from the beginning, placed in the heart of each human being the feelings of love so that, thanks to these feelings, men and women love each other and these two loves may be united together, which gives meaning to the word spouse. So therefore, when the loving soul unites its love to your Love, it becomes your spouse for eternity. To be spouse is to unite together two loves who, loving each other, form only one, to the point of becoming inseparable. From that comes the word spouse, people ...

## 28 August 1946

*Marcel*: Little Jesus, what did I write yesterday without understanding (722) it? I wrote without stopping and the words just seemed to flow.

I was speaking of the word 'spouse', but I had to stop without finishing, since the time was up. My Jesus, while listening to me, did you understand? But, here's a very strange thing, the more I wrote, the more the words flowed, as if you had written everything, in advance, in my heart. When I finished writing one word, I noticed that another word was there waiting for me to write it immediately.

Ah! Little Jesus, my Lover, your conduct towards me is very clever, but I have discovered your trick; I now know it very well. You speak to me without wanting me to know that it is you who speaks. So, when I have finished writing, you deem that what I wrote has come from me. I am no longer surprised by your stratagem, little Jesus. However, we can act in complete freedom with each other because we understand one another perfectly. Is that not so, little Jesus?

There are still fifteen minutes left, so I will continue. Regarding the term *Bạn trăm năm*\* that men dare to use to indicate those whom they love, that is really a great abuse of words. In fact, little Jesus, the world only knows how to lie to itself. Only a little examination is necessary to see it. On this earth, it is impossible for human couples to love each other intimately, it is impossible for their mutual love ever to be joined together for a period of a hundred years; and yet they dare to give to each other the name of spouse, of 'friend for a hundred years'.

(723) First of all, because their physical beauty fades from day to day, their love also diminishes bit by bit. Then, it is certain that one of the two spouses will die, then their love will be divided and, in a hundred years they would consider each other as total strangers. However, they dare to give each other the name of spouse, friend for a hundred years. If they called themselves passing friends, I would find that easier to understand and then little Jesus, the words *Bạn trăm năm* would be reserved solely to you and me, as well as to the souls who would offer their love to you to be united to your Love. We alone are able to call ourselves, truly, *Bạn trăm năm* because we make but one together in a single infinite love. We would even be able to call each other eternal friends. Besides, that is the true meaning of the word 'spouse'. It is therefore better to continue using it. Little Jesus, it is a fact that the world has stolen our word 'spouse', friend for a hundred years, because their love can never last for a hundred years; at the most it can last until death. And after a hundred years, surely nothing more will remain of their love.

For us, the longer our love lasts, the more we understand each other and the more the bond of our love tightens. Furthermore, this love produces such a union that we are one, both of us, and no force is capable of separating us. Little Jesus, that is what it is to be a 'spouse'

---

\* Literally 'friend for a hundred years', that is to say, spouse.

and, consequently, we are the only ones who can have this name. People of the world have stolen this word which is ours alone, since there is no one among them who can have a friend for a hundred years. You are the only one who can be their Spouse. Little Jesus, they are quite arrogant to dare to usurp our Love in this way. What is wrongly acquired does not last. The word spouse is reserved, therefore, to those loves alone who join themselves to your Love ... It is now time, little Jesus ...

Do you know, little Jesus, that I was lucky enough to enter Carmel the other day? I have already told the story to our Mother. If you wish to hear it, ask her to tell it to you. On that day I went to the cemetery carrying a candle; and as this candle was long enough, at the moment when I was about to reach the cemetery, it hit a sweetsop that was hanging from the tree. It was on looking up that I saw it. My candle nearly went out. I had a mad urge to laugh but I dared not do so. (724) Seeing that the fruit was already ripe and that the bees had begun to eat it, I thought to myself, with their lowered veils, how would the sisters be able to see it? And I still wanted to laugh. All the sisters had their veils lowered and yet they saw better than I. It was they who had to point out to me the whereabouts of the ditch. There was a very small sister there. According to the brothers, she was the Mother Prioress. As for the sisters who had spoken with me a little before my entrance into religion, I do not know if they were there. They have probably forgotten that conversation with me in the Carmel parlour. If they remembered it and knew that it was I who was there, they would certainly have wanted to laugh.

On that day* I thought at first that my sister Thérèse had appeared to me and I had a momentary fear. But after having listened a while I realized that it was not she. Indeed, my sister Thérèse speaks Vietnamese very well. As soon as I hear her, I recognize her voice and I immediately understand. On that occasion, it was only by paying great attention that I succeeded in catching clearly one or two words. The sisters only knew how to laugh; they did not know how to speak. When one said something, the other laughed. At least that's what I guessed, since there was no order to what they said. I preferred, however, to hear them laugh without understanding them, than to hear them speak without hearing them laugh.

Little Jesus, I thought at the time that, probably, you had allowed the sisters to welcome me more by their smiles than by their words so as to

---

* When he spoke to the Mother Prioress and her community at the cloister grill to ask for their prayers before his entry into religion.

make me happier and to give me the strength to shed some tears in the parlour of the Community of the Redemptorists. Little Jesus, it is because you are very skilled in providing me with sufferings that you manage to make me your little spouse.

(725) On that day, little Jesus, I again asked the Carmelites to pray for me and I told them I had no money. At that time, I thought that when one asked religious for their prayers, it was necessary to give them some money since, only being able to pray for people, they need alms to live on. It is for that reason that I said I had no money. However, I promised to pray for them in return ... That's all, little Jesus, it is now time. I am going to take a siesta. My little Jesus, I love you a lot. I will speak to you again shortly.

Little Jesus, I have absolutely nothing to say to you. It is only after really thinking hard that I succeed in finding something. Since this is how it is, I am going to ask you some questions.

When will the Redemptorist sisters come to Indo-China? Your Thérèse of the little Jesus would really love to see them come as soon as possible. The other day, she wrote to me: 'I have not made friends with anyone; little Jesus is my only friend.' Little Jesus, are you happy to hear these words? You are surely very happy, since naturally, who does not like to see oneself loved and regarded as a friend? In my opinion, these words of my little sister do not mean that she has already established a friendship with you. If she spoke in this way it is simply because she has an inclination for such a friendship. In fact, no one has instructed her to choose you as Spouse. Little Jesus, teach your little spouse how to love you. Not knowing what more to say, I am stopping now and I am going to relax a bit.

## 29 August 1946

*Marcel*: Mother, why do I feel so full of disgust today?

(726) Little Jesus, a short while ago my Mother Mary taught me an easier method of saying the rosary. First of all, I said to her: 'Mother, people say that to say the rosary well and gain indulgences, it is necessary while reciting the prayers to meditate on the mystery proper to each decade. It is impossible for me, Mother, to say the rosary by following this method, since I do not at all know how to meditate. Even if I try, I never succeed in doing so.' So, this is what Mary taught me: 'In this case, my child, offer me the Hail Mary that you are saying' (I was at that time saying my rosary). Then, she added: 'My child, do as follows: when you begin a decade, say to me: "Mother, I offer you this *Our Father*, and then this first *Hail Mary*, this second *Hail Mary*, this third *Hail Mary*" and do

the same until the end of the decade. Then you begin again as before. When the first decade is finished, offer the second to me, saying once again: "Mother, etc." then continue in the same vein. You, therefore, do not need to know how to meditate on such or such mystery. The method which is most pleasing to me, and that I wish to see used by people, in preference to all others, is that which consists in each one offering to me his prayers and his thoughts during the saying of the rosary.'

That is all, little Jesus. And since then I no longer feel any difficulty in saying my rosary. When I have finished my first *Hail Mary*, I offer to her the second, and so on, until the tenth *Hail Mary*, and the *Glory be to the Father*. I then move on to the second decade, following the same method. It is very easy, little Jesus.

My Mother spoils me a lot. If she forced me to meditate on the mysteries, I would find it very difficult and, then, I would no longer like to say the rosary. Little Jesus, this new method will also be very useful to children who do not at all know how to reflect. Thanks to this method, the daily recital of the rosary will, without doubt, become very easy for them.

That's enough. From now on I will no longer have to worry about meditating on the mysteries; I will be happy to offer everything to Mary as she has taught me, and it will be good like this ...

## 1 September 1946

**Marcel**: My Mother, I have finished writing down what I intend to say to little Jesus after my profession. I have not written the graces to ask for; I am leaving to you the responsibility of asking little Jesus for them for me.

The words I have written have no great style; my sole aim in writing them was to be able to remind little Jesus what I wish to say to him on the occasion of my profession. There is nothing extraordinary in that. Is that not the case, Mother?

Yesterday, bearded Jesus forbade me to tear up what I had written. I think that, even without this prohibition, I would not have wanted to tear it up, since, what I say to little Jesus in this piece of writing, I wish to conform to exactly. For that to be so, it is necessary that I save it. Is that not so, Mother? No, I will not tear it up. Bearded Jesus is still afraid that I might tear it, that is why he has imposed this prohibition on me. I do not wish to tear it up but will carefully save it until the day when the Spouse of my soul will take me with him to the wedding banquet in heaven; then I will give it back to bearded Jesus ...*

(727)

---

\* This text is in Appendix 3, p. 385.

Mother, the voice from on high still rings in my soul; yes, Jesus' voice does not cease to call me to ascend to heaven. Unfortunately, I am hearing a serious and powerful voice which cries to me: 'You will still have to live a long time.' Mary, my Mother, while waiting for the day when I will be able to participate in the wedding banquet with the Spouse of my soul, I will certainly still have to pass through paths sown with thorns and climb mountains of suffering. Only then will I be introduced to my divine Friend in heaven. Whatever may be, even if my body must be torn into pieces for Love, I would agree to sacrifice it through love for my Jesus. I have already heard his voice clearly which continues to call me to him. This voice sounds closer from day to day and I am certain that Jesus is on the point of taking me with him. Is that not so, Mother? However, I can only hear his voice without seeing him . . .

Mother, on the road that leads me to heaven with Jesus, I am sure to meet many difficulties and obstacles, but I will continue to go forward without being discouraged. In spite of all the windings of the road, I will not cease to face the danger until the moment when I shall catch sight of my Beloved and will squeeze him to my heart to satisfy the love that I bear for him who loves me infinitely.

(728) Mary, I continue to walk straight towards the dwelling place of my Beloved. Guided by the sound of his voice, I will walk in his footsteps until the day when I shall be privileged to rest in peace with him in your sweet arms. However, I am certain that little Jesus will not allow his call to be drowned out by the other voice that tries to hold me back until later. Yes, I am certain that he will come to look for me.

Incidentally, Mother, today is the feast day of my brothers and sisters, the Vietnamese martyrs. I have an ardent desire to die like them but, at this time, the Vietminh dares not to persecute religion openly, so I am sure that I am not going to die as a martyr. One thing is sure, however, – that I will die consumed with the Love of Jesus, which always burns in me. Although this kind of martyrdom is longer, I am not afraid, and this prospect can in no way diminish my love for Jesus.

On this subject, Mother, I have asked my sister Thérèse to offer me as a victim to the Love of Jesus. Not at all knowing how to make this offering, I simply said to my sister: 'My sister, offer me in the same way as you offered yourself.' Mother, I am certain my sister Thérèse has carried out my request.

This pen is hopeless. Tomorrow I will ask for another one; all right Mother? When I write the ink does not flow. There, I can write now. With a little care, it will work.

The time is up, Mother. I am giving you a kiss.

## 2 September 1946

*Marcel*: Today, Mother, I have absolutely nothing to say to you. Ah! Today the Vietminh are having a big demonstration. Continually, since this morning, I have heard gunfire and, in the streets, shouts of this kind ringing out: 'We have decided to fight … ' 'Long live this … ' 'Long live that … ' and many other things, Mother. I would like to imitate them and to say, inwardly, to little Jesus: 'Little Jesus, relying on the strength of prayer, I, also, have decided to make of my fatherland, Vietnam, a country that belongs to you, the King of Love.'

Mother, for that it is, first of all, necessary to see to it that union is re-established between France and Vietnam. There are those who say: 'France's attitude at this time is simply a front so as to establish its domination once again over Vietnam. No good will come of it. Where can you find anyone who does not covet riches and where is the country that does not pursue its own interests? At this time the French are working to seduce the Vietnamese and as soon as they have won them over, they will once again impose their domination. Ah! They are not as stupid as us … ' I also think that that is true, but true only for those who have no faith because if anyone has faith and is sufficiently well-informed, he would never think in that way. However, Mother, the one who speaks that way is none other than a postulant about to enter the novitiate. I have already warned bearded Jesus. As for me, I continue to believe in the words that Jesus said to me. All Jesus wants is the union of France and Vietnam, with the aim of spreading the reign of his Love, and not to re-establish the domination of France over Vietnam as before. And if France had this intention, surely its government would not be stable. Jesus said that clearly, did he not, Mother? (729)

Furthermore, on reading the prayers for France that my sister Thérèse dictates to me, it is clear that the Love of Jesus wishes to change France so that she makes the universe the kingdom of his Love. Jesus wishes to make use of French priests to defend the truth in France, as it says in the prayer for the month of August. Mother, it follows from this that French priests will necessarily also have to defend the truth in Vietnam, my country, since Jesus wishes that the two countries might be united together. After that, Mother, why be concerned?

The only thing people of the world fear is to lose their possessions; their only preoccupation is to no longer have the freedom to give themselves up to bodily pleasures. As for those who have been victims of (730) their bad habits for a long time, they do not want to be answerable to anyone; they do not want to be disturbed in attending to themselves; they do not want the truth which will drag them from their vicious habits. So, they give themselves over without restraint to licentiousness.

And then all they know how to do is to open their mouths wide to shout unceasingly: 'We have decided to fight ...'

Alas! If just for once they decided to fight against their bad inclinations, how happy they would be! Mother, it is really unfortunate. These people speak in this way without a single blush. They do not yet know how to fight; they don't even have the strength to fight against their wretched bodies, and they have the cheek to say: we have decided to fight against men. In speaking in this way, I do not really think they know what they are saying. If one asked them what their intention is in speaking this way, they would without doubt reply very clearly; but if they were asked if they understood what they were talking about, they would obviously be incapable of replying in accordance with truth.

Mary, my Mother, graciously snatch these souls from the darkness of hell. I am going to pray for them in a very special way, above all on the days when I should pray for France and for Vietnam, my dear fatherland.

(731) I also know, Mother, that a certain number of Vietnamese harbour in their hearts a personal hatred for the French because they have been harshly oppressed by them in the past. However, if these people knew how to respect the truth and listen to reason, one would be able, nevertheless, to induce them to set aside their hatred. If they were able to understand the difference between the France of former times and that of today, I am sure that they would not retain these feelings of hatred much longer. I know very well what the French of Indo-China were like before; I have seen with my own eyes how they treated the Vietnamese ... But I also know that now France has already drawn God's mercy to itself. Jesus made use of suffering to correct his country, France, so that, at this time, this country is not only the country of France but also still the country that Jesus cherishes in a special way. Is that not so, Mother? Now I understand ...

I am going to pray that France and Vietnam may be united in such a way as to form only one whole. Even when I am in heaven, I will not cease to remind little Jesus of this business so that his will may be done ...

Mother, I am giving you a kiss. The time is up. I have had to summarize and still I cannot say everything. I am stopping. It is sufficient that you understand me. Mother, I love you a lot. Amen ...

## 3 September 1946

*Marcel*: Mother, yesterday in his sermon, the preacher spoke in passing about extreme nationalism, which is like an exaggerated opinion of oneself, and consequently, pride. I find that completely true. Yes, Mother, it really is so. I see that people of the world, above all pagans and communists, say that religious are people who are completely useless to a country. They think that such a one is truly patriotic who moves from town to town, from village to village, shouting at the top of his voice: 'Comrades ... Let us save our homeland ...' They think that that is patriotism. But if someone has some responsibility, which obliges him to remain at his post and which makes it impossible for him to act as they do, they consider him a traitor to the fatherland.

Oh! World full of deceitfulness, you only know how to look for excuses to oppress good people. Mary, how can one call these men (732) patriots when they oppress their own compatriots? While good men work peacefully to earn a living, they sow hatred in their hearts, spreading disorder everywhere. And they call that patriotism!

Mother, the devil is very skilful in deceiving people, but his wretched face is now unmasked and people know his tricks only too well. However, he still tries to hide his game under cover of certain external activities. One sees people who only know how to cling to riches and who, however, cry loudly: 'Let us be patriots ... let us fight ... Let us die, if necessary.'

Alas! Mother, graciously have pity on Vietnam which presents at this time such a distressing spectacle. Mary, my Mother, I love my homeland very much; I am going to use all my efforts to build a quantity of reliable and durable arms, so as to drag it from the slavery of hell. I am speaking of prayer which causes damage to no one, but which can triumph over all obstacles ...

Mother, the time is up. I am going to take a siesta.

Little Jesus, why are you so cruel? My tongue hurts and you do not even think of curing me. This morning, at communion, I reminded you about it, but you have not cured me. If, by some chance, the pain had been too much and prevented me from receiving you, then what would we do? No longer being able to unite ourselves to each other all we could do is stay there and look at each other. I would then be sad and cry. And you, little Jesus, I am sure that you would cry also. Mary, seeing us both crying and not being able to comfort us would cry in her turn. And finally my sister Thérèse, seeing our Mother crying, would not be able to prevent herself from crying too. Then, seeing nothing but tears everywhere, little Jesus, where would we find again something to (733) cheer us up? And who would be the cause of all that? None other than you, little Jesus, that is quite certain.

You must therefore, first of all, cure my tongue so that it no longer hurts me. You must also cure my heart, which at this time hurts me a great deal, above all during these past few days; and I always forget to go and speak of it to bearded Jesus. Besides, I do not know how to express myself. When I feel sorrowful, I forget to speak about it and when I think about speaking of it, the sorrow has disappeared. Little Jesus, play with my heart as much as it will please you; but wait until I have made my profession to take me with you, all right? Besides, I must still welcome, in your place, Thérèse of little Jesus! Little Jesus, I think of you a lot; I sigh ardently for heaven. Little Jesus, do not forget to take me up with you soon. The sooner I get to heaven, the sooner will your apostolate among children bear fruit. Nevertheless, I am not forcing you to take me to heaven immediately, as I would like to. I am leaving you completely free; otherwise, you would say that I continue to be violent towards you. Sooner or later, however, you must keep the promise you made to me, all right? That's enough. I do not know what more to say. I am leaving you ...

## 4 September 1946

*Marcel*: My Mother, I have just made a general confession; at this moment there is no longer the slightest stain on my soul. Mary, my Mother, I pressed my head on Jesus' heart, the Spouse of my soul and I asked him, sincerely, to pardon all the sins and negligences of which I have been guilty since I reached the age of reason until now. I shed tears, I opened up to him my wretched heart and, with all the sincerity of my soul, I asked him not to allow, from this day forward, his little spouse to be guilty of anything towards him, nor to willingly

(734) cause him the slightest displeasure, for fear of obstructing our mutual union.

Mary, I am asking you, also, to hide me from now on under your immaculate mantle and not to allow the slightest thing to come and trouble my soul ...

Mary, I do not know what more to say. Little Jesus, the love of my heart, from now on I wish to love only you; only a pure love remains in my heart, waiting for the day of our spiritual marriage, when I shall give this heart to you, my eternal Beloved.

Oh! Jesus! Jesus! Keep my love unceasingly in all its purity ... That is all I ask of you; for the rest, I do not at all know how to express myself. I am staying here doing nothing; it is sufficient that you understand my heart's feelings.

## 6 September 1946

**Marcel**: Mother, in two days I will be able to call myself in all honesty the spouse of little Jesus. Mother, I love little Jesus very much. Today, when I went to confession, Jesus with the ginger beard* said to me: 'Jesus loves you dearly; in two days time you will consecrate yourself entirely to him.' That is all he said to me yet his words comforted me a lot.

Mother, on the day of my profession, allow me to meet your Thérèse of little Jesus. Arrange things so that my little sister can come to witness the spiritual nuptials of little Jesus with your little Marcel. Outwardly there will certainly be nothing unusual but, interiorly, I am certain that many wonders will be taking place between little Jesus and me, since it is on this day that we will enter into an eternal friendship. Mother, is that not so? So, therefore, little Jesus will have, without doubt, to work great wonders in me to show me his love. I will gladly ask for all the graces it will be possible for me to ask for on that day. However, Mother, I am confiding this task to you; graciously ask little Jesus for them on my behalf. I am asking for each bearded Jesus a special grace that little Jesus will choose instead of me, as he sees fit. I am asking in the same way, for my natural parents, a particular grace of little Jesus' choosing, for each of them. I am asking the same thing also for my benefactors, for your Thérèse of little Jesus, for the Redemptorist sisters, without forgetting the Carmelites because last year when I met Mother Prioress in the parlour, I promised to pray for her in gratitude for the prayers she had said for my intentions. Since I have not yet had the opportunity to keep my promise, I will not forget on that day to ask for the Carmelites a special grace of little Jesus' choosing.

(735)

Incidentally, Mother, I will also ask for a grace for Pauline, the sister of my sister Thérèse. The other day I heard bearded Jesus say that Pauline is still alive. Yes, I will ask a special grace of little Jesus' choosing, for her. I learned also that one of our Fathers had met her, that he had chatted with her, that she is now eighty-four years old, which makes her more than five times my age. She told this Father that she had a great desire to go to heaven quickly to join her little sister, but that her wish had not yet been granted.

Mother, between your Pauline and your little Marcel, let us see which of the two will go to heaven first. Your Marcel is still young and very quick at running; he will certainly arrive close to you before your Pauline who is already elderly and without doubt walks very slowly.

---

\* Father Louis Roy.

(736) Yes, allow me to go up first, and then I will tell my sister Thérèse and little Jesus, to bring your Pauline to paradise very quickly. Yes, Mother, that would be good. So, tell little Jesus to take me to heaven with you before Pauline, so that she can read what my sister Thérèse has taught me and see if it is correct. Mary, my Mother, I will certainly go to heaven before your Pauline. Tell little Jesus to take me to heaven first, and then I will help him to bring your Pauline. It is probable that, having suffered a great deal, she is now tired and can only walk with difficulty. Perhaps, also, little Jesus and my sister Thérèse are not capable of carrying her by themselves and they will have to wait until I am there to help them. Mother, tell little Jesus again to take me to heaven, then, I ...

Mother, a moment ago, in conversing with you, I went over the time without noticing and you did absolutely nothing to warn me. That was not very nice of you. If bearded Jesus had not alerted me, I might have missed my siesta.

But, Mother, look at me about to reproach you. It is very impolite on the part of your little Marcel. Do not get angry I beg you, since I love you a great deal. Mother, make sure you tell Jesus what I asked you to a short time ago. Yes, Mother, it is good that he takes me to heaven a little earlier, so that I can give him some help when it will be time to bring up your Pauline. Without that, Pauline, Jesus' spouse, being already very old ... Ah! I forgot, the soul cannot get old, Mother. Whatever, it is absolutely necessary that little Jesus sees that your Marcel is in heaven first; then we will make your Pauline come up ...

Oh! Pauline, Pauline, my sister, be patient a little while longer. When I rest on the heart of our divine Spouse, I will unite myself to little Jesus and to your little sister Thérèse of the Child Jesus, in order to lead you to our eternal Spouse.

Mother, how do you explain this? Each time I converse with you on paper, how does the time fly so quickly? Before I have the chance to say what I want to say, the time is already up. Mother, it is very sad.

(737) Ah! A moment ago I forgot one thing. Why did I call Pauline by the name of sister? I was mistaken. But I do not know how to correct my mistake. Your Pauline was indeed the Mother Prioress of the Carmel. Consequently, her little sister Thérèse had to call her Mother. But, that's enough, one can, nevertheless call her sister; it is the same thing.

Mother, that reminds me of a story, somewhat similar, that happened to me some time ago with your little Thérèse. Seeing at that time that she loved me like a mother, I thought that it was all right to give her the name of mother, as she had done herself with Pauline; but she protested immediately, saying to me: 'My dear little brother, you have only one true Mother, our Mother Mary. As for me, I behave towards you like a mother, but I am only your sister and not your mother ...' Mother, I found my sister's words correct; then she told me how to conduct myself in my relations with you. Without that, I would not have dared tell you my little stories in all their detail as I do now.

Actually, the situation has changed; so I no longer wish to call little Thérèse by the name of mother; I call her, quite simply, my sister. So, then, there is nothing inappropriate either in my calling your Pauline my sister. Indeed, if she is the Mother Prioress of the Carmelites, she is not my Mother Prioress. So, I can continue to call her my sister, without having to worry.

The other day, while making the Stations of the Cross and having arrived at the fourth station, I thought of you. On that day it was Brother Mark who was reciting the prayers and I felt much disgust on hearing him, so that all I could do was distract myself. I then thought of you and seeing you dressed in a red habit, I said to myself, interiorly: 'So then, Mary was the first Redemptorist sister; I am sure of it since she is wearing a red habit.' I said that to myself but, straight away, my sister (738) Thérèse, who was standing nearby, heard me and she added: 'Yes, Mary your Mother, was the first Redemptorist sister, in Nazareth.' I really wanted to laugh but I had already reached the fifth station; so jokingly, I asked my sister Thérèse this question: 'So, our Mother is not a Carmelite? If that is the case, the Carmelites will be very sad and they will no longer like the Redemptorist sisters. What do you think?'

***Thérèse***: Little brother, the Rule of the Redemptorist sisters draws its inspiration from the spirit of the Carmelite Rule. If you do not believe me, ask your father Saint Alphonsus, and you'll see. I do not intend to say that the two Rules are similar, but your father Saint Alphonsus has drawn the spirit of the Redemptorist sisters' Rule from the spirit of Carmel, and not elsewhere, since Jesus wished it so.

***Marcel***: After that my sister stopped speaking. On my part, I intended first of all to ask bearded Jesus for verification. But at the same time, giving credibility to my sister's words, I said to her, jokingly: 'Let me first of all ask bearded Jesus.' I was trying to tease her, but she was content to smile without adding anything.

Mother, my little Thérèse has a lot of affection for me. Her only desire is that I pray a lot for France, her fatherland. She recommends also that I pray a lot for my country, Vietnam. Mother, I am therefore asking you that my sister's wish may be realized completely, in accordance with the Love of Jesus.

As I am tired, I need a little diversion, so I am going to make a visit to the Blessed Sacrament. Today, I am not as sad as yesterday. That's enough. I am saying goodbye to you on this paper.

## 7 September 1946

(739) *Marcel*: But, little Jesus, is today a fast day? Why was meat eaten in the refectory? This morning I heard the Brother cooks saying that it was the fast of the rule; I was dying of hunger. Bearded Jesus has obliged me from now on to fast like the other brothers. Although I find that a bit difficult, since my director wishes it, it is not possible for me to follow your will any longer. Do not be sad because of it, little Jesus. Even if it were necessary for me to die of hunger through obedience, I would gladly offer up this sacrifice. I will no longer have to suffer from hunger in heaven, is that not so, little Jesus? Today, I was so hungry that I felt dizzy, so much that I no longer wished to speak, and laughing was out of the question. However, there is joy in my heart as usual, and I was happy to follow my director's wish. By that, little Jesus, I have obtained a double joy for you, is that not so?

As long as I remain on this earth, I will continue to make all the sacrifices I can possibly make to offer to you, for fear that, in heaven, I will no longer know what to offer to you in sacrifice.

Mary, in a little time I will go up to heaven with little Jesus. This is what he said to me last night: 'My little spouse, in a little more time I will take you to heaven with me.'

I answered him: 'But, little Jesus, the bearded Jesuses are away, how could I go up to heaven with you?'

*The superiors of the communities of Hanoi, of the Student house of studies and of the Novitiate were, at the time, in Saigon for a meeting of Superiors.*

*Jesus*: Little brother, do not worry yourself, I will find an excellent means of taking you to heaven with me.

*Marcel*: And that is all. We then kept silent, both of us. Little Jesus reposed in peace in my soul and I, my heart overflowing with joy, went to give myself the discipline.

Mother, little Jesus said this again to me: 'Little brother, you will still have to suffer some time on this earth; but, I will come, yes, I will come to lead you with me and take part in the wedding banquet in paradise...'

So Mother, I was very hungry this morning; and when bearded Jesus asked me a question on the subject, I did not know what to reply, not daring to tell him that I was hungry. In fact, as he wants me to fast like the other brothers, I thought I should not tell him that I was hungry since it was the fast day.

Mary, tomorrow is the feast of your birthday. How happy for you! Following my sister Thérèse's example, I also wish to say to you: 'Little Mother, today is the exact day when you offered the little flower to little Jesus.'

Tomorrow is also the anniversary of my sister Thérèse's profession. Ah! What happiness! It is not only the day of my little Mother, but also that of my little older sister. Is it not clever on little Jesus' part in having chosen this day to join himself to me? What happiness, dear Mother! Beginning tomorrow, each year I will celebrate on this day a triple anniversary: that of your Birthday, that of the religious profession of my sister little Thérèse and finally that of my own profession, which will make three anniversaries on the same day.

Ah! Little Jesus really has a talent for choosing. That's enough. I no longer want anything outwardly extraordinary to happen tomorrow; what I have just enumerated is already sufficient to make me happy. Oh! Mary, my little Mother, tomorrow is the day when you will offer to little Jesus the little flower of little Thérèse. Fancy, the words *nhỏ mọn, con*,* all three have the same meaning although they are spelled differently.

The very day when my sister, little Thérèse, accepted little Jesus as her true Spouse, I, also, will have the happiness of accepting little Jesus as Spouse. Ah! Thérèse! We have both received the same happiness on the same day, so that your anniversary coincides with mine and vice versa. What happiness is comparable? On the same day, little Jesus gave us . . .

But, my sister Thérèse, what, therefore, has he given to us. I have forgotten. Perhaps he has not given us anything, since in fact, I do not know. I am going to think a bit in order to see . . . Ah! I've got it. All on the same day he has given you his infinite Love and he has accepted yours; on the same day he will also give to me his infinite Love and will accept mine. That is exactly what I wanted to say earlier but I had forgotten completely. Time passes so quickly. Ah! Perhaps, also, little Jesus will choose to take me with him the same day as he introduced you to the wedding feast in paradise. Do you think so, my sister? Perhaps that's how it will be; I think so but I do not know if it is correct. Whatever may be, I am always ready. I agree in advance that little Jesus may come to look for me at whatever time he wishes.

My sister Thérèse, I no longer know what to write. I am really thirsty. Let me first of all take a little drink.

* Little, very little, small or child.

## 8 September 1946

*Marcel*: Little Jesus, I no longer know what to say,
My dear little Spouse, a moment ago I did not know how to express myself, but now I do know what to say. Truly, little Jesus, I have received today all the graces you have so very generously granted me. From this day I will no longer have any other concern than to love you eternally, you the Spouse of my soul.

On this day, everything contributed to fulfil my desires; I am very happy my Spouse and I thank you with all my heart. And to thank you worthily, allow me to take all my feelings of love merged into one in order to offer them to you. O Spouse of my soul, now we are one ... Oh, accept my gratitude. Today, from the sermon to the religious chants, everything was as I would have wished it. For one thing I wanted, you gave me three, and even more still. Indeed, how many other spiritual favours have you not showered on me today. I have not noticed these favours for myself but for the others for whom I had asked you. ... Oh! I am entirely satisfied; I am beside myself, intoxicated as I am with love for you, my Beloved ... Little Jesus, so it is done, our spiritual marriage is accomplished. Nothing more remains for us than to give ourselves to each other in mutual love. Nothing more remains than to await the happy day that the wedding banquet in heaven will be for us both.

Little Jesus, it seems to me that today my father Saint Alphonsus looked down on me in a very special way. But, while I was pronouncing my vows, I do not know why I trembled so. It was impossible for me to read and it was only with a lot of effort that I was able to manage it. It is lucky that I did not die at that moment. My heart was panic-stricken as if it wished to throw itself straight into the tabernacle, so strong and frequent were its beatings. Happily for me, I was allowed to live to go and meet your Thérèse of little Jesus.

So, I must first of all eat, since I feel a little hungry. At midday, not feeling at all hungry, I ate almost nothing ... But now that I feel hungry, I am going to eat. It goes without saying that I will bring you along with me; you don't have to worry since we are but one.

## 10 September 1946

*Marcel*: Little Jesus, Thérèse of little Jesus has not yet been able to leave, it is still raining. You must see to it, little Jesus. I really want the rain to stop, so that my mother can return and that, tomorrow, the washing day, I will be able to dry the linen. If you allow it to continue to rain it will be impossible to do anything. Yes, you must see to it, little

Jesus; as for me, I am not concerning myself with it. Do what you think is right. Right now, the community doesn't have a lot of linen; if you have not stopped the rain by tomorrow, what will your spouses have to wear next week? (743)

Little Jesus, I am asking you to pay a little attention to this point. It is not for me to think about it and attend to it in your place. I already have my work cut out for me and I have not the strength to attend to your business; that's your concern. If you do not see to it, too bad for you. Little Jesus, try to see to it from my point of view. Otherwise, I will not be pleased with you. Since I am now really your spouse, you must attend to these things for me.

Ah! There is still the business of the photograph to take; do what you wish, that does not concern me ...

Little Jesus, Thérèse of little Jesus is very joyful and very simple; she only knows how to laugh, she does not know how to speak. If she were asked a question, she would be able to reply, but, of herself, she cannot ask any question. If I were allowed to chat with your little spouse, even for a whole day, I would be able to do so. Here are the questions that I asked her.

'Do you know how to love little Jesus?'
'Obviously, why would I not know?'
'So, do you wish, like me, to become little Jesus' spouse?'
'Yes, I wish it.'
'Come, tell me, what is a spouse?'
'It is someone one loves.'

I continued to question her in this manner and she understood everything. Bearded Jesus also told me that my little sister is very simple.

As for my older sister,* it appears that she has now lost her simplicity and her frankness; she has a stubborn character and no longer likes me very much. She thinks, naturally, that bearded Jesus does not yet understand Vietnamese very well, and she often includes jokes in her conversation, so that bearded Jesus does not understand it. If I had not been there last night to repeat the questions he posed to my sister, he would probably not have understood what she was saying. (744)

*Quite true.*

* Lê.

I know the cause of her attitude, but my mother does not yet know. It is that my sister often visits the parish priests and they usually allow jokes to be told that are inappropriate among young girls. Because of that, the respect due to priests has diminished as far as my sister is concerned and she has become accustomed to thinking that priests everywhere act in the same way. However, my mother is not aware of this and she continues to believe that these visits to the parish priests and catechists are good things. In itself it is a good thing, but what is bad is the way in which these priests and catechists behave.

That's enough, little Jesus, time is almost up. Listen to me and save my dear sister from these unsuitable things which do not make sense. My little Spouse, I am asking this favour of you; try to see to it because she is my big sister.

## 11 September 1946

*Marcel*: Little Jesus, I am, without question, called Brother of the Novitiate. Truly you love me a great deal. As you do not wish to be parted from me for a moment, it is no surprise that you are against my leaving the Novitiate. Ah! It is necessary, first of all, that I write a letter to Jesus with the white beard.*

## 13 September 1946

*Marcel*: Little Jesus, this evening I will go to have my photo taken. Be careful to stand beside me, and when the photographer takes the photo we will both be on the same film.

Little Jesus, I love you a lot. Why are you now so indifferent towards me? When I was still a novice all you did was call me to go to heaven with you; but now that I have made my profession, and the spiritual wedding has taken place, you stop calling me to go up to heaven with you. Be careful, little Jesus, if you do not keep the promise that you made to me, I am going to tell our Mother.

I have finished my letter to Jesus with the white beard. I said to him in this letter: 'It is probable that little Jesus will take me soon to the spiritual wedding feast in heaven ... ' So, little Jesus, it will be necessary to act in such a way that my words are carried out according to the promise you made to me.

---

\* Father Edmond Dionne, Vice-Provincial, Vietnam.

Spouse of my soul, I love you a lot. The other day I could not get out of my mind the memory of my little sister, 'Thérèse of little Jesus'. Being your spouse I must necessarily remain with you, must I not? In fact I do not wish to go anywhere, since there is only one place for me to go, and yet, I will not go there on my own because it is you, the Spouse of my soul, who will take me there. I am not concerning myself about anything; I am happy to remain in peace on your heart and to love you, without any wearisome business. My own business is to love you; for the rest, that's your business. However, it may sometimes happen that you forget me, and it is only after having been warned several times, that you will listen to me.

In spite of that, it is not important, little Jesus, since together we are but one and we understand each other perfectly ...

Little Jesus, there are a lot of stories that I would really like to write down; unfortunately, I have not got the time. Besides, you already know all these stories which I tell you about unceasingly; what more do you want? But, little Jesus, you are a Spouse with a difficult nature; (746) what I have already told you, you still make me write down. I am, nevertheless, very pleased; since you wish it so, I wish it also.

Time is almost up. I am going to rest. I will continue on Sunday; I will then have plenty of time. I ask myself what there can be that interests you in what I tell you, since they are things that I have already told you a hundred times. What more do you want? That's enough. I am going to lie down.

Little Jesus, I have already had my photograph taken. I am sure that it will be nothing special, since I found it difficult not to laugh. The photographer complained that my eyes were too small. He called me Father and because I laughed my eyes appeared even smaller. Little Jesus, if my photo is spoilt, try to retouch it so it may be beautiful, so that bearded Jesus is pleased and the photographer also.

Today, on going to the town, nothing unusual happened. I have, therefore, nothing more to tell you; or, rather, I would have but I have forgotten everything. When I remember something I will tell you.

## 15 September 1946

*Marcel*: Are you pleased, little Jesus? Today I finally have time to write to you. Right now I have a lot of work and not much free time. And when I have a little free time, I must still do certain jobs. It's really sad. However, I am also lucky because, were you to speak a lot to me again, I would not know how to find the time to write down your words ...

Incidentally, little Jesus, the photo taken the other day is very beautiful. Bearded Jesus has shown it to me already. I am going to ask him to give one to Thérèse of little Jesus. And you, little Jesus, do you want me to send you one? I do not think it is necessary. All my being, with all I possess, already belongs to you; what more do you want? So, you do not need my photo.

(747) The other day, I went to check the rooms occupied by the novices who have just come down to the community, so as to be able to give out the linen. I then asked Brother Mark: 'So where is your room?' Brother Mark's room, he said to me, is the one where there is a picture of Jesus crying with his head in his hands. After this reply, while laughing, I said to him as a joke: 'But, you have not put your name above the door so that I can find it more easily.'

'Do it for me.'
'Not at all.'
'Go up yourself and look for it in the novitiate.'

But the Brother, while walking, murmured: 'I thought that, being the Brother of the Novitiate, you could do this little service for me. Who would have thought, being the Brother of the Novitiate, you ...' I thought that Brother Mark was right. So, I gave him a smile before leaving the kitchen. Although there was not much joy in my smile, I nevertheless put into it all my good will.

Last night I certainly pleased Brother Mark, since I brought down his name and I placed it, as required, above his door, without his knowing who was responsible. Afterwards as the Brother wished to have two tea towels to clean the dishes in the kitchen, I sewed two of them and I went to take them to him. By doing that, I am sure I made him forget my words of yesterday morning. Possibly Brother Mark is very tired right now because he becomes irritated very easily and appears rough in his manners. Little Jesus, graciously help him a little, all right? He must have a lot on his mind in the kitchen since he is now head cook and there aren't enough brothers working in the kitchen. Graciously come to his aid.

As for me, I am still working in the tailor's shop and I attend to the needs of the Novitiate. It often happens, however, that I completely forget the Novitiate.

(748) But, little Jesus, why is it always raining? Tomorrow we don't need any more rain. I must wash the linen, you remember. Otherwise I shall be very sad, because if the linen does not dry, how can I give to the fathers and brothers what they need to wear? You understand me, don't you?

However, there is one thing that bothers me and which you must always remember: it is the promise you made to me. If you forget it, I am going to tell my sister Thérèse to laugh at you ... Time is almost up, I am going to take a siesta.

Little Jesus, a short while ago I met the former novice Brother Augustine Phan. He wears short trousers and a shirt with short sleeves. He seems to be in very good health. With his hair well parted, he is happy and says he has no fear of anything. He asked us to pray for him, threatening us in these terms: 'If you do not pray for me, I am going ...' then, going through the motions of shooting Brother Andrew, 'I am going to shoot and it will be over.' I was really afraid and I thought that sooner or later, he would certainly be a persecutor of religion. Little Jesus, have pity on him.

## 29 September 1946

'Jesus, arrange things so that France and Vietnam are animated by a mutual confidence based on your Love.'

'Mary, our Mother, so arrange things that unity reigns between French and Vietnamese priests, so that Vietnam understands the truth clearly.'

## 6 October 1946

*Marcel*: Father, my sister Thérèse of the Child Jesus made this promise to me: 'Little brother, I am going to ask a favour for you, to help you understand that little Jesus will soon come to take you with him.' However, she has not specified the moment when she would ask for this favour. She was happy to speak in general terms, without even saying what favour she would ask for. Now, on the Friday when you returned from Saigon, the V.R. Father Vice-Provincial sent a very beautiful picture of Our Lady of Perpetual Succour for each Father and Brother; and it so happened that on that day the Father Minister forgot to give me one of them. After having cleared the table, on returning to my place, I saw that I had no picture, whereas all the others had one. At that moment I considered myself fortunate to have been forgotten on such an unimportant occasion. However, be that as it may, I almost cried. I then acted as if I had received a picture, appearing as happy as if I had really received one. But, inwardly, I suffered a lot. Fortunately, I did not cry. (749)

My sister Thérèse, on seeing me sad, but happy nevertheless, said to me immediately: 'Little brother, the favour I promised to ask for you yesterday – you have just received it.'

But, my sister, it was not a favour at all, I have not received a picture.

***Thérèse***: And that, precisely is the favour. Indeed, if you had received a picture, you would not have known that I had asked the favour for you. As I said to you yesterday, the favour I intended asking for you was to let you know that Jesus will soon come to look for you to take you with him. That being the case, little brother, what need have you of a picture of our Mother Mary? In a short time you will possess her in person, you will be able to contemplate her at your leisure, not so much in a picture but face to face. She will carry you in her arms with little Jesus. So, therefore, why still ask for her picture, when you will have what is best in possessing her, herself.

(750)

***Marcel***: At that juncture I was very joyful and I was certain that little Jesus would soon come to take me with him. Truly, my Father, I regard this favour as joyful news sent from heaven to your humble child.

One more story that Brother Placide told me in these words: 'Brother Louis said that at Saigon the Fathers treat the Brothers as common coolies who must carry the goods ...' On hearing that I could not believe it and I asked little Jesus this question: 'Little Jesus, is it really true what Brother Placide said?'

Then little Jesus answered me clearly: 'Little brother, you are asking me if Brother Placide's words are true, if the Fathers really treat the Brothers as coolies ... Know this well: those who speak in this way are not true Redemptorist Brothers; they possess absolutely nothing of the spirit of the Congregation. Indeed, if the simple thought that they can be treated as coolies upsets them, what would their reaction be if they really were treated as such? The spirit of the Congregation consists in the perfect abnegation of self. Not only is it necessary to renounce oneself entirely but, also, it is necessary, to allow others to consider one as nothing. If, therefore, only the thought of being treated like coolies – without it being a fact – if, I say, this single thought is so disagreeable to them, what would they do if they were regarded as nothing?'

(751) Little Jesus told me again that I should not believe these words because they came from the mouths of certain brothers who do not possess the spirit of the Congregation. If only the thought of being regarded as coolies upsets them to this extent, with much greater reason would they be upset if they were really considered as such. And, simply being treated as coolies is bad enough; but what would it be like if they were regarded as nothing?

These brothers, by their profession, have renounced themselves but there, once again, they attach themselves strongly to their self-will and their self-love. Although they have not even begun to put into practice the vows they have taken, they think that they have already done too much. Before even having taken the first step, they believe they have already reached the limit. Truly, little brother, those who act in this way are not true Redemptorist brothers and you must not believe the words coming from their self-will.

My Father, that is all. At these times I forget very easily. On the other hand, little Jesus often answers my questions in an unexpected way so that I can understand but cannot remember.

## 13 October 1946

***Marcel***: Father, the other day, I believe it was 10 October, before the bell for rising, although I was sleeping, seemingly in a deep sleep, I saw myself in a dream at the Hữu-Bằng presbytery where I had formerly lived. I do not know why but I was running from the entrance to the village when I spied, in the distance before me, a beautiful cross of very large dimensions. To the left of this cross there was a tree that appeared very old. This tree had dense foliage, with a reddish trunk and adjoined the cross. It was beautiful to behold, with its green leaves, but of a green different from the usual leaf green. A little further on, there was another tree similar to the first but without a cross; and further still a third tree. It all formed a magnificent landscape. Enchanted by this beauty, I turned my gaze in the direction of the cross, and I noticed that it had disappeared. I then looked once again in the direction of the third tree and I saw it also disappear, bit by bit. This phenomenon seemed very strange and the idea came to me to go to the very spot to see what this wonder was. But when I started to walk, a storm arose which darkened the sky so that I no longer saw anything beautiful. Since it was raining, I returned, running, following the same path that led to the entrance to the village; but I could no longer see the entrance. Then spying a house, I went to take shelter there and, a moment later, I saw, running towards me, an innumerable group of children who were coming from I do not know where. A large number of them formed a circle around me, calling me their big brother. Then we left all together to go to a certain house that we did not know. We did know, however, that once we arrived there, we would receive a reward.

During the course of the journey a child asked me: 'My brother, what kind of flowers are there in summer, what kind in spring, what kind in autumn and what kind in winter?' Noticing a clump of fresh dazzling chrysanthemums, I immediately answered: 'In summer there are chrysanthemums.'

(752)

(753) We had just arrived at the house to receive our reward when I heard the bell for rising; and so my dream came to an end. Once I got up, I naturally felt joyful. However, I am convinced that this dream has no special meaning. It is probably because I like to play with children that I think of them all the time, even during my sleep. In the group of children who came to me were boys and girls, and they were all happy. That's all I remember.

## 17 October 1946

*Marcel*: My Father, yesterday you asked me what I thought of the words of certain people who say that it is impossible to imitate Saint Gerard because he performed many miracles and he often had ecstasies ... I gladly answered these words. I do not know at this time what to write, but what I will write for you will conform with what my sister Thérèse said to me in speaking of our father Saint Alphonsus.

Previously, I used to think like everyone else that it was impossible to imitate the saints, but now I know and understand clearly the truth of this. Nevertheless, my Father, if I were able to write all that I understand, I have the feeling it would be very difficult. I am afraid I might write unwarranted things that do not have much meaning. Allow me to sum up the question, but it is possible that my reply might contradict what is said in the life of Saint Gerard. That is a supposition I am making without being certain of it. If my supposition is false, I will not worry too much, because it is possible, I know, that the author of Saint Gerard's life knows these things better than I.

(754) For myself, I am stating that Saint Gerard did not perform any miracles, that he did not enter into ecstasy a single time. He loved, he sacrificed himself, he performed acts of mortification, he prayed, he worked, he ate and slept, he travelled, he spoke and, in one word, he acted simply like an ordinary man, he acted like your little Marcel. It is therefore possible for us to imitate him by our work and our conduct. As for the power to work miracles, this is not the work of Saint Gerard, but really the work of God himself, of whom Saint Gerard was only the instrument to show to souls the goodness of God's heart.

The miracles are, therefore, God's work and not that of Saint Gerard. Now, being the work of God, it is not necessary for us to imitate them, since that is something beyond our natural powers and God never asks us to do anything beyond our power. So, in reality, the miracles do not belong to Saint Gerard but to God himself who allowed Saint Gerard to perform them; and that not with the intention of glorifying Saint Gerard but with the intention of being glorified himself in Saint Gerard.

I regret not having any comparison to prove this. All I can say is that the virtues that Saint Gerard practised to reach sanctity, we can also imitate. But the miracles, it is God alone who performed them in Saint Gerard. So, one never says that Saint Gerard performed miracles or entered into ecstasy, one says, quite simply, that he dedicated himself to prayer, to mortification and to other virtues.

The works that he accomplished for God with much generosity appear really frightening, however, I dare to affirm that Saint Gerard never did anything beyond his powers. Although his works may have been beyond the strength of others, they were never beyond his own power. If someone does something beyond his power, in reality, he is a madman and not a saint. Consequently, to imitate Saint Gerard it is not necessary that we do as he did; but we can imitate him very well in (755) another way. That is, in doing what he did, but in being aware of the strength that has been given to us by God.

What I have just said is sufficiently clear. We must not say, as people sometimes say in seeing the saints perform miracles, that it is impossible to imitate them. It is not because they are perfect that the saints are able to perform miracles. The Blessed Virgin, for example, was really the most perfect creature, after her son Jesus; so why, during her earthly life did she not perform any miracles and did not have any ecstasies? Is it because she could not or because she did not want to? One thing is certain, and that is that God did not wish her to do so because, in those times, it was not necessary that God should show men that he was still very much alive in all creation.

However, because of the fact that Saint Gerard performed miracles, I can assume with certainty that in his time there were many unbelievers who refused to believe in God's presence in all things; people who denied miracles and only saw purely natural phenomena in all that happens. It is for that reason that God showed himself in one of his creatures, wishing by that to teach men that he has the right over life and death, over all that exists. It follows from this that God only performs an obvious miracle when the thing is necessary to give proof of his goodness to men.

When one reads the life of Jesus, one notices, in the same way, that in his time there were two or three groups, of which one believed this and the other denied that. If it had not been so, I am sure that Jesus would not have performed a single miracle to reveal his presence. His words were sufficient.

Ah! My Father, the time is up already. That is all I can say on the subject.

## 20 October 1946

*Marcel*: One Sunday, as I was saying to Jesus: 'Jesus, ordain things so that your Love spreads rapidly throughout the world', little Jesus added for me: 'And above all in the hearts of all men'.

One Tuesday when I was praying for sinners and for pagans, as Jesus asked me to, I pointed out to him that he had not yet fixed the day when I should pray for children. Jesus replied to me: 'I want you to pray for children on Tuesdays especially.' So what is the day to pray for pagans and sinners?

*Jesus*: You will do that also on the same day.

*Marcel*: I again remember that one Saturday my Mother Mary told me that apart from the first Saturday of the month, when she wanted me to pray especially for her little apostles, she wished that on all the other Saturdays I remind Jesus of the same intention so that her little apostles might progress more rapidly.

## 23 October 1946

(756) *Marcel*: My Father, my sister Thérèse has just given me the prayer (*prayer for the month of November*). She said to me: 'Little brother, ask for this: My Jesus, make French and Vietnamese priests act in such a way that the Holy Father is pleased with Vietnam, my fatherland.'

'Mother, deign to make Vietnam, my fatherland, know and love only truth; release it from the communist yoke and support it as you support France, your kingdom.'

My Father, that is all my sister said to me, before you came to administer my medicine, because at that moment I reminded my sister what you had said to me.

## 3 November 1946

*Marcel*: Some days ago, while reading the book entitled *Jesus and adolescence*, I came across a sentence in the Bible translated as follows: 'Be therefore cunning as serpents and simple as doves.'*

As I found these words strange and did not understand them, I

---

* Matthew 10, 16.

complained to little Jesus in these words: 'Little Jesus you say some things that are difficult to understand.'

And I wanted to question him on the meaning of this text. At midday, before the particular examination of conscience, suddenly remembering this same text, I questioned little Jesus who answered me as follows: 'I did not say that the serpent is prudent. The serpent is cunning by nature, but because he is cunning without being simple like the dove he is called the deceitful one. My intention is to say to souls that, if they wish to be prudent, they must be cunning as serpents and simple as doves.

Guile without simplicity, is deceitfulness and not prudence. On the other hand, simplicity without cunning, is not simplicity but madness. My intention is to say that, to be prudent, one must be at the same time cunning and simple. If one of these two elements is missing, there is nothing more than deceitfulness or madness. (757)

The Holy Spirit is at the same time infinitely cunning and infinitely simple and it is for this reason that he is called Infinite Wisdom. Because of this a soul inhabited by the Holy Spirit can be deceived only with great difficulty by the devil, since Infinite Wisdom will make known to this soul the deceitfulness of the devil.'

My Father, after these explanations of little Jesus, I find this thing very easy to understand, and it is the same for the words of the Gospel. That is all.

## 10 November 1946

*Marcel*: My Father, this particular day, on hearing the Brothers speak of those who have left the Congregation to return to the world, this thought came to me: 'As all these brothers left truly through their own fault, I ask myself why everybody says that it is God's will?' I then posed this question to little Jesus who answered me in this way: 'Although all of these brothers may have returned to the world through their own fault, it can be said, nevertheless, that it is God's will. Obviously, I never wish that those who have left the world should return to the world. But neither do I wish to have people in the Congregation who conduct themselves like people in the world and give bad example to their brethren. It follows that in not wanting to tolerate these things, I must allow these worldly religious who give bad example and do not want to correct themselves, to return to the world. So, although naturally I do not wish that, justice obliges me to allow it. Otherwise, where would I be able to find fervent communities to give me sanctuary?' (758)

## 17 November 1946

(759) *Marcel*: My Father, for a long time now, as I have already told you many times, I often think of heaven and, when I think of it, I desire to die very soon to go with little Jesus. Until now, however, I did not want to make Jesus aware of this desire for fear of forcing him to follow my will. Once or twice, however, I have made known this wish, but only indirectly. Apart from that, my Father, I have spoken of it only to Mary, to my sister Thérèse and to you. But, in the course of the morning while you were at the particular examination, I went to pay a visit to little Jesus, and then this thought came to mind: even if I hide this wish from little Jesus, he certainly knows it, since we form only one. So, I said to him: 'Enough's enough, little Jesus, since you and I make but one, I do not wish to have any secrets from you. My little Jesus, I really want to die, I really wish to see you.'

But little Jesus did not reply. I even asked him to make me die, taking care to add: 'It is not necessary to go to extremes to grant this wish; consider the favour I have asked for like all the other favours. If it conforms to your will and if you freely grant it to me, that is fine; but I do not want to force you.' At that, little Jesus again did not answer. Nevertheless, I am certain to obtain what I am asking, since my intention is not to compel little Jesus to follow my will, but simply to unite my will to his. Besides, even if I had not manifested this desire, he would nevertheless know it quite well. Consequently, it seems to me that there is more frankness in explaining it to him in this way and, had I not done so, I would give the impression of lacking simplicity with him.

Then, basing my argument on the fact that we two are but one, I asked him this question, just to see: 'Little Jesus, since we make but one, can I say: "Marcel, I love you"?' But again, little Jesus did not answer with a single word. In fact, each time that I intended to say: 'Marcel, I love you', I had such a strong urge to laugh, that I could not say it, although I was able to say quite easily: 'Little Jesus, I love you.'

(760) In these last few days, when I eat, I find nothing appetizing; but when I receive Jesus, I find a sweet taste. Is it because of the host or because little Jesus wishes to console me a little? It is surely because he wishes to comfort me, since on the two preceding days when I received communion, I did not taste this flavour. The two days when I received communion in my room, after communion, I asked my Mother Mary and my sister Thérèse to thank Jesus for me. I even asked Jesus to make my thanksgiving for me, after which I fell asleep; it is the only time when I succeeded in sleeping well without having any terrifying dream.

## 27 November 1946

*Marcel*: I once asked Jesus this question: 'Why does the translator of the Gospel into Vietnamese use the word *Tao* so often? If you were speaking Vietnamese, how would you express it? Would you use the word *Tao*?'

*Jesus*: No, I would never use the word *Tao*. If I had spoken Vietnamese in past times, I would express myself as I do now. Since there are no words corresponding to *Tao, Ta, Cha, Thầy*,\* in the Jewish language, I spoke as ordinary people speak. But I had to speak sometimes with firmness, sometimes with gentleness and sometimes in an intimate or comforting tone. If I had had to express myself in Vietnamese, I would sometimes have used the word *Thầy*, sometimes the word *Cha*. Normally, I would have used the word *Thầy* but I might also have used the word *Cha* with my apostles and those close to me. (*I have forgotten, writes Brother Marcel*.) ... I spoke like everybody and I behaved towards men like a father with his children. Consequently, while referring to myself under the name of Father, I acted in the same way as a father does with his children. And at that time, I also acted as the Father of all souls. Not only did I give the name of Father to God the Father, but I gave it to myself, also, as I do in speaking with you, Marcel. (761)

## Prayer for December

'O Jesus, make all the French and Vietnamese understand that they must form but a single heart so that the two countries may together enjoy a true peace founded on your Love.'
  'Mother, free France and Vietnam from the communist yoke which is the crushing yoke of hell. Make everyone clearly understand that the words of the communists are a dangerous venom which they never cease to spew forth to make people lose true peace and mutual confidence ... '
  'O Mary, graciously feel pity for the fate of our two countries. Amen.'

Father, there is a lot of confusion in what I have written earlier; I am not certain that it conforms exactly to Jesus' words. I have forgotten everything. Perhaps I was mistaken. However, Father, as I have already told you yesterday, I cannot express myself with more clarity.

---

\* I (superior and impolite), I (superior), father, brother in religion but also master.

## 1 December 1946

(762) *Marcel*: The other day,* after communion, I thought suddenly of my Holy Father.† I did not pray for him at all since, wishing to sleep, all I could do was doze. Once the Mass was over, I went to tidy my room and it was only then that I remembered what I had previously thought about. So I said to little Jesus: 'Little Jesus, I am sure that my Holy Father is at this time plunged in sadness.' I then offered my Holy Father to little Jesus, asking him to comfort him in my place. All I can say is that he is sad, without knowing the cause of his sadness.

Then little Jesus replied to me in these words: 'So, then, from now on you will dedicate the whole of Thursday to praying for the Holy Father, but while keeping the other intention that I have already suggested, namely to pray that many Christians might communicate every day, since, if you pray for this intention, the prayers said for Pius XII will be more numerous from day to day.' That is all that little Jesus said to me.

## 8 December 1946

*Marcel*: When I was small, I did not like going to church because I was afraid of being beaten. And it was the same for all the other children; if they dozed a little, they were beaten. Jesus said that it is never necessary to beat children. The Blessed Virgin also said: 'If the natural law forbids the maltreatment of animals, with what greater reason does it forbid the beating of children.'

## 24 December 1946

(763) *Marcel*: My Father, each time I have asked your permission to re-read the words that Jesus addressed to me, my mind was obsessed by a worrying thought. Indeed a thousand troublesome thoughts invaded my mind on the subject of these words, which seemed to me to be a figment of my imagination that I would then write down for you. Although my soul was then plunged into darkness, I felt, with some certainty, that these thoughts were an invention of the devil who wanted to throw me into turmoil. However, after having re-read what I had written, I recovered my composure and I was sure that I could not have invented words so full of meaning. You also know, Father, that

---

\* Thursday, 28 November.
† Pius XII.

during the times when Jesus no longer talks to me, I am unable to write a single sentence with any style. Furthermore, I cannot even relate to you the ordinary facts that come up each day. Consequently, I am sure I was not able to write, by myself, words like those that Jesus dictated to me.

## 4 January 1947

*Marcel*: Little Jesus, do you know what is actually happening in my heart? If you had to submit to the same fate as me, what would you do? Oh! Friend of my heart, I do not really know how to express myself to make you understand the state in which the immense desire I have to see you has thrown me. This desire has become a serious wound for me and I can do nothing to alleviate the pain. My Mother Mary and my sister Thérèse can do nothing either; even bearded Jesus does not know what remedy to apply to this serious injury. I hear words of comfort but they only increase my sorrow. What's to be done now? My Beloved, I desire more to see you than to enjoy the delights of heaven. My wound is serious and at each moment, at each beat of my heart, at each of my breaths, this wound continues to get worse. (764)

Oh! My Jesus, it is to you alone that I wait for the cure of this wound of Love. Yes, you alone, Jesus, are capable of curing me of this wound. Why so, Jesus? May I be certain that you will soon take me with you? How can I tolerate that you still leave me with the impression that I have been mistaken? Or, if I have been mistaken, Jesus, I nevertheless offer all of it to you, so that souls who do not believe in heaven can, nevertheless, enter there like those who do believe ...

My Beloved, I do not know if you understand what I have just said; however, graciously remind yourself that I am carrying a serious wound in my heart that has been inflicted on me by my burning desire to see you ...

That is all. The time is up, but, the time of my life on this earth is not yet over for me. Oh! Jesus, Jesus, graciously understand the feelings of my heart at this time.

## 11 January 1947

*Marcel*: My bearded Jesus! My sister Thérèse just gave me the prayer to be recited for Vietnam and for France during this month.

'Jesus, may Vietnam and France enjoy peace together under the sweet yoke of your Love.'

'Mary, arrange things so our two countries carry this yoke together for all eternity. Amen. Mary, may it please heaven that it may be so. Graciously remember this.' It is finished.

At the end, my sister Thérèse added: It is finished. I do not understand the meaning of these words, but I feel totally at peace. My sister spoke to me at the time when I was about to get washed after having passed along the rooms to awaken the brothers. I had just taken my towel when I heard the words 'the sweet yoke of your Love'. Knowing that it was the voice of my sister little Thérèse, I asked her a question but, without replying to me, she continued to recite the prayer until its end so that I might know it by heart. Then she said to me: 'It is finished'.

My Father, it is very fortunate for me, because perhaps it is the sign that the time of my exile draws to its close.

## 12 January 1947

(765) *Marcel*: Alas! My little friend why must my heart live in this way always weighed down under the weight of my immense desire? It is only because of this desire that I do not stop moaning in your presence. 'Whoever asks obtains, who desires sees his wish granted'. And I, I ask without obtaining, I desire without seeing my wish granted ... Where, therefore, is heaven? Where is my eternal Beloved? Who is he after whom I sigh? Could I sigh simply after something which does not exist? Jesus, Mary, if you exist, come to my aid at this moment, if not, my heart will suffer another wound which would consist of loving only things which do not exist, not knowing what Love is ...

My Jesus, why have I spoken such lunacy? I do believe that you exist; I do believe that Mary is my true Mother. You are my little Spouse, you are the one whom my heart loves; yes, Jesus, you know well that I love you. And you, Jesus, you love me in the same way and you always remain with me. But why, a short while ago, did I utter such madness? Forgive me, since I believed in this way, labouring under an illusion and loving things which do not exist. Jesus, your Marcel is very foolish, and I do not know how I could write such things so spontaneously. I was wrong and, from now on, I will be more careful. I am suffering a lot.

(766) Nothing in this world can obtain for me the least joy. I wish all the time to die, but without ever daring to inflict on myself the slightest bodily harm with the intention of hastening my death. Jesus, if I knew that by holding my breath I would be able to die before the time decided by your will, I would never hold my breath. Although I ardently sigh after you, my little heavenly Spouse, I am, however,

content to wait as long as you wish. However, Jesus, I beg of you, also, to have pity on me. If you do not grant me heaven at this time, deign at least to give me the grace to accept cheerfully the sufferings of life in this valley of tears.

It is time ... Oh my Jesus! I am tired of waiting for you; the memory of you draws tears from me, day and night ...

## 14 January 1947

*Marcel*: My little Jesus, how? Could you have forgotten your little Marcel? Day just like night is a profound darkness. I see absolutely no one; it is total emptiness. I am alone and abandoned; all that happens in me is hidden in this deep night. Also my desire to see you becomes more and more ardent. But the more my desire grows, the more I feel I have been deceived.

Ah! My beloved Jesus, this is how you will know, or rather the world will know that I love you with an unselfish love. Far away as you may be, I still love you. It is really so, my little Jesus, it is obvious. In spite of the suffering, nothing can assuage the ardour of my love. In sorrow and suffering, I will not continue to love you less. Although a specific thought may come to make me doubt your real existence and your true love for me, I love, nevertheless, this doubt, since this doubt, for me, it is you, Jesus. Do you exist, Jesus? Certainly you exist, since if you did not exist, how would I be able to love you so intimately and sigh after you as I do? That's enough. The time is up. I am going to pay you a visit. It is, therefore, the proof that you really exist, little Jesus. I love you. (767)

## 15 January 1947

*Marcel*: My beloved Jesus, I feel a little joy in seeing that the French have arrived here. However, I still feel sadness and disgust, because, after having longed for you for a long time, still I do not see you come. What can I really say to you now, since all that was the object of my desires has become as if it did not exist ...

Jesus, you who love me in heaven, remember me, have pity on me. Let me see soon, in paradise, him after whom I sigh. O my Beloved ... Grant me at least the grace to accept joyfully the sufferings I am enduring at this moment because of my ardent desire to see you ... Jesus, Jesus ...

## 15 February 1947

(768) *Marcel*: My Father, for about two or three weeks, at the times when I really want to see Jesus, the friend of my heart, be it when I am walking, be it when I am working, as soon as I think of him without seeing him anywhere, all of my body suddenly becomes frozen, my limbs weaken and I am unable to stand up on my legs. I must sometimes go close to a wall and lean against it for several minutes so as to regain a bit of strength to walk. Often also, even when I am very happy, if I suddenly think of Jesus without seeing him by my side, I become incapable of making the slightest movement. The same thing happens also when a single current of air brushes by me and when I turn my gaze towards the sky or on the countryside which surrounds me. And then my glance is not an ordinary one; it is like the gaze of someone who hopes to see a dear friend coming in his direction. When, therefore, glancing thus in the distance, I do not even see Jesus' shadow, I feel as if I've been affected by a polluted current of air that make me lose consciousness, as I said earlier. Each time, this phenomenon lasts only a moment, yet it suffices to make me shed tears for at least fifteen minutes. And afterwards, I must make a lot of effort to control myself. It sometimes happens that I cry, but sometimes, too, I do not shed a single tear.

Ah ...! My Father, I am very happy to bear this wound of Love until the day when I will meet the friend of my heart in the arms of Mary. No remedy is able to cure me of this serious wound ... I agree, therefore, to die of this wound, since the only remedy that will deliver me from it is the actual death of my body. It is because of this wound that I have now lost all feeling, that I know nothing. Although, outwardly, I eat, I sleep, I work, I speak, I laugh, in reality, I am as if inwardly dead.

(769) My Beloved, I still hope in you, I still keep the hope of meeting you one day, as my heart desires. If the things I am writing here are making you sad, my Beloved resplendent with purity, I ask you to put them aside and to make them disappear at the same time as my sufferings.

But despite all my sufferings, I will never consent to give my love to any creature on this earth. Help me to carry joyfully the yoke of suffering which Love imposes on me, and to do so until the day when I shall be no other than one with you on the breast of Mary our Mother. Amen.

## 19 March 1947

If he stumbles, he does not fall, since the Lord holds him by the hand (Ps. 36, 24).

## 20 March 1947

And now, Lord, what can I wait for? All my hope is in you (Ps. 38, 8).

## 30 March 1947

*Marcel*: My father, the night after you began your retreat, I dreamt that I was on the point of dying. On that particular day, I needed sleep so much that I fell asleep as soon as I lay on my bed. But after having slept hardly a few seconds, I awoke and could no longer get to sleep since I really wanted to see Jesus. I did not stop sighing and crying, wishing to be able to die at that very instant in order to see him. While I was sighing in this way I fell asleep, I do not know exactly when, and I immediately felt my feet become cold and stiffen little by little. Seeing this, I was almost certain that I was about to die, but I still doubted, not knowing if Jesus had granted my wish to die, or if it was rather a figment of my imagination. Afterwards, noticing that my body was becoming little by little cold and stiff, I was sure I was dying. I also wished for you to know what was happening and I intended to call you; but remembering that you were on retreat and fearing to disturb you, I decided not to. Lying peacefully, I still waited to see if Jesus would come, since I was certain that I was about to die. Then, seeing that I could no longer move, I called you, crying out twice: My Father! My Father! But the second time, I cried out so loudly that I awoke with a jerk and I still heard the words 'my Father' ringing round my room. It is only when awake that I realized that I was dreaming. An ardent desire to see Jesus came once more to me in the silence of the night. I welcomed it with many tears, then I fell asleep once more while waiting for Jesus ...

... Another day, I do not remember when, I had the following dream. When I was in my room, I heard voices, which were crying: 'A bird which is bringing a letter, a bird which is bringing a letter'. Not at all knowing what this bird was which was bringing a letter, I went out of my room to go and see. I then spied a bird, it was probably a pigeon and I began to follow it to observe it close up. In its beak it seemed to be carrying a branch. I then heard people once again asking among themselves: 'Do the French no longer have aeroplanes, to have to use a bird to carry letters?' But no one replied to this question. The bird continued to fly slowly, looking downwards as if it was looking for some place where it could land. Then it flew a little higher, since I heard voices, which were saying: 'Let us kill it.' It continued to fly straight ahead, but a moment later it turned its head towards the place where I

(770)

(771) was standing and came to rest on the roof of the house. I went close to it to see better. Seeing me approach, the bird began to fly very low as if it wished to invite me to follow it. Seeing it fly very low, I began to follow it and, having arrived at a corner of the wall where there was nobody at all, I saw a letter that had neither a stamp nor an address fall immediately. Then raising my eyes, I no longer saw the bird anywhere. All I heard was a voice that said: 'Deliver this letter to the French.' But, as soon as I had reached the place where the letter had fallen, I noticed someone who was standing hidden near there and who ran as if to grab hold of the letter. However, I was able to seize it before him. Then this man ran after me to take the letter from me, but I, I held it at the end of my outstretched hand, saying: 'Hold on, this letter belongs to the French.' Then, my Father, I delivered it to you.

There, that's all I dreamt.

As for the story of the heap of mud containing a precious pearl, I remember that once, the brethren were speaking among themselves about the French who were like this or like that, but only the French military who behaved badly were targeted. At that moment Brother Andrew, arriving from somewhere, seeing that the conversation centred on the French, told us that he had himself met a French military man who was very good. Then he told how this military person behaved towards him in a very polite manner, as he would have done with a priest ... In short, the Brother said that this soldier was a very good member of the French military and, unlike many others, he was joyful, polite, etc.

(772) I then heard my sister Thérèse give me an example, which puts in a nutshell the two categories of French that were just being spoken of. This is what she said to me: 'Even if throughout the whole of France there exists only sinners, with the exception of one just person, this single just person would be sufficient for Jesus not to destroy France, since he would know that in the middle of this multitude of sinners, there is a pure soul. In the same way who would dare to stamp on a pile of mud which contained a precious stone? It is obvious that it is necessary to preserve this heap of mud to extract from it the precious stone which is buried in it. Jesus acts in the same way. And if a precious stone is buried in a heap of mud, it has much more value and deserves much more attention since it is necessary to avoid treading with one's feet on this heap of mud. Such is the way Jesus behaves.' That's all I remember.

## 13 May 1947

*Marcel*: Mary, how many trials I have endured. My saddened heart is waiting for the Beloved. I am like a young spouse who has had the misfortune to become a widow ... But, Mother, what good is there in showing you my sadness, if it risks saddening you? However, graciously understand also one thing: I am telling you this without exaggeration, my heart feels as if it is torn in pieces. Besides, you also know that your little Jesus has become for me a fiery blade that does not cease to pierce my heart ... Oh! ... My God! ... Oh! My Mother understands the feelings of my heart. I am suffering to the extent of dying from it, but I do not die. It is because of an excess of love that my heart has reached this state of dryness.

## 15 May 1947

*Marcel*: My Father, do you want to know what the feelings of my heart are at this moment? Truly, I do not know how to express to you these feelings. Let me simply say one thing to you: to comfort my heart, I can find nothing other than the sorrow of my heart ... I do not hope to meet any joy on this earth.

## Letter, 25 August 1947

To the dear little Lord of my heart.

Jesus, how long has this friendship lasted? Here we both are, as if totally isolated. After a union of some minutes, it is as if our friendship has been broken by the separation and I now possess in a lonely body an arid soul, resembling the withered stem of the autumn lotus. O my brother, I am certain that you find yourself in the same situation as I. Yes, I know very well that to manage to contain your love for me and to hide it, you must fight against it.

It happened at one time or another, impelled by love and my ardent desire to see you, that I allowed some words to escape which perhaps (773) have caused you pain. However, beloved Brother, as we have but one heart, if, in the excess of my love, I said words to you which by their nature saddened you, I beg of you to pay no attention to them, since with a heart overflowing with love for you, if I have been guilty of some intemperance in my words, it is solely through love for you that I have done so ... I am suffering a lot! Yes, I am suffering a lot ... this suffering is capable of being the death of me, but it is not time for me to die ... ! However, my Brother, remain in peace; I will make use of a smile to veil my sufferings ... !

Allow me to make use of your pretty lips to give a kiss to Mary. Give her this kiss in my place. Do the same also for my sister Thérèse and ask her to teach me to write poetry, since I have many feelings similar to hers, but I do not yet know how to express them. Finally, my brother, let me give you a kiss. This kiss I am giving to you while my tears still flow, but it must not sadden you, since in the middle of my tears, I, nevertheless, hold on to a smile.

J. M. T. of the Child Jesus. Marcel

# Appendix

# 1

## Vision of 26 November 1945 (*Cf. Conv. 162*)

Jesus, travelling through France said to Marcel: 'I give to you all of my sufferings.'

The following day, alluding to this vision, Brother Marcel wrote to me:

My Father, I will have to suffer even more, but you who are the love that Jesus leaves to me to comfort me, you must work to beautify this little flower, you must cover it with love when the storm comes.

My Father, you ask me to give you my sufferings. Ah! I know that you love me a lot and seeing the little flower in this state, you have pity on her fate. My Father, I do not wish to give you my sufferings because, in fact, you will have to suffer even more than me. These sufferings, you will know when they come ...

My Father, my Father! I will also be with you at that time ... I will wipe your tears just as you have wiped mine. My Father, many sufferings remain for me to endure, but yours will be even more numerous.

*(written 27 November 1945)*

My Father! What did I just write down? While I am telling you the story of my vocation, how is it that such things have come from my pen? Have I lost my mind? Is it not true, my Father? Yes, truly, Jesus has taken away my mind in order to leave me only 'his mind', which remains with me. O 'mind of Jesus' look after everything instead of me ... if I mislead myself, you will understand and will forgive me, since I have lost my mind. Perhaps, being too small, Jesus has not yet given me the use of reason, which explains my ignorance and my lack of experience ...

Now, I am continuing the story of my vocation ...

## 1 December 1945
*Disgust – Call for Help*

My Father, at the moment I feel disgust, a great deal of disgust. I want to cry without being able to cry. I force myself to laugh but I do not wish to laugh either. Oh! My Father, I do not know what state I find myself in, I do not know what illness affects me. Sometimes I am joyful, sometimes I am shedding tears. My breathing is sometimes slow, sometimes fast. My mouth is half tense, half smiling; I do not know what is happening.

My Father, I do not wish to work any more; neither do I wish to rest. I am tired and sick at heart. I feel a little pain in my stomach and a little warmth in my chest. My limbs are trembling a little. My Father, take pity on me! Come to my aid. Why am I in this state? Where is Jesus? Why has he left me like this? Oh! Jesus! Jesus! Jesus! Do you understand the love of my heart? Why do you remain so far from me?

My Father! My Father! You, the love which comforts me, come very quickly. What state am I in and what is it that comes into my throat like this. Father, come quickly. I feel so much disgust. I am not crying, but if no one comes to comfort me, I will have to cry. My Father, comfort me. Quickly, quickly, my Father. I can only press you to come very quickly, since I am incapable of going to find you. Oh! My Father, take pity on me. My Father, I am calling you, and Jesus has told you to come close to me. My Father, when you are there, my heart feels relieved and comforted. My Father, have pity on me, think of my disgust, please love Jesus in my place. My Father, my Father, I love you. In heaven, I shall be privileged to see France. My Father, France, I agree to suffer for France! My Father, give me peace. My Father, I love you. My Father, you must comfort me in my deep disgust. I cannot write any more. My Father, see my heart full of disgust, and understand everything.

*Bless me with holy water*. Trace the Sign of the Cross on me with holy water. My Father, I love you. I am suffering so much that I can no longer write.

## 2 December 1945

Father, I do not know why I wrote so badly yesterday. For myself, I do not understand a word. I do not know what you are going to do to decipher it. Please pardon me, Father, since Jesus has enabled you to understand my heart on this occasion.

*(A little later: more disgust and interior pain.)*

My Father, I feel much disgust today. I no longer wish to write the story of my vocation, since I no longer know how to write. I feel something that comes into my throat all the time and then goes away after a while. It takes me almost fifteen minutes to recite a single 'Hail Mary', and it is only with a lot of effort that I succeed in reciting the invocations for France that my sister Thérèse asked me to say with her. My Father, on this day when I pray for France, I must also suffer for her. I am inclined to worry but I do not know how to tell you these things. However, when you question me, I know what to answer. Ah! My Father, when will I be privileged to go to heaven? Jesus is still absent and my sister Thérèse too. My Father, I am feeling the bitterness that comes even more to my throat. In my disgust I haven't the taste for writing; I only do it to distract myself. I am going to take my siesta. I am still waiting for Jesus' love to come to me. I no longer have the strength to hold my pen firmly. That's enough; I am going to stay seated and rest myself.

Alas! The love of Jesus has already closed his door to take his rest. It's a waste of time to wait for him further, he will not come. My Father, spiritually send me your blessing. I see my table covered with dust and I do not know what to do to dust it, such is my feeling of disgust. My Father, you are already lying down, it is useless to wait for you. Father, I love you. My face is very hot and I feel pain in my chest. I am going to take a rest ...

My Father, why does my heart change so? I am hardly seated for a moment when I sometimes feel joy, sometimes sadness, sometimes pain and sometimes suffering. My Father, when I am close to you, when I can see you, although I do not know what to say to you, I feel, nevertheless, more at peace. I would like never to be far from you; I greatly love to see you with me.

# 2

## Excerpts from a letter to Father Boucher

Saigon, 21 March 1950

The intention that Jesus gave me for today is to pray for children. He asked me not to forget them, so, I thought only of them.

During prayer this evening, while meditating once again on the goodness of Jesus towards children, I remembered the words that Jesus spoke to me concerning children not yet baptized ... But I was very worried, asking myself if that was really the case or quite simply a figment of my imagination. So, Jesus came to me immediately to free me from this concern, saying clearly to me:

'That is not a figment of your imagination but a true doctrine which, as I wish it, must be recognized as true by the Church. Yes, I want the Church, as a good and kind mother, to open her arms to welcome these little ones and admit them to the number of its children, like many others who have had the happiness of receiving baptism. If, because of circumstances, they were not able to receive baptism like the others, they have, however, the right to receive it.

Further, it is original sin that prevents them from enjoying sanctifying grace. Now, by virtue of my merits, original sin has been largely atoned for. On the other hand, I have given the Church the power to retain and to remit sin. So why would the Church not have sufficient power to remit the original sin of these children, even if, because of circumstances, they cannot receive baptism like other children?

If the Church wishes it, these children are purified immediately, since the Church alone on earth possesses this power. Consequently, in this domain, no spiritual power can oppose her authority, even if non-religious parents did not wish their children to enjoy the grace of Redemption, since in this case, the parents' will would be unjust in regard to an innocent child who does not yet have the use of reason. That is why the Church can freely exercise its authority and nothing can oppose it.

Little brother, remain in peace. What I have communicated to you is not something that should trouble you, but really a point of doctrine which I wish to make known to my venerable Spouse, the Church.'

***Marcel***: So, why have the holy Doctors, like Saint Thomas, held a contrary opinion?

*Jesus*: An opinion and a revelation are two different things.

*Marcel*: So, do you intend to scorn Saint Thomas for having held an erroneous opinion?

*Jesus*: Not at all, little brother. I am not saying that it was an erroneous opinion, but clearly a truth which was not yet known. That is why I wish to reveal it so that the Church may publicly recognize it. Do not be troubled. I am the Truth. Continue to follow me, without fear of ever being lost.

*Marcel*: Yes, but is there no extraordinary sign to make these things known, then ...

*Jesus*: Remember, little brother, what I said to my apostles: 'Let the little children come to me, since the kingdom of heaven belongs to them.' Did these words, said on that day, concern only those children who were then present, or all the others to come? The extraordinary sign, which surpasses all imagination, is the infinite goodness of God in three Persons.

My Father, what do you think of that? What Jesus repeated to me in this way, I am hurrying to communicate to you, and I beg you to give me a response so that I know what to hold on to. I am also taking advantage of this opportunity to ask you to send to me a copy of the words that Jesus said to me previously on this same subject, and also what I wrote on your request to confirm the things I understood. I do remember, however, that there are one or two things which are not right – this one for example: 'We can deliver the souls from purgatory ...' etc. Although it may be true, it proves nothing here, since the souls in purgatory already possess sanctifying grace. Be kind enough, therefore, to set aside this argument, which proves nothing here.

J. M. T. Marcel, C.Ss.R.

# 3

## The Day of My Spiritual Marriage (8 September 1946)

... My Father, you wish to know what I said to my little Jesus on the day of my religious profession. Let me write it down for you here. If, on reading these lines, you feel neither joy nor emotion, attribute it only to my simplicity.

Jesus, divine Spouse of my soul, I wish to express to you at this time all the love of my heart, since it is at this precise moment that I have become your little spouse, and from now on my love is closely united to yours, you, my divine lover.

But, alas! My friend, I do not know what to say to you to convey all the tenderness of my love. When I look at you, the sight of your infinite beauty intoxicates me with love and the marks of affection that you are giving to me at this time throw my soul as if into an ecstasy, so that I cannot even say a single word to you. I can only remain silent to contemplate you at my leisure, remain silent to listen to the quickened beatings of our two hearts overflowing with mutual love, remain silent, finally, to hear each of your breaths.

Jesus, my sweetheart! I throw myself into your tender arms. I hold you tightly, desiring that the slightest movements of my heart may pass into yours and that I am not the only one to notice them but that you too, my divine lover, can also detect them.

Tell me, Jesus, why are you keeping so silent? Could it be that, in your excessive love for me, you no longer know what to say to me? Yes, that is surely the reason; you love me so much that you also no longer know what to say to me.

Because we love each other, we have become a single love; now, being no more than ONE, it is no longer necessary that we speak to each other since we are ONE. You understand me, Jesus, just as I understand you; we therefore have no need to speak to understand each other.

My Jesus, I really love you dearly. We are inebriated with love for each other. Love joins us both, to the extent of no longer being able to do anything but love each other. Yes Jesus, I no longer know what to do except to love you. I no longer know anything, neither you, Jesus, nor your little Marcel; the only thing I know how to do is to love you, Jesus. It is as if my heart is charged by a strong current of love which agitates my soul. Jesus, if you do not look after me carefully, later, you will no longer see my hand continuing to write down your words.

Jesus, my only wealth is the love I have for you. If I was not able to love you, if my love for you should be rejected, our heavenly Father would have to destroy us both at the same time; if not, my soul would suffer for all eternity from a wound of love that no power could cure.

My divine lover, starting from this moment, we are both engulfed in your infinite love. Only reciprocal love will be, eternally, the food of our life; only Love possesses the power to keep us alive for our mutual love. Jesus, my very dear friend, I am pressing you to my heart and I will hold you clasped there eternally.

This day of my marriage is going to lead me to the eternal wedding banquet with you and, while waiting for this happy day, Jesus, I beg you never to allow my love to fragment or weaken. Clasp me in your arms, place my feet in your footsteps so that I may arrive at eternal life; and once I have arrived at this place of rest, my beloved, I will give you an eternal kiss, and I will receive yours in return. Then both standing embraced in our love, we will rest in peace on the sweet bed of love: THE ARMS OF MARY.

Your little spouse Joachim-Mary, Thérèse of the Child Jesus Marcel
On the day of my spiritual marriage,
8 September 1946

My Father, on reading these words you will surely want to smile. However, in them I have not been able to express completely my love for Jesus. I will have to wait for the banquet of our spiritual wedding in heaven to do so perfectly with Jesus.

On the day of my profession, I have also asked for special graces for children; it would be too long to enumerate them here. Allow me not to speak of them. Later, in heaven, I will obtain what I have asked particularly for them.

Your humble child: J. M. T. Marcel

# 4

## Redemptorist Fathers and Brothers Close to Van at Hanoi

Father Antonio Boucher, *bearded Jesus*
   Born on 7 March 1907, Father A. Boucher left for Vietnam in 1935, one year after his ordination. In 1944 he saw the arrival of the young Joachim Nguyen Tan Van whose Master of Novices he became and whom he guided during all of his life. It is Father Boucher who collected all the Writings that we have today and who spent twenty years of his life, on his return to Canada, translating all of them into French. He died on 4 July 1991, after having introduced the Cause for the Beatification of Van.

Father Edmond Dionne, *Jesus with the white beard*
   He arrived in Vietnam at the beginning of the Canadian foundation there. He was the first Superior and founder of the Hanoi monastery before becoming the first Vice-Provincial, a post he held for seventeen years. He possessed sound intuition and he laid the foundations of the mission including the independence of the Vice-Province of Vietnam. Van loved to write to Father Dionne. He died, exhausted, at the age of 55.

Father Roméo Gagnon
   A tireless missionary who distinguished himself with a great competence in foreign languages. Van witnessed a certain lack of flexibility on Father Gagnon's part towards certain Vietnamese confreres.

Father Jacques Huberdeau
   Father Huberdeau was a great missionary personage, whom Van was very much aware of. All were drawn to him by his gentle and friendly personality. It was said of him that his care of the little aspirants that he looked after in a special manner was quite maternal.

Father Maurice Létourneau
   Father Létourneau was the Father Minister (bursar) when Van sought to enter the Redemptorists. He played an important role in his admission. He 'obeyed' Saint Thérèse unwittingly.

## Father Pierre Nguyễn Xuân Lộc
One of the first Vietnamese Fathers. Later he was called to important responsibilities.

## Father Henri Bạch Văn Lộc
One of the first Vietnamese Fathers.

## Father Irénée Marquis
Father Marquis demonstrated ability in many areas, above all in the field of diplomacy. In the *Conversations* one finds a beautiful conversation with Van on childlike simplicity (Conv. 494).

## Father Louis Roy, *Jesus with the ginger beard*
Father Roy was so tall that Van reached only to his waist! Van loved the simplicity and the sense of humour of the Rector of the Hanoi monastery. Father Roy had already shown his gift for the spiritual counselling of religious and communities. He became Vice-Provincial in 1952. He was the one who, after much hesitation, authorized Van to go back to the North in 1954. He acknowledged jocularly: 'I was the one who authorized Brother Marcel to become a saint!'

## Father Jean Nguyễn Văn Thính
Father Thinh was one of the first Vietnamese to receive a post of authority in the Vice-Province of Vietnam.

## Father Alphonse Tremblay
After having been prefect of studies at Hanoi from 1942–1946, he became Vice-Provincial from 1946–1952. He perceived something of Van's interior life since, in 1947, he wrote to Father Boucher on the subject of Van's letter which he was charged to pass on to Pius XII: 'For the time being I must admit to being inclined to keep it for my own edification.'

## Brother Alexander – Alexander Grenier
Brother Alexander arrived in Vietnam in 1930. In 1948 he returned to Canada and was sent to Rome in 1950 to accompany the Vietnamese brothers who did not speak French very well. This brother left behind, in Vietnam, the reputation of a man of high quality. Van cannot find words to express his admiration and his attachment to Brother Alexander. He is the one who called Van: 'holy Brother Marcel'.

**Brother Andrew**, *became a priest* – Father Joseph Lê Quang Phụng
Brother Andrew was a very close confrere of Van's. They were postulants and novices together, and then they took their first vows, made their second novitiate and their perpetual profession. Van wrote to Brother Andrew: 'Among the brethren of the community, I consider myself as being your very close little brother.'

**Brother Anthony** – Anthony Nguyễn Văn Toàn
Brother Anthony, who was much older than Van, looked after the sick. He became ill himself and died in Hanoi before Van left for Saigon.

**Brother Augustine** – Augustine Phan
This novice was often in conflict with Van. He left the Congregation before taking his vows.

**Brother Báo**, *choir brother* – Father Ignatius Nguyễn Văn Báo
Brother Bao's health was very weak. This delayed his priestly ordination. He worked with Father Antonio Boucher in editing a text relating Brother Marcel's last months.

**Brother Basil**
Brother Basil was very good at sewing. He learned more quickly than Brother Marcel and suggested helping him.

**Brother Bonaventure** – Pierre Vũ Minh Ngữ
He was skilful in his work and Van asked him to take his place. Later, in a letter (16 September 1952), Van said of him that he had been his 'Guardian Angel'.

**Brother Eugene** – Joachim Nguyễn Đức Hóa
Brother Eugene entered the monastery at the same time as Van. Together they made the postulancy, the novitiate, then their first vows, the second novitiate and their perpetual profession.

**Brother Gregory**
Brother Gregory was a brother in the same novitiate as Van. However Van prayed at the same time that he would leave and that, if he stayed, the Holy Spirit would invade him.

**Brother John Baptist** – Arthur Beaudoin
Van wrote: 'I like Brother John Baptist a lot and Brother John

Baptist likes me a lot.' This indicates all the admiration the Vietnamese brothers had for the simplicity of this old brother who taught everything to the youngest.

Brother Louis
Brother Louis let slip that at Saigon, the fathers treat the brothers as coolies.

Brother Mach, *choir brother* – Pierre Vũ Văn Mạch
Brother Mach was preparing for the priesthood. Van had made some critical remarks to him concerning the Rule. This brother left the Congregation before pronouncing his vows.

Brother Mark – Bernard Trần Văn Đàn
Brother Mark entered the novitiate at the same time as Van. They were postulants and novices together and together made their first vows, their second novitiate and their final vows.

Brother Placide Nguyễn Văn Truc
Brother Placide was happy to repeat Brother Louis' accusatory words towards Van, and Jesus, in his response to Van, said severely: 'Those who speak in this way are not true Redemptorist Brothers; they possess absolutely nothing of the spirit of the Congregation.' In fact he left in 1949 before his perpetual profession.

Brother Simon
He made his first vows in 1942 and left the Congregation in 1946.

Brother Thaddeus – Thaddeus Trần Tấn Đạo
Brother Thaddeus was very willing to help Van. Being older than Van he was like an older brother to him.

Brother Thuấn, *choir brother* – Joseph Nguyễn Thế Thuấn
He was a choir brother, a little older than Van. He was in the novitiate at the same time as Van.

Brother Vitus – Joseph Hà Văn Chính
Van often 'had a go' at Brother Vitus and would have been pleased to see him leave the Congregation. But he pronounced his vows in 1942 and still lives in the Monastery at Saigon.

# Les Amis de Van

The Association of the **Friends of Van** (Les Amis de Van) is recognized as a 'private association' of the faithful.

Through its international vocation it participates in the communion between the Churches and in the building of the universal Church.

Its main activities are:
- The sponsorship of Vietnamese seminarians.
- The publication of Van's story and his writings in several languages.
- The preparation of the dossier for the beatification of Van.
- The setting up of a Marcel Van house in Vietnam.

The cause for the beatification of Van as a Confessor of the Faith began on 26 March 1997 in the diocese of Belley-Ars.

If you have any testimony to give, if you have received a grace through Van's intercession, or if you have any information on his life, you can write to:

> Les Amis de Van
> 15, rue de l'Orangerie
> 78000 Versailles
> France
> Tel: 33(0) 1 39 51 30 90
> Fax: 33(0) 1 39 51 30 89
> e-mail: cause@amisdevan.org

www.ingramcontent.com/pod-product-compliance
Ingram Content Group UK Ltd.
Pitfield, Milton Keynes, MK11 3LW, UK
UKHW021316180426
11947UKWH00015B/1257